DECODING THE NEW TALIBAN

Decoding the New Taliban

Insights from the Afghan Field

Editor

Antonio Giustozzi

Columbia University Press
New York

Columbia University Press
Publishers Since 1893
New York   Chichester, West Sussex
Copyright © 2009 C. Hurst & Co (Publishers) Ltd
All rights reserved

Library of Congress Cataloging-in-Publication Data

Decoding the new Taliban : insights from the Afghan field / editor, Antonio
Giustozzi.
    p. cm.
    ISBN 978-0-231-70112-9
    1. Afghanistan—Politics and government—2001– 2. Taliban. 3. Insurgency—
Afghanistan—History—21st century. I. Giustozzi, Antonio. II. Title.

    DS371.4.D43 2009
    958.104'7—dc22

                            2009015843

∞

Columbia University Press books are printed on permanent and durable
acid-free paper. This book is printed on paper with recycled content.
Printed in India

c 10 9 8 7 6 5 4 3 2 1

References to Internet Web sites (URLs) were accurate at the time of writing.
Neither the author nor Columbia University Press is responsible for URLs
that may have expired or changed since the manuscript was prepared.

CONTENTS

ACKNOWLEDGEMENTS

The present volume is in a sense a continuation of the project which led to the publication of *Koran, Kalashnikov and Laptop* in 2008. Already in the preface of that book, I warned that it was not going to be my last word on this subject. *Decoding the New Taliban* is not my final word either. The ambition of this book is of expanding the horizon of knowledge and of contributing to the debate about the nature of the Neo-Taliban and their modus operandi.

The task of thanking all those who have contributed to the realization of this volume is not easily achieved. I have first of all to thank the contributors, particularly those who agreed to produce chapters to tight deadlines in order to replace other contributors who had dropped out of the project. Special thanks are deserved by Thomas Rutting, who apart from writing his own chapter also helped crucially in recruiting some of the contributors. Thanks also to Mina Moshkiri of LSE's cartography department, who once again redrew my maps professionally. The book would not have been produced without the financial support of the Crisis States Research Centre, for which I thank its director, James Putzel. Niamatullah Ibrahimi, the Kabul-based research officer of the Centre, accompanied me in my trip to Herat, which resulted in the chapter included in this collection. Thanks also to Wendy Foulds, administrator of the Centre, for her support and administrative help. I and the contributors to the volume also have a debt of gratitude to all those unnamed individuals who made the research possible by responding to our enquiries.

Antonio Giustozzi

GLOSSARY

Achakzai	Pashtun tribe of southern Afghanistan, part of the Durrani confederation.
Ahl-i Hadith	revivalist school of Islamic thought.
Aimaq	an ethnic group of western Afghanistan, of Dari language and Turco-Mongolic features.
'Ali Shura	see *Rahbari Shura*
Alim	Islamic scholar.
Alizai	a Pashtun tribe of southern Afghanistan, part of the Durrani confederation.
Alokozai	a Pashtun tribe of southern Afghanistan, part of the Durrani confederation.
Amir	leader, king.
Amir-ul-momenin	Leader of the believers.
ANA	Afghan National Army, acronym used to indicate the internationally trained Afghan army (2002–).
Andiwal	"followers" in Pashto.
ANAP	Afghan National Auxiliary Police, local militias incorporated into the Afghan National Police in 2006.
ANP	Afghan National Police, acronym used to indicate any Afghan police unit, particularly after 2003.
Arbakai	community guards, active in some regions of southeastern Afghanistan. Pl. *Arbaki*.
Barakzai	a Pashtun tribe of southern Afghanistan, part of the Durrani confederation.
CIMIC	Civil-Military Cooperation.
DDR	Disarmament, Demobilisation and Reintegration, a UN-sponsored programme to disband official militias in Afghanistan in 2003–5.

ix

Deobandi	an Islamic revivalist movement based on strict adherence to Sunna and Shariah.
DIAG	Disbandment of Illegal Armed Groups, a UN-sponsored programme to disband unofficial militias in Afghanistan, which started in 2005.
Dilgai	"front" in Pashto.
Dilgai meshr	front commander.
Durrani	tribal confederation in southern and south eastern Afghanistan.
EFP	Explosively Formed Projectile.
FATA	Federally Administered Tribal Areas (Pakistan).
Ghilzai	tribal confederation in southern and south-eastern Afghanistan.
Harakat-i Inqilab-i Islami	"Movement of the Islamic Revolution", a Jihadi group active in the 1978–92 conflict, from whose ranks came many leaders of the Taliban.
Harakat-i Islami	"Islamic Movement", Shi'ite Jihadi group led by Sheikh Mohseni in the 1980s and 1990s.
Hawala	an informal banking network.
Hawaladars	traders in the *Hawala*.
Hazara	an ethnic group in central Afghanistan, Dari-speakers of Shi'ite religion and Turco-Mongolic features.
Hizb-i Islami	"Islamic Party", an Islamist group based in Afghanistan and one of the protagonists of the conflict started in 1978.
Hotak	tribe of the Ghilzai confederation.
IED	Improvised Explosive Device.
IMU	Islamic Movement of Uzbekistan.
ISAF	International Security Assistance Force, a multi-national contingent deployed in Afghanistan from 2002 to secure and stabilise the country.
Ishaqzai	a Pashtun tribe of southern Afghanistan, part of the Durrani confederation.
ISI	Inter-Services Intelligence directorate (Pakistan).
Ittehad-i Islami	Islamic Union, an Islamist group led by Prof. Sayyaf.
Jabha	"front" in Dari.
Jabhe-ye-Motahed-e-Milli	United National Front (UNF), a heterogeneous alliance of political groups opposed to President Karzai.
Jaish-i-Mohammad	"The Army of Mohammad", an international Jihadist organisation.

Jamaat-ul Ulema-i Islam	"Society of the Islamic Scholars", a political group based in Pakistan.
Jami'at-i Islami	"Islamic Society", an Islamist party based in Afghanistan and one of the protagonists of the conflict started in 1978.
Jami'at-i Khuddam-ul-Furqan	"Society of the Servants of Providence", political group formed by former members of the Taliban in 2002 in Pakistan.
Jawanan-i Muslimin	"Muslim Youth", Islamist movement formed in Afghanistan in the 1960s.
Jihad	holy war.
Jihadi	supporter of a *jihad* movement.
Jihadist	militant in favour of the spread of the *jihad* movement.
Jirga	"assembly" in Pashto.
Jundullah	a Sunni militant group operating along the border of Iran with Pakistan and Afghanistan.
Kakar	a Pashtun tribe of southern Afghanistan.
Karez	underground water channel.
Khan	rural notable, normally a major landowner.
Khugiani	a Pashtun tribe, split into two branches in eastern and southern Afghanistan.
Khuddam ul-Forqan	"Servants of Providence", politico-religious movement formed in the 1960s by a group of *Ulema* close to the Mojaddidi family.
Lashkar	tribally mobilised group of armed men, to wage war against enemies.
Lashkar-i-Tayba (LeT)	"Army of the Righteous", Pakistan-based jihadist group.
Layeha	"Book of rules".
Loy wuluswali	large district.
Loya Jirga	"Grand Assembly".
Madrasa	religious school.
Mahaz	Pashto for "front".
Mahaz-i Milli	Jihadi party created in the early 1980s by Pir Gailani.
Malik	tribal leader.
Mawlawi	Islamic religious title.
Mehsud	a Pashtun tribe in Pakistani Waziristan.
Mohmand	a Pashtun tribe of eastern Afghanistan.
MRRD	Ministry of Rural Rehabilitation and Development.
Mujahidin	holy warriors.
Mullah	religious leader or teacher, preacher.

NDS	National Security Directorate (Afghanistan's intelligence agency after 2001).
Noorzai	a Pashtun tribe of southern and western Afghanistan, part of the Durrani confederation.
OMAR	a de-mining NGO.
Pai Luch	"barefoots", Kandahari brotherhood active in the 1980s *jihad*.
Pashai	ethnic group in eastern Afghanistan, speaking its own language.
PDPA	People's Democratic Party of Afghanistan, leftist party in power in Kabul in 1978–92.
Pir	Sufi leader.
Popolzai	a Pashtun tribe of southern and western Afghanistan, part of the Durrani confederation. The tribe of President Karzai.
PRT	Provincial Reconstruction Team, a mix of foreign military personnel (usually 80–150) and civilian elements intended to tie together the military and developmental aspects of security enhancement.
Qazi	Islamic judge.
Rahbari Shura	"Leadership Council" (of the Movement of the Taliban).
RPG	Rocket-Propelled Grenade, type of Soviet-designed rocket launcher.
Safi	a Pashtun tribe of eastern Afghanistan.
Sepah-i Pasdaran	"Army of Guardians", a pro-Iranian militant Shi'ite group based in central Afghanistan.
Sepah-i Saheba	a Militant jihadist group based in Pakistan.
Sharia	Islamic law.
Shura	"council".
Shabnamah	"night letters", tracts distributed as propaganda or threats.
Tablighi	a Muslim missionary revivalist tendency.
Takfir	doctrine that declares unorthodox or imperfectly practicing Muslims as apostates and therefore *kafirs* (unbelievers).
Talib	religious student. Pl. *Taliban*.
Tanzim	"organisation"; term used to indicate the Jihadi parties of the 1980s in Afghanistan.
Taraki	a Pashtun tribe of eastern and southern Afghanistan, member of the Ghilzai confederation.
Tarana	vocal music composition.
Tehreek-e Nafaz-e Shariat-e Mohammadi (TNSM)	"Movement for the Enforcement of Islamic Law", Pakistani militant group.

Tehrik-i-Nafaz-i-Shariat-i-Muhammadi Wazir	a Pashtun tribe in Pakistani Waziristan.
Tehrik-i Taliban-i-Pakistan (TTP)	Movement of the Taliban in Pakistan, umbrella organisation gathering several Taliban groups in Pakistan.
Tehrik-i Tulaba-yi Harakat Wilayat	student wing of Harakat-i Enqelab-e Islami. province.
Tehrik-i Taliban-i-Pakistan (TTP)	"Movement of the Pakistani Taliban".
Ulema	pl. of *'alim*
UNAMA	United Nations Assistance Mission to Afghanistan.
USAID	United States Agency for International Development.
Ushr	religious tax usually consisting of 10 per cent of agricultural produce payable.
Wahhabi	a Sunni sect characterised by the strict observance of the Koran.
Zakat	religious tax on assets and liquidity.
Zadran	a Pashtun tribe of southeastern Afghanistan.

INTRODUCTION

Antonio Giustozzi

Every age has its follies; perhaps the folly of our age could be identified as an unmatched ambition to change the world, without even bothering to study it in detail and understand it first. Although study and scholarship have never been widespread passions as far as humanity was concerned, what is surprising in the attitude of contemporary policy makers is the readiness to enter countries and set out to transform ("modernise") every remote corner of the world. This fever to turn everything upside down was already seen during the colonial age, but at least at that time it was accompanied by a determined effort to improve knowledge and understanding of the objects of conquest. The texts that we use to study Afghan society, culture and traditions, for example, are still the 'Elphinstones' who were dispatched by the British Empire to investigate its borderlands. No comparable effort seems to have been undertaken for contemporary Afghanistan, certainly nothing that has involved the scholarly community and produced results observable in the public domain. It falls therefore to the "scholarly community" to pick up this effort, with the limited means available in a context of underfunded research, so that the public debate will be informed by more in-depth information.

Writing and analysing unfolding events carries some risks, including one of bias against one or more of the parties in a conflict. Another major risk is the adoption of a short-term perspective, missing out the wider picture and the long-term dynamics. However, writing and analysing as events unfold also carries one huge advantage over waiting half a century: that is, the possibility of gathering information directly from the protagonists, most of whom would be dead or too old to be of any help if the dust of the events was allowed to settle. Some contributors to this volume managed to reach higher levels of objectivity than others; indeed some of us are, I think, admirably unbiased given the circumstances and the fact that all the contributors know somebody

1

who has fallen victim in the post-2001 Afghan conflict. On the whole, the volume may well fall short of Thucydides, but we hope it will remain a valuable contribution to understanding of one of the main wars of the early twenty-first century. The idea of this book first emerged in early 2008, as a follow-up to my previous work on the subject. During my research I realised that a good deal of knowledge about the Taliban existed in a dispersed form, among the many people who had been researching into them for one reason or another over the years. They are journalists, diplomats, military officers, academics and political analysts, who for a number of reasons were not motivated to put all their knowledge and thoughts on paper. At the same time it was obvious that the public debate on the Afghan crisis was dominated by superficial or plainly wrong assumptions. I therefore decided to make the effort to bring together as many of them as possible to contribute to a volume on the new Taliban, which would try to throw light on their most controversial and least understood aspects. The present volume is the result of this effort. Not all those who were contacted to contribute were willing or able to do so. Some were prevented by the policy of the organisations which employed them, forbidding the publication of material related to their work. In other cases, even if there was no explicit prohibition of publishing, the long lead required for internal clearance made it impossible for the chapters to be included in this book. Others still were unable to contribute because of unexpected professional commitments. Nonetheless, the final output more than justified the decision to proceed with the book.

Afghanistan is a very complex country, most of all because of its division into regions which vary tremendously among themselves in terms of population, culture, geography and history. Expertise on Afghanistan tends therefore to be quite regionalised: even countrywide experts tend to be better informed about a specific region or two, particularly as far as recent and contemporary developments are concerned. This characteristic of Afghan scholarship dictated that most chapters in this book are dedicated to particular regions or provinces, even if this might not be the most reader friendly approach. There was no strict logic in determining why one province deserved a chapter, while some other chapters covered whole regions. Various factors contributed to the decision, ranging from the expertise available, the importance of the province, the homogeneity of a group of provinces to be pooled together as a region, and so on.

The contributors were briefed to focus as much as possible on a number of topics, which, in the view of the editor, are key to understanding the Taliban as a movement and their internal dynamics. In particular, I stressed the need to look in as great a depth as possible at their command and control structure. To what extent is this based on personal relations? Do abstract "institutions" (like a party or an organisation) play any role? To what extent is the leadership able to impose changes of strategies and tactics on the rank and file, and how? How do they maintain the degree of unity which they have? When we study the organisation of a non-state armed group and particularly one engaged in a political insurgency, we need to verify the existence of a formal structure of command, with people obeying "ranks" as opposed to specific individuals, more or less charismatic. The rigidity or fluidity of territorial control by individual commanders is another benchmark of organisational strength, as is the consistency of patterns and shapes in the formation of military units. The more consistent, the more organised. The strength of command and control from above is also shown by the ability of the leadership to rotate commanders away from one location and/or away from a group of fighters and to avoid the emergence of "warlords", that is field commanders displaying growing autonomy from the leadership. Other signs which should be taken into account are the ability of the leadership to restrain banditry and undisciplined behaviour within the movement's ranks, and the nature of its logistics—centralised or managed individually by commanders, run as a free market enterprise where money is offered to whoever will bring weapons and ammunition, or as a complex logistical system in place with caches, safehouses, etc. managed directly by the Taliban themselves, and so on.

The task imposed on the contributors was of course not easy; by definition the internal organisation of subversive organisations is not widely publicised. Still, the Taliban are not the most secretive organisation to have walked the planet, and as the chapters of this volume show, it is possible to cobble together a picture of how they operate. The contributions inevitably have to deal with a number of other issues, in part because of the need to provide some background for readers, in part because organisational aspects cannot be isolated from wider considerations, and finally because the quality and specificity of the forthcoming information varied greatly from region to region. The style of the individual authors also varies greatly from one chapter to the other, as some of the titles make explicit. As an editor, I felt that it would have been inappropriate to impose a particular style on all authors. Hence some chapters are more academic in character, others are more journalistic in style, others still are witness reports from people who have an extensive experience of living and working in a province or region. I felt that this diversity of approaches and authors' backgrounds was a source of richness and not a liability; I also think it makes the book more entertaining to the average reader. However, together with the objectively uneven availability of information and material, it meant a very flexible policy with regard to the sourcing of the chapters. In some cases the contributors have been able to footnote the whole text; in most cases sources are indicated in the text, but since interviewees were almost always disinclined to be mentioned by name, it appeared superfluous to burden every text with an extensive apparatus of footnotes. Some contributions are mainly based on the personal experience and knowledge of the authors and should be read as "eye witness statements" or historical memoirs.

I shall revert to this point in the conclusion, but it is important to stress already at this stage that there are several points of view from which the organisational skills of the Neo-Taliban can be judged. Of course it makes sense to compare them with an abstract ideal of subversive organisation and conclude, rather unsurprisingly, that the Taliban are no match for Maoist or Leninist movements in terms of organisational skills. But it makes even better sense to compare them with other models of non-state armed groups which have operated in the past in Afghanistan or in the region. The reader should bear this in mind throughout the book.

The volume also includes two thematic chapters, one by Joanna Nathan of ICG on the Taliban's propaganda and another by Gretchen Peters on the links between the Taliban and the narcotics trade. I would have liked more thematic chapters, but for a number of reasons it was not possible to bring more authors to contribute on themes such as the Taliban's military tactics, attitude towards negotiations, etc. Books like this have to come out quickly to avoid the ageing of the contributions; those who have never edited a book do not realise how complicated a task it is to get everybody to deliver on time and meet the deadlines. Sacrifices are necessary in order to achieve this indispensable aim; I apologise to readers and to contributors-who-never-were for having been ruthless, but the task demanded it. The two thematic chapters that I did manage to include do address some of the most important aspects of the Neo-Taliban as an organisation. The propaganda and public relations aspect of insurgent movements is usually neglected by scholars, but it can in reality tell a lot about the way they operate and think. Joanna Nathan's chapter typically derived from a more policy-oriented output (an ICG report), but I believe she has successfully demonstrated how rewarding a focus on propaganda activities can be.

Gretchen Peters' chapter on the Neo-Taliban and narcotics was bound to be controversial, as I was aware from the beginning. For a while I even considered having two chapters on the same topic, illustrating different points of view. Much of Gretchen's chapter is matter of fact, but the degree of the Taliban's involvement in the narcotics trade remains a matter of debate, perhaps inevitably. Because of this, I shall discuss it extensively in the conclusion.

Helmand province has been given a special place in this book, with the longest chapter among those dedicated to a single province, for two reasons. The first is that Helmand is of particular interest to the British public, for obvious reasons. The second is that the author, Thomas Coghlan, contributed such a wealth of extremely informative material, all specifically relating to Helmand, that I did not feel like making any substantial cut. The south-eastern region is also covered by an exceptionally long chapter, divided into two sections. Part of the material is historical in character and initially I was inclined to cut it, but one of the authors (Thomas Ruttig) compellingly argued that there is a dearth of published information about the "Haqqani network" and its historical origins and that the gap should be filled. One reason which convinced me to leave the material as it was is the importance of Haqqanis in analysing the structure of the Taliban. I apologise to those other authors whose chapters I savagely cut in order to bring the book back to a more manageable size; as a rule I did not enforce a draconian discipline in terms of respect for the original specifications to which the chapters were commissioned, but I removed parts and sections which were not relevant to the analysis of the specific region or province. Elyas Osman Tariq, for example, had contributed his knowledge of other parts of Afghanistan to his chapter on the central region (Logar, Wardak and Kabul), but for the sake of discipline I have had to sacrifice some parts of it. Most other authors too saw some parts or bits of their chapters being sawn away; I hope they will not harbour resentment! In my defence I shall say that the only contributor who wrote the chapter exactly to the specifications (and on time too) was Martine van Bijlert, whose piece stands almost immaculate in the book.

One exception to the rule of "specificity" is Sippi Azerbaijani Moghaddam's piece on north-eastern Afghanistan, because some of her arguments have a wider applicability than the region she is analysing. The reason why I "tolerated" this deviation is that her argument was not repeated elsewhere in the volume; in addition, to the extent that it applies beyond the north-east, the chapter concerns mostly provinces of northern Afghanistan which are not covered in this volume. The volume was not necessarily planned with the intention of covering every single region or province, but I would have liked to include the important province of Nangarhar. However, the contributor scheduled to write on Nangarhar had unfortunately to drop out.

A number of chapters are derived or summarised from other pieces of work. My own chapter on western Afghanistan owes much to my contribution to DFID's "Understanding Afghanistan" exercise (2008). Gretchen Peters' chapter is based on her USIP-funded research, which is also resulting in a USIP report and in a full size book. As mentioned already, Joanna Nathan drew her chapter from her ICG report and I thank ICG for having given the green light to Joanna contributing to this book. Sébastien Trives' section is taken from his article published in French in 2006 in *Politique Étrangère*, whose publisher kindly consented to have it reproduced here. Finally, David Kilcullen's chapter is extracted and slightly modified from his recent book *The Accidental Guerrilla*, with the kind consent of the publisher. He uses the example of Kunar to discuss more general dynamics, for which I invite the readers to refer to his book. The main purpose of including the chapter here was that I wanted to throw light on another Afghan province, which was among the first to be affected by the insurgency and has received little attention. The author of the piece on Zabul, a province disregarded and ignored despite having been the first to fall to the Taliban in 2003, has chosen to adopt a pseudonym for his own safety, as he travels there often. His contribution is the only extensive discussion of post-2001 Zabul politics in the public domain, as far as I know.

Claudio Franco's chapter on Pakistan occupies a place of special interest in the book, as over the last few years the FATA has become as much as of a battlefield as the Afghan Pashtun belt, but it has been neglected even more than Afghanistan in research and analysis. Franco's contribution is the first published attempt to analyse the leadership structure of the Taliban and how it extends to Pakistan and I think that observers of the Taliban will find it of great interest. The conflict is clearly no longer just an Afghan one.

Social scientists enamoured of theoretical elaboration will not find much to their liking in this book, except in the conclusion or in terms of raw material to be used in the development of models and theories. This is deliberate, as the absorption of the Taliban war into theoretical constructs is in my view premature. Scholars need sometimes to be humble enough to recognise that their theories are not sufficiently refined or informed by empirical material and be patient. Understanding the Taliban is still very much work in progress.

1

THE TALIBAN AND THE OPIUM TRADE

Gretchen S. Peters

To fully comprehend the astonishing resurgence the Taliban have made since being toppled by US-led forces in 2001, it is critical to investigate the economic miracle that financed their comeback. From one of the world's most remote and backwards regions, where the transport network and infrastructure are almost completely shattered, Taliban insurgents and drug traffickers with whom they collaborate have managed to successfully integrate an agricultural product into the global economy.[1] In terms of market share, this coalition has quickly become dominant: opium produced in southern provinces where the insurgency reaps financial benefits accounted for roughly 80 percent of global supply in 2008.[2]

While the wider world may outlaw their product and shudder at their methods, it is important to recognize that insurgents and traffickers in southern Afghanistan have triumphed at something neither the Afghan government nor the international community could implement: creating a farm support network and an export network. There are obvious reasons why an illicit crop like poppy would succeed where legal crops like wheat and pomegranates tend to fail: poppy is a sturdy, drought resistant crop and, once harvested, opium does not rot. But there is another factor important to recognize here. From importing precursor chemicals to getting farm loans to thousands of small farmers to providing security for the shipments as they move across borders, coordinating and managing Afghanistan's expanding opium trade is an organizational feat of the very highest order.

The Taliban are often stereotyped as a rag-tag militia, made up of unkempt, backward villagers, who lack sophistication in the ways of the modern world. Meanwhile, little is known about the thousands of traders and trucking net-

7

works who for decades have controlled a vast commerce in commodities—some legal and some not—between Pakistan and Afghanistan. Opium forms a major percentage of the total trade, which has never been accurately quantified. Suffice it to say that billions of dollars worth of goods are traded annually across the rugged border without the use of Blackberries, computers, fax machines or even widespread literacy, so that many outsiders dismiss this commercial network as unsophisticated. Yet it is a mistake to underestimate the powerful role of this unregulated commerce, and the traders who profit from it most, in keeping both Pakistan and Afghanistan unstable.[3]

The Taliban did not create this trade network, although the movement is said to have received its original funding in 1994 from members of this trucking and trading mafia.[4] And although insurgents have expanded and diversified their activities to expand their profits from the narcotics trade since 2001, they still do not control it. It is more accurate to say that major traffickers and traders, who at times have sat on the senior *shura* with the Taliban leader Mohammad Mullah Omar, continue to have powerful influence over decision-making at the top levels of the core movement, now often referred to as the Quetta *shura*.

It is difficult to make sweeping generalizations about the Taliban today, as the movement has diversified greatly on both sides of the border. Because of this diversity, it is often described as a loosely structured organization where regional commanders maintain relatively high degrees of independence to conduct operations and raise funds. Operational autonomy is reported to have increased in the post-2001 phase of the movement.[5] Yet in terms of how money filters through the hierarchy, the Taliban remain remarkably rigid, according to dozens of interviews with Taliban fighters, smugglers and Afghan officials. Strict control over financial flows appears to allow the top tier leadership—the Leadership Council—to maintain a greater degree of authority over dispersed and sometimes loosely affiliated Taliban commanders. According to local sources and Afghan officials, it appears that such loosely affiliated gangs have little connection to the central leadership other than the dues they must pay.

How opium funds the movement

Examining the various ways senior Taliban commanders and members of the top leadership earn profit from narcotics, and how they have expanded their role in the trade, illustrates how the myriad drug earnings enter the system. A central source of Taliban revenue comes from *ushr*, the 10 per cent tithe collected from poppy farmers in kind, since few of them hold hard currency.[6] At the village level, where each Taliban sub-commander carts off his share of opium, every farmer will receive a handwritten receipt for the amount of tax paid. Poppy farmers say they do not get charged more than once, since the Taliban hierarchy is strict in assigning regions of influence. Researchers for this project heard of multiple cases where farmers complained to the Taliban hierarchy over being charged twice by rival sub-commanders. In most cases, the Taliban leadership responded by punishing the sub-commanders.

Village level field commanders use personal contacts to develop information about people in their control zone, paying as much as $10 a tip to informants.[7] They work over the local community much like *mafiosi*, even using the "good cop bad cop" routine. In one typical exchange, Haji Bado Khan, a landowner in Kajaki district in northern Helmand, described how the local Taliban sub-commander wanted to start billing him $3,000 a season. He appeared late one night at Khan's house with a group of armed men. "We hear you're growing your own poppy and buying it from others to trade," he said. "You will have to start sharing some regular money with the *mujahidin*." Since the two men had known each other most of their lives, he told Khan, "I am here as your friend, but if you fail to pay this, I'll have to report you to my commander. No matter what I say, I know he will get someone to come after you." Khan bargained the rate down to $1,500, and said he paid it in the form of two motorcycles.[8]

Although it is impossible to calculate an accurate total dollar figure, Taliban commanders at the village level appear to receive each year millions of dollars worth of material supplies collected as tax from villagers and smugglers. These often include vehicles, like motorcycles, SUVs or pick-up trucks. Many commanders demand satellite and mobile telephones, or will collect top-up cards with talk-time credit from local shopkeepers. Other supplies they take as payment include weapons, ammunition, petrol, food, shelter and even medical care for wounded soldiers.

Across the southern poppy heartland, Afghan and NATO officials believe the Taliban maintain opium warehouses where insurgent commanders can deposit and later withdraw quantities of opium, much like using an ATM machine. In December 2007, NATO forces that retook Musa Qala, in Helmand province, following a brief period of Taliban control found warehouses that stored 11 tons of opium, which they say the insurgents maintained.[9] This author heard about Taliban opium stashes from dozens of sources, from the early years of the movement. Using opium as a form of currency is not unique to insurgents. Opium is routinely traded as a form of currency across the poppy-rich south.[10] A shopkeeper, for example, might accept payment for groceries, petrol or other supplies in the form of a chunk of opium, and some keep weights and measures to calculate the correct rate.

Taliban foot soldiers and sub-commanders captured in battle have told Afghan intelligence officials that *ushr* proceeds and commodities collected in barter agreements cover the bulk of their operational needs, including salaries for fighters and transport, fuel, food, weapons and explosives. Each sub-commander has to pay a percentage of the proceeds he collects to his military commander at the district level, who in turns pays off the district-level Taliban governor. A portion of these funds—still often transferred in the form of raw or partially refined opium—then filters up the Taliban chain of command to the provincial commander, who will hand over a portion to the Taliban's central financial committee.[11] Some Afghan officials complain the Taliban system seems to work more smoothly and with less corruption than the Afghan government network. "It's very organized," says an Afghan intelligence official tracking the drugs trade in the south.[12]

In addition to *ushr*, Taliban commanders collect a percentage on every drug shipment—as well as other illicit and licit commodities—that moves through their control zone. It is not unusual in Afghanistan for a local power broker to take a cut of commodities moving through his patch, or to receive payments for providing armed protection for a shipment as it passes. Escorting illicit consignments earns the Taliban tens of millions of dollars a year in protection fees, which often range as high as 20 per cent a consignment. The Taliban have broadened their role in the protection racket since 2001, moreover, by starting to take an active military role in protecting drug shipments. According to Afghan and NATO officials, Taliban units started attacking security checkpoints to allow drug convoys to pass, and have come to the protection of drug labs being raided by an elite paramilitary counternarcotics unit. There have even been cases where insurgents launched diversionary strikes to draw Western troops away from an area where a major consignment was passing. Campaigns for territorial gain, such as a 2007 Taliban push into Dehrawud district in Uruzgan, often support smuggling activities.[13] Dehrawud is perched along the most important drugs- and arms-trafficking route in Uruzgan, connecting to Iran in the west and Pakistan in the south. The shift in battlefield tactics, from passively taxing a trade taking place in their region to actively supporting it militarily, is a strong indication that Taliban leaders work closely with traffickers, who appear to have tremendous influence over their military strategy.

Traffickers and Taliban also appear to collaborate to dictate farm output. They began distributing night letters, or shabnamah, in 2004, offering protection to farmers who grew poppy and threatening dire consequences for anyone who did not. "The one who is not cultivating poppy in their lands and accepting the governor order for destroying their poppy cultivations will be killed by Taliban," read one message found pinned to a mosque door and later obtained by UN officials. By the autumn of 2008, the UN's Office on Drugs and Crime (UNODC) reported the Taliban and their collaborators appeared to have reversed course, taking a "passive stance" or even discouraging poppy planting.[14] They may have been trying to reduce the amount of opium produced, possibly to drive up prices, which had softened after several years of bumper crops.

According to farmers and Afghan officials, traffickers have also used Taliban fighters to guard thousands of poppy merchants, dispatched to pre-purchase poppy crops at planting time for prices below what the farmers could fetch at the time of harvest. The so-called *"salaam"* system provides the funds that poor sharecroppers and small farm owners need to buy food for their families during the winter. It is designed to trap them in debt at harvest time, thus forcing them to grow poppy the next season. Many get caught in a vicious cycle of owing more and more every year, and there are appalling tales of farmers selling off their daughters to settle their arrears.[15] The Taliban also provide security for poppy farmers, building defensive positions around the poppy fields, or planting mines and IEDs ahead of visits by the Poppy Eradication Force.[16] "The Taliban will make people grow opium but they also provide security for their fields," said a security official in Helmand. "They do this on behalf of the drug dealers, who pay them in the form of 4X4s and weapons."[17] Such deals are likely to be done locally, but they appear to happen across the region where the Taliban operate.

Continuing a practice they implemented while in power, the Taliban also collect taxes at drug refineries located near the Pakistan and Iran borders. Eventually, some Taliban commanders took up running refineries themselves. "Big commanders now have their own mobile labs," said a senior Afghan security official in 2007. The number of sites turning opium into crystal heroin, the high-end product exported to the West, climbed from 30 to 50 by 2008. More simple rigs making morphine base operated off the back of supped-up pick-ups that can hurtle across the rocky terrain hugging the Pakistan border.[18] When Afghan and international troops retook Musa Qala in December 2007, they found that the militants oversaw or offered safe haven for heroin production at as many as 50 heroin labs—and that the number of labs in operation expanded during their time in power. Some employed as many as 60 men.[19]

Insurgent commanders also expanded their protection racket into the business realm, charging shop-owners and national enterprises for the right to operate safely. When the provincial director of one mobile phone network refused to pay his monthly "tax" in Zabul province, Taliban fighters blew up three distribution towers in the Shah Joy district, cutting service for a week.[20] Shopkeepers must pay as much as 10 per cent of their earnings. The highest "taxes" are incurred on the highways, where truckers can expect to get charged by both the Taliban and corrupt Highway Police.[21] Taliban fighters patrolled the streets of Musa Qala by the hundreds during their time in power, extorting funds for the insurgency. Fariq Khan, a Musa Qala resident who owned a telephone shop there, said the Taliban would take about $8 from each family every month during a collection at the mosque. Trucks passing through paid $50 each.[22]

How the poppy informs villagers' decisions to support or join the Taliban

Apart from coercion, a complex blend of motives appears to inform decisions by Afghan villagers to engage the protection of the Taliban or even take up arms and join them. Toronto's *Globe and Mail* conducted a video survey of 42 Taliban foot soldiers in Kandahar in 2007, finding the overwhelming majority were poppy farmers. About half said that their fields had been targeted by government-led poppy eradication teams, a striking statistic in a province where just eight per cent of the entire poppy crop was eradicated that year.[23] The critical question is whether they joined the Taliban because their fields were targeted or whether their fields got wiped out because they were Taliban.

There are also signs that iniquitous eradication policies tend to benefit rich landowners and tribal federations close to the provincial and federal power structures. This has divided communities across the southern poppy belt and driven many poor farmers to join the Taliban. Southern Afghan tribes allied with the Karzai administration tend to suffer less eradication; rival tribes often are pushed into the arms of the insurgents. "The farmers have never benefited from poppy cultivation," said Haji Mahuddin Khan, a tribal leader in Helmand. "The profits are taken by those [officials] who tell farmers to engage in cultivation but then threaten their crops with eradication. The international mafia is the main benefactor, while we are being held responsible for it and portrayed as criminals."[24]

The number of fighters interviewed by the *Globe and Mail* was small, but the uncanny similarity of their responses indicates that Taliban leaders—and perhaps their financial backers—play a powerful role indoctrinating low-level foot soldiers on a number of issues, including poppy cultivation. Almost one-fifth of the respondents said they grew poppy because their mullahs ordered them to, and 16 said they hoped to make addicts of non-Muslims. "It is obvious to everyone that the Americans hate poppies," said fighter #18. "And if we grow it in this era, it will be better for us and worse for the Americans." Many acknowledged that Islam forbids growing or trading narcotics but said they were financially desperate. "Islam says not to grow it and we are not opposed to Islam," said Soldier #19. "But our *ulema* [Islamic clerics] say to grow it as it is harmful for non-Muslims." When the interviewer asked how it got transported to the West, the soldier replied: "They have their own businessmen who take to their own countries."

The UNODC has also surveyed poppy farmers about their reasons for growing an illegal crop. In southern and western Afghan provinces, the high sale price and poverty alleviation were the dominant reasons farmers gave in 2008 for the decision to cultivate opium.[25]

How drug money filters through the Taliban hierarchy

Although it appears that Taliban commanders at the village and district levels might have considerable room for manoeuvre when reporting their earnings to those higher up, the leadership seems to strictly enforce routine reporting sessions when the regional commanders must send a representative to report earnings to the Finance Committee. "Each commander has his own financial representative—the guy who looks after the money side of things," says an Afghan intelligence official based in the south. "He will have to come to

Quetta and deal with the Taliban's finance committee."[26] Small, nondescript guesthouses in Quetta (and Peshawar on the eastern front of the insurgency) are routinely used as temporary meeting points for massive, drug-related financial transactions, which take place roughly once a month to six weeks, according to multiple sources on both sides of the border.

The powerful committee, which decides how funds are spent, has tremendous influence over which sub-commanders rise or drop in the rankings, since fighters will win appointments to more lucrative postings according to their fund-raising ability. Money can travel in both directions. Sub-commanders from poppy rich areas might have to pay into the central coffers, while others in strategic regions with less earning potential might collect a monthly stipend for operational expenses. NATO officials estimate that the Taliban pay contract soldiers more than $150 a month, a solid wage in a country where the average annual income is less than $500 and a local policeman takes home just $80 a month.[27] One source described a sub-commander who controlled 20 fighters from Helmand as collecting $5,000 monthly to pay salaries of his troops and their supplies.[28]

Major traffickers who own refineries and smuggle tons of opium annually also pay directly to the top Taliban leadership, often to the tune of millions of dollars per year, according to Western officials and locals on the border. In meetings with Taliban leaders, they also get contracted to provide a certain number of 4X4s and Toyota Hilux pickup trucks each year. A few have built *madrasas* in neighbouring Pakistan where recruits can be trained, or hotels where Taliban fighters can escape for R&R. Traffickers also get billed for medical expenses incurred by Taliban injured on the battlefield, and at least one major dealer runs his own health clinic in Quetta, which is reportedly filled up at any given time with wounded fighters.[29]

Competition between rival Taliban sub-commanders has on occasion erupted into internal violence, as was common during the anti-Soviet resistance.[30] In 2007, eight died in a remote district of Kapisa province during fighting between two Taliban commanders over rights to collect tax there. In April of the same year, Pakistani Taliban in South Waziristan allegedly clashed with fighters from the Islamic Movement of Uzbekistan (IMU) over land and smuggling rights.[31] Despite efforts to rigidly control money flows within the Taliban, researchers for this project heard multiple reports of rival commanders clashing over drug spoils. There were also tantalizing indications that high-level Taliban officials may have competed violently for drug profits since 2001. Mullah Obaidullah Akhund, who was responsible for Taliban military and financial supplies, worked closely with senior opium traffickers to move drugs out of the region and bring weapons back, according to US military intelligence documents. Sources close to the Taliban say Obaidullah clashed with the late military commander Mullah Dadullah Lang after Dadullah independently tried to take charge of money and resources in the south.[32] Dadullah also struggled for power with the late Mullah Ahktar Osmani, who was killed in a December 2007 air strike. Mullah Osmani, it was reported, took charge of collecting money and other resources for the Taliban in Baramcha, the rough-and-tumble Helmand border town that is a centre for heroin production and home to numerous refineries. After Osmani's death, rumours circulated among insurgents that Mullah Dadullah had indirectly passed information about Osmani's whereabouts to NATO authorities so that he could take control of the lucrative Baramcha market. Dadullah himself was killed in a May 2007 clash with US-led forces in Helmand.

Although the central earning region for opium is in southern Afghanistan, the system for tax collection and the way in which drug income filters though the insurgent hierarchy function in much the same way across the other two central fronts of the Afghan insurgency—the east and the southeast. In these zones there is far clearer evidence that networks linked to top leaders such as Gulbuddin Hekmatyar and Jalaluddin Haqqani have long collaborated with foreign *jihadis* linked to Al Qaida, Pakistani traffickers and individuals within Pakistan's intelligence services to move narcotics and other contraband out of the Afghanistan.[33] This is precisely where the profit margins are greatest. Hizb-i-Islami (Gulbuddin) reaps extensive income from smuggling timber and gemstones, while Haqqani's group earns the majority of its profits smuggling weapons, according to local residents and Afghan and Western officials. Both Hizb-i Islami (Gulbuddin) and the Haqqani group have been deeply involved in smuggling of all sorts since the days of the Soviet resistance, and little has changed in their operations since then.

Smugglers have long backed the Taliban

Because of the Taliban's one-year ban on poppy cultivation in 2000, there is a widespread misconception that the movement was anti-poppy. In fact, there is clear evidence that smugglers, traders and the Pashtun trucking mafia which controls transport between Pakistan's southern port city Karachi and Central Asia backed the Taliban well before Islamabad tried to muscle in. Taliban officials have themselves described Haji Bashar Noorzai, the son of a leading member of the Quetta Alliance of traffickers and himself a former *mujahid*, as Mullah Mohammad Omar's original sponsor. Noorzai raised eight million Pakistani rupees (then about $250,000), a half-dozen pickup trucks and leftover weapons from the resistance to help launch the movement.[34] Mullah Omar never forgot the favour, according to former Taliban and declassified US government documents. Noorzai came to sit on the eight-member senior Taliban *shura*, which made all policy decisions. Another original *shura* member was Haji Baz Mohammad, who today is incarcerated in the United States, having pleaded guilty in 2007 to charges that he smuggled heroin for the Taliban.[35]

In *The Taliban*, the Pakistani journalist Ahmed Rashid has mapped out how the Pashtun trucking mafia poured money into Taliban coffers, financing among other initiatives, the advance on the western Afghan city of Herat. The author Anthony Davis reported how generous bribes helped the Taliban buy their way across Afghanistan, seemingly capturing town after town without firing a shot. The same has been true in the post-2001 phase of the Taliban's resurgence. The movement has been deeply dependent on, and highly receptive to the needs of, major opium traffickers.

The clearest case in point is Haji Juma Khan, a member of the Mohammad-Hasani tribe of the Brahui people, a Sunni Muslim ethnic group nearly two million strong spanning the tri-border region.[36] Alhough Haji Bashar Noorzai appears to have enjoyed dominant influence over the Taliban *shura* during the early years of the movement, Juma Khan's wealth and influence were clearly established by midway through the Taliban regime, when he erected a palatial compound in Zaranj, the capital of western Nimruz province. His citadel, which was heavily fortified and guarded by dozens of armed men, dwarfed even the provincial governor's mansion across the street. His massive 100–plus vehicle convoys crossing the Iranian desert soon attracted the attention of foreign counter-narcotics officials. By the late 1990s, British officials regarded Haji Juma Khan as the trafficker who moved the most opium shipments from Pakistan's Makran Coast into the United Arab Emirates, where he later took up residence. He ferried opium and hashish along the narrow channel of the Arabian Sea that separates Pakistan from the Arabian Peninsula, coming ashore on the stretches of empty coastline between Oman and the UAE. "They would land along the remote beaches and bury their shipments in the sand," said a former British official.[37]

Before long, Juma Khan's authority eventually came to rival that of Bashar Noorzai, although there are no reports of the two men actually fighting over drug turf. "Haji Juma Khan was number three in the Taliban by the end," said a US official.[38] US officials believe he also became close to Al Qaida during the late 1990s, and there is evidence that he helped move Al Qaida operatives around the region after the US-led invasion in 2001.[39] US forces briefly arrested Haji Juma Khan in late 2001 near Kandahar, and although he was known to be involved in drugs, US military intelligence let him go, believing him to be insignificant. It was a decision they would come to regret. By 2004, Western intelligence agents identified Haji Juma Khan's drug network as a principle source of funding to the Taliban and Al Qaida—and a key conduit for their weapons and ammunition. He ran massive heroin refineries and maintained huge underground storage depots in Baramcha. At the height of his power, Haji Juma Khan moved as much as $1 billion worth of opium traffic annually.[40] After Afghan and international law enforcement units began cracking down on Baramcha, Haji Juma Khan established large heroin-producing bases in the remote Chahar Borjak district of Nimruz and along the mountainous border with Iran, according to Afghan officials. He also maintained large, hidden weapons caches in those areas. He was one of the first to develop mobile drug refineries, often built in the bed of Toyota Hilux trucks or hastily erected in people's homes.[41]

Once notorious for his 100–vehicle drug convoys, Haji Juma Khan had to adjust tactics once NATO troops moved into Helmand. He began sending smaller caravans—just 15 to 20 SUVs—normally guarded by fighters armed with heavy machine guns and RPGs. "We often tried to intercept his convoys," said a senior Interior Ministry official in Kabul, "but his connections are very good within the government and police. He'll get a tip off that we are coming, and pass that information onto the Taliban and they will come out in force."[42] Internationally, his preferred method of moving contraband was by sea, and for years he ran shipments between Karachi and Sharjah in the United Arab Emirates, where the kingpin lived for several years after the Taliban government fell. The UAE authorities eventually ejected him from Sharjah under pressure from the US, but until that point, US intelligence officials believed his boats carried contraband out of Karachi and returned laden with weapons—including plastic explosives and anti-tank mines which were shipped overland to the militants.[43]

Sources close to the movement say a trafficker like Haji Juma Khan maintained a symbiotic relationship with the insurgents, providing weapons and funding for their operations, while receiving protection for his massive drug shipments and military muscle to back the farm output he demanded. Where smaller traffickers were content to contract the insurgents to protect their drug shipments, Haji Juma Khan played an active role in organizing the insurgency, counternarcotics officials say. "For some time, we knew that Haji Juma Khan was meeting directly with Taliban officials who would then sit down with Al Qaida about battle plans," a US official said.[44] In return, the Taliban put pressure on farmers to increase poppy output, distributing night letters that warned Afghan villagers against the consequences of not growing poppy. Taliban fighters helped protect Juma Khan's drug shipments as they snaked down through southwestern Afghanistan, but Afghan security officials said there was some degree of overlap between the insurgents and Haji Juma Khan's personal army. He was known to maintain a force of up to 1,500 armed men, who operated mainly in the western provinces of Farah and Nimruz, where they were often referred to as "Taliban" by the locals.[45] "They pretend to be Taliban," says an Afghan police official. "But they are just Juma Khan's thugs." One such loose associate identified by Afghan security officials was a commander who protected Juma Khan's convoys as they travelled west through the parched plains of southern Nimruz. In return, Juma Khan paid him cash, Toyota Land Cruisers, Thuraya telephones and weapons.

Using this finally, and other henchmen, Haji Juma Khan also branched into in kidnapping, people smuggling and the extortion from local businesses, according to security officials. He funded a large *madrasa* in Pakistan which schools as many as 1,500 students at a time, according to Western officials, who said he used the school to talent spot potential employees or fighters for his private army. Haji Juma Khan's illustrious career came to an end on 23 October 2008, when he was arrested, according to news reports, at Jakarta

Airport on a flight from Dubai. The Taliban kingpin was swiftly handed over to US officials and extradited to New York City, where he appeared just 24 hours later before a federal judge to plead not guilty. US, Afghan and Pakistani officials say he was not only the dominant smuggler in the tri-border area, but also a critical coordinator between the insurgency and the opium trade. It may be years before the effects of his removal from the scene are truly understood. More than any other individual, Haji Juma Khan signified the powerful role played by shadowy businessmen backing the Taliban. Although his influence was well known to counter-narcotics agents, he never became a household name (as did senior Taliban leaders like Mullah Dadullah or Mullah Omar) either among the wider Afghan public or even among many policy-makers working on Afghanistan and Pakistan.

Smugglers are the link between insurgents and corrupt officials

Major traffickers like Haji Juma Khan and their associates play critical roles in negotiating the movement of illicit shipments across Afghanistan, acting as the go-betweens among insurgents and corrupt government officials who are unable to meet in person or communicate by phone, according to interviews with truckers and low-level smugglers, as well as Western officials. Deals brokered by smugglers, including elaborate arrangements made by Haji Juma Khan to protect his consignments as they passed from Taliban territory into regions controlled by the government, are a central reason why the opium trade makes up almost half of Afghanistan's GDP: the booming commerce creates a perverse incentive for leaders on either side of the battlefield to create a stable Afghanistan. There is simply too much money to be made.

The corruption does not end at Afghanistan's borders. Iran, which battles one of the world's highest opium addiction rates, spends more than $400 million a year trying to prevent Afghan opium from entering its territory. Tehran has erected massive ramparts along its border with Afghanistan to block drug convoys, and some 3,400 soldiers and police have died in the past six years battling heavily armed drug convoys that pass through Iran on their way to Turkey and the lucrative European market.[46] Yet there is considerable evidence, according to Western officials and smugglers along the border, that corrupt Iranian intelligence agents protect traffickers, even moving drug shipments in their vehicles, which have special plates and do not get searched by Iran's anti-drug police. Sources along the border also identified a handful of major traffickers, mainly ethnic Baluchis, who cooperate with Iranian secret agents to coordinate Taliban attacks on NATO troops. This would suggest that the problem is more than just an issue of corruption, but rather a covert effort within Iran's wider strategy to disrupt NATO, and specifically US, activities in Afghanistan. This phenomenon was linked to the June 2007 accusation by US Defense Secretary Robert Gates that Iran was supplying plastic explosives being used in deadly IED attacks.

The corruption problem is equally severe in Pakistan, which in 2007 was quietly added to the US State Department's list of major trafficking countries. Just as Islamabad is reticent about going after the Taliban, so it is rare to hear of high-level drug traffickers getting apprehended. "Not arresting them is a passive form of assistance," says a Western diplomat. Many believe the cooperation goes much deeper: as in Iran, elements of Pakistan's Inter Services Intelligence, or ISI, are widely believed to help protect the drug trade. Multiple smugglers interviewed along the border were able to identify specific agents in specific regions, and even knew the sums of money they had been paid. Ex-President Pervez Musharraf once admitted that "retired" Pakistani secret agents supported the insurgents, and some Western officials believe these "retirees" facilitate the drugs trade to keep the Taliban and other local *Jihadi* groups funded.

It is hard to get clear data about what happens to drugs proceeds earned by the insurgency once they have been converted from opium into hard currency. Sources close to the movement identify Karachi as the place for Taliban money transfers to pay for weapons supplies and to launder drug proceeds. Officials also believe drug money earned by the Taliban is invested in real estate in Quetta and nearby districts of Baluchistan province. Authorities believe Taliban insurgents transfer cash using the bustling *Hawala* network that operates between Afghanistan, Pakistan and the UAE. Given the unregulated nature of *Hawala*, it is impossible to know how much money the militants transfer through the network, still more to pinpoint how much of those funds are connected to drugs, donations or payments for weapons or other supplies. The World Bank and the UN calculate that *Hawala* dealers in Helmand and Kandahar alone move more than $1 billion of drug money annually. Surveyors identified 54 *Hawaladars* in those provinces as "specialists" in laundering opium money. Most traded exclusively in Pakistani rupees, indicating that most payments flowed from Pakistan.[47] Senior Pakistani officials believe a staggering one-third of their country's $8 billion annual *Hawala* trade is related to drug traffic.[48]

However, *Hawala* is not the preferred method for laundering drug proceeds. Most Afghan opium is actually bartered for commodities, which means that there is virtually no money trail to follow. There is little use for hard currency in the Afghan market, which is instead desperate for basic goods like vehicles, electronics and construction materials. From Smugglers Creek in Dubai, where hundreds of dhows are loaded with commodities bound for Pakistan, to the teeming Karachi port, where tiny rowing boats unload goods off larger vessels, and then on to the chaotic Chaman border where trucks bursting with goods stream into southern Afghanistan, one begins to understand the complexity of trying to regulate regional trade, let alone isolating the "bad" from the "good." As with *Hawala*, it is not possible to calculate a total annual dollar figure traded by traffickers who are associated with the insurgents.

Drugs-for-commodities scams provide smugglers with a critical "legal" front for their activities. Until his arrest, Haji Juma Khan was one of the largest importers of Toyota Land Cruisers in southern Afghanistan. He also owns an electronics import-export firm in the UAE, according to authorities. Haji Bashar Noorzai was Afghanistan's largest tyre importer, until he was arrested in the US in 2005. It is said that an empty truck never passes over the rugged Durand Line, the disputed border between Pakistan and Afghanistan, although neither country is terribly successful at collecting customs revenue from this steady stream of traffic. "The Pakistanis often complain about the Afghan Transit Trade Agreement," says former US Special Treasury Agent John Cassara. "Basically, it is drugs going out and commodities going in."[49]

Estimating Taliban drug earnings

There is no doubt that traffickers backing the Taliban earn the lion's share of profits from Afghanistan's booming opium industry. Yet it is pertinent to try to estimate how much the insurgents collect on an annual basis. The UNODC estimates about 98 per cent of Afghanistan's 7,700 metric ton opium yield in 2008 came from regions affected by the Taliban insurgency and sold at an average of US$70 per kilogram. This would have netted the Taliban up to $54 million in *ushr* revenue alone, although it might be excessive to assume that the Taliban were able to tax all of the output, as not all fields are under their control even in the south.

Additionally, insurgents collect about $250 for every kilogram refined in labs located in their control zones.[50] The UNODC estimates those refineries produced 666 metric tons of heroin and morphine base in 2007, which would have yielded up to another $133 million.[51] There are no available estimates yet for the amount of drug refined in 2008. The Taliban are estimated earn as much as $250 million annually providing armed protection for drug shipments moving through their region, as well as receiving tens of millions of dollars worth of material supplies from smugglers including vehicles, food, and satellite phones.[52] Added together, the profits could come to close to a half a billion dollars per year in cash and commodities—similar to what Colombia's FARC is estimated to earn annually in cocaine revenue.

When putting numbers on criminal activity—especially in a region where few paper records are kept—even the best estimates are just that. However, the fact is clear: Taliban insurgents are earning astonishingly large profits off the opium trade. As the Afghan government and the international community search for ways to put an end to the insurgency, eliminating their means of raising and transferring funds will be critical. Simultaneously, Afghan villagers who cultivate poppy, either by coercion or by choice, or who in some way engage in the illicit drug trade will need to have legal alternatives made available to them.

Notes

1. This chapter examines how the Taliban profit from the opium trade and considers the relationship between the insurgents and the traffickers. Many Afghan power

brokers apart from the Taliban, including regional strong men and senior members of the Kabul government, also profit from the drug trade. This chapter does not aim to suggest that the Taliban are the only actors in the drug trade, nor that they reap more profits than individuals allied with the Kabul government.

2. According to figures extrapolated from the 2008 UNODC *Annual Opium Survey* and the *World Drug Report 2008.*

3. The outside world—and particularly Western forces fighting in Afghanistan—has similarly underestimated the Taliban's public relations campaign, which displays similar sophistication. For more on this see J. Nathan's chapter in this book.

4. For further discussion on this, see also Ahmed Rashid, *The Taliban: Militant Islam, Oil and Fundamentalism in Central Asia*, New Haven: Yale University Press, 2000; and Anthony Davis, "How the Taliban Became a Military Force", in *Fundamentalism Reborn*, ed. Bill Maley, London: Hurst and Co.,1998, p. 44.

5. Maj. Shahid Asfar, Maj. Chris Samples and Maj. Thomas Wood, "The Taliban, An Organizational Analysis," *Military Review*, Naval Postgraduate School (Monterey: May-June 2008), p. 64.

6. The United Nations Office on Drugs and Crime (UNODC) estimated there were 2.4 million people involved in poppy cultivation in Afghanistan in 2008, or about 10 per cent of the population.

7. Interview by research assistant 2, Lashkar Gah July 2007.

8. Interview by research assistant 2, Lashkar Gah. July 2007.

9. Stephen Grey and Anna Schecter, "Exclusive: 11 Tons of Opium Discovered in Taliban Town", ABCNews.com, 20 December 2007.

10. This was also true during the Taliban era and during the Soviet resistance in *mujahidin*-held areas.

11. When the petals drop off the vivid opium poppy flower, they expose a green pod containing a thick, milky sap: opium in its purest form. Farmers harvest the sap as they have for centuries, by scoring the buds with a curved scraping knife and collecting the sticky brown resin that dries on the buds. In rudimentary "laboratories", often nothing more than a mud hut with metal mixing drums and a brick stove, the raw opium is mixed with lime and boiled in water to make morphine base. Once poured into moulds and sun-dried into hard bricks, it has reduced in weight and volume by a factor of 10, making it easier to smuggle. Depending on the region, Taliban sub-commanders may collect sticky raw opium gum or partially refined morphine base. In this discussion, it is uniformly referred to as opium for simplicity's sake.

12. Interview by research assistant 1, Kabul July 2007.

13. Moore, Molly, "NATO Confronts Surprisingly Fierce Taliban," *The Washington Post*, 26 February 2008.

14. http://www.unodc.org/unodc/en/press/releases/2008–11–27.html

15. Hayatullah Gaheez, "Daughters Sold to Settle Debts," *Institute for War and Peace Reporting* ARR No. 155, 30 December 2004.

16. Tom Coghlan, "Even the School Playground Has Been Turned into a Poppy Field." *The Telegraph* (8 February 2007) and author's interviews with local farmers in Helmand.

17. Interview by research assistant 1, Kabul July 2007.

18. Abubakar Siddique and Salih Mohammad Salih, "Afghanistan: Poor Helmand Farmers Find Themselves in Eye of Drug Storm," *Radio Free Europe/Radio Liberty* (10 October 2007), and authors' interviews.

19. Noor Khan, "Taliban Collected Taxes, Ran Heroin Labs, Had Own Judge in Afghan Town," *The Associated Press*, 12 December 2007.
20. Interview by research assistant 1, Kabul August 2007.
21. Interview by research assistant 2, Kandahar August 2007.
22. Khan, "Taliban Collected Taxes..." (note 19).
23. Graeme Smith, "Air Strikes and Drug Eradication," in "Talking to the Taliban: Globe Special Report," *The Globe and Mail* (24 March 2008). See: www.theglobe-andmail.com/talkingtothetaliban. The figure of eight per cent comes from the UNODC *2007 Opium Survey* p. 6.
24. Abubakar Siddique and Mohammad Salih Salih, "Afghanistan: Poor Helmand Farmers Find Themselves in Eye of Drug Storm", Radio Free Europe/Radio Liberty, 10 October 2007.
25. http://www.unodc.org/documents/publications/Afghanistan_Opium_Survey_2008.pdf p. 17.
26. Interview by research assistant 1, Kabul July 2007.
27. Lobjakas, Ahto, "Afghanistan: NATO Downplays 'Conventional' Threat In South," *Radio Free Europe*, 23 January 2007.
28. Interview by research assistant 2, Helmand July 2007.
29. Interviews by research assistant 4, in Quetta 8–9 October 2007.
30. In the late 1980s there were epic internecine battles over control of drug between *mujahidin* commanders like Hizb-e Islami's Gulbuddin Hekmatyar and Mullah Nasim Akhundzada of Helmand.
31. Bill Roggio, "The Taliban's Internecine War in Waziristan," *The Long War Journal* (6 April 2007) http://www.longwarjournal.org/archives/ 2007/04/the_talibans_interne.php
32. Obaidullah's current whereabouts are uncertain. He was reported as being arrested on 2 March 2007 in Quetta, although Pakistani officials would never officially confirm his capture. Obaidullah was later reported to have been traded for the release of Pakistan's Ambassador in Kabul, Tariq Azizuddin, after the envoy was kidnapped near Peshawar on the road to the Afghan border.
33. The day-to-day running of the Haqqani Group is now run by Jalaluddin's son Sirajuddin.
34. Author's interviews and US Embassy (Islamabad) Cable, "Finally, a Talkative Talib: Origins and Membership of the Religious Students' Movement" (20 February 1995), Taliban File. 9/11 Sourcebook., *National Security Archive*, George Washington University.
35. Press release from US Attorney's Office, Southern District of New York, "First Heroin Kingpin Ever Extradited from Afghanistan Pleads Guilty to Smuggling Heroin into the United States," *Department of Justice*, 11 July 2006.
36. Historians believe Brahuis migrated to the remote area about 3,000 years ago from the Indus Valley region. Linguists interpret their language, which is distinct from Dari and Pashtu, as grammatically derived from ancient Dravidian tongues. Today, territories the Brahui inhabit are as forbidding and isolated as any on earth. Smuggling is the central livelihood in the tri-border area, where official boundaries between the three countries scarcely exist. Virtually everyone associated with HJK is also Brahui. It is not an easy clan for outsiders to penetrate.
37. Interview by author with a former British official, November 2007.
38. Interview by author with a US official, Kabul 30 June 2004.
39. Interview by author with a US official, Washington DC July 2007.
40. Interview by author with a US official Lashkar Gah, May 2006.

41. Interviews by research assistant 1 in Afghanistan. July 2007.

42. Interview by research assistant 1, Kabul July 2007.

43. Tim McGirk, "Terrorism's Harvest," *Time Asia Magazine* (9 August 2004); and author's interviews.

44. Interview by author, Kabul, May 2004.

45. Interview by research assistant 1, Kabul July 2007.

46. Interview by author, Kabul February 2007.

47. Edwina Thompson, "The Nexus of Drug Trafficking and *Hawala* in Afghanistan," in *Afghanistan's Drug Industry* William Byrd and Doris Buddenberg, eds, United Nations Office on Drugs and Crime/World Bank (2007), pp. 177–9.

48. Interview with author, Rawalpindi, February 2008.

49. Interview by author, Washington DC, 29 June 2007.

50. David Rohde, "Second Record Level for Afghan Opium Crop," *The New York Times*, 28 August 2007, and author's interviews.

51. Interview by author, Kabul 4 March 2008. The figure of $133 million is based on the assumption that 80 percent of the opium also gets refined in Taliban-dominated territory.

52. According to multiple interviews by the author and research assistants.

2

READING THE TALIBAN

Joanna Nathan

Perceptions are vital in an insurgency, and as the Taliban leadership has regrouped since its 2001 overthrow it has devoted increasing attention to communications. During its time in power the Taliban had been mindful of their image—nationally and internationally—but usually appeared confused how to shape it beyond censorship and crude punishment of those they believed to be misrepresenting them. Today, when they lack territorial control and state institutions and have to compete in the market place of ideas, speaking to the population both through the mainstream media and through their own work is crucial. In attempting to frame the current fight as a *jihad*, the one time southern commander Mansur Dadullah points out that communications are considered on a par with fighting: "[I] have a message to the Afghan people and to all Muslims: They must continue to wage jihad, wherever they may be—whether it is jihad of the pen, of the tongue, of the sword, or of money."[1]

Taliban communications reveal some broader aspects of the revitalized movement. First, the regional dimension and the importance of cross-border logistical support are very obvious, with all the early spokesmen providing Pakistani contact details and magazines, DVDs, audiotapes and websites all bearing Pakistani addresses. The internal aspects of the insurgency, which have been vital to the geographic spread and upswing in violence, are also seen, with increasingly bold spokesmen switching to Afghan telephone numbers and an almost solely nationalist message relentlessly spotlighting the poor state of local governance and questioning the motives of foreign "invaders".

Finally, the Taliban movement is shown for the diffuse movement it is, with a number of networks and fellow travellers disseminating their own communications output. Recent statements show the leadership—styling itself in the name of the former regime, the Islamic Emirate of Afghanistan (IEA)—attempting to increase control. Approaches to such work may even be a point of friction within the movement. Most of the media "stars" to emerge in recent years, such as Ustad Mohammad Yasir and the Dadullah brothers, are those more closely linked with the media-friendly Al Qaida rather than the more traditional Taliban leadership which has always remained largely in the shadows.

This chapter will focus on work in the name of the IEA and examine what it seeks to portray of the movement. Examining the image the leadership tries to project is obviously somewhat different from the reality of the movement, but provides insight into what is publicly highlighted—and what is hidden. It must also be acknowledged that in a largely illiterate, rural culture the messages that reach those on the ground come largely from community networks and not from the more formal media. Further, looking at what a movement says about itself is very different from examining the effects this has on the wider population. Graeme Smith's research does however suggest a large measure of vertical messaging, and over time communications are presumably increasingly tailored to what is perceived to best appeal the intended audience(s).[2]

Most broadly, communications can be seen as embedded at the very heart of Taliban operations, with actions undertaken for their wider impact on perceptions. A Taliban commander in Wardak province recognised the publicity value of attacks in the central regions relative to other areas of the country: "[B]eing near Kabul allows the news and military events that happen here [Maidan Wardak] to reach all the international media outlets. For instance, when we destroyed 54 logistics vehicles in July, local and international journalists rushed to report the event."[3]

High-profile attacks, including targeting the Serena Hotel (January 2008) and a military parade (April 2008), garnered international attention, demonstrating new levels of technical capacity in small but complex operations. In reality they demanded little in the way of manpower or community support and did not change the situation on the ground. However, the widely reprinted photographs of the (unarmed) Afghan National Army soldiers running from the latter event dealt a severe blow to local perceptions of their new security forces. The June 2008 Kandahar jailbreak was the subject of accounts in many Taliban outlets and appears to have entered insurgent lore, celebrated as a psychological victory:

The performance of this operation had a heavy negative effect on the psyche of the enemy forces both foreign and interior, and their spirits were completely crushed after the mujahidin were able to perform an operation in such an accurate technical manner that did not result in any casualty in the ranks of the mujahidin.[4]

In its communications work the Taliban leadership targets a number of different audiences through its own output as well as contact with the mainstream media. The vast majority of material is in Pashtu, the language of the ethnic constituency from which the movement sprang and continues to draw most of its supporters. Here it seeks to fuel often quite legitimate local griev-ances among sympathisers as well as providing powerful and violent images of battlefield exercises and operations to mobilise recruits and intimidate those who may oppose them. Smaller-scale Arabic language activities would seem intended to draw personnel and resources from wider transnational networks. There has been active outreach to Arabic language media as well as its own productions and publications featuring personnel from the *mujahidin* period, including Yasir. A former member of Abd al-Rabb al-Rasul Sayyaf's Ittehad-i Islami, he is a fluent Arabic speaker and presents himself as a fiery ideologue.[5]

More recently there has been increased output and outreach directed at Western audiences through English language efforts. This demonstrates an appreciation that popular opinion in international capitals is crucial to the staying power of a multinational alliance. Such efforts are increasingly well translated, with idiomatic expressions indicating the involvement of native speakers by late 2008. A relatively new phenomenon has been blood-curdling statements directed at countries in the multinational Coalition who have suf-fered losses, emphasising the intractability of the conflict. Following the August 2008 murder of two Canadian aid workers in Logar, after first claim-ing that the women were military personnel, the Taliban website proclaimed: "Afghans have not invaded Canada to kill Canadians, but it's the Canadians who have invaded Afghanistan for murdering, torturing and plundering of Afghans and Afghanistan, so they can satisfy the craving of the fascist mode of neo-crusaders."[6]

There has also been a marked increase in monitoring what the outside world is saying about events in Afghanistan. Almost daily there are now translated—and heavily edited—highlights from foreign news items and commentaries on the state of the insurgency on the Taliban website. Material in other West-ern languages is also watched, pointing to further external assistance.[7]

Tracing the emergence of Taliban communications following the 2001 fall of the regime begins with a chaotic period as the remnants of the leadership regrouped and rethought their strategy. With the senior members in hiding and no infrastructure available to them, statements first appeared as *shabnamah* (night letters—pamphlets or posters spread at night containing statements and/or threats). These were able to attract wider attention and audiences when shared with the mainstream media, authenticated through their delivery by purported spokesmen. One of the first apparently reliable representatives called himself Mohammad Mukhtar Mujahid; in early 2003 he faxed journal-ists in Pakistan a statement in the name of Mullah Omar, calling for *jihad*,[8] and further announced the formation of a new 10–man leadership council.[9] A confused plethora of self-proclaimed spokesmen and commanders contin-ued to invoke the regime's name. A February 2004 statement expressed frus-tration and named Hamed Agha (which may be an alias for Qudratullah Jamal)[10] as the sole authorised representative.[11]

It was however Latifullah Hakimi, a Taliban-era official, who emerged as the movement's most prominent voice, telephoning journalists from a Pakistan number in contrast to previous faxed communiqués.[12] He was detained in Quetta in October 2005, and although he was freed in a March 2007 prisoner exchange, little has been heard from him since. Hakimi's successors were the previously unknown Qari Mohammad Yousaf Ahmadi (subsequently referred to as "Qari Yousaf") and Mohammad Hanif ("Dr Hanif"). The Taliban-era head of the department of Information and Culture in Kandahar, Abdul Hai Mutmain, stated that he would be the overall "political" spokesman,[13] although he has rarely spoken. With insurgent violence on the rise in Afghanistan the two everyday spokesmen became increasingly boastful and confident, available at all hours to make exaggerated claims about incidents. "Dr Hanif", a young Nangarhari in his mid-20s who had taken to his role with enthusiasm, was arrested in January 2007, apparently soon after entering the country from Pakistan. He was paraded on television in subsequent weeks denouncing the movement and its tactics.[14]

Presumably to spare such humiliation being repeated, the two main points of contact today—Qari Yousaf, for the south, and Zabihullah Mujahid, for the eastern and central regions—are aliases used by a variety of people according to journalists who deal with them. These "spokesmen" maintain regular contact with the mainstream media through email, SMS and telephone calls and provide online reports of incidents, often within minutes of them taking place. One Kabul-based editor described being so deluged in claims that he asked them to stop contacting him so regularly.[15]

With the Taliban leadership now having to compete to be heard, Taliban-era strictures on television, the internet and pictures of living images were quickly dropped. Supportive publications began springing up within a year or so—a tradition for all factions from the *mujahidin* years—featuring pictures of "American atrocities".[16] From around 2005 there were increasingly confident moves to take advantage of new media such as the internet and DVDs, as well as outreach to the mainstream media. Relations with journalists had never been easy during the Taliban's time in power, and amidst the growing insurgency the battlefield has been kept largely off-limits to independent verification. Instead it is largely a battle of press releases, with the Taliban unleashing a deluge of exaggerated military tolls. In most cases there is a real incident at the core of claims, but numbers are massively skewed. It was stated for instance that 30 foreign troops had been killed in an August 2008 assault on an American base in Khost[17] when far fewer deaths were later reported in reputable media.[18] The same month, Taliban statements put the number of French soldiers killed in an ambush in Sarobi at 95, refuting the French government's figure of ten, but offering no evidence.[19] The Taliban have even sought to claim attacks that they did not commit, with Qari Yousaf telling a news agency that the Taliban had killed the district chief of Chora in Uruzgan in September 2008, when it actually apparently occurred amidst a firefight involving foreign soldiers as the result of a fatal misunderstanding.[20]

Menace hangs over local correspondents in particular if it is felt that their work is unfavourable or inadequate editorial space is provided. In 2006 Mullah Dadullah demanded: "Many news sources cruelly treat the Taliban. For example they do not air our reports... We will kill anyone who mistreats us like this. What we demand is that the media should impartially and independently air our reports."[21] A Taliban-linked magazine gave an even more sweeping condemnation of the state of the post-Taliban media scene, in an article entitled "Independent Journalists or Spies of the Crusaders?", claiming:

Some years back there were few government TV channels in the region and today there are dozens. The only aim of this evil conspiracy is to disseminate poisonous propaganda against the mujahidin in a secret way, to stop the sympathy and support of the nation in favour of the jihad.[22]

A number of reporters have been kidnapped when seeking interviews with Taliban figures, and a local journalist and driver were gruesomely killed in Helmand in 2007 after the release of their Italian colleague. It is not clear whether such actions are carefully planned or are due to the diverse range of actors and communication difficulties. Some individual commanders have granted media interviews apparently on their own initiative,[23] but access has for the most part been limited to a few selected "embedded" reporters,[24] and it is clear that the leadership, as well as presumably fearing for its safety in arranged meetings, prefers to closely control its image.

There certainly appears to be some kind of guiding hand behind the broader scheme of the Taliban's evolving output. The Taliban's Arabic-language magazine *Al Somood* claims that an official media unit began as early as September 2002, led by former Information Minister Qudratullah Jamal until his replacement in May 2004 by Yasir.[25] In March 2008 *Al Somood* outlined a new "administrative structure" with Amir Khan Muttaqi, the former regime's first minister of Information and Culture (later its Education minister) now heading a "cultural commission" with duties to:

a. Establish relations with media channels and agencies to notify them on important military events
b. Issue Jihadi magazines and newspapers
c. Oversee the internet website related to the movement
d. Issue and publish Jihadi books
e. Prepare Jihadi films and publish them on Jihadi websites.[26]

It is unclear how this fits with a "media bureau" described in an *Al Somood* update of the Taliban media scene in July 2008 (marking the publication's third year). This states that the bureau is headed by the magazine's chairman Nasiruddin "Herawi", who "enjoys a special status and dignity in his relation to the *Amir ul-Momineen* (Commander of the Faithful)" and who must employ an alias "as he works in more than one sphere, his original name appears at the head of the Americans' list of main wanted persons belonging to the Taliban".[27] This media bureau's role was stated as:

- the production and publication of Jihadi films
- their transmission on Jihadi websites
- putting in order and publishing the archives of important issues related to the Afghan cause
- the gathering of photos, videos and military reports from within the front by *Al Somood* correspondents
- the setting up of explanatory media sessions on important subjects for reporters and journalists from within the military frontlines, such as in Musa Qala district in Helmand province, Panjwayi district in Kandahar province, Tora Bora in Nangarhar province, Sayedabad district in Wardak province, Askar Kut as-Sakhina in Ghazni province, Sabari district in Khost province and the other regions of Afghanistan if and when the need arises
- the publication of the special announcements of the Amir with regard to urging *jihad* against the Crusaders, and directives and orders for the *mujahidin*
- the starting up of educational, cultural and Islamic courses in the *mujahidin's* camps
- the preparation of books on jihadi thought and their distribution to the *mujahidin*
- the accumulation and organisation of data and statistics concerning the martyr-soldiers against foreign forces in Afghanistan
- the gathering and organisation of the data and statistics of martyrs and orphans of martyrs (both civilian and *mujahidin*) who died in the battles fought between the *mujahidin* and the Americans
- the accumulation and ordering of data concerning the activities of the Christian evangelical organisations operating under the cover of humanitarian aid to the Afghan people, research into ways of confronting these activities.[28]

While not systematic, or on the scale suggested, there do now appear to be efforts in nearly all the areas highlighted, with increasing attempts at "branding". The white flag of the Taliban and the imprint of the "cultural affairs commission of the Islamic Emirate of Afghanistan" appear on a variety of material. There also seems to be something of a physical entity working on output linked with the operational sphere, with a 2007 Al Jazeera documentary showing Mullah Dadullah touring a roomful of young men working on computers.[29]

Al Somood in particular has always sought to portray a more coherent, hierarchical structure of the re-emerging movement than is otherwise apparent. Its March 2008 schema included some 10 alleged commissions overseeing everything from recruitment to looking after "martyrs'" families.[30] There is little to suggest that these are truly functional and for the most part the inner workings of the leadership remain opaque, the sacking of Mansour Dadullah being one very unusual and very public exception.[31] Mullah Omar is rarely heard from except in communiqués issued in his name marking important occasions. It is his deputy Mullah Baradar who in the last two years has taken an increasingly public role announcing the launch of "operations".[32] In September 2007 he boasted of a strategy of targeting the country's regional centres and the access roads to Kabul, as was somewhat borne out:

1. Our military operations will focus on the capital cities of the four regions of the country including Kabul
2. Most of these operations will be allocated to martyrdom-seeking attacks and roadside blasts, as these tactics are the most effective at inflicting the most losses upon the enemy
3. The primary target of our attacks are the Crusader invading forces and then secondly the high ranking officials of the Karzai administration
4. In order to keep national and foreign forces surrounded in Kabul, the initial stages of surveillance/control of the roads leading to Kabul from Maidan Shar (capital of Maidan Wardak), Kapisa and Char Asiab have begun. This tactic will soon be put to the test in the Maidan Wardak and Sarobi areas.
5. Before the implementation of this military strategy, all members of the slave army of the Karzai administration are notified to leave and join the *mujahidin*.[33]

Spokesman Qari Yousaf admits that the Taliban leadership does not have full operational command and control, while insisting that this is changing:

On fundamental issues, all orders and decrees are coming from the centre, all *mujahidin* are bound by the stance of the leadership, although in some daily, simple affairs and issues the commander of each area can himself make decisions… as our areas of control expand, the leadership's watch improves and stances become coherent, having control over simple issues becomes possible too.[34]

Central to the leadership's "branding" of statements and claims has been the website Al Emarah (The Emirate). While it will be accessed by very few in a largely offline country such as Afghanistan, it plays a particularly useful role in guaranteeing that output comes from a single source. It thus acts as a distribution centre for leadership statements which can be directly downloaded and shared by interested individuals or followed up on by the mainstream media. A 2007 statement attributed to Mullah Omar showed frustration at continuing claims outside officially recognised channels, demanding that "The international community and the people of the country should not term each comment to be those of the Islamic Emirate. The comments of the Islamic Emirate are those which are released by our official spokesmen and our Al Emarah web page."[35]

Started in mid-2005, Al Emarah has a banner on the front page proclaiming "The Voice of Jihad" (*Da Jihad Ghag* in Pashtu) and stating that it is a product of the Cultural Affairs Commission of the Islamic Emirate of Afghanistan (*Da Afghanistan Islami Emarat Da Farhangi Charu Kummisiyun*). It is fairly basic, without the forums and password protection of some of the more globalised extremist sites—or even links to them. This is however, no small-scale effort, being currently updated several times a day in five languages (Dari, Pashtu, Arabic, English and Urdu). As well as news, statements and longer features, Al Emarah contains expanding sections of poetry and *taranas* (emotive, martial unaccompanied songs) showing how modern technology can help facilitate the spread of age-old art forms and their active promotion by the Taliban.

A few videos began appearing on the site in late 2008 and there are also links to a number of online versions of magazines which, while not all official organs of the movement, would appear through such endorsement to be viewed at the very least as supportive. These are also available in glossy-covered hardcopy, more easily found just across the border in Pakistan, particularly Peshawar, with a Pakistani rupee cover price (although the currency is routinely used on both sides of the border). They are regular and topical, and while aimed at a literate elite would presumably seek to circulate ideas and themes to be picked up elsewhere.[36] Interestingly a link to *Tora Bora*—one of the longest-running monthly magazines, having recently marked four years of publication[37]—was removed in October 2008, presumably demonstrating a grievance with its backer, the Tora Bora Military Front. Those still linked as of November 2008 were:

- *Srak* (Beam of Light): Pashtu-language monthly which says it is the produced by the "Afghanistan Islamic Literary Association" as an "Independent, Impartial, Scientific, Cultural, Social and Islamic Publication". It is among the longest running publications, having started in 2004 with its editor listed as Lutfullah Momand. It offers an address in a Tajik-dominated neighbourhood in Kabul with a 20 rupee cover charge.
- *Shahamat* (Courage): mainly Pashtu language, issued every two months with many of the articles also appearing in Al Emarah. It is not stated who is behind it although the Tora Bora website, which also links to it, says that it is published by "Afghanistan's Islamic Cultural Society".[38]
- *Elham* (Inspiration): A Pashtu-language weekly. It lists its chief editor as Salim Sohail and its publisher as "Afghanistan's Islamic Cultural Society", with a launch date given as 2005. Again an address in Khair Khana is provided.
- *Al Somood* (Standing Firm/Perseverance): A glossy-covered Arabic-language monthly, also available in PDF format; it is filled with colour photo galleries. "Issued by the Media Centre of the Taliban Islamic Movement" under the "guidance" of Nasiruddin "Herawi" as discussed above. It recently entered its third year of publication. The simple standard of the Arabic would suggest it is written by those to whom it is a second language, although the cover pages are of a noticeably higher standard.
- *Murchal* (Trench): A military-focused quarterly launched in 2006; it is published by the "Islamic Emirate of Afghanistan" and the editor is Mullah Khabir Ahmad Mujahid. The address given is simply "Kabul".

- *Zamir* (Conscience): *Tora Bora* says that it is a weekly published by the "Association for the Protection of Islamic Culture in Afghanistan".[39] The link is broken and there is little further information.

Despite some bold claims there has not been widespread use of radio by the Taliban in Afghanistan. There have been reports of broadcasts by Radio Voice of Sharia (Da Radio Shariat Ghag) sporadically in Kandahar since 2005,[40] and later more sustained use of mobile radio in the south east and east.[41] However, presumably fearing potential targeting and possibly in the face of jamming technology, this has not been on a large-scale. Other media include DVDs, some of which are produced in the name *Da Jihad Ghag*, like the website, although there are a variety of studios with more prolific output whose links are not always clear. These discs—or MP3s in urban areas—tend to feature scenes of groups of men in the mountains walking, battle scenes, attacks (particularly on foreign forces) and displays of captured "booty". In a largely illiterate culture, and for the young they presumably seek to recruit, this is an attractive visual medium. Indeed it is here that most communication efforts appear to go into appealing to suicide bombers, with kitschy "martyrdom" tributes to the fallen and appeals by Dadullah and Yasir. There are some examples of "wills" by alleged suicide bombers, although still relatively few by comparison with other arenas.

In one series of apparent suicide wills from 2006, "Khalid" is pictured sitting under an IEA sign with apparent makings of a suicide vest before him stating: "I am from Khost province and here [in Afghanistan] there are attacks from all sides. Allah says that Jews and Christians are the enemy." He speaks not just to potential bombers, but to their families: "Well done to those mothers and those families who rocked these sons in the cradle."[42] Often such DVDs feature emotional *taranas* appealing to nationalist sympathies and seeking to shape perceptions of recent events into traditional narratives. These chants are also available widely on audio cassettes, and even mobile phone ringtones, produced by numerous studios, most apparently across the border in Pakistan.

In April 2008 there was a statement advising those producing such material in the name of the IEA without approval to seek endorsement:

Recently a number of writers, religious scholars and poets have compiled books, Jihadi CDs and recorded *taranas* and publicly distributed them. They referred to their personal work in the name of the Islamic Emirate, in particular the cultural affairs commission, while they had not informed any authorised official of the Islamic Emirate. The Islamic Emirate hails their efforts, however recommends that those who compile books, Jihadi CDs or songs and want them to be released in the name of the Islamic Emirate should get the approval of the Islamic Emirate cultural commission.[43]

Much of this "unofficial" output can be attributed to enthusiastic supporters and local level groups seeking the legitimation of their criminality or protest through use of the Taliban name. It is clear however that there are also distinct elements determined to maintain their own national—or even international—profile.

Anwar ul-Haq's Tora Bora Military Front (*Tora Bora Nizami Mahaz*)—which emerged from the remnants of his father Mawlawi Khalis' faction of Hizb-i Islami upon the latter's 2006 death—seeks a particularly high profile. Indeed with the long-running *Tora Bora* magazine, a rapidly expanding website and regular claims for attacks in its name, its communications would appear to far outpace its battlefield achievements in the eastern region. While Al Emarah recently removed the link to *Tora Bora*, which suggests tension, the faction goes out of its way to emphasise its allegiance to the Taliban, its website stating: "Tora Bora has been established by the efforts of loyalists of the late exalted Khalis *Baba* [a respectful honorific, literally meaning father] and fulfils its jihadi mission within the framework of the Islamic Emirate".[44]

Gulbuddin Hekmatyar's Hizb-i Islami also acts autonomously in its communications work, but with no such claims of allegiance. About its links, Hekmatyar has stated: "We neither have organizational links with Al Qaida nor with the Afghan or Pakistani Taliban…We have asked our mujahidin to call every mujahid his brother, fight the enemies jointly [and] not to spare their help to any good mujahid."[45] More recently relations appear tenser, with Hekmatyar's 2008 Eid message accusing the Taliban of leaving the country open to foreign intervention through refusing alliances with it in 2001 and earlier in the 1990s: "If at that stage the Taliban…had joined the rows of the loyal mujahidin of Hizb-i Islami, then without any doubt, the Northern Alliance might have perished and the war would have fully ended forever."[46]

Hizb-i Islami's long-running newspaper *Shahadat* can still be found in Pakistan, as well as a new online version which operates uninterrupted with the contact details for a Pakistani webmaster displayed. It does not mention Taliban activities or statements but rather focuses on interviews with Hekmatyar and what it claims are Hizb-i Islami operations throughout Afghanistan. There are increasingly often competing claims for attacks with, for instance, both the Taliban and Hizb-i Islami saying that they were behind the August 2008 Sarobi ambush of French soldiers. In November the Taliban released footage to Al-Arabiya satellite television in continuing efforts to disprove Hizb-i Islami's claim and back its own.[47]

In contrast, Jalaluddin Haqqani's network in the south-east has not been nearly so self-promotional, despite being regarded as closely involved in the more complex and high-profile attacks. The widely publicised March 2008 video of the veteran *mujahidin* fighter, alive and defiant albeit with laboured breath, was brought out under the joint imprint of the cultural affairs commission of the Islamic Emirate of Afghanistan and *Manba al-Jihad* ("The Source of Jihad" in Arabic). The latter was the name of the Haqqani's glossy monthly magazine during the earlier years of war, although links with the studio, which maintains a fairly steady stream of DVDs, remain unclear.[48] His son Sirajuddin has recently sought a somewhat higher profile with a few interviews in 2008. In these he portrays the network as part of the Taliban, while seeking to publicly distance it from foreign backers, despite his father's well-known long-time relationship with Osama Bin Laden and

Pakistan's InterServices (ISI) (see Chapter 4). For instance when asked specifically about relations with Bin Laden and Zawahiri, he claims they have not met "because we are very busy in our own war" but that "we are in contact with one another".[49]

Al Qaida, for its part, maintains its own distinct Arabic-language outlets focused on Afghanistan, demonstrating the importance of the area to its global narrative.[50] This includes a magazine *Vanguards of the Khorasan* (a historic name for the region) started in 2005 and the DVD production unit As Sahab, which has an international focus, even occasionally producing material with English subtitles. Some "cross-promotion" with at least elements of the Taliban movement is evident with Yasir appearing in a number of Al Qaida DVDs. Abu Yahya al-Libi, an Al Qaida member who presents himself in DVDs as a hard-line ideologue following his 2005 escape from Bagram prison, in turn endorses *Tora Bora* magazine, appealing to readers to "support it to the best of your ability with money, articles and reports, and by distributing it among the people, in order to bring the voice of the mujahidin to as many Muslims as possible in Afghanistan, Pakistan and the rest of the countries around the world."[51]

Al-Libi further claimed that in 2002 he had a hand in early Taliban online efforts, stating: "My mission was to transmit the word of the mujahidin through the internet and the special website (*Al-Imara Al-Islamiyya*)".[52] It is notable, however, that the only members of the Taliban name-checked by Al Qaida's top leadership are the Dadullah brothers and Mullah Omar, with the latter carefully respected as *Amir ul-Momineen*. Answering public questions, Al Qaida's deputy leader Ayman al-Zawahiri however put something of a caveat on this, declaring that Mullah Omar is "the leader of the Islamic Emirate of Afghanistan, and of the mujahidin who have joined him. Sheikh Osama Bin Laden—may Allah protect him—is one of his soldiers. The leader of the Muslims around the world is the Imam of the Caliphate state and we strive for its return."[53]

The Dadullah brothers in turn spoke regularly of their ties with Al Qaida. Indeed Mansour Dadullah specifically referred to these links upon his brother's death when seeking to bolster his own legitimacy: "The most recent proof that Osama bin Laden is alive and well is that he sent me a letter of condolence after my brother's martyrdom, and advised me to follow in the footsteps of my brother, Mullah Dadallah."[54] In contrast Mullah Omar has been circumspect about the relationship with Al Qaida, although the Taliban's media commission did offer condolences on his behalf upon the death of Al Qaida's leader in Iraq, Abu Musab al-Zarqawi.[55]

Indeed, given the Taliban's nationalist credentials, and demands for Karzai's foreign backers to leave, there is always a public rejection of suggestions that it receives outside assistance. One magazine insisted that such claims were part of age-old foreign propaganda:

The surprising point is that when the former Soviet Union and its handpicked Kabul communist regimes had received blows from the mujahidin or if the mujahidin had captured a piece of land, the black-hearted KGB network and its related intelligence circles would state that it was done by the neighbouring country Pakistan…Americans and their puppets use the same excuse that the Russians and communists used, that Pakistan is involved in the resistance and help them directly. They are trying to distract the public from their defeat.[56]

The so-called Pakistan Taliban are also kept at arm's length. Qari Yousaf, when asked specifically about the group, said: "We have sympathy with each and every Muslim and our official policy is not interfering in others' affairs, our military program is for our homeland's independence from an unjustified invasion."[57]

The few times the Taliban have ventured into the sphere of international affairs have not proved successful. Hard-line bloggers were apparently up in arms at perceived support for the concept of nation states in a rare statement by a so-called political commission of the Islamic Emirate of Afghanistan,[58] which said that: "The Islamic Emirate is eager for good relations with all foreign countries and neighbours and wants to live with them in peace, in the light of the provisions of the holy religion of Islam. Similarly the Islamic Emirate expects that all other countries will reciprocate good relations."[59]

Internally in Afghanistan the Taliban's continued quest for some form of legitimacy and public support can be seen in the leadership's denial of involvement in attacks that have resulted in numerous civilian casualties. This includes the November 2007 Baghlan bombing and the July 2008 attack on the Indian embassy. Thus while keen to project a powerful image and demonstrating little regard for innocent bystanders in violence that it does claim,[60] the appearance of indiscriminate terror has not been the aim of the Taliban's communications. While gruesome tactics such as beheadings continue to be used, despite public condemnation by Mullah Omar in February 2008,[61] there are however few examples—other than Mullah Dadullah—of the practice being videotaped.

Such mixed messages are also to be found on schooling. A large-scale campaign by the Taliban—and others—has targeted teachers and schools in recent years with explicit threats made (and acted on) in local night letters in the Taliban's name. In public discourse however, such actions are denied, attacks on child-centred community institutions apparently being seen as hard to justify. One magazine displayed the logic often put forward, simultaneously condemning the post-2001 education system as being "prepared in such a way as to demolish jihadi and cultural values" while also stating that the Taliban "do not torch books, not the schools of Muslims, nor kill students or teachers".[62] On a number of occasions Taliban spokesmen have even talked of efforts to build schools, although there is no evidence of this to date.[63] At least some school attacks are undertaken by groups engaged in local quarrels or "foreign elements" for whom popular consent is not such as issue, but the scale of such incidents would also suggest that the Taliban leadership is disingenuous. In his 2008 Eid message, Mullah Omar went so far as to claim that the acts attracting the most public outrage were a deliberate smear campaign, pointing the finger of blame elsewhere even as he warned supporters to exercise care to:

…strictly avoid every action that is not in harmony with Islamic commands or is not appropriate to Islamic morality and the dignity of Islamic society and which is carried out by your enemies dressed as you, such as blasts in mosques and gathering places, seizing property of ordinary people on the highways, cutting noses and ears of people…burning religious books and similar actions. Whoever commits such irresponsible actions outside our organizational structure should reveal their faces and should not slander our mujahidin.[64]

The Taliban leadership taps wells of resentment from the early days of international intervention and the structure of the post-2001 settlement. These include anger over the revenge attacks on northern Pashtun communities and the treatment of Taliban prisoners in 2001/02—and international silence on these issues. The events in the northern fortress of Qala-e Jangi and Guantánamo Bay have entered the local folk culture of an "oppressed nation", with alleged letters from prisoners regularly appearing in many Taliban magazines and the subject of widespread poetry and songs. The re-empowerment of the warlords and commanders—many of the very same people whom the population so hated that they supported the Taliban the first time around—is highlighted repeatedly, with DVDs splicing together new and old footage. Events in which the Uzbek commander General Dostum defied police from the rooftops before the national media in February 2008 are highlighted as an example of the weakness of the current administration: "[if] nobody dares to bring him to justice, how will they stop other ordinary people?"[65]

Similarly civilian casualties is a very deeply felt issue among the population, which is capitalised on. Speedy responses, often lacking ground facts but unable to be checked, or not properly investigated by the fledgling local media, have meant the Taliban have often been able to set the news agenda and drive wider narratives. Events are overblown and inflated to present ideas of a violent, invading force inflicting deliberate harm. Amidst the hyperbole U.S forces are accused of having "committed the most horrible crimes and massacres in human history."[66]

Vocabulary is carefully chosen to condemn those working with the Karzai administration as *munafiq* (hypocrite), *ghulam* (slave/servant), *ajir* (agent) and *gaudagai* (puppet). Particular effort goes into undermining the Afghan police, already not popular amongst the people, who have been subjected to a relentless campaign of violence and invective, with Mullah Omar demanding: "If the police of a state consist of people who are immoral and irreligious, who are drug addicts and who are turned away by their families, how can they protect the property, dignity and honour of the people?"[67]

In turn they seek to cast themselves as "*mujahidin*", often using this name in preference to Taliban, reaching out to those involved in previous eras of fighting.[68] This broadens their appeal as well as tying the fight today into a grand historic narrative of Afghans' "victories" over great powers such as the British and later the Soviets, which are constant points of reference. Indeed a constant theme is the invincibility and omniscience of the movement, with hyperbolic accounts of military action emphasising the high cost and intractability of the conflict, both for local and foreign audiences.

However, just as they did during the movement's rise to power in the 1990s, they deny that they seek power for themselves. Qari Yousaf, asked about future plans, responded: "Our war is not for dividing the government positions, but it is for terminating the occupation and for an independent and Islamic government...Now we are very busy with the resistance and talking about things at governmental level would be untimely and very early now."[69] A rosy view of conditions under their last administration is however constantly presented, glossing over corruption and nepotism under the regime, and overlooking the paradox that it is the Taliban that are the source of much of the current insecurity. Harking back to the rough justice of the period has indeed become an increasingly common sentiment on the streets of Afghanistan, given the lack of functioning judicial systems today. This checklist in an article on Al Emarah encapsulates many of the major messages it highlights, all overwrought and exaggerated, but grounded in deep-seated feeling over the current absence of the rule of law:[70]

Activities of the Islamic Emirates of Afghanistan	The circumstances of the current imported administration
Afghanistan was an independent Islamic country and had absolute Islamic rule;	Everything is under the control of foreigners, the name of Islam is only used to deceive people;
Everyone's life, property and honour (namoos) was secure, there was no stealing or abductions;	No one's life, property or honour is secure, kidnapping, stealing and sexual assaults happen not only on adults but on children;
Everyone's rights were protected in the light of Sharia law and everyone had equal privileges and punishment before the law;	"Right" is now in the hands of those with money and power, those who do not have financial means are deprived of their rights;
Sovreignty was enforced—the entire system was administered from a single centre in accordance with the law, and all decisions were made by the Afghanistanis themselves;	The current administrative corruption has also surprised the foreigners. Moral corruption has increased to the level that cases of AIDS have jumped to thousands in the last few years—and this is only the people whose blood has been checked;
There was no moral or administrative corruption at all;	The mines of the country are exploited in various ways because the aim of the foreigners was to seize the mines. On the other hand the so-

The interests of the country were protected and socially uplifting activities were underway. Those mines for whose exploitation Afghans lacked equipment were kept as country's [future] capital;

There was security at that time.

called aid money mainly goes in the pockets of foreigners and the little that remains goes into the bank;

Given the current feeling of strategic momentum lying with the insurgents, their demands for foreign forces to leave and Karzai to go, and for the imposition of Sharia law, are expressed in absolutist terms. This demonstrates high morale and has the advantage of distracting from the lack of a real programme. Talk of negotiations is always resolutely denied. With stories swirling of meetings in Saudi Arabia in September 2008 Al Emarah proclaimed:

The Islamic Emirate of Afghanistan rejects all these false claims by the enemy who is using this propaganda campaign, the aim of this programme is to create an atmosphere of disunity among the Muslims in order to weaken the Ummah. Our struggle will be continued until the departure of all foreign troops.[71]

There has been none of the softening of rhetoric which could indicate that the leadership is preparing its support base for some form of power-sharing or settlement.

The focus of their communications is above all a nationalist one. This has the advantage of holding wide appeal without highlighting the more divisive aspects that the regime stood for. This has allowed for broad recruitment in what has become a diffuse protest movement. Tribal disenfranchisement may be used at a localised level as a recruiter, but the leadership has never presented or fostered the movement as a wider tribal uprising. Similarly ethnic rhetoric is not used. The vast majority of material is in Pashtu and some of the folk poetry and *taranas* talk of Pashtun pride, but ethnic slurs have not overtly entered communiqués despite virulent anti-Shia sentiment directed at the Hazara population when the Taliban were in power in the 1990s. While the movement holds little appeal to other ethnic groups the stance at the moment appears to be not to antagonise them, with an instruction to "poets and singers" that: "efforts should be made so that the ideals of the current jihad should not be sacrificed to regional, linguistic or personal aspirations and the country's lofty interests and Islamic unity should not be harmed".[72]

Such a broad appeal holds the seeds of potential difficulty in maintaining clarity of purpose. Indeed statements from the leadership show frustration at a lack of control and attempts to consolidate. Despite claims to the contrary, the increasing level of sophistication that has fairly quickly evolved in the last seven years, particularly in new forms of media, would suggest outside assistance and "capacity building". But at their heart Taliban communications have been predicated on understanding of local audiences, amplifying pre-existing perceptions and misperceptions and tapping popular and deep-rooted narratives and networks created by decades of conflict and conspiracies.

Notes

1. "New military commander of the Taliban Mansour Dadullah: Bin Laden is alive and well", Al Jazeera, broadcast 17 June 2007. Translated transcript Middle East Media Research Institute (MEMRI) TV, Clip No. 1490.
2. See Smith's chapter in this book.
3. Abdullah Farid, "Al Somood Interview with Military Commander for Maidan Wardak province", *Al Somood*, September 2008, pp. 8–13. This gives an autobiography stating that since the founding of the Taliban Mawlawi Ahmad Taha Khalid had held positions as Nangarhar provincial deputy military commander, Nangarhar provincial security police chief, Paktika provincial governor, Bamian provincial military commander, Laghman provincial security police chief, and Kunar provincial military division commander.
4. "The conquest of the Kandahar prison and its effect on the military situation in Afghanistan", Translated by Dar Al Murabiteen publications, taken from *Al Somood*, published by the Media Centre of the Taliban Islamic Movement, July 2008.
5. Yasir was arrested August 2005 in the North West Frontier Province (NWFP) and handed to Afghan authorities before being freed in a March 2007 swap for a kidnapped Italian journalist. Taliban-era head of the department of Information and Culture in Kandahar, Abdul Hai Mutmain was quoted telling Radio Tehran that the detention of Yasir and spokesman Latifullah Hakimi (also later released in the prisoner exchange) was against international conventions on the freedom of the press as they did not have military designations. "Extradition of Hakimi, Yasir to Afghanistan against INT'L laws: Taliban", *Pak Tribune*, 29 October 2005. At the start of 2009 Yasir was reported re-arrested in Peshawar, "Pakistan says senior Taliban official arrested in Peshawar", Radio Free Europe, 3 January 2009.
6. "Islamic Emirate of Afghanistan address to the Canadian people in connection with killing of two of its female citizens", Al Emarah, 17 August 2008. Similarly it was demanded of France: "The Islamic Emirate of Afghanistan has always asked those countries, particularly France, that have sent soldiers to Afghanistan in violation of international norms but to make the despotic US regime happy, that such big and independent countries should not sacrifice their national and international reputations to the interests of the US, so that Afghanistan and the brave people of Afghanistan can seek to have good relations with them." Zabihullah Mujahid, "Interesting and updated information on the French casualties and deaths in Sarobi", Al Emarah, 18 August 2008.
7. This would appear to be communicated back to the field; an interview with the Dutch commander of the PRT was reported to have been discussed by the Taliban on their walkie-talkies within an hour of its broadcast on a Dutch station. "Taliban monitors Dutch media", Radio Netherlands, 10 October 2007.
8. Rahimullah Yusufzai, "Taliban call for holy war", BBC News, 8 February 2003.
9. Amin Tarzi, "Neo-Taliban free to communicate with media in Pakistan", Radio Free Europe, 9 August 2005.

10. Graeme Smith, "The Taliban", *The Globe and Mail*, 27 November 2006.
11. Amin Tarzi, "Neo-Taliban free...", cit.
12. Ron Synovitz, "Pakistan hails capture of Taliban spokesman as breakthrough", Radio Free Europe, 5 October 2005, says Hakimi had been the head of the Justice department and then oversaw the department of Information and Culture in Herat (1999–2000).
13. "Mr Mutmain said Mr Yousuf and Dr Hanif would provide information on militant activities in different parts of Afghanistan. They would speak on military matters only, he said, adding that he would be the spokesman on political issues." "Taliban 'appoint new spokesmen'", BBC News Online, 14 October 2005.
14. See for instance "Mullah Omar 'hiding in Pakistan'", BBC News, 17 January 2007 and Aryn Baker "A Taliban Spokesman's Confession", *TIME*, 17 January 2007. After release he and some family members were killed in eastern Afghanistan, although it is unclear by whom, with the finger pointed at a personal feud. "Taliban's ex-spokesman shot dead", BBC News, 28 November 2008.
15. Interview with editor, Kabul, 6 May 2008.
16. An article in the Taliban media provides a timeline for various—often short lived—publications. See "The Media Activities of the Taliban Islamic Movement", *Al Somood*, December 2007, pp.5–6.
17. Statement on Al Emarah website, 16 August 2008.
18. Carlotta Gall and Sangar Rahimi, "Taliban escalate fighting with assault on US base", *The New York Times*, 19 August 2008. This quoted Afghan authorities saying that three American troops had been wounded along with six members of the Afghan Special Forces, with a further 12 Afghan workers killed in a suicide attack outside the base the previous day.
19. "A day after the incident the so-called ISAF occupier force which has command of foreign forces in the country published a press release that said that only 10 French soldiers were killed and 21 others wounded. But we have to say that in fact 100 French ground troops who were with 18 armoured tanks were ambushed by hundreds of fresh Taliban recruits...in the successful attack while mujahidin were firing light and heavy arms, five armoured tanks and eight military vehicles were torched on the spot and caused 100 French casualties and five other vehicles were left in the battlefield. According to a verified report from a battalion of 100 French soldiers only five were able to make their way to safety." Zabihullah Mujahid, "Interesting and updated information over French casualties and deaths in Sarobi", Al Emarah, 18 August 2008.
20. "ISAF forces reportedly kill Afghan district chief, two other people", Peshawar-based Afghan Islamic Press (AIP) news agency, 18 September 2008. Translation: BBC Monitoring.
21. "Taliban supreme commander demands 'impartial' treatment by media", Pakistan-based Afghan Islamic Press News Agency (AIP), 4 September 2006. Translation: BBC Monitoring.
22. Q.M., "Independent journalists or spies of the crusaders: Killer hiding in the garb of reporter", *Tora Bora*, August 2008, p. 1.
23. "What's important is to kill the Germans", *Der Spiegel*, 21 May 2008. This is an interview with Qari Bashir Haqqani, self-proclaimed Taliban military commander in Kunduz, who said he controlled 500 men. Eric De Lavarene, "Our journalists found the Taliban who killed 10 French soldiers", *Paris Match*, 3 September 2008. This commander who called himself Farouki and said he was from Laghman province. Lisa Myers and the NBC Investigative Unit, "An interview with a Tali-

ban commander", 27 December 2005. Here Commander "Ismail" claimed to have downed a Chinook and provided video footage.

24. See for instance David Loyn's "Travelling with the Taliban", BBC News, 24 October 2006; James Bays "Taliban 'in control' in Helmand", Al Jazeera, 24 June 2007; "Special report from Musa Qala", Institute for War and Peace Reporting (IWPR), 27 November 2007; and Sayyed Saleem Shahzad, "In the land of the Taliban", Asia Times Online, December 2006.

25. "The media activities of the Taliban Islamic movement", *Al Somood*, December 2007, pp. 5–6. Translation: Afghan-Wire.

26. Ahmad Mukhtar, "Administrative structure of the Taliban Islamic movement", *Al Somood*, March 2008, p. 17.

27. "The media activities of the Taliban Islamic movement", *Al Somood*, December 2007, pp. 5–6 Translation: Afghan-Wire.

28. "Al Samood begins its third year", *Al Somood*, July 2008, pp. 1–3.

29. "Neo Taliban", Al Jazeera documentary, screened 5 July 2007. Translated transcript MEMRI TV, Clip No. 1508.

30. Ahmad Mukhtar, "Administrative Structure of the Taliban Islamic Movement", *Al Somood*, March 2008, p. 17.

31. A statement on the website announced: "Mullah Mansur Dadullah is not obedient to the Islamic Emirate of Afghanistan in his actions and has carried out activities which were against the rules of the Islamic Emirate of Afghanistan, so the decision [-making] authorities of the Islamic Emirate of Afghanistan have removed Mansur Dadullah from his post." "The decision by authorities of the Islamic Emirate of Afghanistan to remove Mansur Dadullah from his position as the Commander in Charge of the Taliban", Al Emarah, 29 December 2007. Translation: AfghanWire. His personal spokesman Shahabuddin Attal rejected this, telling the media this was "a conspiracy by some elements within the Taliban movement against Mansur Dadullah." "Taliban member dismisses 'sack' claim", Agence France-Presse, 30 December 2007.

32. For instance "Kamin (Ambush) Operations Declared against domestic and external enemies", Al Emarah, 27 May 2007. Translation: AfghanWire.

33. "Interview with the deputy and exalted mujahid of the Islamic Emirate Mullah Baradar", Al Emarah, 27 September 2007.

34. "Detailed interview with Qari Yousuf Ahmadi, Official Spokesman of Islamic Emirate of Afghanistan", republished on Al Emarah, June 2008 (in Pashtu), from East and West website.

35. "Message of Amir ul-Momineen to the nations of Afghanistan and Iraq", Al Emarah, 12 May 2007 Translation: AfghanWire.

36. "The media activities of the Taliban Islamic Movement", op. cit. discusses the history of some of these publications and previous more short-lived organs.

37. Its masthead says it is founded by Ghazi Ajmal and edited by Mawlawi Hatem Tayi.

38. Toorabora.com accessed 6 October 2008.

39. Ibid.

40. See Amin Tarzai, "Taliban radio back on the air", Radio Free Europe, 9 May 2005.

41. See Pam O'Toole, "Taliban radio station back on air", BBC News, 21 June 2007, further information from interviews in Kabul with organizations and individuals working in the eastern regions.

42. "Voice of Jihad" (*Jihad Ghag*), Islamic Emirate of Afghanistan Cultural Affairs Commission, audio and video department). Dated 14 May 2006.
43. "The announcement of the Afghanistan Islamic Emirate Cultural Affairs Commission", Al Emarah, 8 April 2008.
44. "About Tora Bora Military Front", Tora Bora website, accessed 16 October 2008. While emphasising the links, it also introduces its own spokesman: "The head of the Tora Bora Military Front is respected Mawlawi Anwar ul-Haq (Mujahid) who undertakes jihadi activities in Nangarhar and some other regions. Each region has its own chief who also sends his own reports to the official spokesman of the Islamic Emirate. Sometimes, to ensure the immediate release of the news, the respected Qari Sahib Sajjad also reports."
45. "Interview with Esteemed Mujahid Brother Hekmatyar", republished undated on www.shahadatnews.com, early October 2008.
46. Hekmatyar, "Eid ul-Fitr Congratulations Message", undated September 2008, www.shahadatnews.com
47. See "Taliban leader threatens Paris in video dating from August", *L'Express*, 18 November 2008.
48. A website supportive of the Taliban has operated under the *Manba al Jihad* name, although this has been all but defunct for at least a year and shows no obvious link to Haqqani.
49. Interviewer Rahimullah Yousufzai. Translation: The NEFA Foundation, 18 August 2008.
50. All material is apparently distributed through the al-Fajr Media Centre. Hanna Rogan, "Al Qaida's Online Media Strategies", Norwegian Defence Research Establishment, 1 December 2007, pp. 98–101.
51. An interview with Yahya al-Libi conducted by Mawlawi Hatem Al-Tayi (Tora Bora's editor) in a November 2005 issue of Tora Bora was distributed in April 2006 around Islamist websites. Translation: MEMRI, Special Dispatch No.1160, 10 May 2006. Al-Libi has since appeared in multiple Al Sahab and Labbayk productions as well as writing tracts on Afghanistan, Iraq and Palestine.
52. Ibid. Al Emarah did not exist in 2002 but there was an Arabic language website *Sawt al-Jihad* (Voice of Jihad in Arabic) which had a section for the Islamic Emirate of Afghanistan consisting of statements by the spokesmen. This has not been updated since mid-2007 and the exact relationship remains unclear.
53. "Selected Questions and Answers from Dr Ayman al-Zawahiri—Part 2", released on 17 April 2008. Translation: The NEFA Foundation.
54. Shown on Al-Jazeera Television, 17 June 2007. Translation: MEMRI Special Dispatch No. 1630, 21 June 2007.
55. "The condolence message of his Excellency Amir ul-Momineen on the martyrdom of Zarqawi", Al Emarah, 9 June 2006.
56. Khabir Ahmad, "Army Swelled by Power of Media", *Shahamat*, June-July 2008, p. 28.
57. "Detailed Interview with Qari Yousuf Ahmadi, Official Spokesman of Islamic Emirate of Afghanistan", republished on Al Emarah, June 2008, from East and West website.
58. Ron Synovitz, "Al Qaida Bloggers' Sparring With Taliban Could Signal Key Differences", Radio Free Europe, 12 March 2008.
59. "Statement by the Political Commission of the Islamic Emirate regarding certain developments in Afghanistan and the world", Al Emarah, 5 March 2008.

60. In suicide attacks, for instance it was estimated in 2007 that while 76 per cent of such incidents had targeted international and national military forces the greatest impact was on civilians. Out of 183 Afghans killed in such incidents in the first half of 2007, 121 were civilians. "Suicide Attacks in Afghanistan (2001–2007)," United Nations Assistance Mission to Afghanistan, 1 September 2007, p. 10. The Afghanistan NGO Safety Office (ANSO) estimated until the end of September 2008 that 970 civilians had been killed by armed opposition groups. This compares to 373 killed by international military forces: ANSO Third Quarter Report, 1 January–30 September 2008, p. 15. Many of the latter deaths are also attributable to the fact that Taliban operate in civilian areas.

61. Janullah Hashimzada and Akram Noorzai, "Omar to Taliban: Stop beheadings", Pajhwak Afghan News, 3 February 2008 and "Taliban chief orders change in mode of executions", IRIN, 4 February 2008.

62. Hasaand, "Does the true Taliban set books and schools ablaze? No, Never, No", Al Emarah, 3 September 2008. Also published in Srak, September 2008.

63. See "Taliban issues new school curriculum", Al Emarah, 16 January 2007, translation: AfghanWire, and M. Ilyas Khan, "Taliban 'to build Afghan schools'", BBC News, 23 January 2007.

64. "Message of His Excellency Amir al-Momein on the occasion of the arrival of Eid al-Fitr", Al Emarah, 29 September 2008.

65. "Detailed Interview with Qari Yousuf Ahmadi, Official Spokesman of Islamic Emirate of Afghanistan", republished on Al Emarah, June 2008, from East and West website.

66. "Obama's visit and his policy on Afghanistan", Al Somood, August 2008, p. 3.

67. "Message of his Excellency Amir ul-Momineen on the occasion of Eid ul-Fitr", Al Emarah, 29 September 2008.

68. "There is no doubt that former jihadi commanders and leaders had given many sacrifices in the path of Islam and independence….if they find the truth, the Islamic Emirate can reconcile with them, and the Islamic Emirate's heart is open for them." "Statement by the Political Commission of the Islamic Emirate regarding certain developments in Afghanistan and the world", Al Emarah, 5 March 2008.

69. "Detailed Interview with Qari Yousuf Ahmadi, Official Spokesman of Islamic Emirate of Afghanistan", republished on Al Emarah, June 2008, from East and West website.

70. H.N. "I tell in brief the long story I have heard and seen myself", Al Emarah, 23 August 2008.

71. "Statement of Islamic Emirate of Afghanistan regarding the untrue news about peace talks", Al Emarah, 28 September 2008.

72. "Some advice from the cultural affairs commission of the IEA to poets and singer", Al Emarah, 5 May 2008.

3

THE RESURGENCE OF THE TALIBAN IN KABUL

LOGAR AND WARDAK

Mohammad Osman Tariq Elias

Introduction

The content of this chapter is based on information gathered through the author's personal contacts in Logar and Wardak. The focus of this paper is mainly Kabul, Logar and Wardak Provinces. Kabul is the capital of Afghanistan and it is different from, as well as similar in many ways to, the other two provinces. It is located in a mountainous area and has an estimated population of 3.2 million.[1] Kabul has 13 rural[2] districts and 22[3] urban or municipal districts. Kabul is the main area of residence for more than 6,000 international expatriates and specialists working in Afghanistan. Its social structure is very diverse, with neighbouring provinces exercising a significant influence. Different neighbourhoods of Kabul are populated mostly by people from the surrounding provinces. For instance, in the west side of Kabul city there are more residents from Wardak province and other provinces located along the highway leading south and west; physical access to the west of Kabul will be easier for people from Wardak province rather than from other provinces. Similarly, there is still considerable influence of Logar province in Kabul. Indeed the capital reflects the political, economical, social and religious structure existing in the country generally. As a result, it was only a matter of time before the Taliban developed some influence in the city as well as in the rural districts of the province, particularly those mostly populated by Pashtuns or located on the border of Logar, Wardak, Nangarhar, and Laghman provinces. Criticism of the presence of foreign forces in Afghanistan by religious scholars,

43

preachers and Imams started in Kabul city after groups like Jami'at-i Islami started to oppose the government. Previously this had not been possible because the National Security Department, which is mostly staffed by ex-communists and Jami'atis, would have intervened and arrested them, as they did in a few cases in 2002–3.

This preaching is now enormously helpful to the Taliban. I remember when one of the BBC journalists had a series of interviews with inhabitants of Kabul about the level of corruption in the government and the state institutions; most interviewees, a mix of Pashtuns and other ethnic groups, answered that the Taliban regime was better than the current regime. Nowadays, Kabul is witnessing a strong popular shift towards Islam and Islamic studies, as can be realized from the existence of more than 20 Islamic studies centers for women and hundreds mosque-based centers for boys and girls; the mosques are full.

Wardak and Logar are provinces influenced by the culture of Loya Paktia and their religious background; Pashtun are the majority of the population, even if there is a strong minority of Hazaras in Wardak and a minority of Tajiks in Logar. These two provinces are recognized as centers of strong religious sentiment; there were more than thirty study centres in each province during the 1950s-1970s period, run by Deoband graduates.[4] This makes them different from the southern provinces of Loy Kandahar where most people are fighting according to their tribal rivalries[5] and the number of religiously educated people is not as large, nor is the number of *madrasas*. The table below shows the number of official *madrasas* in the different regions:

Table 1: Number of Islamic schools, students and teachers by region

Region	Schools	Students	Teachers	Students to school ratio	Students to teacher ratio
East	69	15,547	492	225.3	31.6
Central	40	13,514	539	337.9	25.1
Northeast	56	10,162	401	181.5	25.3
West	25	6,008	163	240.3	36.9
Southeast	39	5,371	266	137.7	20.2
Northwest	27	3,785	152	140.2	24.9
Kabul	11	2,137	16	194.3	133.6
Southeast	6	1,561	45	260.2	34.7
Central Highlands	2	443	5	221.5	88.6
Total	275	58,528	2,079	212.8	28.2

Source: Ministry of Education of Afghanistan, educational statistics.

The central region is the third highest in terms of the number of schools and the highest in terms of teachers, despite having a smaller population. There are no statistics for private *madrasas*, but my research in Mohammad

Agha district of Logar shows that their number is seven times higher than that of official *madrasas* (based on unpublished research carried out for CPAU, a research organization based in Kabul).

During the time of *jihad*, support for the leftist government in Kabul was always very weak in Wardak and Logar; Kabul was never able to form significant militias here, as it did in a number of other provinces.[6] The interest of the Taliban in these provinces stems from a number of reasons, such as their proximity to the capital, the fact that they are crossed by two very important highways, and the natural resources of Logar (chrome and copper).[7]

The Taliban in the region before 2001

During the Taliban's early years, the movement enjoyed the support of President Rabbani, who said they were a "self-motivated movement and the members are angels".[8] Rabbani supported them financially in order to get them to remove his rivals of Hizb-e-Islami in the south, southeast and east.[9] The Taliban were also popular among ordinary people, who wanted to get rid of abusive and undisciplined armed groups. They indeed defeated Hizb-e-Islami and even captured its strongholds of Wardak and Logar provinces. Initially, the Taliban membership from the region was limited and did not count more than one or two hundred people from both Wardak and Logar, and even less than this in Kabul. After the fall of Kabul to the Taliban, however, Jami'ati Pashtun commanders such as Anwar Dangar from Shakardara District of Kabul and Habib Afghan from Nejrab District of Kapisa joined the Taliban. Gradually, however, ethnic divisions, specifically fomented by Massud in Parwan, polarized the confrontation, and the Tajiks of Parwan, Kapisa and the North of Kabul largely joined the resistance against the Taliban. The Taliban lost more than 3,000 people in the fighting in Kapisa and Parwan, including many real *taliban* from *madrasas*, and also from Logar and Wardak provinces, such as Mawlawi Khushaal who was the Chief of Police in Kapisa.

Before 2001 the Taliban members from Logar and Wardak provinces never occupied important positions in the movement's leadership, despite the influence that these two provinces had had in all Afghan governments (except in the 1980s). The famous commanders of the Taliban were Kandaharis and Helmandis, but Taliban from Logar and Wardak were appointed as district governors in other provinces under the control of the Taliban, as well as directors of the departments and other public institutions, including at least one deputy minister.

The Taliban after 2001

After the fall of their regime in 2001 the Taliban were scattered and fragmented, but they promptly recovered and by the winter of 2002 they had established contacts with many of their members in different locations of Pakistan and in some provinces of Afghanistan.[10] They were even paying expenses for those members who could not provide for themselves. They were getting ready for military attacks against Coalition forces, even in Kabul, Logar and Wardak, but were still afraid that the Pakistani government would make a deal with Karzai's government and arrest them and hand them over. The situation quickly changed in 2003 and 2004 and military activities started escalating; they were able to conduct and organize some attacks even in Kabul, Logar and Wardak provinces. At this point they were working with three- to five-member groups in these areas. Logar was less affected than Wardak, possibly because the Taliban were using Logar for transit to other provinces (especially Wardak) and because their provincial commander for Logar was weak and passive. He was later criticized by other Taliban from Logar as not qualified for that position.[11] The first districts to be affected by the intensification of Taliban activities in late 2005, with the formation of larger groups of insurgents, were mountainous ones such as Jaghato in Wardak, Kharwar in Logar and Sorobi in Kabul.

The weakness of the government and the widening gap between the people and the state in these areas were due to a number of reasons:

- The arrest and torture of some former commanders and religious scholars by security institutions of the state without any evidence
- Little attention to and government recognition of religious scholars and former commanders, who had influence in society
- Corruption of state institutions, including the judiciary, as described by the Tiri and Integrity Watch anti-corruption organizations (2007)
- Bad local governance (Afghanistan Social Outreach Program Assessment done by the Asia Foundation, 2008)
- Weak and non-committed security forces with imbalanced ethnic composition (Giustozzi 2007).

In 2006 and 2007 the Taliban made more progress in Logar and Wardak provinces by establishing more armed groups in new districts such as Charkh, Baraki Barak and Puli Alam in Logar and Chack, Nirkh, Sayed Abad and Jalriz in Wardak. This in turn provided them with more opportunities to plan their infiltration of the rest of the districts in Logar as well as in Wardak. During 2008 in Wardak they started approaching the main highway leading south and west, attacking the convoys supplying ISAF and Coalition forces. The power of the Taliban on the Kabul-Kandahar-Herat highways is very well described in the report by Abdul Ahad Ghaith from Wardak published by the *Guardian* (14 December 2008); here the District Commander of Sayed Abad declared that "Salar is the new Falluja".[12]

Generally it can be said that the strength of Taliban forces correlates with the weakness of the government; in the absence of positive changes addressing bad governance, one can expect the Taliban to gain more ground in the

Map 1: Security and governance in Logar and Wardak, 2008, according to IDLG.

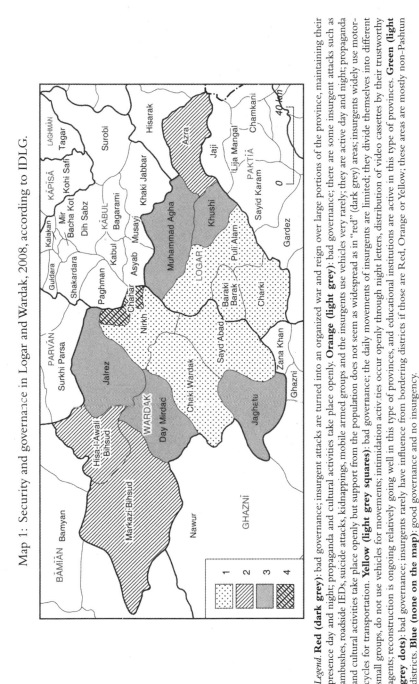

Legend. **Red (dark grey):** bad governance; insurgent attacks are turned into an organized war and reign over large portions of the province, maintaining their presence day and night; propaganda and cultural activities take place openly. **Orange (light grey):** bad governance; there are some insurgent attacks such as ambushes, roadside IEDs, suicide attacks, kidnappings, mobile armed groups and the insurgents use vehicles very rarely; they are active day and night; propaganda and cultural activities take place openly but support from the population does not seem as widespread as in "red" (dark grey) areas; insurgents widely use motor-cycles for transportation. **Yellow (light grey squares):** bad governance; the daily movements of insurgents are limited; they divide themselves into different small groups, do not use vehicles for movements; intimidation activities occur openly through night letters, distribution of video cassettes by their trustworthy agents; reconstruction is ongoing relatively going well in this type of provinces, and educational institutions are active in this type of provinces. **Green (light grey dots):** bad governance; insurgents rarely have influence from bordering districts if those are Red, Orange or Yellow; these areas are mostly non-Pashtun districts. **Blue (none on the map):** good governance and no insurgency.

future. The only action taken by the government is the Afghanistan Social Outreach Program (ASOP), which was implemented in Wardak at the time of writing, but it is doubtful if it will be successful. Interviewees from both provinces compared the current (2008) security situation in Logar and Wardak with the early stages of the Soviet occupation (1980); the expectation was that 2009 would look like 1981, when the government could not secure the highway any longer. According to the mapping produced for the assessment of the Afghanistan Social Outreach Program, implemented by the Independent Directorate of Local Governance (IDLG) in Wardak, no province in Afghanistan has good governance. The situation in Logar and Wardak looked pretty dismal by 2008 (see map).

The security situation usually improved over the winter, but then worsened again in spring. The government tried to address the situation in Logar with the appointment of a new governor, raising new expectations for a secure Logar, free of Taliban, or at least inverting the existing trend toward greater insecurity. The governor does indeed have special relations with the Taliban in Logar, but it is not clear who will benefit from this and he plays a game in which no-one knows who will be the winner especially by appointment of a Wardak residence as governor for Logar by Taliban, recently. Wardak looks more stable because the two major Hazara populated districts are safer, but the Pashtun districts are as bad as Logar.

Who's who in the Taliban

Particularly in these provinces, the Taliban are largely composed of religiously motivated militants, a fact that motivates them in the fighting and facilitates the maintaining of unity. The tendency seems to increasingly infiltrate the state apparatus, making possible attacks such those during the 28 April 2008 anniversary, the prison attack in Kandahar and the Indian embassy attack and recently the large scale Justice Ministry attacks. Some types of action are coordinated centrally, but in others small commanders are given much freedom. The Taliban rely on personal relations as an organizational tool. Every lower level commander is responsible to report to the higher level and the same path has to be followed until the report reaches the Emam or Nayeb Emam, that is Mullah Omar and his deputies.

The provincial commander for Logar province was initially Mawlawi Adbul Rauf from the Dobandi area of Khushi district, but he ended up being discredited because of his lack of activism in establishing groups and organizing attacks. Moreover, his brothers were driving tankers supplying oil to the Americans in Bagram. He was replaced by Mir Ahmad Gul from Padkhab area of Puli Alam, capital of the province; in late 2006 and early 2007 Mullah Abdullah (known as Mullah Toor) also appeared, claiming to be a provincial commander: competition started between the two and ended with a physical clash at a meeting in Peshawar. Mullah Abdullah was injured by Mir. This struggle continued until Mullah Abdullah was asked to go to Khost province in early 2008 by the leadership. Mullah Abdullah is reported to be close to Sirajuddin Haqqani and working for him. The whole incident, therefore, can be taken as an example of a bigger and higher-level split within the Taliban movement.

People who had earlier joined the Taliban for various reasons lost their interest in frontline fighting, and the new members come from the youngest teenagers who can easily accept to die and believe what they have learned from their teachers. The Taliban in the battlefield are a new brand of people and they enjoy and exercise total power locally, in the way the *mujahidin* did during the first years of the communist era between 1978 and 1980. The top rank people based outside the country, who started to move towards regrouping Taliban in these three provinces in 2002–4, are old Taliban. Examples are the former deputy foreign minister Abdur Rahman Zahid, Mawlawi Abdul Rauf and Mir Ahmad Gul. The inexperience of those in the frontline affects the ability of the Taliban to cope with issues such as accusations of spying for the government against local people; as a result there are frequent executions of alleged culprits even when the accusations might actually derive from local feuds.

Warlordism plays a little role in the Taliban. Three basic elements are essential to the emergence of warlords: weak leadership, non-ideological mindset of the members of the group, and independent financial resources. To judge from the experience of the Jihadi period (1980s), the first two elements are the fundamental ones. Their existence was to pave the way for creation of warlords. For example, one can rarely find a warlord who was from start to end of the period a member of Gulbuddin Hekmatyar's Hizb-e-Islami, because that party had strong leadership and its membership was indoctrinated ideologically. Some Hizb-e-Islami commanders had autonomous financial resources or received some foreign financial assistance, but they never became independent from their leadership and the hierarchy of their organization. The formation of warlords took place in other Jihadi groups, which lacked strong leadership and an ideological membership. As for the Taliban movement, it has a strong leadership with a strong hierarchy and ideological mindsets. Therefore, the chance of warlords emerging is small even if in specific areas of Afghanistan financial resources are available to fund independent warlords: the chromites of Logar, the poppy of Helmand, the logistical convoys of Coalition forces and NATO in Khyber Agency areas. Even external financial support might be available to such figures. Mullah Dadullah in Helmand was in fact gradually emerging as a warlord, thanks to the revenue from the narcotics trade, but Mullah Omar resisted his ascent. There are widespread rumors that his murder was assisted by those who were loyal to Mullah Omar. Mullah Dadullah's brother Mansur tried to take his place, but he was arrested by the Pakistani authorities.

Relations with elders, the population and local authorities

The relations between Taliban and elders as well as the people in general are correlated to the structure of the tribes in a province or a district—whether they are unified and well structured or fragmented. In Loya Paktia, for example, the Taliban will strongly consider the power of tribal elders and leaders and will not be very free in their actions within the communities. This was already the case in the late 1990s, when the Taliban were not able to impose their orders on the tribes of Loya Paktia as they did in the rest of the country. In other provinces where there is no strong tribal structure, the Taliban will have more freedom to impose what they want on elders and people, although they will still be limited by the extent of sympathy that they receive. This sympathy can derive from the conviction of the elders that although the Taliban are not able to provide them basic services, at least they will provide the most needed physical security. There will be no corruption or illegal impositions, as practiced by state officials. There will also be some elders who believe that the Taliban will give them back the political rights usurped by groups like Jami'at and the government backed by the Americans.

Often the first demand placed on elders when the Taliban start having influence in an area is to take over dispute resolution, as long as the environment is not conductive to the establishment of a Taliban court or the deployment of one of their mobile judges. For instance, in the summer of 2008 in the Sheniz area of Sayed Abad district of Wardak province, the Taliban asked community representatives to come to the mosque at a specific time. When the elders came to the mosque the Taliban's group leader asked them to not go to the state courts anymore, and to have disputes resolved instead by elders and *ulema*. When Taliban approach them, elders can either choose to accept what they are asked and assist the Taliban, or refuse and leave the area and move to the place where the Taliban are weak and cannot reach them. The attitude of the Taliban towards local authorities depends on whether they have good relations with individual officials or not. If they have, the official can stay on with a guarantee that he will not be attacked. If not, he will be targeted in the assassination campaign.

How the Taliban are organized

The Taliban leadership is able to impose whatever changes it wants both at the strategic and technical levels. Such ability is demonstrated by the gradual spread of new fighting strategies and tactics from top to bottom, by the ability to change individuals as well as commanders from one front to an other or even from one province to another, as in the cases of Wardak and Logar which appointed two non-locals as governors. The latter aspect is particularly important.

When the Taliban grow, expand and gain more control the establishment of more organized military, administrative, judiciary structures become greater priorities. The expansion period can be described in different phases:

Phase One: small groups of 3–5, then 10–20 members. Military activities are limited to guerrilla action; there is no organized structure yet. It is not possible to establish courts at this stage. When the Taliban consider that they are ready to move to phase two they will ask people not to go to state courts; they have to refer their issues and disputes to the elders in the areas as they did in Sayed Abad District of Wardak in the spring of 2008. It is worth noting that even in those areas where there is no insurgency 80 per cent of the cases are referred to the local and traditional justice system.[13]

Phase Two: the Taliban introduce more military, administrative and judiciary organization. The military structure will reach up to front level (*jabha* or *mahaz*), which may be divided into district level commands. In Logar they established in 2008 two *mahaz*, the southern one under the command of Mir Ahmad Gul and the northern one (which includes some areas of Wardak) under Mullah Abdullah (known as Mullah Toor). Wardak's provincial commander is Mawlawi Taha, originally from Paktika, and he is also responsible for the western part of Kabul province. Other organizational aspects include some local centres in charge of printing night letters and other necessary documents, and the establishment of mobile courts. As has been described, people are happy with Taliban courts and prefer to go there.[14]

Phase Three: the Taliban gain control of the area in daylight. They introduce permanent courts, with *ulema* from the area who are not members of Taliban group. The reason is clear: these *ulema* have to be in contact with the people and be exposed to them. However, only those cases that do not have a political or military character will be judged in these courts, the others remain within the competence of the mobile courts.[15]

The Taliban are said to be divided into three big factions. Mullah Omar's faction is against the burning of public infrastructure and the involvement of personal rivalries in the war. This faction is strongest in the central region, but the faction of Seraajudin Haqqani is also present; as indicated earlier, it had a separate structure at least as long as Mullah Abdulla alias Mullah Toor was present.[16] The third faction, called Lashkar-i-Dadullah Shaheed (Army of Dadullah-e-Shaheed), has only limited contact with people in the central region or indeed anywhere outside the south. This group is often accused of being funded by ISI or even of having been created by Western intelligence services to divide the Taliban.

In the early stages of the insurgency, the effort is by its own nature unsophisticated and unstructured. Recruitment starts at the individual level and then groups of three to five people are formed. Such groups carry out attacks based not on orders from above, but on their own ability and understanding. For example, if the group recognizes someone as a person to be killed, there is no need for confirmation from a higher level authority. The victim will then be described as an American spy and the news passed on to the Taliban's spokesperson. The group's membership grows once the situation goes out of the government's control. Support from people, such as shelter and food, becomes more forthcoming. As the security posts disappear, the Taliban can start operating in broad daylight. Once they achieve full control, as they did in 2008 in Kharwar of Logar and some areas of Wardak, they will start offering services such as guaranteeing physical security of the people and referring disputes to the *ulema*. The groups' leaders are not allowed to interfere in the judiciary cases. They will also take some steps towards managing the Bazaara and implementing taxation.

The Taliban's fully developed organizational structure looks as follows:

1. Regional level
2. Provincial level
3. Front level (which consists of two or three districts)
4. District level
5. Sub-district level

For Wardak province and the west part of Kabul is Mawlawi Taha, for Logar province he is Mawlawi Abdul Karim from Sayedabad district of Wardak. They have their district level commanders and appointees, based on their personal relations. Responsibilities are clearly divided between different ranks of Taliban and no one is able to interfere in another group's area or target. There are two different types of logistics. In an emergency, logistical needs are allowed to be satisfied at the local markets and weapons dealers. Ordinarily, however, they rely on an organized, complicated logistics system where strict rules apply.

The Taliban seek tax and other financial help and assistance from the people where they are strongest; sometimes they can ask ransom after kidnapping people. Even the code of conduct issued by Taliban on 8 January 2007 states that, with the permission of the leadership, the Taliban can ask for money for the release of government, NGO and private company staff who work on governmental projects and even drivers of trucks carrying supplies for the Coalition forces or the government. It is worth pointing out that area authority is determined among the leaders and commanders and is not same as it was under the Taliban government. The military coordination structure is not constant; in particular the Jabha (front) organization is not based on any special geographic regions or areas. Members, particularly those who have religious knowledge, have a lot of influence in that organization and they can be active in different regions with no geographic restrictions; the members of the Jabha do not have any specific residence. If the Taliban are not strong enough to have a structure in each district, then a Jabha commander is appointed to lead more than one district. There is no evidence of frequent shuffling or changes of commanders. The members of the groups maintain relations and cooperate with other groups for their material and spiritual benefit; the leaders usually indoctrinate their rank-and-file, saying that no disputes are possible with other groups because the fight is for a common purpose; that is, defending religion, country and purity. Cooperation is advocated with all the groups fighting the central government. New groups of

Taliban are established by recruitment of new members, but old groups' leaders are rarely changed.

As during the *jihad* of the 1980s, when the anti-government opposition appears in a region bandits and gangs become active, leading to an increase in criminal activities. Even at the time of the first Taliban movement in 1994 the author of this paper, when passing through Ahmad khil Jiji district in Paktia, faced a group of gangs[17] who took all valuables from the people in the vehicles they stopped. Local inhabitants will be scared more by the criminal activities of the bandits than by the insurgents. In Wardak from the summer of 2007 bandits and gangs increased their activities and took advantage of the gap between people and government, and the still weak relationship between Taliban and local communities. Once the Taliban consolidated their hold on an area, they got rid of the gangs and punished them by death. This duly happened in our region, in places like Kharwar and Baraki Barak in Logar and Nirkh district of Wardak (2008).[18] However, in some cases they also used the gangs and purchased kidnap victims from them, when they expected political and financial benefits. In other cases the Taliban refused to buy kidnap victims because they could not see any gain, as in the case of a BRAC staff member from Bangladesh kidnapped in Logar. There can also be stronger relations, direct or indirect, between the Taliban and armed groups, criminals and gangs. This goes back to the existence of different fictions inside Taliban. The main group of Taliban led by Mullah Omar does not recruit criminals as members.

Processes like DDR and DIAG have benefited the Taliban, who recruited the demobilized and jobless militiamen into their ranks, where they represent a significant percentage. These former militiamen are often experienced and could compare well with inexperienced ANA and ANP members. One example is Fazel Rabi, a group commander of Jami'at-i Islami, who joined the Taliban after he was DRRed. He became very active in raiding the road between Wardak and Logar and attacked several ISAF and Coalition military convoys, until he died in 2008 at the hands of the Coalition. The situation on the highway improved after his death.

There are obvious signs that other jihadist armed groups opposed to the government are active in areas under the control of Taliban. Taliban give them full freedom and encourage them; all they might demand is an oath of obedience to the Amir (Mullah Omar). The best example is represented by Hizb-i Islami: there is no unity and not even good relations between the leadership of Taliban and Hizb-e-Islami, but in some areas Hizb-i Islami local commanders prefer to work closely with Taliban and accept the conditions imposed on them for moving free in the area—that is, acknowledging Mullah Omar's leadership. That may be because there are some former Hizb-e-Islami members or their relatives appointed as commanders of Taliban such as Shafiq, son of Mawlawi Abdul Baqi, ex-commander of Hizb-e-Islami in Wardak province. The Taliban also have relations with foreign elements, mostly Arabs, who provide material and spiritual support for the Taliban. Relations with the foreign fighters are at the higher level; the leadership of

Taliban officially does not allow ordinary members of the movement to have direct relations with Arabs, although some people developed relations with them on a personal basis.

Conclusion

The Taliban developed a strategy of gradual infiltration and growth for the provinces of Logar and Wardak as well as Kabul. The local people's social and religious mindsets facilitated their task, as did the corruption of the state administration. The Taliban have been cautious in dealing with the local population and have mostly behaved well. The organizational structure of the Taliban might not look too sophisticated from a Western standpoint, but it is appropriate to the human resources they have and to the tasks they face. They are also ready to intensify such a structure as they make more gains or consolidate what they have gained already. By the end of 2008, most of both provinces was under *de facto* Taliban control. In Logar and Wardak, the composition of the Taliban seems to be more strongly ideological/religious-minded than in the south. However, this has not prevented the Taliban from displaying some pragmatism in dealing with bandits and criminal gangs. The threat represented to the Afghan state by the Taliban on the outskirts of Kabul cannot be underestimated: three of the four gates of Kabul are being threatened.

Notes

1. According to estimates by of Central Statistics Organization of Islamic Republic of Afghanistan.
2. It was said that recently some of these rural districts are to be changed to urban districts.
3. According to the latest updated number from Municipality of Kabul (02/ March/2009).
4. My previous research report to PRIO on Trans-border Religious Networks: the Case of Islamic Education in Afghanistan and Pakistan; Informant: Mawlawi Sharbat Muhtamim of Darul Uloom Ziaul Madaris a newly established *madrasa* in Logar; and Informants: Mawlawi Ahmadullah, Haji Gula Jan
5. Marten De Boer, New Perspectives for Conflict Transformation: Development and Diplomacy: Implementing a Cautious and Fully Balanced Approach against the Odds in Urozgan, 2007; CAPS (Center for Conflict and Peace Studies), Kandahar Provincial Profile; Produced for IDLG (the Independent Directorate of Local Governance), 2008. This profile is not publicly available but I was in charge of supervising its quality.
6. See Giustozzi, 2000, pp. 198ff. on this point.
7. An informant has close links to the current head of Taliban's Intelligence Department.
8. Ex-President Rabbani's Interview with BBC and National Radio and TV of Afghanistan (1994).

9. This is taken from some sources of Taliban in (1999); and sources from Jami'at-i-Islami in (2004).

10. The author was living in Peshawar and was in contact with some of the Taliban members for various reasons.

11. This person is Mawlawi Abdul Rauf from Dobandi area of Khushi Distric of Logar; he was criticized because his brothers' transport operations are supplying logistics to coalition forces in Bagram, and he was replaced by Mir Ahmad Gul who is fired by Mullah Omar and replaced by Mawlawi Abdul Karim who is originally from Tangi Wardak an area in the border of Wardak and Logar but related officially to Wardak.

12. Salar is a village with a small bazaar on the main highway of Kabul-Kandahar-Herat.

13. USIP (2007), "Informal Justice and Formal Justice in Afghanistan".

14. Sarhadi Nelson, 'Taliban Courts Filling Justice Vacuum in Afghanistan', NPR December 2008.

15. These existed already in the 1980s during the *jihad* and were called Mahkama-e-Sahraee.

16. Mullah Toor was recently dismissed and no longer has any position in the movement, as is the case for Mir Ahmad Gul.

17. Even they will call themselves Taliban when they need.

18. The Interviewees from Wardak.

4

LOYA PAKTIA'S INSURGENCY

(I) THE HAQQANI NETWORK AS AN AUTONOMOUS ENTITY

Thomas Ruttig

Within the post-2001 insurgency, Loya Paktia (Greater Paktia)[1] represents a quasi-autonomous region. Its three constituent provinces, Paktia, Paktika and Khost, are one of the three major Pashtun regions of the country, along with Southern (sometimes called South-Western) Afghanistan around Kandahar and Eastern Afghanistan around Jalalabad. Located a relatively easy two and a half hours' drive south-east of Kabul, with only one pass to cross, it is the Pashtun region closest to the Afghan capital. During the regime of the Soviet-backed People's Democratic Party of Afghanistan (PDPA) and the subsequent *mujahidin* and Taliban regimes, the three provinces constituted a semi-official administrative unit, a "region" (Dari/Pashto: *tanzima*) or "zone".

Loya Paktia is inhabited by a number of Pashtun tribes, the most important ones being the Ahmadzai, Zadran, Zazi, Kharoti, Mangal, Sabari, Sulei-mankhel, Tani and Wazir and the smaller tribes of the Khost basin, sometimes put under one label as Khostwal. There are also small Tajik and Sikh minorities, mainly in urban areas, as well as small Shia groups, among both Pashtuns and Tajiks. Most South-Eastern Pashtun tribes are distinct from their Southern and Eastern brethren. Except for the Ahmadzai, the Kharoti and the Suleimankhel who are Ghilzai, they belong to neither of the two most famous Pashtun tribal "confederations", the Durrani and the Ghilzai.[2]

The non-Ghilzai tribes of the South-East live mainly in mountain valleys. The limited space for settlement provides that they are relatively small and closely knit. Their traditional tribal institutions—the tribal leaders (the *khan*), the tribal intermediaries with government (the *malik*), the tribes' egalitarian (but male-only) decision-making body, the *jirga*, and their enforcement organ, the volunteer-based *arbakai* (plural: *arbaki*)—are significantly stronger than those of the lowland tribes. However, even among the South-Eastern Pashtuns these institutions have been partly weakened and superseded by powerful newcomers during almost 40 years of violence, coups d'état, civil war, occupation and resistance, mainly by former *mujahidin* commanders.[3] The South-Eastern Pashtuns strongly adhere to their ancient code of behaviour, the Pashtunwali, although it might differ slightly from tribe to tribe.

The Pashtuns of the South-East consider themselves as the traditional king-makers in Kabul and are in fact deeply pro-government. This is mainly due to two historical events. First, the South-Eastern tribes, who in 1929 had just contributed to the overthrow of the reform-minded King Amanullah, revolted against his successor Habibullah II, a Tajik and the first non-Pashtun ruler since modern Afghanistan's emergence in 1747, and resurrected the Pashtun monarchy by helping General Nader Khan (ruled 1929–34) to ascend to the throne. Secondly, historiographers from the region also claim that the uprising against the PDPA regime started in Loya Paktia.[4] As a reward for their services to the kings, the tribes of Loya Paktia have been exempted from paying taxes and conscription by central governments for over 100 years and have also been free from most other forms of state influence. This feeling of power has contributed to an extremely strong sense of independence and self-confidence among the Loya Paktia Pashtuns.

Loya Paktia was never a stronghold of the Taliban movement, neither during their Islamic Emirate of Afghanistan (1996–2001) nor in the phase of its new incarnation, the post-2001 neo-Taliban insurgency. As a movement that had emerged from the South-Western region ("Greater Kandahar"), it was alien to Loya Paktia. Furthermore, the leadership around Mullah Mohammad Omar, made *Amir-ul-momenin* by a gathering of *ulema* in Kandahar in 1996, had jealously protected its superiority in the movement, only allowing a few token non-Kandahari into their inner circle that really takes the decisions. The Taliban did not have to conquer most of Loya Paktia on their advance towards Kabul in 1995. They took Paktia, Paktika and Khost without a fight in the last days of January. Paktika's large Suleimankhel tribe called them to take over the province's centre, Sharana, after they had conquered Ghazni (on 20 January 1995)[5] from a particularly abusive *mujahidin* commander, Qari Baba. Khost town followed on 15 February. The mujahidin-led administration of the province went to receive the Taliban advance party at the Seta Kandao pass in neighboring Paktia, stepped down and handed over provincial affairs to the newcomers. Lacking a consistent supra-tribal leadership, the Loya Paktia tribes were hoping that the Taliban would put an end to the post-1992 political chaos in their region, and also assumed that they would support them in escaping the influence of the mainly non-Pashtun Northern Alliance[6] that ruled in Kabul. In some areas, however, the Taliban had to fight local forces like those of Hekmatyar's Hizb-i Islami Afghanistan (Islamic Party of Afghanistan) in Eastern Khost in August 1996.[7]

Loya Paktia's four-pronged insurgency

The post-2001 insurgency in Loya Paktia has not been homogeneous. It is composed of four different strands. There are two networks led by the Haqqani and the Mansur families respectively. Besides them, there are Taliban groups acting independently from these two networks, led directly by the Taliban *Rahbari* or *'Ali Shura* (Leadership or Supreme Council) or by individual influential commanders in Quetta. Organisationally even further apart, separate structures of Hizb-i Islami have an insular operational base in Loya Paktia. While Taliban and Hizb structures are distinct from each other, the leadership of the former reportedly has instructed its fighters not to attack the fighters of the latter early on after 2001. All insurgent organisations field a number of small armed groups headed by local commanders who mostly operate in their own tribal areas. Some control only a dozen men, others up to a few hundred. For Khost province alone, a number of some 150 commanders is given, 95 per cent of them linked to the Haqqani network.

In contrast to the Taliban's and Hizb's country-wide structures, the Haqqani and Mansur networks are regionally based and traditionally have not operated outside the South-Eastern region (including Ghazni province which is not part of Loya Paktia). Afghan security organs, however, claim that this changed. They point to a number of commando-style operations in Kabul in 2008—the attack on the Serena Hotel on 14 January, the sniper attack against the VIP stand during the 7 Saur (27 April) National Day parade, and the suicide car-bomb attack on the Indian Embassy in Kabul on 7 July. For these extremely daring operations, the Haqqani network also claimed responsibility. The same network seems now to be operating in Logar, Eastern Ghazni and, to a lesser extent, Wardak too, coopting other jihadis (see Chapter 3 in this book). These developments were preceded by an expansion of the Haqqani networks in Loya Paktia at the expense of other insurgent structures. It took over parts of Taliban structures that were operated directly from Quetta before, and at least a part of the Mansur network's *ulema* base. Prominent Taliban commanders from the region like Mullah Kabir, the deputy chairman of the former Taliban Emirates' Council of Ministers and governor of Nangrahar—a Zadran from Nika district—left the region. While there were still two parallel Taliban structures in Loya Paktia in 2003—one run by Jalaluddin Haqqani, the head of the Haqqani network, the other led first by the Taliban Emirate's former Minister of Finance and Economy, Taher Anwari from Kulalgo village (in Zurmat district of Paktia province), and later by Kabir—this competition was decided in Haqqani's favour by October 2007, when Kabir was appointed head of the Taliban forces in Eastern Afghanistan.[8] Apart from Haqqani's military strength, the fact that Kabir had been one of his sub-commanders during the *jihad* was supposed to have influenced the decision. Also other South-Eastern Taliban commanders like Mawlawi Sedrazam, Kabir's deputy as governor, moved to the East. This also could indicate that the Haqqani network asserts some influence in Eastern Afghanistan now.

The Haqqani and Mansur networks divided operational areas in Loya Paktia among themselves, with one exception: both use the mountainous Shahikot area (in Zurmat) as a hideout and staging area. In contrast, there are overlaps between the different Taliban strands and Hizb-i Islami. For example, the Haqqani network also carries out operations in Sabari (a.k.a. Yaqubi) district (Khost province) which has a larger Hizb presence. But it is not clear whether this is result of some coordination or not. Furthermore, both the Haqqani and the Mansur networks and Hizb-i Islami have established influence across the border in Pakistan, in the Pashtun-inhabited region called the Federally Administered Tribal Areas (FATA). From the 1970s, they developed extensive links with the local tribal population, the Pakistani authorities—first of all the army and its Inter-Services Intelligence (ISI)—and various Islamist political parties. These links were reactivated after 2001 by the neo-Taliban and other insurgent groups that had only temporary been paralysed by the US-led invasion of Afghanistan after 9/11.

One, two or many insurgencies?

There has been a lot of argument about whether the Haqqani network is an integrated part or a distinct organisation within the Afghan insurgency. A Pentagon report issued in June 2008 talks of a "potential for two distinct insurgencies in Afghanistan": apart from "a Kandahari-based insurgency dominated by the Taliban in the south (…) a more complex, adaptive insurgency in the east", described as "a loose confederation of affiliates such as the Haqqani Network [note the capital "N" in Network—*the author*] and like-minded groups that are prepared to cooperate" with the mainstream Kandahari Taliban like al Qaida, Hizb-i Islami and the Pakistani groups Jaish-i-Moham-mad, Lashkar-i-Tayba and Tehrik-i-Nafaz-i-Shariat-i-Muhammadi. Seth Jones of the Rand Corporation speaks about "a range of insurgent groups such as (…) the Haqqani network".[9] Already in late 2004, Kucera had quoted an anonymous[10] US defence official along the same lines, adding that these "two insurgencies (…) definitely talk, (…) have a common cause (…,) coordinate at the strategic and operational level (…). They've kind of broken the country up and operate in one area and the other operates in a different area."[11]

According to UN analysts in Kabul, the insurgency consists of "several distinct groups" with "numerous fault-lines" among each other (among them what they call the "Haqqani tribal organisation or HTO"), while other UN officials in the South-Eastern region call Jalaluddin and his son Serajuddin Haqqani "Taliban commanders".[12] The UN Sanctions Committee also labels Haqqani an "active Taliban leader".[13] These analyses also must have informed the Policy Action Group (PAG), a body formed in 2006 by the representatives of countries with troops in Southern Afghanistan (Canada, Netherlands, UK, US) and Afghan top politicians to develop a counter-insurgency strategy. PAG documents seen by the author also speak of the Haqqani Network as a separate entity in the insurgency. A British analyst concluded that the different insurgent groups are only under a "certain degree of central leadership".[14]

Exactly how big this "certain degree" is remains uncertain. The background for this uncertainty is that Taliban structures in general remain extremely secretive and elusive. For obvious reasons, they are not very transparent, there is no regular contact with leading figures, and if they speak publicly they give a lot of contradictory information, so that it is not clear what is truth and what propaganda. Afghan and international analysts largely agree that there are four insurgents' councils (*shura*) below the leadership level—the "Amir", Mullah Mohammad Omar Mujahid, and the Leadership Council—that direct day-to-day operations in certain geographical areas: the Quetta Shura for "Greater Kandahar" and the areas further west up to Herat, the Peshawar Shura for Eastern Afghanistan, the Haqqani-led Miramshah Shura for Loya Paktia and provinces north towards Kabul, and a separate *shura* for the North and North-East. Often the Leadership Council and the Quetta Shura are confused because they are based in the same area. There also seems to be a significant overlap of the membership of both.

Although it is mentioned often, it seems far from clear (at least to this author) whether Jalaluddin Haqqani is really a member of the Taliban Leadership Council, and if so, whether this council can convene so regularly that it really counts in decision-making. Also a report from May 2006 that Jalaluddin Haqqani has been appointed the overall Taliban "head of military operations" contradicts what is known about the general Taliban structure and might have been deliberately placed to boost Haqqani's standing. Some Taliban leaders reject the notion that Jalaluddin Haqqani is the commander of all Taliban fighters, call Serajuddin Haqqani "a main commander" (not *the* main), and insist that he "always coordinates his actions with the Taliban and is completely subject to the Taliban's [supreme council's] discipline."[15] The last part, however, sounds more like wishful thinking; other reports speak a different language. According to Mullah Abdussalam Zaeef, the Taliban's former ambassador to Pakistan and currently one of the most prominent "reconciled" insurgents, "Jalaluddin Haqqani and Abdullatif Mansur both listen to Mullah Omar", i.e. respect him as their spiritual leader, the *Amir-ul-momenin*. It has to be noted that he talks of "respect" towards a spiritual leadership, not about obedience to a commander in the military sense. The veteran Pakistani journalist Rahimullah Yusufzai reported that major commanders of the network endorsed Serajuddin Haqqani's leadership role in 2005 and also "reiterated their trust in the leadership of Taliban leader Mullah Mohammad Omar".[16] Note again: "trust", not "subordination". Even one Western intelligence source accessed by this author says that Jalaluddin Haqqani "always stood outside the Taliban chain-of-command". Another US-based author describes the Haqqani network as based on "a more ethnically diverse fighter corps (e.g., Pashtuns, Uzbeks, Pakistani, Chechens, and "foreign Arabs") that is operating out of Peshawar and Waziristan".[17] The body directing its operations, the Miramshah Shura, appears to be composed not only of Afghans, but also of Pakistani Taliban and, possibly, foreign fighters. This makes it more of a transnational Jihadi body that transcends the mainly national orientation of the Kandahari mainstream Taliban. Consequently, this *shura* has the capability to operate independently of the Taliban Leadership Council. Its exact composition, however, remains largely unknown.

The Haqqanis: 'Taliban warlords'?

The Haqqani network is the strongest insurgent structure in Loya Paktia and is responsible for most of the armed activities there.[18] An increasing number of analysts agree with those US and Afghan officials quoted in a US magazine report that Serajuddin Haqqani has become "the most active, aggressive and powerful [insurgent] commander along the border" between Afghanistan and Pakistan. A US commander in Afghanistan says: "Siraj[uddin] Haqqani is the one who is training, influencing, commanding and leading [...] Kidnappings, assassinations, beheading women, indiscriminate killings and suicide bombers—Siraj[uddin] is the one dictating the new parameters of brutality associated with Taliban senior leadership."[19] The US military put a bounty of US$200,000 on his head and published this on posters distributed all over the area covered by its Regional Command East.

The Haqqani network's main area of operations is the Zadran territory that stretches over nine near tribally homogeneous districts at the border triangle of Paktia, Paktika and Khost provinces (see Map). This so-called Zadran Arc has direct access to the staging area in Zurmat district, and in fact constitutes a corridor to it from Pakistan through Spera, Gayan and Zurmat and further on to Ghazni and Logar provinces. The Shahikot area of Zurmat, theatre of the 2002 Operation Anaconda, and possibly the non-Zadran Sabari district—with small guerrilla groups led by commanders Mohammad Khan Gurbuz and Khenjo—are the only areas inside Afghanistan where Haqqani fighters are constantly present. In late 2007, US forces identified the Zambar area in the northern part of Sabari as the "main insurgent safe haven" in Khost province "for some time".[20] There are even not any permanent bases in the Zadran Arc, including the Haqqanis' home village of Srana in Gerda Tserey district. Instead, most of the networks operations are carried from temporary staging areas set up by cross-border "patrols", from safe houses in Loya Paktia villages or completely as cross-border attacks.

The network itself is led by the veteran Afghan Islamist and *mujahidin* commander Jalaluddin Haqqani, a Zadran Pashtun[21] from the Gerda Tserei area, an unofficial district of Paktia province, and one of his sons, Serajuddin Haqqani (a.k.a. "Khalifa"), born to the elder Haqqani's Arab wife. Owing to

Map 2: Tribes and insurgents in Loya Paktia, 2008

Note: The boundaries of the networks are meant to be indicative only and should not be assumed to imply a compact area of activity or influence, particularly in the case of the Hizb-i Islami network.

old age (he was most probably born between 1930 and 1938[22]) and illness, Serajuddin Haqqani has taken over the responsibility for day-to-day operations from his father. In February 2005 he identified himself as the head of the Taliban military committee for the provinces of Paktia, Paktika, Khost, Ghazni and Logar.[23]

Serajuddin is often is described as less ideological, but more radical (or ruthless) than his father; however he clearly lacks his standing. Jalaluddin Haqqani is still lending the authority of his familiar name and his long-standing resistance credibility to his son. This is meant to stabilise the network vis-à-vis possible challengers to the young Serajuddin's leading role. Indeed, Serajuddin's takeover was not accepted unanimously, even within the family. There were reports coming from the Afghan intelligence community that Ibrahim Omari, one of Jalaluddin Haqqani's three brothers—and as such senior to his nephew Serajuddin—unsuccessfully tried to take over control over the networks fronts in the summer of 2007. Since then, he seems to have withdrawn from the insurgency, but still lives in Pakistan. Until then, reports had suggested he was responsible for the networks liaising with Arab and Chechen fighters in Miramshah.[24]

Other members of the wider Haqqani family play a leading role in the network also. Among them is the second brother, Haji Khalil. Some intelligence sources call Haji Mawlawi Abdurrahman Zadran, a cousin of Jalaluddin Haqqani, the network's head of operations. The second son of Jalaluddin Haqqani, Badruddin, seems to be a commander in the network while the third, Nasruddin (also from his Zadran wife), is called a commander by some sources.[25] There are some individuals that are reported the network's deputy commanders: Sangin Zadran operating in Spera, Mawlawi Bakhta Jan, also a Zadran from Gian district, operating from Urgun (Paktika), and Hakim Khan. None of them seems to belong to the Haqqani family.

Beyond this, there is very scarce information about how exactly the network is led. It is clear only that the operational planning is done by the so-called Miramshah Shura. But, again, the composition of this body is not known—including whether there are only the Haqqani sub-commanders or also representatives of the wider Taliban movement or even other insurgent groups. Reportedly, Janbaz Zadran heads the Haqqanis' office in Miramshah. Together with Mawlawi Gul Badar, a Wazir, he is said to be responsible for coordinating suicide attacks. Another Wazir, Mawlawi Sadeq Nur, supposedly coordinates the deployment of car-bombs. There is only one report from early 2005 that mentions some other of the network's commanders' names—in connection with the endorsement of Serajuddin Haqqani as their commander; they are Maalim Jan, Ghani Mohammad, Mawlawi Naebsalar, Mawlawi Abdurrahman (Zadran), Mawlawi Zaman, Haji Darin, Sher Mohammad. Also Sher Khan Mangal, a former provincial head of the Taliban intelligence, is reportedly among the most influential commanders.

Where Haqqani came from. Jalaluddin Haqqani was one of the earliest Afghan Islamists. He obtained his education first in a private *madrasa* in Afghanistan and later in the famous Dar-ul-Ulum Haqqania of Akora Khattak, situated halfway between Peshawar and the legendary Khyber Pass, in Pakistan's North-West Frontier Province. With the first group of Afghan Islamists, he went to Pakistan a few months after Daud's 1973 coup d'état to get military training in order to take up weapons against the new regime. He settled in Miramshah, barely 15 kilometres inside Pakistan and less than 50 kilometres from his home in Srana.[26] Among the 500 "fighters and commanders" who were trained in Pakistan by the Frontier Corps led by Nasrullah Babar (who, in the 1990s, as Interior Minister under Benazir Bhutto became the first mentor of the Taliban) at that time, were future prominent *mujahidin* leaders like Gulbuddin Hekmatyar and Ahmad Shah Massud.[27]

On 22 July 1975, some groups from this contingent started an uprising simultaneously in different parts of Afghanistan. It was suppressed quickly because of its lack of popular support. Jalaluddin Haqqani led the most vicious attack. A small band of fighters under his lead ambushed the convoy of the governor of Urgun *Loy Wuluswali* in the Mandzkai gorge in Ziruk district of today's Paktika province.[28] The governor, one of the Parchamis allied with President Daud, survived but twelve members of his administration were killed. This incident established Haqqani's Jihadi credentials. From 1976 to 1979 he was a member of the executive committee of Hizb-i Islami Afghanistan when it still was the unified Islamist organisation with most future *tanzim* leaders as members, including Hekmatyar, Khalis and Rabbani.[29] In an even more spectacular operation in early 1979, he lured the PDPA Minister for Tribal Affairs, Gen. Faiz Mohammad, into a trap in Paktia and killed him. Ostensibly inviting him for negotiations, Haqqani served the minister and his team a rich meal, after which the guests fell asleep and were slaughtered. At that point, Haqqani already belonged to Hizb-i Islami Afghanistan/Khalis (Islamic Party of Afghanistan/Khalis faction), a loosely structured *tanzim* that mainly relied on the Eastern Afghan Khugiani tribe and was led by conservative tribal *ulema*. In January 1979, the Paktia tribes held a *jirga* in Miramshah (Waziristan), where they allowed the different *tanzim* to operate on their territories. Haqqani became the only significant commander of Khalis' party in the South-East and was virtually independent of it. His main base inside Afghanistan then was already situated in the Shahikot Mountains.[30]

Haqqani's rival Hekmatyar was still the ISI favourite among the Afghan *mujahidin* at that time. On 31 March 1991, two years after the withdrawal of the Soviet troops, the *mujahidin* captured their first important provincial capital, Khost, from the Najibullah regime. Haqqani's fighters were the backbone of this attack but ISI made sure that Hekmatyar was able to present himself as the real victor.[31] Haqqani inherited Hekmatyar's position only after the latter had taken an anti-US position in the first Gulf War.

After the fall of Dr Najibullah's regime in March 1992, Jalaluddin Haqqani was appointed Minister for Justice in the first *mujahidin* cabinet led by Interim President Prof. Sebghatullah Mojaddedi (the same in which the current President Hamed Karzai served as Deputy Foreign Minister later). Under the subsequent government of the Islamic State of Afghanistan under Rabbani, he was the quasi-warlord in the Khost/Paktia area. When the Taliban marched towards Kabul, he first opposed them taking over the area but soon joined them in 1995, allegedly prompted by ISI. He became one of their strongest battle commanders, taking part in the conquest of the Eastern region and the fighting against Massud's forces in the Shamali plain north of Kabul in the winter of 1996/97. When the Taliban made him Minister for Tribal and Frontier Affairs in 1998, this was mainly a symbolic gesture. They honoured Haqqani's fire-power but kept him away from the real decision-making process in Kandahar at the same time; the cabinet in Kabul only had limited governing authority. Even on the military side, Haqqani was kept on the sidelines. When he raised troops to attack Mazar-i Sharif again after the Taliban defeat in 1997, he nevertheless was "powerless to take military decisions" because "Kandahari officers" had the supreme command at that front.[32] After 9/11 but still in September 2001, Mullah Omar appointed Haqqani to lead all Taliban forces in their effort to resist the expected US attack. The Kandahari core forces, in the meantime, started to melt away into their villages or across the border to Pakistan.

Between 9/11 and the Bonn Conference on Afghanistan that started in late November 2001, there apparently were attempts to encourage a "moderate" faction of the Taliban to break away from the mainstream movement and to become part of the following political process. It was reported that US and British agencies saw Haqqani as the possible leader of such a group and offered him a leading role in a future Afghan government. A spokesman of the Pakistani Foreign Ministry confirmed that Haqqani had visited Islamabad "as part of a search for a "broad-based government" to succeed the Taliban's, and that his meetings involved at least one with representatives of the former Afghan King.[33] It can be assumed that this idea had been planted by ISI, which counted Haqqani among its most reliable allies in Afghanistan.

This initiative failed, but it remains unclear why. Possibly it was a case of lack of coordination between different US authorities: one report indicates that Haqqani's younger brother Ibrahim Omari was arrested by the military while other agencies negotiated with him.[34] After a visit to Pakistan from 17 to 21 October 2001, Jalaluddin Haqqani rebuffed any such plans and declared that he would start a guerrilla war against the expected US invasion. He even became the "key organiser" of the al Qaida escape.[35]

The Haqqanis' comeback. After the fall of their regime and their retreat from Kabul on 13 November 2001, the Taliban's leadership went into hiding or exile in Pakistan. It had suffered a defeat and was not sure whether the movement could be sustained. Some groups and individuals changed sides, gave themselves in to the US-led Coalition or stretched out feelers towards the new Karzai administration in Kabul. Among them were protagonists of the Haqqani and Mansur networks, the latter ones re-emerging in the form of a political party, Jami'at-i Khuddam-ul-Furqan (Society of the Servants of Providence), established in Pakistan in January 2002. Its participation in the Loya Jirgas of 2002 and 2003 and its registration as a political party were rejected by the Karzai administration. Currently, it exists in the form of a circle of some 30 "reconciled" Taliban lodged in government guest houses in Kabul and consulted by the President on reconciliation issues from time to time.

Jalaluddin Haqqani also retreated to Pakistan, where he resided in Danday Darpakhel, a suburb of the town of Miramshah in North Waziristan (FATA) in the neighbourhood of the Pakistani Army's 11th Corps HQ with its ISI office. In the 1980s, he had built a mosque and a *madrasa* there, the Manba-ul-Ulum. Afghan sources allege that in those years he resided under the protection of the Pakistani military or even in a compound reserved for Pakistani army officers. The Haqqani network was not represented at the Bonn Conference on Afghanistan in late 2001. Instead, Jalaluddin Haqqani's arch-enemy

Pacha Khan Zadran, a commander from a rival Zadran subtribe and a US ally with 600 of his men hired as auxiliary troops, was invited there—as the only member of the royalist Rome group delegation based inside the country. When, as a result of the conference, Pacha Khan's brother Amanullah Zadran was awarded the Tribal and Border Affairs portfolio—the same that Jalaluddin Haqqani had held under the Taliban—in the new Karzai-led Interim Administration, he was very likely further alienated from the political process.[36] By mid-2002, however, Haqqani's followers among the Zadran still had not broken their links with the UN mission in Kabul. His cousin Haji Abdurrahman Zadran, today said to be the network's head of operations, still participated in a delegation of Loya Paktia tribal elders meeting high-ranking UNAMA staff in April 2002, complaining about US bombings of villages. From then onwards the Haqqanis slowly drifted back into the insurgency, soon becoming known as "the Haqqani network". As a result, the security situation in Loya Paktia was gradually to deteriorate every year.

It started in Paktika province, which had already become volatile by 2003. When UNAMA undertook a security assessment mission to the province in September that year, it was able to visit only ten out of 22 districts; twelve were already inaccessible. The paucity of effective government presence there had led to Taliban influence in various degrees; at least one district (Barmal) was already without even a symbolic government presence and completely in the hands of the Taliban. Elsewhere in the province, their forces were becoming more aggressive and extended their activities beyond border districts, setting up embryonic parallel administrations in some areas, mainly Barmal, Gayan and Terwa districts, sometimes with the tacit support of some district officials. Ten of the 12 Paktia districts and all districts in Khost were still accessible for the UN then. However, the UN reported operations by anti-government elements "throughout the region with high infiltration [rates] at [the] border areas with Pakistan", and coordinated attacks on police posts often involving more than 100 fighters, also mainly in areas close to the border, as well as regular attacks against Coalition forces, governmental installations and NGOs, including IED attacks on Coalition vehicles in Gardez. Attacks on US supply convoys on the road between Sharana and Ghazni province had started by 2003.

In January 2003 the Taliban's radio *De Shariat Ghag* (Voice of Sharia) had temporarily started broadcasts for the South-Eastern region.[37] On 19 June 2007 it came back with a daily 30–minute FM programme of better quality that, however, could be received only in some areas of the region. It was not clear whether it transmitted from one of the dozens of Islamist-run FM stations just across the border in FATA or from a mobile base inside Afghanistan.

In June 2003, Taliban spokesman Mohammad Mukhtar Mujahid announced that a new 10–member Supreme (or Leadership) Council had been established that included Jalaluddin Haqqani and Abdullatif Mansur from the South-East.[38] One month later, in July 2003, reports came in about a new command structure of the Taliban in the South-East and a visit by Jalaluddin

Haqqani to villages in the Zadran gorge in Spera district. In Khost the Taliban, the Haqqani network and Hizb were reported to have divided the districts into distinct operational areas among themselves. Towards the end of that year, increasing infiltration of Haqqani fighters into Paktia was noticed, in particular through Tsamkani district, just about ten kilometres from the Afghan border and the Pakistani town of Parachinar, a major insurgent base.

In 2004 the Haqqani network was "waging small-unit, small-arms, hit-and-run attacks on U.S. bases just a mile or two across the border" from Pakistan.[39] In April 2005, 50 Taliban showed up on 30 motorbikes in Paktika. However, UNAMA still spoke of "extremely high levels of support for Karzai" during the elections process of 2004/5. In early 2005 the governors of Khost and Paktia—Merajuddin Pattan, a Western educated liberal businessman, and Assadullah Wafa, a conservative tribal elder from Kandahar province close to President Karzai—publicly claimed to be in contact with Haqqani commanders or even Jalaluddin Haqqani himself for reconciliation efforts, a fact strongly denied by the latter. At approximately the same time, some Afghan officials reported that communities in the Panjshir valley had started to sell government-owned weapons stocks to the Taliban, including those active in Loya Paktia.[40]

When this author visited the region in April 2006, the Haqqanis and Mansurs had consolidated their networks for broader operations. The regional Taliban *amer* Taher Anwari—there were still two different Taliban networks in the South-East then—and other Taliban commanders moved freely in the region, without being involved in direct combat operations. They were mainly networking and conducting propaganda activities. These included a call from Jalaluddin Haqqani to all those working in the government, the Afghan army, the occupation forces and the administrative system to terminate their involvement. Pro-insurgency propaganda, particularly in two border districts of Paktia, also was increased by mullahs in official mosques, who incited the population against "foreign occupiers" and openly justified the killing of pro-government locals and government employees. Newly recruited Taliban groups became visible in the Zadran areas. In the first week of April, Taliban shot at the convoy of the newly-arrived UNHCR country director when it passed Gerda Tserey district, the Haqqanis' area of origin. A first suicide attack occurred in Paktika, in Barmal district, against an ANA checkpoint, while a larger Taliban group tried unsuccessfully to take over Dila district centre, also in Paktika. A mission from the EU Special Representative's office in Kabul in July 2006 still assessed Khost and Paktia as "relatively secure and stable, despite intense efforts by insurgent commanders to mobilise former networks and increase attacks against government and international targets". But the number of incidents had already doubled in relation to the previous year, from 87 in the whole of 2005 to 97 between January and June 2006 alone. According to this report, the South-Eastern insurgency was still "in the hit-and-run phase". It also noted that the government tried to stem this rise by increasingly involving the tribes through the creation of *arbaki*. By early 2006, the governor of Paktia had agreed with the main tribes of the area to appoint 30 *arbaki* members per district, which were supposed to be paid 50 US$ per month from his operational funds. This was later increased to 200 US$ per district. But at that point, most of the *arbaki* already were unpaid for four months, which might help to explain why the number of attacks doubled nonetheless.

On 10 September 2006 a suicide bomber sent by the Haqqani network succeeded in killing the highest-ranking Afghan official by then, Paktia governor Hakim Taniwal. When insurgents also bombed the governor's funeral in his home village of Tanai the next day, killing seven more people, the Haqqanis' reputation suffered a significant setback among the population. A UN report in March 2007, however, saw the situation further deteriorated. Areas most affected by the insurgency were Zurmat in Paktia and the border districts of Khost, Paktia and Paktika. The groups operating there, it stated, were still "not beyond the scope of dialogue". A month later, a UN official in the South-East summarised the state of the insurgency there as follows: "The networks are already there and only need to be mobilised." According to him, they drew on "a class of disenfranchised, jobless, frustrated young men, and there are incentives [for them] to fight; but there are very few incentives not to fight." Still, there were no open, large-scale attacks. There was more distribution of pro-Taliban propaganda, but most of the still relatively few IEDs planted were recovered with the help of the local population. UNAMA was working intensely with the Zadran tribe, in particular with Jalaluddin Haqqani's sub-tribe in Gerda Tserey, and there was still hope that an indirect dialogue could be maintained. Even the US troops in the area seemingly held themselves back vis-à-vis the Haqqanis. To describe the situation, Paktia governor Rahmatullah Rahmat quoted a Pashtun proverb: "The bear doesn't climb down from the mountain; the hunter doesn't climb up on the mountain." The above-mentioned UN official stated that this district's *shura*, with some close Haqqani relatives as members, "has never been closer to the government than now".

However, the shortcomings of the government were already too visible. A local UN official summed up the reasons for the growing insurgency at this time as follows: "the non-existence of visible reconstruction projects of significant scope, weak and resource-starved province administrations, increasing threats to the presence of district administrations on the ground and the almost complete non-presence of foreign NGOs [that] led to the perception among the tribal population that the peace process has no impact on their lives and that the central government doesn't care about them." Governor Rahmat, a former UNAMA political officer, was kept at arm's length by the Kabul government. When he took over his position, he was not paid the operational funds his predecessor had received.[41] This deprived him of crucial means in counter-insurgency, like public outreach, contact and hospitality as well as pay for *arbaki*. While in Paktia the *arbaki* were still in being, hoping for a resumption of payments, those in Khost already had dispersed around the same time. Corrupt and openly criminal members of the administration did their share to discredit the reputation of the Kabul government and its local representatives. In one striking example the Zurmat chief of police, a former Khalqi, raided a mosque during prayer in the district in February 2007. His men robbed the congregation of money and watches. When those being robbed staged some resistance, one of the policemen was killed. The police chief radioed to Kabul that he had been attacked by Taliban and had lost one man. Although UNAMA reported the incident, the police chief was still not removed when the author visited Gardez in October of the same year. In late 2007, there were reports from Paktia that the *wuluswal* and the police chief of one district were setting up illegal checkpoints and dividing the "taxed" money between them on the basis of a daily quota.[42]

During 2007, the situation deteriorated drastically. According to UNAMA, the outreach for civil servants declined in 34 of the 43 official South-Eastern districts[43] between March and June 2007. Paktika was described by a tribal elder from neighbouring Paktia as "lost" and "a black hole". But now also Paktia and Khost were deteriorating rapidly. By April 2007, groups of Haqqani fighters were regularly operating in non-Zadran districts like Dand-e Pattan and Zazi Aryub (Paktia). Insurgents' ambushes were better prepared and coordinated and resulted in a higher number of casualties. Khost province experienced the biggest increase in security incidents in the whole South-East and had the third highest suicide attack rate in all Afghanistan. July 2007 saw a 250 per cent increase in security incidents along the Gardez-Khost road, a reflection of Serajuddin Haqqani's intention to destabilise the road's construction that had been delayed at least since 2003 for the lack of sufficient funds. The US PRT had subcontracted an Indian company to carry out the work—a welcome target for the Pakistani-backed Haqqanis. Towards the end of the year there was an increase in direct attacks on district centres and police posts, civilians involved in the political process were targeted more often. There were "large concentrations" of insurgents in Western and Northern Paktia and "prolonged combat situations" on the rise in Paktia and Paktika. The Haqqani network was more and more effectively able to constrain governmental space in Loya Paktia and, from there, in Wardak and Logar since the end of 2006. It still relied, according to UNAMA, on small, relatively isolated cells and mainly carried out cross-border attacks.

A non-governmental organisation with good contacts in the region registered more Taliban visibility and contacts with tribal elders in October 2007. As a result, elders were increasingly intimidated; many moved into urban centres. That reduced the inclination of local tribes to prevent the insurgents from using the twelve infiltration routes that led through Khost province alone.[44] At approximately the same time, in September 2007, UNAMA found out that 35 per cent of the 7,000 police officers in the South Eastern region's structure were there on paper only, with commanders pocketing the salaries of the ghost policemen. In the problematic district of Zurmat, only 25 out of a theoretical 174 were on duty.

In the summer of 2008, the deterioration in Paktia and Khost continued. Local families warned relatives working for NGOs not to travel to the area any more; more NGO and UN personnel moved their families out of the region. Afghans from the region reported *shabname* in Pakistani-coloured Pashto sanctioning the "execution" of US troop translators as "Islamic" and warning teachers and officials that if they continued working for the government it would be "their own responsibility" if they were hurt. Youths on motorbikes openly intimidated government officials by following them to their homes. Propaganda video cassettes and DVDs proliferated, although the insurgents were not able yet to openly use mosques for propaganda as in Paktika or Southern Afghanistan. According to Afghan newspaper reports, mullahs in Khost, enraged by US air strikes causing civilian casualties (among them a member of the celebrated Afghan cricket team), had started a "campaign" that appealed to the local population no longer to cooperate with Coalition forces trying to identify insurgents.[45] In June 2008, insurgents attacked the US/ANA base in Laka Tiga at a strategic bridge on the Khost-Gardez road. Haqqani groups that had infiltrated the margins of Paktia's provincial capital Gardez (including the area just outside the local UNAMA office) were carrying out a series of armed raids, kidnappings and executions around the town throughout 2008. In their boldest attack yet they entered Khataba village mosque in a suburb of Gardez, selected five men from the assembled worshippers and took them with them on 23 September (they were released later). Since the spring of 2008 in particular, the Haqqanis' fighters had been reinforced by a large number of Pakistani Taliban from the Wazir, Dawar and Mehsud tribes.[46] Some sources speak of up to 4,000 of them, mainly based in the Zadran Arc.

District centres started being targeted more aggressively. According to the governor of Khost and local Afghan intelligence officials, there still was not a single attack on a district centre in that province by the autumn of 2007. In neighbouring Paktia there had been only one, on Shwak in June. In Paktika the situation was much worse: in June, insurgents temporarily held the centre of Yahyakhel district, and on 30 August they even tried to storm the provincial centre in Sharana. The district centre of Dila was abandoned by government.[47] This changed in 2008. During this year, Haqqanis' fighters also attacked the district centres of Waza Zadran, Shwak (both Paktia), Spera (Paktika) and Zazi Maidan (Khost) and temporarily took over those of Gayan (Paktika), Gerda Tserey (Paktia) and Sabari and Qalandar (Khost).

Meanwhile, the operations also affect the main road between Kabul, Gardez and Khost. There are also frequent attacks on both main passes along this road, Tera Kandao and Seta Kandao. Construction sites for secondary roads to the district centres and the workers on them are attacked. In May 2008 the Haqqani network issued a decree banning any road construction in Zurmat district (Paktia) altogether. *Shabname* ("night letters" or leaflets) are distributed in order to intimidate government officials and civilians who sympathise with the government or work for international actors, both military and civilian.[48]

In late 2005, local sources reported that premiums of 15,000 Pakistani rupees were being offered for the assassination of Afghan officials and 100,000 rupees for a foreigner.[49] In April 2007 a UN official said that the Haqqani network "researches international organisations in the South-East" for their internal structures in order to identify possible targets. These threats did not remain empty ones. In 2008 alone, insurgents killed the spokesman of the Paktika governor, the head of the Khost appeal court, the district attorney of Zurmat, three security officials in Khost (among them the provincial security head) and tribal elders in Alisher (also known as Terezai, Khost), Wormamay and Urgun (Paktika). On 13 August 2008 Taliban killed three female international staff members of the NGO International Rescue Committee (IRC) in Logar province, on the Gardez-Kabul road. After this incident, the UN stopped all its personnel in the South-Eastern region moving by road except for larger convoys for well-prepared missions.

How does the Haqqani network function? The coherence of the Haqqani network is based on a combination of tribal and ideological loyalties. The initial core of its fighters was recruited from the Haqqanis' sub-tribe among the Zadran, the Mezi. Immediately after the Soviet invasion, it was described as "very tribal in character".[50] Its basis was broadened during the anti-Soviet struggle when *mujahidin* were also recruited from other South-Eastern Pashtun tribes. A foreign observer noted in 1984 in Paktia how closely Jalaluddin Haqqani worked with local tribal leaders, "sharing jurisdiction with them and allowing them to apply customary tribal law to resolve internal disputes". Another speaks of "some tribally mixed fighting groups" in Paktia under Haqqani's command by 1985.[51] It also became known that a commander from Keshm (Badakhshan) in Northern Afghanistan, a Tajik, fought alongside Haqqani in Paktia during the 1980s.

After 2001, but possibly earlier also, the Haqqani network additionally included Zadran and other Pashtuns from across the border in Pakistan. One of them, Darim Sedgai, acted as his liaison to Baitullah Mehsud's Pakistani Taliban. He was reported as killed in January 2008 but the fact was rejected by Taliban sources. Another was 'Id Niaz Borakhel, killed in late 2007. [52] According to recent reports from the area, the Haqqanis still give financial support strategically to tribal elders (*khans* and *maliks*) in Loya Paktia.[53]

As of late, fighters with a background in nomad (*kuchi*) tribes are gaining more prominence among Haqqani's fighters in Khost and Paktia.

The tribal base of the Haqqani network, though, is also a cause of one of the major fault lines in the insurgency: the lack of inter-tribal confidence between the Kandaharis and the Paktiawal (those from Paktia). The Haqqani network draws its support mainly from the latter. In contrast, from the outset in 1994, the Taliban leadership was mainly made up of "Kandahari" Pashtuns, i.e. Pashtuns from the provinces of "Greater Kandahar", comprising Helmand, Uruzgan, Zabul and Kandahar itself. They belong to either of the two most well-known Pashtun tribal "confederations", the Durrani and Ghilzai.

Although there were some representatives of other Pashtun tribes and ethnic groups in the official Taliban leadership (the Leadership Council in Kandahar and the cabinet in Kabul), the closest circle around Mullah Omar was dominated by brothers-in-arms from his home province of Uruzgan whom he knew and trusted from their common anti-Soviet struggle. The others had difficulties in gaining Mullah Omar's full confidence. On the all-Afghanistan level, this Kandahari-Paktiawal fault-line within the Taliban seems to be much stronger then the much-discussed Durrani-Ghilzai gap. During the Taliban regime, occasionally Loya Paktia tribes openly resisted what was perceived as Kandahari dominance. There were at least two revolts in 2000 when Taliban officials tried to suppress a local tradition to celebrate the new year, the so-called "egg fighting", perceived by them to be un-Islamic—a conflict followed that evolved into open fighting. Seeking appeasement, the Taliban were forced to take recourse to the same means as other regimes who did not want to alienate the local tribes: convening local *ulema*, tribal leaders and people's representatives who were persuaded to voice their support for the government—in return for the government's tacit climb-down on the issue.[54]

It seems that the elder Haqqani owed his rise to become one of the strongest *mujahidin* commanders more to his military prowess (and his political and supply links in Pakistan) than to his religious status. It was his firepower that allowed him to oust and replace the traditional Zadran khans from the Babrakzai family.[55] His (rather formal) membership in Hizb/Khalis mainly ensured that he had direct access to Western and Arab military and financial supplies distributed through ISI as a monopolist. One can only speculate about Jalaluddin Haqqani's motivation to continue his fight with the Taliban. Although he is one of Afghanistan's Islamist pioneers and an Islamic scholar, and has founded a number of *madrasas*, some people who have met Haqqani over the past decades doubt that he is mainly motivated by religious feelings. Some also claim that he runs his *madrasas* more for fund-raising then for Islamic purposes, knowing their attraction for Arab donors.[56]

The elder Haqqani is undoubtedly a religious conservative who does not see much of a difference between the current US-led NATO intervention in his country and the Soviet occupation before. His growing intransigence, however, can possibly be explained by a series of political about-faces for which he might feel victimised. In 1989, Haqqani was one of the central figures in the anti-Soviet resistance. For the US, he was among the "less publicized CIA favourites", located "[a]t the centre of [the] border nexus" of "interlocking networks of Pakistani intelligence officers, Arab volunteers, and Wahhabi *madrassas*". He "was seen by CIA officers in Islamabad and others as perhaps the most impressive Pashtun battlefield commander in the war", had "the CIA's full support", received payments and supplies and was entrusted with testing new weapon systems and tactics. According to Steve Coll, he was a so-called "unilateral asset" of the CIA in 1988 and 1989.[57] His switch to the Taliban, however, turned him into an enemy of the US. As a Taliban minister, he was included on the UN sanctions list against al Qaida and the Taliban already before 9/11, on 31 January 2001.[58]

Today, Haqqani's fight might be increasingly motivated by feelings of revenge. During various bombing raids and predator drone attacks against his houses and *madrasas*, in both Afghanistan and Pakistan, starting in early 2002 and with the latest strike on 23 October 2008 on his *madrasa* in Danday Darpakhel near Miramshah, many of his family members, among them women and infants, and students lost their lives. In early July, his youngest son Omar was fatally injured during a skirmish at Sata Kandao pass at the border between Paktia and Khost provinces, which, it was reported, he had been videoing.

The Haqqani network is definitely on the rise. It has expanded its area of operations further north, towards Kabul. There are reports that the Haqqanis are trying to reach out to "some Northern Alliance groups" and Hizb-i Isla-mi.[59] This is quite possible. As one of the major resistance commanders and later a minister in the *mujahidin* government, Jalaluddin Haqqani has good personal relations with many former *mujahidin* leaders. Such relations count a lot in Afghan society. Former Haqqani sub-commanders are members of post-2001 institutions, like the Khost Mujahidin Shura, the Shura of Khost's three unofficial urban districts (Matun, Lakan, Shamal), and even of the lower house of the Afghan parliament. Moreover, many northern commanders who are officially part of the new Afghan institutions harbour bad feelings towards Karzai and his external backers because of their perceived exclusion from the political set-up. Being religious conservatives, and often even Islamists, they secretly reject the (far from blameless) international involvement in their country as an occupation and an attack on Afghan culture.

On the military side, the Haqqani network's main *modus operandi* is still asymmetrical warfare, using means of terrorism and guerrilla warfare including the use of IEDs, mines and suicide attacks. Spectacular operations aim at showing that it is able to "hit everywhere" and to catch international media attention. Meanwhile, open military combat operations remain sporadic and an absolute exception. Apart from some insular bases, it has not been able to organise permanent fronts on Afghan territory and does not control any district centre or even village full time, as the mainstream Taliban in Southern and Eastern Afghanistan do. The use of terrorist means is a copy of Islamist militant tactics elsewhere and perhaps puts the Haqqani network much closer to al Qaida than even most of the Kandahari Taliban leadership. This increasing ruthlessness carries the message to Afghans: we are not trying to win hearts and minds any more, like the Taliban of the 1990s. It is "shock and awe" *à l'afghane*. It might also represent the attempt of hawkish Taliban elements to sabotage possible negotiations.

However, this also deepens rifts within the insurgency. There are more and more reports that old-time, "pious" Taliban commanders internally express abhorrence at the bloodshed among the Afghan civilian population caused by car bombs and suicide attacks. Some of these reports emanate from Loya Paktia.[60] This is perhaps reflected by Mullah Omar's 'Id address of 2008 which also is distributed as a *layha* (instruction) among Taliban ranks:

"I once again give you the same guidelines, to stand in front of the enemy like steel. But be very careful when you face the general people and your innocent countrymen. Don't go for an attack which has a possibility of harming the general people. All your operations must be in the light of the sayings of Allah and the way of Mohammad (Sallaho Alaihe wa Sallam). Always leave your personal and emotional feelings behinds.

Every act which is not in harmony with the teachings of Islam or is not according to the Islamic civilization or does not look good with the Muslim Ummah [...] like blasts in [mosques] and where there are a gathering of the general people, looting of the properties on the highways, cutting noses and ears in the name of [sectarian] differences which Islam forbids [...] or the burning of Islamic books must be strongly countered."[61]

This seems to be an attempt by the Taliban leadership to indirectly distance itself from Haqqani's practices (although some of its commanders like the late Mullah Dadullah also used them) and remedy growing concerns in its own ranks. Whether leaflets bearing Haqqani's signature and criticising Mullah Omar for jeopardising the future of the Taliban, which appeared in Eastern Afghanistan in mid-2008, really originate from this source or are part of the psy-ops battle cannot be finally answered. It can be said, though, that such open and personal criticism, even putting Mullah Omar's Islamic credentials in question, would be very unusual in Pashtun society.[62]

Links with foreign Jihadis and Pakistan. Significantly, Haqqani was the first Afghan *mujahidin* commander who welcomed and incorporated Arab Jihadi volunteers into his groups. This happened as early as 1987.[63] Already before that, he had established durable connections with wealthy Saudis during *hajj* pilgrimages, as well as with the Saudi intelligence service, and run fund-raising offices in Persian Gulf countries. One of Haqqani's two wives comes from the United Arab Emirates. All this laid the ground for his extremely close relationship with Arab sponsors, including Osama bin Laden personally, whom he met during the construction of the Zhawara base in Khost province (carried out by Bin Laden and his company),[64] as well as ISI and later the al Qaida network. According to some sources, the Arab influence on the Haqqani network might have even increased recently with the younger Haqqani's rise. He has no personal experience of the anti-Soviet resistance and mainly grew up in the FATA's radicalised environment. It can be assumed that most of the no more than "150 to 500 hard-core Qaeda fighters" in Pakistan's tribal areas "financing, training recruits and facilitating attacks into Afghanistan" are closely linked to the Haqqani network.[65]

The second pillar of the Haqqanis' support—their symbiotic relations with Pakistani power structures, the military, ISI and the Islamist parties—largely remained intact after 2001. A high-ranking police officer in Loya Paktia says that ISI has maintained an extensive contact network amongst the region's tribal leaders since the 1980s. The Haqqani network today uses these connections to bribe those elders with "cash payments, passports, houses in Pakistan and trips to the Gulf", to recruit fighters and to request that those tribes reject access to their territories for fighters of other groups (and the government).[66] A US news magazine reported in September 2008 that American officials "say they have evidence that some elements of Pakistan's ISI are protecting and even helping the Haqqani network". It carried a story of how a Haqqani sub-commander travelled in a five-vehicle convoy to Pakistan to get supplies and instructions from Serajuddin Haqqani, passing various Pakistani military checkpoints just by calling an apparent minder of the Haqqanis. The commander concluded that the younger Haqqani "seems to feel invulnerable" in Pakistan and that "[t]he ISI protects him". Senior Pakistani officials still hold their hands over the Haqqanis. They are quoted in the same report as saying that "now is not the time to move against [them]". In July 2008, US military and CIA officials confronted their Pakistani counterparts with evidence of ISI links to the Haqqani network at least in two meetings.[67] "Pakistan is like your shoulder that supports your RPG", said a Taliban commander quoted by *Time* Magazine.[68]

Obviously Haqqani is still seen as a valuable ally by the Pakistani Taliban sympathisers within the ISI and the Frontier Corps. They repeatedly used his influence among the Pakistani Taliban to pressure them to cease attacking the country's security forces—and attack Afghan and Western forces in Afghanistan instead.[69] Afghan sources also reported a meeting between representatives of Haqqani, Hekmatyar's Hizb and Arabs in Parachinar in the early spring of 2007 that was protected by Pakistani military. In 2006, ISI requested Jalaluddin Haqqani and the famous Kandahari Taliban commander Dadullah (killed in May 2007) to mediate in bloody clashes in South Waziristan between factions of Pakistani Taliban, one of which supported militants of the Islamic Movement of Uzbekistan (IMU) of Qari Taher Yuldushev. More than 2,000 Uzbeks, including families, were living on the Dawar tribe's territory around Mirali alone.[70] This conflict reflected the rivalry about who would lead the still diverse Pakistani Taliban movement and was, at the same time, an ISI-instrumentalised tribal conflict between a part of the local Wazir tribe and the Massud tribe from outside the area. Haqqani sent in his son Serajuddin and the former head of the Taliban Supreme Court, Nur Mohammad Saqeb.[71] Their involvement led to the North Waziristan peace agreement of 5 September 2006. After its conclusion, Jalaluddin Haqqani issued a declaration in the name of the Islamic Emirate (i.e. Mullah Omar) "not to fight against Pakistan, because this is in the interest of the US". This clearly served Pakistani interests.

Behind this ISI initiative stood a broader aim: "to marshal the different tribal Taliban chieftains into a movement coherent enough to abide by a truce".[72] The initiative succeeded when on 14 December 2007 the Tehrik-i-Taliban-i-Pakistan (TTP) was founded. Its leader, Baitullah Mehsud, is a close ally of the Haqqanis. The Haqqanis gained considerably from these events. Their successful intervention strengthened their hand on all sides. They managed to save their Uzbek allies, whom Jalaluddin Haqqani had earlier asked

Mehsud to harbour.[73] And they proved their influence on both sides of the Pakistani Taliban rivalry: on Mehsud's TTP and on its rival, the ISI-financed splinter group of Haji Mawlawi Nazir. Nazir, from the Kakakhel sub-tribe of the Ahmadzai Wazir in Waziristan, is particularly close to the Haqqanis. He owns property not only in Paktika but also in Kandahar. After a stint with Hizb-i Islami during the anti-Soviet *jihad*, he had joined the Taliban after they established their regime and fought alongside the Haqqanis.[74]

Another part of the Haqqanis' Pakistan link is their involvement with Kashmiri and sectarian Punjabi Jihadis. Fighters of the Kashmiri Harakat-ul-Mujahidin (HuM) were running a training camp in Afghanistan,[75] most probably Yawar camp in Khost province, as early as in the mid-1980s when it initially was under the authority of Hizb-i Islami/Khalis and Jalaluddin Haqqani.[76] Haqqani admitted that he trained Kashmiri fighters in an interview in 1991.[77] This and another HuM camp were attacked by US cruise missiles in 1998 after Al Qaida commandos had bombed the US embassies in Nairobi and Dar es Salaam. The Kashmiri-Haqqani connection still operates. It was reported in early June 2008 that about 300 fighters from Jihadi groups had secretly gathered in Rawalpindi and "agreed to resolve their differences and commit more fighters to [...] Afghanistan". A HuM leader was quoted as saying that the *jihad* in Kashmir was "not the most important right now" but Afghanistan was "the fighting ground, with the Americans there". According to this report, the sectarian terrorist groups Jaish-i-Mohammad and Lashkar-i-Tayba were also present at the meeting.[78]

Most foreign elements linked with the Haqqani network inside Afghanistan are based in Mata Khan (Paktika), the Kulalgo area of Zurmat district where they maintain a supply base and in Eastern Ghazni.[79] One of the last reports of Uzbek IMU fighters active inside Afghanistan came from Sarobi district in Paktika province in October 2007.[80] Many Arabs and Uzbeks have married local wives, bought land, settled down and learned the Pashto language. Also, the obscure Uzbek-Turkish İslami Cihad İttehadi (Islamic Jihad Union) seems to operate—at least partly—under the Haqqani network. When one of its members, Cüneyt Çiftçi, also known as Saad Abu Furkan, a German of Turkish origin, blew himself up in front of a US military installation in Sabari (Khost) on 3 March 2008, his last statement was published together with a video message from Jalaluddin Haqqani. In its statements, however, the group refers to the leading al Qaida member Abu Laith al-Libi as its *sheikh* instead of Haqqani, so that it might be closer to al Qaida itself. Its leader is said to be an Uzbek (possibly of Tajik ethnicity), Najmiddin Jalolov.[81]

The Haqqani networks' links to the Arabian peninsula and to Pakistan also provide the bulk of its financial supplies. These money flows are reportedly collected in Parachinar (Pakistan) by a religious figure linked to the network. Additionally, religious taxes (*zakat* and *ushr*) are raised from businessmen, shopkeepers and also government officials in Khost and other areas. Income from the drug trade also plays a role, mainly from transit shipments originating in Southern Afghanistan.

The Mansur network

The second insurgent strand in Loya Paktia is the Mansur network, which is led by members of the family of the same name. Its original leader was the late Mawlawi Nasrullah Mansur, an Andar Pashtun from the small Sahak sub-tribe, which lives in the village of the same name in Zurmat. He received a religious education at Nur-ul-Madaris, the *madrasa* founded by the Mojad-dedi family, one of the most well-known (and conservative) abodes of Muslim learning in Afghanistan, located a few kilometres outside Ghazni city in Andar district. At least two cousins, Latifullah and Bashir Mansur, as well as the three sons of Nasrullah Mansur, Saifurrahman, Seyyedurrahman and Fathurrahman, were or still are operating prominently in Loya Paktia. Latifullah Mansur's deputy reportedly is Mullah Matin.

The Mansur network is also part of the Taliban-led insurgency without organisationally being fully integrated into it. It maintains a degree of organi-sational autonomy from the Taliban movement. But with many of its leading representatives killed over the last few years, it has been weakened consider-ably and has clearly passed its heyday. Some local observers think that it has almost completely lost significance. Others maintain that although the Mansur family has been partly wiped out and has lost its best fighters, the attraction of the name still creates some cohesion. The losses have certainly diminished its autonomy from the "Kandahari" Taliban core, but the current head of the family, Abdullatif Mansur, still seems to be a member of the Tali-ban's Leadership Council—which confirms that the network is still important to them.

The Mansur network, like the Haqqani one, is not active countrywide and is only of sub-regional importance. Historically, it is limited to areas in north-eastern Ghazni, south-western Paktia and pockets in Logar province. Its main operational area stretches across the so-called central corridor from Sarhauza district in Paktika and this province's most populated areas (around its capital Sharana and the district of Mata Khan) through Zurmat to Kharwar district in Logar, and also includes an area towards Paktia's centre at Gardez. This makes it even less extended than the Haqqani network. In Zurmat and Sha-hikot, it overlaps with the Haqqani network's area of influence. While the Shahikot Mountains in Zurmat constitute the Mansur network's main base and staging area, the districts of Kharwar (Logar) and Dehyak (Ghazni)—al-most devoid of any even token government presence—are other safe havens. Those areas coincide almost completely with the Ghilzai Andar tribe's terri-tory that comprises a few districts in Ghazni province (Andar, Dehyak, Giro, Qarabagh, Waghaz, Zana Khan), parts of Zurmat and Mirzaka areas in Paktia as well as of Mata Khan in Paktika. From those areas, the networks' fighters—operating in small groups and able to seeking shelter in surrounding villag-es—attack government and UN employees, and threaten, kidnap and kill Afghan government and UN employees as well as ISAF contractors.

In early 2007 there were 29 groups of 15 to 30 fighters operating in Zur-mat and 150 to 200 fighters in Shahikot again. [82] Possibly, it was Mansur's men in Zurmat who fired the first shot at a UN vehicle there in July 2003, narrowly missing an international staff member. In late 2006/early 2007, they temporarily imposed a total ban on the use of vehicles in the same district as an answer to the governor's attempt to forbid the movement of motorcycles, the insurgents' weapon of choice for assassinations. This show of force was clearly won by the insurgents although the ban—with some damage to the insurgents' image—had to be lifted after a civilian car carrying a pregnant woman to hospital ran over a mine.

Nasrullah Mansur's eldest son Saifurrahman stayed in Shahikot after the fall of the Taliban regime in November 2001. In the Taliban Emirate's time, he had commanded the Armoured Regiment No. 15 in Paktia and later the important 4th (Qargha) Division in the north-western outskirts of Kabul. In March 2002, he led the embittered resistance of over a thousand fighters, including his own men, those from the Haqqani networks, Arabs, Uzbeks, Tajiks and Chechens, against a large US military operation, codenamed Anaconda, that started on the last day of the Muslim 'Id-ul-Azha festival. During two weeks of massive fighting, his and Haqqani's forces were pushed out of the area. Jalaluddin Haqqani's brother Ibrahim Omari surrendered to Afghan troops under the command of the local Ministry of Defence representative, Gen. Gul Haidar.[83] This fighting forced the entire civilian population to leave the area. Four-fifths of its 2,642 families remain displaced in Pakistan to the day. With 235 civilian casualties and 2,500 houses, 21 mosques, two *madrasas* and all the infrastructure like bridges and *karez* destroyed, this operation was an early example of the excessive use of air power.

Apart from the alienation of local Pashtun populations by the US military and the activities of the Mansur network, a UN official quoted the following reasons for the instability in Zurmat in April 2007: the corruption in local government, the district's function as a major transit corridor for Taliban fighters moving from Pakistan to Ghazni province and more central Afghan areas, intra-tribal conflicts, and the strong position of conservative *ulema* in the area. "This is not the people's government: the chief of police is a thief, the *qazi* is a thief, the district governor is a thief," said a tribal elder from area, adding, "this makes it effectively a Taliban nursery".

Tribally, the area of Zurmat is highly fragmented, with a different subtribe of the Andar, Suleimankhel and others in almost every other village. The area was accessible for convoys then even so, but that situation has changed in the meantime. The Provincial Council's members from Zurmat were not able to attend the body's meetings in Gardez in the spring of 2008 any more; the UN has suspended all road movement in the whole region.

Furthermore, the relatively small district of Zurmat was strongly represented in the structures of the Taliban's Islamic Emirate. There were at least three ministers (Abdullatif Mansur for Agriculture, Taher Anwari for Finance and later for Economy and Amir Khan Muttaqi—whose family was originally from Zurmat but had been resettled to Kunduz—for Education), four deputy ministers (Abdulhakim Munib, from the Mamozai subtribe of the Suleimankhel, for Tribal Affairs; Mawlawi Rahmatullah Wahidyar for Martyrs and Refugees; Arifullah Arif for Finance; Mawlawi Rahimullah Zurmati for Information and Culture) as well as Khalilullah Firozi, a Suleimankhel, and Maulana Pir Mohammad Rohani as president of the Academy of Sciences and chancellor of Kabul University respectively. That made it possible for the area to be governed by Zurmatis themselves, not by Kandaharis, which earned it the nickname "Little Kandahar". This situation replicated itself after the Taliban comeback to the area in late 2005. According to sources familiar with the area, there is "complete local Taliban command in Zurmat". Local commanders get their orders from the remaining members of the Mansur family, mainly staying in Pakistan.

The Mansur network is a successor of one of the oldest Islamist groups in the country, the Khuddam ul-Forqan, or "Servants of Providence". [84] It predates the Taliban movement considerably. The Khuddam ul-Forqan emerged in Afghanistan in the mid-1960s from within the *ulema* under the influence of the head of the Mojaddedi family, Ibrahim Mojaddedi.[85] Its spiritual centre was the Nur-ul-Madaris *madrasa*. Its main aim was to counter the rising Marxist groups of the time. In 1978 the group contributed to the formation of Harakat-i Inqilab-e Islami (HII/Movement for an Islamic Revolution) as one of the seven major Sunni *tanzim* fighting the leftist regime in Kabul and the Soviet invasion. According to participants, its founders were "mullahs with Khuddam-ul-Forqan links from Helmand, Kandahar, Paktia and Paktika". They elected Mawlawi Mohammad Nabi Muhammadi, an Andar Pashtun from Logar, who was the member of parliament for Marja district in Helmand in the King's time,[86] as Harakat's leader. The raison d'être of the new organisation was the *ulema's* rejection of the spiritual authority of the self-proclaimed *jihad* leaders Gulbuddin Hekmatyar and Burhanuddin Rabbani to issue a *fatwa* for *jihad* against the Soviets.

In 1982 Harakat split into various factions. Most of its commanders joined the faction led by Nasrullah Mansur, officially called Harakat-i Nawin-i Inqilab-i Islami, or New Harakat, but usually known as Harakat/Mansur. Pakistan, however, refused to recognise it officially. This deprived the new group of a share of the Western and Arab countries' military and financial aid distributed by ISI. It therefore advised its commanders to join other—recognised—*tanzim*. It also made overtures to the Iranian government. Tehran rejected any cooperation, most probably because Harakat/Mansur was the one *tanzim* seen to be closest to the radical, anti-Shiite Deobandi doctrine of Sunni Islam. It also was fervently anti-monarchist and opposed more moderate groups like Prof. Mojaddedi's Jabha-e Nejat and Gailani's Mahaz-e Melli. One of its most popular slogans read: "In Islam, moderation is *kufr* [infidel]." Also in the 1980s, Mansur's Harakat was the main ally for Kashmiri Jihadis amongst the Afghan *mujahidin*, in particular for Harakat-ul-Mujahidin (HuM) and its successor organisation Harakat-ul-Jihad-al-Islami (HJI), founded in 1984. Their main contacts were Maulana Rohani and commander Arsala Rahmani, a Kharoti from Sarobi in Paktika.[87]

The HuM/HJI fighters "constituted a significant part of the Taliban forces in Afghanistan", known as the Punjabi Taliban. The HJI central leader Maulana Qari Saifullah Akhtar, a Pashtun from Waziristan, stayed with Mullah Omar in Kandahar up to the US attack started in October 2001. Its first leader, Maulana Ershad Ahmad, was killed fighting Soviet-backed Afghan government troops alongside Harakat in Sharana (Paktika).[88]

In 1992, *mujahidin* Harakat's various factions reunited under Nabi Muhammadi's leadership. When the *mujahidin* took over the government from the Najibullah regime in the same year, the Mansur family re-established its grip over Zurmat and suppressed all other competing organisations, particularly Hekmatyar's Hizb which had many local members killed by Mansur's fighters, but also Pir Gailani's Mahaz. He successfully urged local tribes to block supplies from Pakistan for Hizb at the behest of his allies Rabbani and Massud. Shortly afterwards, on 8 February 1993, Nasrullah Mansur was killed when his car hit a mine in his home Zurmat district after his return from a meeting with Interim President Rabbani in Kabul. The suspicion for Mansur's killing fell on Hekmatyar's Hizb. Thereafter, Nasrullah's brother Abdullatif Mansur became the leader of the Mansur faction; he was perceived as "more of a politician, an orator not a commander".[89] A year later, in 1994, Harakat's student wing Tehrik-e Tulaba-ye Harakat—with many Khuddam-ul-Forqan sympathisers—took the initiative to explore the new Taliban movement. A group comprising the later Taliban foreign minister Mullah Wakil Ahmad Mutawakkil and his deputy Abdur Rahman Zahid "went to Quetta to see what the Taliban were really about". Finding that "respected people" were with them, they decided to join. In late 1994, the Harakat leader Nabi Muhammadi followed with a public statement of support for the Taliban that declared his own organisation dissolved into the new movement. Khuddam-ul-Forqan, however, maintained distinctive structures even during the Taliban Emirate's time. The author encountered several Taliban officials in 2000/01, among them young men who identified themselves privately as Khuddam-ul-Forqan members. Some of them rose to high positions in the Taliban administration. Nasrullah Mansur's three sons—Saifurrahman, Seyyedurrahman and Fathurrahman—used the advance of the Taliban to start regaining influence in their region of origin.

Watching the decline of the Taliban even before 9/11, Harakat announced in Quetta that the movement would resume its own activities in July 2001. According to a participant in the events, its leaders wanted to avoid being dragged into an anti-US war. After the fall of the Taliban regime, many Mansur commanders associated themselves with the Karzai government. In some cases, this happened from a position of power: Qari Baba in Ghazni and Mohammad Ali Jalali in Paktika, who had been the governors of these provinces under the *mujahidin* government and had been pushed out by the Taliban, simply moved back into these positions. Others were Khial Mohammad, Ghazni governor for a while and now an MP, and Arsala Rahmani, who was appointed a Senator by the President. Mawlawi Seyyed Ahmad Shahidkhel joined the reconciliation programme and was released from prison in May 2008. This weakened the Mansur network's firepower significantly. However, it also provided them with links into the government camp. It was assumed that some of these commanders were playing in both camps.

The Mansur network became militarily active again in Zurmat only in late 2006, after about a year of preparations. Earlier, a broad meeting of representatives of different insurgent groups—al Qaida, the Haqqani and Mansur networks, pro-Taliban tribal commanders from Pakistan, Taliban commanders from Kunar, Zabul, Kandahar and the South-Eastern region in Yargulkhel (Waziristan)—had decided to step up operations in the South-East again. Following this, Abdullatif Mansur with 35 men visited his home village of Sahak (in Zurmat), met elders of various local tribes, among them the Baramkhel and Uryakhel, and announced *jihad* against the Karzai government, arguing that it was a puppet of the US. Also in 2006, Mansur fighters re-established their base in Shahikot.[90] The mood of the population, however, had deteriorated much earlier and provided a fertile ground for the Mansur network's comeback. This was linked to the arrest of a prominent tribal leader from the area, commander Mohammad Naeem Faruq, by US forces in January 2002, and that of Dr Hafizullah Shahidkhel, the head of the Zurmat tribal *shura*, who also had served as the first district governor under the Karzai administration, in April 2003. Both were detained in Guantánamo; Faruq was released in mid-2003. The population suspected that both fell victim to intrigues by the highly unpopular chief of police of the province, Abdullah Mujahid (who, ironically, also ended up in Guantánamo later); he was linked to Jami'at which wanted to keep control over this province. Dr Hafizullah had worked with Jalaluddin Haqqani during the *jihad* and later switched allegiance to the Mansur networks. A prominent figure locally during the Taliban period, he also signalled readiness to cooperate with the new Karzai administration initially. This was abruptly ended by his detention.

In early 2008, the Mansur network suffered a serious setback when one of the sons of Nasrullah Mansur was killed. An Afghan press report from January 2008 quoted an Afghan National Directorate for Security official as saying that Saifurrahman Mansur died during sectarian clashes in Parachinar in Pakistan's Kurram Agency in December 2007.[91] UN analysts, however, consider these reports as unconfirmed and assume that the victim was in fact Seyyedurrahman, and that the quoted Afghan report had confused the names. The youngest Mansur son, Fathurrahman, was reported inactive at the same time, although still involved in active fighting in mid-2003.

Like the Haqqani network, the Mansur network is based on tribal affiliation in the first instance. This constitutes the substratum of its internal cohesion and solidarity, coupled with a shared political outlook which, in this case, even goes further back than the shared experience of *jihad*. Owing to the Mansur's copycat "entryism", an approach that in Afghanistan has mainly been employed by Maoist anti-Soviet groups, it has very strong links into most of the other important *mujahidin tanzim*. For example, commander Arsala Rahmani was a member of Sayyaf's Ittehad executive committee in 1987.[92] Last but not least, it can be assumed that ISI has infiltrated this network through the Harakat youth, which was strongly influenced by Abdullah Zakeri a.k.a. Saheb Jan Sahebzada, one of the Taliban's later chief ideologues.

Other Taliban

There are, particularly in Southern Paktika, some Taliban structures that belong neither to the Haqqani or the Mansur network but are directly linked to Taliban Leadership Council. They guard the strategic crossing from Pakistan of an old *mujahidin* supply route that starts in Khama Ghar (Pakistan) and leads through Nika, Ziruk, Gayan and Spera districts to Shahikot and further on to Ghazni and Zabul areas. These groups are firmly rooted in the local tribal society dominated by the large and partly nomadic Suleimankhel tribe, which constitutes almost 100 per cent of the inhabitants of this thinly populated and isolated area, known as Southern Katawaz (with Wazakhwa and Terwa districts). Currently, their overall commander is reported to be Mullah Nawab Khan, a Suleimankhel Pashtun from the Mahmudkhel sub-tribe. He is active in Wazakhwa district.

In 2003, there still was a whole range of—sometimes well-known—Taliban commanders operating in Paktika border districts who were not integrated into the then still evolving Haqqani network. Among them were prominent former Taliban, like Mawlawis Kabir and Toha. The latter was a chief of police in Laghman and Nangrahar provinces under the Taliban Emirate, and is now operating further north in his Zadran tribe's territory in Nika, Gayan and Ziruk districts, from a base in Narey-e Manzakey in Nika.[93] There were also a number of smaller commanders like Maula Jan (Zadran from Gayan) and Ibrahim, as well as commander Arafat, who later joined the Afghan government's reconciliation programme. According to some reports, the Zadran commanders among them, in particular, have drifted towards the Haqqani network.

Under Nawab Khan, a cluster of smaller Taliban groups were reported to be starting activities in mid-2007. Its sub-commanders are said to be Mawlawi Adam Khan (with two deputies, Abdul Baset Agha and Abdul Hamid, with Mohammad Bassir Sahebzada as the head of operations), Saadullah Khadilai, the Taliban regime's district governor for Katawaz, Mawlawi Hamidullah, a former member of the Taliban's Supreme Court in Kandahar and Mawlawi Mohammad Gul Jega'i, originally from Khushamand. These groups are based in the Shahghra Mountains of the unofficial Terwa district (a part of Wazakhwa), close to the Pakistani border. Probably, it constitutes rather a staging and transit area for Southern Ghazni and Zabul. A group originally led by Engineer Abdul Majid Faizani (he was killed in early 2008), a former Sayyaf commander, operating in the Marzak Mountains of Sarhauza district since

2004 with some 250 fighters including Chechens, Arabs, Uzbeks and Tajiks, might be a separate structure.

Shortly before these groups started operations, Taliban emissaries had simultaneously visited mosques in the area and had usually told local teachers not to accept government money. They emphasised that they did not oppose education in general, but appealed to the people to pay the teachers themselves and to hold lessons in private houses. As a result, most Katawaz schools were closed in mid-2008. This is another example of the Taliban's *modus operandi* of sending first unarmed "propaganda" groups and then, a few weeks later, weapons and funds that are handed over to newly-won local sympathisers who then start a new front.

Thirdly, there is a Taliban network in Paktika operated by Mullah Nazir from South Waziristan (Pakistan). Organisationally, he is neither linked to the Pakistani Taliban movement nor to the Haqqani network, but allied with the latter.

For Afghanistan, the existence of the separate Southern Paktika structures illustrates the fact that there are peripheral areas where Taliban are still not consolidated and competition between various commanders and networks is continuing. These structures also might be the remnants of a formerly much broader network that was diminished as a result of the Haqqani network's expansion.

Hizb-i Islami in Loya Paktia

During the anti-Soviet war, Hekmatyar's Hizb-i Islami was only of local importance in the Afghan South-East. There were a handful of commanders, mainly in Paktika province and in Sabari. Among the better-known was Khaled Faruqi, who was a strong Hizb commander in Paktika during the *jihad*, became the first leader of a Hizb-i Islami wing that applied for registration as a legal political party in 2004, and—after a painful process of official dissociation from Hekmatyar's leadership role under pressure both from the international community and the Karzai government—was finally registered in October 2005.

Today, the influence of Hekmatyar's Hizb-i Islami in the South-East is still limited geographically to small "islands". The most important areas of influence are mountainous parts of Sabari, Bak and Terezai districts which are close to the Afghan-Pakistani border. Most of Hizb-i Islami's military operations in Loya Paktia take place here. From there, Hizb has been expanding north more strongly in 2008, towards Zazi Maidan and Tsamkani districts, both known for political Hizb influence, and even into the hitherto stable Mangal areas. Isolated operations, however, have been reported from here earlier, like temporary checkpoints for passing cars on side-roads in the Surkhab area of Zazi Maidan district. In Seyyed Karam district, minor Hizb groups have been active even since late 2003. These groups are led by Mullah

Haji Jailani, a Tutakhel from this area, who officially joined the government's reconciliation programme in July 2005 but is reported to be continuing his anti-government activities from this shelter.

Although Hizb-i Islami was reported to have appointed a new commander for the South-Eastern region in June 2006 (his name is not known, but Abbas Khan from Zambar in Sabari district is the strongest in the region [94]), the party's main activity continued to be political and ideological up to 2008. This included maintaining networks of former and/or current commanders, activists and loyalists and their networks, sending in small propaganda teams, threatening government officials directly or by so-called *shabname*, and recruitment. Reports from the region speak of increasing pressure on teachers and construction companies not to cooperate with the central government and international actors. There were reports of Hizb political agents recruiting fighters to support the Sunni side during the sectarian clashes in Parachinar (Pakistan) that continued throughout most of 2007 in tribally mixed Tsamkani as well as among the Zazi and Mangal tribes. In particular after the Sabari suicide truck bomb and heavy US retaliation with air strikes, not only the Haqqani network but also Hizb-i Islami are reported to be making more inroads into the area of other tribes, among them the Terezai who had still backed President Karzai strongly during the presidential elections.[95] There is also known political influence of Hekmatyar's Hizb among former *mujahidin* in the towns of Khost, Gardez and elsewhere. Of late, there are reports that Hizb is creating parallel governmental structures in those areas.

Backed by elements of the Pakistani authorities, Hizb fighters have easy access to Afghanistan from safe havens in Pakistan from where they cross the border on a daily basis. Hizb-i Islami (and also Taliban) militants are reported to be still able to use the Zhawara base in Gurbuz, close to the border with neighbouring Tani district, and Spina Shega in Zazi Aryub district. Both were famously built with Osama bin Laden's involvement in the 1980s, temporarily taken and destroyed by a spectacular Soviet operation in April 1986 and during the US Tomahawk raids in 1998, and partly rebuilt later. Zhawara, a complex of caves on a mountain slope facing east, is accessible only from the Pakistani side of the border, just 15 minutes away from Miramshah.

Hizb commanders Abbas Khan Sabarai (a.k.a. Major Abbas) lives in Pakistan and cooperates with the Haqqani network and the Taliban. Inside Afghanistan, he has a base in Zambar (Yaqubi district) not far from the border, from where he operates into Bak and Zazi Maidan districts. From the spring of 2008 onwards, Hizb-i Islami expanded its activities from its Sabari base into all the neighbouring districts of Khost and Paktia provinces, where it seems to have established some permanent presence. Earlier inroads were attributed by regional observers to relatively weak tribal structures in the affected areas (like Gurbuz),[96] as well as a creeping radicalisation of at least some elements of these religiously conservative but originally non-militant and rather pro-monarchy and pro-central government tribes, due to their forced migration to camps in the Pakistani tribal areas from 1978 onwards. In other areas, strong tribal structures have prevented the infiltration of insurgents into certain districts, sometimes with the help of *arbaki*. According to reports from the region, this changed in 2008. Armed Hizb activists are now even able to move freely in the territory of the highly centralised Mangal tribe. This is possibly a sign that this tribe—after years of neglect by the central government and international donors—has given the green light for more insurgent activities. Hizb has been clearly better funded than ever since 2001. Afghan security sources allege that international jihadist groups offer money to Hekmatyar in order for him to cooperate with the Haqqani network in Khost and, by that, strengthen the insurgency there as a whole.

The case of the Mangal is particularly striking as an example of the neglect of the Pashtun tribes by Kabul's post-2001 policy and the lack of understanding of tribal society by the international community. As early as 2003, the Mangal Central Shura took and implemented a decision that no poppy should be grown on the tribe's territory. This was completely ignored by the Kabul government and external donors who failed to reward the Mangal for this unilateral decision even in the slightest way. At this time, the UK-led anti-narcotics programme concentrated on the Eastern region. Later, the Mangal committed themselves by a traditional Pashtun undertaking (*tarun*) to defend their territory against the Taliban. The Mangal also played a prominent part in the Tribal Solidarity Council which brought together Paktia and Khost's major tribes during 2003/4, an initiative that was met with the same ignorant response from Kabul.[97] Kabul's fateful decision to start paying *arbaki* through governors' discretional funds in the first quarter of 2005 undermined a tribal institution that had stabilised Pashtun areas whenever there was a lack of government presence. Even the Afghan leaders apparently failed to understand its character. "In the King's time it was an honour to be member of an *arbaki*," explained a tribal elder from the region to this author in April 2007. "Its members were provided with *e'ana* [rations, weapons and ammunition] by the *jirga*." This made the *arbaki* an instrument controlled by the tribe; to pay it means to remove it from the tribal setting and renders it uncontrollable when payment stops. Even though there are some examples of South-Eastern *arbaki* that continued to carry out their duties for months without pay, this process turns tribal volunteers into pseudo-tribal militias.

Equally counterproductive is the American approach to the South-East. After the region had remained almost without resources during the first post-2001 years, Washington started to pour enormous amounts of money into it from early 2007 with the aim of making it a model of success, the "crown jewel in the American counterinsurgency".[98] When a new US PRT commander visited the volatile Zurmat district in April 2007 he promised projects worth US$100 million, but it remained unclear whether the money would cover just Paktia province or the whole of the South-Eastern region that also includes Ghazni. The region was subsequently flooded with projects. Zurmat alone was reported to have received $63 million of US aid by early 2008.[99] Many projects were faulty, though. Inhabitants of the region reported substandard school buildings and roads: there were also some "white elephants", like a specialised hospital in Khost inaugurated during a visit of the then NATO commander for Afghanistan, Gen. Karl Eikenberry, that remains largely unused. The claim that 72 of the 86 districts of the South-Eastern region supported the central government in mid-2008[100] seems to be largely exaggerated.

Another factor in growing Hizb-i Islami influence is a strong political polarisation between former *mujahidin* and PDPA activists in Loya Paktia, which can be felt in meetings on the ground. Intellectuals from local tribes like the Mangal, Tani, Zadran, Ahmadzai and others were strongly represented in the party and state leaderships between the so-called Saur revolution of 1978 and President Najibullah's fall in 1992. Among them were former Interior Minister Mohammad Aslam Watanjar and Eng. Nazar Mohammad, both from Zurmat; Seyyed Mohammad Gulabzoi, also a former Interior Minister and a Zadran from Nadershahkot; Shahnawaz Tanai from Khost province, the Minister of Defence who unsuccessfully tried a coup d'état against Najibullah in 1990; former PDPA Politburo member Habib Mangal (from Musakhel/ Khost) and also Khial Mohammad Katawazai (from Paktika), a former deputy foreign minister who spent many years in prison under Presidents Karmal and Najibullah. Khost town was dubbed "Little Moscow" then. But in addition Najibullah (from the rival Parcham faction), an Ahmadzai from Seyyed Karam district, was from Paktia. Many second-line as well as some first-rank PDPA activists, including many army and police officers, have played a prominent role in post-Taliban Afghanistan. Being educated, they often possess better chances of obtaining administrative posts. Former ministers and generals like Nur-ul-Haq Ulumi, Abdurrashid Aryan and Abdurrashid Jalali lead political parties; Gulabzoi and Ulumi have been elected members of parliament since 2005.

In Khost, until recently former Khalqi military officers even commanded militias, known as Khost Protection Force and Afghan Security Guards. They are paid by US Special Forces for guard duties but also accompany them during counter-insurgency operations or do patrols on their own. This foreign patronage makes them untouchable for disarmament through the DDR/ DIAG process. These groups became known for their ruthlessness and human rights abuses—and for the impunity with which they can act. The prominent role played by former Khalqis created suspicions among former *mujahidin* that they or their communities are deliberately targeted by their former foes. One episode occurring against this background could have contributed to the re-emergence of the insurgency in Sabari: Shahid Gul Sabarai, a Taliban commander based in Waziristan, had returned to the area with some 40 of his men in mid-2007, was integrated into the Khost police and even given training at the US-run regional police training centre, but shortly afterwards was accused by other policemen of involvement in IED attacks and arrested by US troops.[101] Reciprocally, the insurgents—possibly in conjunction with former *mujahidin*—target former PDPA members. In one case, the district governor of Qalandar district (Khost), Mirza Jan Nimgerai, a former PDPA member who was accused of having passed wrong information to U.S. forces, was killed in June 2008. Even former anti-Soviet activists like the late Hakim Taniwal and Merajuddin Pattan, who had become provincial governors in the South-East under Karzai, were accused of "pro-communist" leanings because they are simply Western-educated and politically liberal.

Conclusion

The Haqqani and Mansur networks are clearly part of the Taliban universe. Their leaders, commanders and fighters consider Mullah Omar as their spiritual leader (*Amir-ul-momenin*) but their *modus operandi* is that of semi-independent warlords who have joined the rather heterogeneous insurgency movement for reasons of expediency. At the same time, there are clearly visible fault-lines and differences in approach, in particular between the mainstream Taliban and the Haqqani network. The increasing closeness of the Haqqanis to al Qaida, underpinned by distinct tribal features, seems to be deepening the divisions currently. But the symbiotic relationship still holds because it is mutually beneficial. The mutual benefit outweighs the shortcomings. It allows the Haqqanis to maintain organisational semi-independence and gives them access to the label of the Taliban, as the most popular insurgent organisation, while the Taliban gain access to Loya Paktia, a region that has never been a core area of their movement. This gives them the chance to present themselves as more than a purely Kandahari movement.

The Haqqani network could theoretically stand on its own feet. Its independent links to Arab financial sources, to al Qaida and to Pakistan's ISI give it command of sufficient resources to operate autonomously of the Taliban supreme leadership. But this would also be risky. For the purposes of being full-scale warlords, the Haqqanis lack a clearly defined area of control within Afghanistan. Even their own home village is not under their full control and is regularly accessed by Western and Afghan forces, even if only in heavily armoured convoys. That would not be compensated by the fact that some of the tribal territories on the Pakistani side of the border constitute a safe haven for the Haqqani network and hence a *dar-ul-islam* free from non-Muslim influence—which, according to the Wahhabi version of Islam, is a theological *conditio sine qua non* for leading a *jihad*. However, if they were only relying on foreign bases and supplies, it would make them look too much like Pakistani-handled puppets in the eyes of the very anti-Pakistani local population. Therefore, it would be realistic to speak about a "tactical alliance" between the Haqqani network and the Taliban movement which does not need to last for ever. Even the Taliban can only rent a Pashtun, never buy him.

(II) ROOTS OF THE INSURGENCY IN THE SOUTHEAST[102]

Sébastien Trives

The insurgency is rooted in the activities of a number of local Taliban and Hizb-i-Islami networks, largely supported and supplied with resources from across the border, and structured around different tribal, religious and political networks. These networks are not organized around disgruntled or under-represented groups, but are for the most part purely ideological, structured around traditionalist religious groups, or more modern Islamist networks. To understand the articulation and geographic distribution of the insurgency in the South-East it is first necessary to take a closer look at the internal factors underpinning it, five of which are essential.

Relative strength of tribal structures

With one notable exception, the strength of tribal structures can generally help explain whether the insurgency is carried on by Hizb-i Islami or by Taliban based in a given area, Hizbi networks being dominant in strongly tribal areas and Taliban networks stronger in more detribalized zones of the region. Two factors account for the degree of integrity of the tribal structure of the Pashtun tribes of the South-East: the administrative status of the province under the old regime, and the nature of the terrain.

Because of the power of its tribes, Greater Paktia benefited from a special tribal administrative status until the revolution, while Ghazni did not.[103] In areas under special tribal administrative status, because state penetration and encapsulation of the local Pashtun tribes took place later than in the rest of the country, the tribal structures are generally stronger, and hence the grip of factional and associated religious networks on the politics of the area is comparatively weaker. Where it was in force, the special administrative status helped preserve the integrity of Pashtun tribal structures to an extent unseen elsewhere in Afghanistan, giving these areas unique features such as the resilience of a real element of "rule of law" thanks to a still functioning system of informal justice based primarily on Pashtunwali; the resilience of the *arbakai* system (tribal self policing mechanism); and the preservation of signs of tribal identity (the flags). Hence, Greater Paktia is the only area in Afghanistan where the tribes, although weakened by decades of encapsulation by the government and the outside world, remain to varying degrees the main recipients of power alongside the state.

In contrast, in those areas of the South-East under normal administrative status during the old regime (Ghazni), because state penetration and encapsulation of the local Pasthun tribes took place much earlier, the tribal structures are generally weaker than in Greater Paktia, and the grip of factional and associated religious networks on the politics of the area is therefore stronger. In these areas, although Pashtunwali is still practiced, tribes have generally forgotten where their flag is, the *arbakai* system has ceased to exist and the tribes cannot usually be construed as important independent political entities.

The second variable affecting the strength of tribal structures is geographic: as a rule the tribal structures are stronger in mountainous and remote areas, and weaker in plain areas. The east of Greater Paktia is a remote mountainous zone, peopled mostly by small independent landowners. This has prevented the concentration of economic power, while at the same time insulating against outside influences over the centuries. It has also kept alive the spirit of independence of the tribes and partly preserved the integrity of the tribal structure and of the Pashtun code underpinning it. In Pashtun areas of Ghazni, Western Paktia and Katawaz the land is mostly flat, agriculture being supported by larger-scale underground irrigation systems, and although small landholdings remain the norm, there are some larger landowners. This, together with the greater permeability of plain areas to outside (government and other) influences over the centuries, accounts for a comparatively weaker tribal structure than in mountainous areas.

Degree of tribal unity

A few tribes can claim a sufficient degree of unity to be able to act as political entities with power to decide to prevent or curtail insurgent activities on their territories. The best example of such a politically united tribe having a macro impact on the security of its territory is the Mangal tribe in Paktia and Khost between 2002 and 2004. Such tribal decisions are usually enforced through the imposition of fines and other penalties (banishment of the violator and his immediate family and destruction of his house).

It should be noted that tribal unity is a double-edged sword, as it can also work against the government if the tribe decides to support the insurgency rather than curtail it. This threat of tribes turning against the government has been a central concern of all Afghan rulers since the establishment of the modern Afghan state, a threat which has usually been reduced through a state policy designed to co-opt the tribes to the government's side.

Relative strength of traditionalist religious networks

There are three types of religious networks existing in the South-East:

Sufi networks are organized around the charismatic figure of a holy man and his family. These networks, most often organized around the Gailani family in the South-East, are particularly strong in Paktika and Ghazni. Their strength stems from the fact that often the *pir-murid* relationship is not construed as an individual one, but encompasses the whole tribal group. The Sufi networks most often translate into a strong presence of *Mahaz-i Milli* in many areas, especially Katawaz. Although some of their members may support the insurgency, these networks do not play an important role in it as such.

Tablighi networks exist everywhere but are particularly strong in Khost. These networks are not associated with any factional network in particular, and although they indirectly help the insurgency by preaching a particularly radical brand of Islam, they do not seem to be involved in violent anti-government activities.

Traditionalist religious networks are organized around networks of Deobandi *ulema* and *madrasas*, themselves linked with similar networks south of the border. These networks are particularly strong in Pashtun areas of Ghazni (and other Ghilzai areas neighboring it), a province which has always been a recognized center of conservative religious learning. The traditionalist religious networks most often became Harakat-i Enqilab factional networks (the Nabi and later the Mansur faction, the latter in Western Paktia and Northern Katawaz) during the *jihad*. As a rule, these Harakat networks transferred their allegiance to the Taliban, and Taliban networks of the plain areas are still generally structured around Harakat factional lines and commanders who chose to stay with the Taliban.

Although the degree of interconnection between these groups is difficult to ascertain, only the traditionalist Deobandi networks appear to be playing an important and recognizable role in the insurgency. Indeed, as a rule Taliban networks stem from old or newly created Deobandi networks. Because the strength of the tribal structure and the depth of encapsulation are inversely proportional to the strength of these Deobandi networks and the social status of mullahs, it follows that before the revolution, traditionalist religious networks and the social status of mullahs were weakest in the mountainous areas of Greater Paktia under special tribal administration, medium in those plain areas of Greater Paktia (neighboring Ghazni) under special tribal administration, and strongest in the Pashtun districts of Ghazni under direct government administration.

There is one exception to this: the presence of strong traditionalist religious networks in some mountainous and deeply tribal areas of Greater Paktia (the Zadran Arc and some districts of Khost). This anomaly can be explained by the fact that in the last 27 years, Commander Jalaluddin Haqqani (formerly of the Hizb-i-Islami Khalis faction, who turned Taliban), with much Arab financial support, has patiently woven a new network of traditionalist *madrasas* in areas under his influence, thus creating the conditions for strong Taliban support to emerge in these areas.

Because the South-East was generally not represented in the ruling elite during the old regime, many members of the modernizing class created through the formal education system from the 1950s onwards found themselves embracing various form of political opposition and radicalism: many embraced radical political Islamist ideology, mostly through adherence to Hizb-i Islami, while others joined the PDPA. These modern elites were particularly strong in Greater Paktia, partly because the government made special efforts to co-opt the tribes by enrolling the sons of tribal leaders in the Westernizing elite. The strength of these networks, which helps explain the footprint of currently active Hizbi groups, was strongest in Khost, Paktia and Eastern Paktika, and medium in Western Paktika and Ghazni.

In recent years the successful conclusion of the political transition process has not translated into better government performance in the South-East. In fact, with the exception of the ANA, government performance either stagnated in 2005 or even retreated in some areas where insurgents have been particularly active. The government has major weaknesses which play into the hands of the insurgency. In many districts of the South-East, government presence can be characterized as "non substantial", becoming a presence in name only, and insurgents have optimum operational space. This is compounded by the poorness or absence of the formal education system, and the lack of a state-run religious education system at the provincial levels, both of which make enrollment in well-funded extremist *madrasas* in Pakistan considerably more attractive, especially when sanctioned and encouraged by the local *ulema*. Hence government weakness locally often results in a gradual shift of the balance of power in these areas towards insurgents.

Articulation of the insurgency

From this brief analysis of the five internal factors underpinning the insurgency in the region, the following conclusions can be drawn.

First, in all the mountainous areas of Greater Paktia not under the influence of Jalaluddin Haqqani, where the tribal structure is strong, where there are some united and politically relevant tribes, and where religious networks are weak, Taliban networks are weak or non-existent and Hizbi networks provide the backbone of the insurgency. In these areas, the insurgency tends to be less deeply rooted in the population and generally less virulent.

Secondly, in the remaining mountainous areas of Greater Paktia where the tribal structure is robust, but where strong traditionalist religious networks have been recently created by Haqqani, the insurgency is primarily built around Taliban networks controlled by Haqqani. In these areas, the insurgency is comparatively more deeply rooted in the population and more virulent than in other tribal areas.

Thirdly, in all of the Pashtun areas of Ghazni and surrounding plain areas of Paktia and Paktika under Ghazni's influence (mostly Ghilzai), where the tribal structure is weaker and traditionalist religious networks stronger, although there are some active Hizbi elements the insurgency is articulated around Taliban groups that stem largely from strong traditionalist Deobandi religious networks dating from before the Saur revolution. Taliban groups in Western Paktia and Northern Katawaz are controlled by the Mansur network, while those in Central and Southern Katawaz and Ghazni are directly linked with the Taliban Southern leadership (Dadullah, Baradar). In these plain areas, the insurgency has a deeper and wider social base.

Fourthly, as a rule, whenever the conditions exist for the insurgency to develop it tends to do so particularly well in areas where the government is weakest: Southern and parts of Eastern Paktika, as well as Southern Ghazni.

Dynamics of the insurgency

The insurgency started to raise its head from the spring of 2003 onwards in the South-East, steadily growing in virulence over the years. It is notable that before 2008 it had remained rather marginal, low level and unpopular, as was shown by the success of the political transition process and the very significant popular participation in this. Most important, after the collapse of the Taliban regime, insurgents in this region failed to win substantial popular support beyond their limited political/tribal or religious bases. However, already in 2005–6 the insurgents' operations suggested that they were not only better organized and more effective, but seemed to have adopted a long-term strategy towards reaching their goal of establishing their own Government of Afghanistan. This was predicated on a belief that the international community would soon disengage from Afghanistan and that the Afghan government would be unable to build its capacity sufficiently to be able to survive without a high level of direct foreign support. This new strategy seemed to have two main objectives:

1. To prevent government outreach by estranging the population from it. This is done through an intensification of propaganda, the targeting of government personnel and infrastructure, and the creation of an atmosphere of fear within communities fuelled by intimidation as well as acts of violence and killings targeting individuals seen to be pro-government.
2. To continue to target the international presence, both civil and military, in order to limit its operational space in the short term, while at the same time augmenting the political costs of involvement for the governments of the main contributing countries.

In fact, the insurgency managed to increasingly limit the operational space of traditional reconstruction actors, and complicate efforts to increase government outreach in large areas of the South-East. Beyond limited military pressure and a few ad hoc efforts at strengthening government and co-opting communities locally, there was no clearly articulated counterinsurgency policy on the part of the government and its international backers that would seek to counter the strategy of insurgents.[104] Moreover, although Coalition forces fared rather well in many insurgency-ridden areas of the South-East in terms of not alienating the local people too much, one wondered how much longer the Pashtun population, caught between hammer and anvil and not reaping sufficient reconstruction, security and governance benefits from the central government, would remain faithful to it.

Notes

1. Paktia, Paktika and Khost were a single province prior to the 1978 coup d'état. Paktika was established by the pro-Soviet government in 1979 by merging the southern part of Paktia (the Loy Wuluswali of Urgun) with the Suleimankhel-inhabited Loy Wuluswali of Katawaz hitherto belonging to Ghazni province. Khost was upgraded from a Loy Wuluswali (within Paktia) to a full province in 1985, also during the PDPA regime.

2. Those tribes mainly belong to the Karlani (or Karlanri) confederation. However, this part of their genealogy does not seem to be relevant any more. When the author asked random Loya Paktia Pashtuns, hardly anyone knew this term at all. In general, tribal genealogies are often ambiguous. The Khugiani, for example, are often perceived as Durrani in Southern Afghanistan, while elsewhere they are considered Ghilzai. Actually, the "Ghilzai" should be called "Ghilzi" because this is a plural, like Durrani. This paper, though, sticks to the familiar spelling.

3. There are no real warlords in South-Eastern Afghanistan who control a significant and unified territory and exert quasi-autonomous power. For the discussion of warlords in Afghanistan, see for example: Antonio Giustozzi and Noor Ullah, "The Inverted Cycle: Kabul and the Strongmen's Competition for Control over Kandahar 2001–2006", *Central Asian Survey*, 26 (2007) 2, S. pp. 167–84.

4. It is claimed that the Zadran of Ziruk district already proclaimed *jihad* six days after the 27 April 1978 coup d'état. See: Gul Zarak Zadran, *De Afghanistan Tarikh: stergolidena khateruna, darsuna, 'ebratuna* [History of Afghanistan: witnessed impressions, lessons, warnings], Vol. 2, Kabul: Nomani, 1386 (2007), p. 206.

5. With the help of local Harakat fighters which, in this area, most probably would have been Mansur's (on the Mansur network, see below in this article). Kamal Matinuddin, *The Taliban Phenomenon: Afghanistan 1994–1997*, Oxford and New York: Oxford University Press, 1999, p. 71.

6. Officially: National Islamic Front for the Salvation of Afghanistan, with Prof. Burhanuddin Rabbani as its political and Ahmad Shah Massud as its military leader.

7. Interviews with the then deputy head of the Suleimankhel *shura* and with a leading Hazara who supported the Taliban takeover of Ghazni, Kabul, October 2007; Matinuddin, *The Taliban Phenomenon...*, cit., pp. 259–60; Anthony Davis, "How the Taliban Became a Fighting Force", in William Maley (ed.): *Fundamentalism Reborn? Afghanistan and the Taliban*, New York University Press, 1998, p. 65.

8. Which put him into a new conflict with this region's other semi-autonomous insurgent group, the Tora Bora Front, another remnant of Hizb-i Islami/Khalis, led by Khalis' son Anwar-ul-Haq Mujahid.

9. "Report on Progress toward Security and Stability in Afghanistan", Report to Congress in accordance with the 2008 National Defense Authorization Act (Section 1230, Public Law 110–181), June 2008, p. 10, http://www.defenselink.mil/pubs/Report_on_Progress_toward_Security_and_Stability_in_Afghanistan_1230.pdf(last access: 17 Sept. 2008).; Seth G. Jones, "The State of the Afghan Insurgency:

Testimony presented before the Canadian Senate National Security and Defence Committee on December 10, 2007", p. 2, http://www.rand.org/pubs/testimonies/2007/RAND_CT296.pdf (last access: 18 Sept. 2008).

10. This is a general problem: almost no insurgency-related information, even basic information, is given in a way that it can be attributed. The author met a US military commander in an Afghan province who was not even ready to mention well-known names of Taliban commanders in his area of operations.

11. Joshua Kucera, "Paving the Way to Peace—Counter-Insurgency in Afghanistan", *Jane's Defence Weekly*, 15 Dec. 2004, p. 26.

12. Author's interviews, Kabul, April 2007 and April 2008, Gardez, October 2007.

13. "The Consolidated List of the United Nations Security Council's al-Qaida and Taliban Sanctions Committee", 14 Mar. 2008, http://www.un.org/sc/committees/1267/consolidatedlist.htm#talibanind#talibanind (last access: 18 Sep 2008).

14. Paul Rogers, "The Afghan Summer of War", *Oxford Research Group: International Security Monthly Briefing*, Sept. 2006, p. 3.

15. Sayyed Saleem Shahzad, "Secrets of the Taliban's success", *Asia Times Online* (Hong Kong), 11 Sept. 2008, http://www.atimes.com/atimes/South_Asia/JI11Df01.html (last access: 17 Sept. 2008; this is an interview with the former Taliban deputy foreign minister Mullah Abduljalil); Sayyed Saleem Shahzad, "Iraq and Afghanistan: The changing face of resistance", *Asia Times Online*, 23 June 2006, http://www.atimes.com/atimes/Middle_East/HF23Ak02.html (last access: 17 Sept. 2008).

16. Author's interview, Kabul, Oct. 2007; Rahimullah Yusufzai, "Taliban refute defection reports", *The News* (Islamabad), 16 Feb. 2005, p. 10.

17. Robert C. Martinage: *The Global War on Terrorism: An Assessment*, [Washington]: Center for Strategic and Budgetary Assessments, 2008, http://csbaonline.org/4Publications/PubLibrary/R.20080223.The_Global_War_on_/R.20080223.The_Global_War_on_.pdf (last access: 17 Sept. 2008).

18. On the structure of the Taliban movement, see: Thomas Ruttig, *Die Taleban nach Mullah Dadullah. Ihre Strukturen, ihr Programm—und ob man mit ihnen reden kann*, SWP-Aktuell 2007/A 31, Berlin: Stiftung Wissenschaft und Politik, June 2007.

19. Ron Moreau and Mark Hosenball, "Pakistan's Dangerous Double Game", *Newsweek*, 22 Sept. 2008, http://www.newsweek.com/id/158861 (last access: 22 Sept. 2008); Bill Roggio, "Targeting Taliban commander Siraj Haqqani", *The Long War Journal*, 20 Oct. 2007, http://www.longwarjournal.org/archives/2007/10/targeting_taliban_co.php (last access: 1 Dec. 2008).

20. "ANSF-led combined force arrest suspected Taliban leaders in Khowst", *Operation Enduring Freedom, Combined Joint Task Force—101, Bagram Media Center*, 27 Dec. 2007, http://www.cjtf-a.com/index.php/Press-Releases/ANSF-led-combined-force-arrest-suspected-Taliban-leaders-in-Khowst.html (last access: 1 Dec. 2008).

21. More precisely, the family belongs to the Sultankhel clan of the Prangai subtribe of the Mezi (a.k.a. Batkhel) subtribe of the Zadran.

22. Ludwig W. Adamec, *Historical Dictionary of Afghanistan*, Metuchen, NJ and London: Scarecrow Press, 1991, p. 103, gives 1930 as his year of birth. Jere Van Dyk, *In Afghanistan: An American Odyssey*, San José, New York, Lincoln, Shanghai: Authors Choice Press, 1983, p. 96, gives an age of 43 for the autumn of 1981 when the author visited Haqqani (meaning that he would have been born in 1938). The UN Sanctions Committee gives 1942 as the year of birth, but that seems too late. See: "The Consolidated List…", cit. Sayyed Saleem Shahzad, "Secrets of the Taliban's success", cit. even gives an age of 58 years in 2008 (i.e. born in 1950!). S. Haqqani is said to be in his 20s or 30s, some sources give 34 in 2008. A UN

source, however, put him at the age of 37 in July 2007. In June 2007 there were Afghan media reports, referring to intelligence sources, of J. Haqqani's death and burial in his home village. In a videotape released on 22 March 2008 on al-Jazeera, Haqqani rejected the reports of his demise. See: "Taliban key commander Haqani dies", *Bakhtar Information Agency* (Kabul), 13 June 2007, http://www.bakhtarnews. com.af/default.asp?Lang=E&ContID=1702 (last access: 1 Dec. 2008); "Commander Jalaluddin Haqqani is Dead?", *Pajhwok Afghan News* (Kabul), 14 June 2007, http://www.pajhwok.com/viewstory.asp?lng=eng&id=37895 (last access: 1 Dec. 2008).

23. Rahimullah Yusufzai, "Taliban refute…", cit. Afghan sources from the region reported for 2008 that there were parallel (rivalling) Taliban and Haqqani network structures in Logar and Wardak provinces.

24. Claudio Franco, "A Taliban Resurgence: The Destabilization of Kabul?", *NEFA Foundation Terror Watch, www1.nefafoundation.org/miscellaneous/nefatalibankabul1107. pdf* (last access: 12 Dec. 2008). Earlier, though, after Operation Anaconda in 2002, Ibrahim Haqqani had surrendered to the Afghan authorities, and was held under house arrest by the Afghan Ministry of Defence's South-Eastern zone representative in Logar province and later in Kabul where he met US officials. See also: Kathy Gannon, "U.S. prepares for final fight", *Associated Press*, 12 Mar 2002, http:// careers.thedailycamera.com/news/terror/mar02/12aafgh.html (last access: 3 Oct. 2008). The third brother, Ismail, was killed fighting the Soviets.

25. Other sources say that Nasruddin is too young and stays at home. Author's interviews with serving and former Paktia officials, Oct. 2007 and Oct. 2008. Badruddin Haqqani was the one who denied his father's death in an interview with a private Afghan TV station. "Son of senior Taliban commander rejects his father's death", *Ariana TV* (Kabul), 15 June 2007.

26. See: James Rupert, "Afghan ally Haqqani is now a foe", *Washington Times*, 16 Oct. 2008, http://www.washingtontimes.com/news/2008/oct/16/afghan-ally-is-now-a-foe/ (last access: 1 Dec. 2008).

27. Henry S. Bradsher, *Afghan Communism and Soviet Intervention*, Oxford and New York: Oxford University Press, 2000, p. 17. According to this source, there were 500 fighters and commanders under Pakistani training.

28. Afghans interviewed on this issue do not recall the exact date of this event. As there also seem to be no published renderings of it, it cannot be established whether the Ziruk ambush was part of the planned uprising or a separate incident. A *Loy Wuluswali* (greater district) was an administrative unit in pre-*mujahidin* Afghanistan.

29. David B. Edwards, *Before Taliban: Genealogies of the Afghan Jihad*, Berkeley, Los Angeles, London: University of California Press, 2002, p. 240.

30. Edwards, *Before Taliban…*, cit., pp. 260–1; Van Dyk, *In Afghanistan…*cit., photographs following p. 128.

31. Bradsher, *Afghan Communism*, cit., p. 346.

32. Mawlawi Wakil Ahmad Mutawakkil, *Afghanistan au Taliban* [Afghanistan and the Taliban], Kabul: Baryalai Pohantun, 1384 (2005), p. 33; author's interview in Kabul, May 2008; Ahmed Rashid, *Taliban, Islam, Oil and the New Great Game in Central Asia*, London and New York: I.B. Tauris, p. 60.

33. John F. Burns, "Taliban army chief scoffs at report of peace talks", *New York Times*, 21 Oct. 2001, http://query.nytimes.com/gst/fullpage.html?res=9B07E4DD1E3E F932A15753C1A9679C8B63 (last access: 1 Dec. 2008).

34. See: Daniel Eisenberg, "Are There Any Moderates Here?", *Time*, 21 Oct 2001, www.time.com/time/magazine/article/0,9171,1001072,00.html (last access: 6 Nov. 2008); Jay Solomon, "Failed courtship of warlord trips up U.S. in Afghanistan", *Wall Street Journal*, 8 Nov. 2007, www.online.wsj.com/article/SB1194484723 03085968.html (last access: 6 Nov. 2008).

35. Ahmed Rashid, *Descent into Chaos*, New York: Viking, 2008, p. 268.

36. In contrast to Haqqani, Pacha Khan Zadran has fought the Taliban and supported the late King Zaher Shah. He later fell out with President Karzai and the US. In 2005, he was elected a member of parliament.

37. Robert D. Crews, "Moderate Taliban?", in Robert D. Crews and Amin Tarzi, eds, *The Taliban and the Crisis of Afghanistan*, Cambridge, MA and London: Harvard University Press, 2008, p. 283.

38. Amin Tarzi, "The Neo-Taliban", in Robert D. Crews and Amin Tarzi, eds, *The Taliban and the Crisis...*, cit., p. 295; Rahimullah Yusufzai, "Omar Names Council to Resist Occupation", *The News* (Islamabad), 24 June 2003, quoted in: International Crisis Group, *Countering Afghanistan's Insurgency: No Quick Fixes*, Asia Report No. 123, 2 Nov. 2006, p. 9.

39. Moreau and Hosenball, "Pakistan's Dangerous Double Game", cit.

40. Author's interviews, Kabul, April 2006.

41. Officially, the payment of these funds was stopped altogether. However, some governors with good contacts in Kabul still received them.

42. Author's interviews with government official and tribal elder, Kabul, Nov. 2007 and May 2008.

43. There are a number of so-called unofficial but mostly functioning districts created by the different governments over the last 30 years that are not yet officially recognised. Their officials do not receive any salary but live from locally (most extra-legally) acquired resources.

44. Author's interview, Kabul, Oct. 2007; own observations.

45. "Preachers' Campaign Against NATO", *Paiman* (Kabul), 19 Oct. 2008, p. 1.

46. The Dawar tribe controls the area around the Haqqanis' Pakistani residence in Miramshah.

47. Jason Motlagh, "Coalition moves on Taliban before election", *Washington Times*, 11 Dec. 2008, http://www.washingtontimes.com/news/2008/dec/11/disruptive-operation-coincides-with-voter-registra/ (last access: 12 Dec. 2008).

48. On Taliban propaganda activities see: International Crisis Group, *Taliban Propaganda: Winning the War of Words?*, Asia Report No. 158, 24 July 2008.

49. Claudio Franco, "Islamic Militant Insurgency In Afghanistan Experiencing "Iraqization"", *Eurasianet*, 8 Nov. 2005, http://www.eurasianet.org/departments/insight/articles/eav110805.shtml (last access: 17 Sept. 2008).

50. Olivier Roy, *Islam and Resistance in Afghanistan*, Cambridge University Press, 1986, p. 128.

51. David B. Edwards, *Before Taliban...*, cit., p. 252. See: Van Dyk, *In Afghanistan...*, cit., pp. 97, 125; Roy, *Islam and Resistance*, cit., p. 129.

52. "Coalition forces confirm Sedgai death", *Pajhwok Afghan News* (Kabul), 26 Jan. 2008, *www.pajhwok.com/viewstory.asp?lng=eng&id=49101* (last access: 12 Dec. 2008); Janullah Hashamzada, "Taliban repudiate claims about Sedgai's death", *Pajhwok Afghan News* (Kabul), 28 Jan. 2008; Ismail Khan and Carlotta Gall, "Tribesmen urge Pakistan to halt raids after heavy civilian and combatant toll", *New York Times*, 11 Oct. 2007, *www.nytimes.com/2007/10/11/world/asia/11pakistan.html* (last access: 12 Dec. 2008).

53. Author's interviews with Khost residents, Kabul, May 2008.
54. See: Robert D. Crews, "Moderate Taliban?", cit., pp. 266–7.
55. Roy, *Islam and Resistance…*, cit., p. 152.
56. Author's interviews, Gardez, Khost and Kabul, Oct. 2007 and April 2008.
57. Steve Coll, *Ghost Wars: The Secret History of the CIA, Afghanistan, and Bin Laden, from the Soviet Invasion to September 10, 2001*, New York: Penguin Press, 2004, pp. 157, 167, 202; Steve Coll, *The Bin Ladens*, quoted in Karen DeYoung, "Missiles for Afghanistan, Bin Laden took part in 1986 arms deal, book says", *Washington Post*, 1 April 2008, p. A12.
58. His son Serajuddin was listed on 13 Sept. 2007. "The Consolidated List…", cit..
59. Hamid Mir, "8,000 foreign fighters in Fata ring alarm bells in Islamabad", *The News* (Islamabad), 21 July 2008, http://www.thenews.com.pk/arc_default.asp (last access: 27 Nov. 2008).
60. Author's interviews with Afghans living in or travelling to South or South-Eastern Afghanistan in Kandahar, Tirinkot and Berlin, 2008.
61. Ameer Al-Mu'meneen Mullah Mohammad Omar Mujahid about the pleasure of Eid al-Fitr, http://www.afghanvoice.com/index.php/news/news-in-english/237–ameer-al-mumeneen-mullah-mohammad-omar-mujahid-about-the-pleasure-of-eid-al-fitr (last access: 27 Nov. 2008).
62. The author saw one copy in August 2008 in Kabul. See also: Waliullah Rahmani, "Jalaluddin Haqqani Challenges Mullah Omar's Leadership of the Taliban", *The Jamestown Foundation: Terrorism Focus*, Vol. 5, Issue 25, 1 July 2008, http://www.jamestown.org/single/?no_cache=1&tx_ttnews%5Btt_news%5D=5026 (last access: 12 Dec. 2008).
63. There is at least one report about an Egyptian and a Pakistani former army officer working with Haqqani as early as the autumn of 1981. See: Van Dyk, *In Afghanistan..*, cit., pp. 99, 125. The Syrian-born Al Qaida strategist Abu Musab as-Suri also joined Haqqani's group in 1987. See: Brynjar Lia, *Architect of Global Jihad: The Life of Al-Qaida Strategist Abu Mus'ab al-Suri*, London: C. Hurst & Co., 2008, pp. 84–5.
64. Steve Coll talks of a "long history with bin Laden personally" in the PBS radio programme "Return of the Taliban" (transcript: http://www.pbs.org/wgbh/pages/frontline/taliban/militants/haqqani.html, posted 3 Oct. 2006 (last access: 30 April 2008). See also: Steve Coll, *Ghost Wars..*, cit., pp. 157, 202. In late 1981, Haqqani had already travelled to Pakistan, Iran, Saudi-Arabia and the Emirates, see: Van Dyk, *In Afghanistan…*, cit., p. 109.
65. Eric Schmitt, "Militant gains in Pakistan said to draw more fighters", *New York Times*, 10 July 2008, http://www.nytimes.com/2008/07/10/world/asia/10terror.html?_r=1&hp&oref=slogin (last access: 27 Nov. 2008).
66. Author's interview, Kabul, May 2008.
67. Moreau and Hosenball, "Pakistan's Dangerous Double Game", cit.; Mark Mazzetti and Eric Schmitt, "C.I.A. outlines Pakistan links with militants', *New York Times*, 30 July 2008, http://www.nytimes.com/2008/07/30/world/asia/30pstan.html?hp (last access: 1 Dec. 2008).
68. Ron Moreau and Michael Hirsh, "Where the Jihad Lives Now", *Newsweek*, 29 Oct. 2007, http://www.newsweek.com/id/57485 (last access: 27 Nov. 2008).
69. Moreau/Hosenball, "Pakistan's Dangerous Double Game', cit.
70. Shafiq Ahmad, "The Jihad within", *The Herald* (Pakistan), April 2007, p. 92.
71. Sayyed Saleem Shahzad, "Global jihad splits into wars between Muslims", *Le Monde Diplomatique (English version)*, 2 July 2007, http://mondediplo.com/2007/07/02al-qaida (last access: 17 Sept. 2008).

72. Quoted in Graham Usher, "The Pakistan Taliban", *Middle East Report*, 13 Feb. 2007, http://www.merip.org/mero/mero021307.html (last access: 27 Nov. 2008).

73. "Ahmadzai Wazir Tribesmen Negotiate Return of Taliban Commanders", in: *The Jamestown Foundation: Terrorism Focus*, Vol. 5, Issue 14, 9 April 2008, http://www.jamestown.org/programs/gta/single/?tx_ttnews%5Btt_news%5D=4838&tx_ttnews%5BbackPid%5D=246&no_cache=1 (last access: 27 Nov. 2008).

74. Hassan Abbas, "South Waziristan's Mawlawi Nazir: The New Face of the Taliban", in *The Jamestown Foundation: Terrorism Monitor* Vol. V, Issue 9, 10 May 2007, p. 8.

75. Zahid Hussain, *Frontline Pakistan: The Struggle with Militant Islam*, New York: Columbia University Press, 2007, p. 68.

76. In 1986 it was handed over directly to Harakat: K. Santhanam, Sudhir Sreedhar and Manish Saxena, *Jihadis in Jammu and Kashmir: A Portrait Gallery*, New Delhi: Sage Publications/Institute for Defence Studies and Analyses, 2003, pp. 100/1, 106.

77. Mike Winchester, "Terrorist U", *Soldier of Fortune*, April 1991, quoted in Roy Gutman, *How We Missed the Story: Osama bin Laden, the Taliban, and the Hijacking of Afghanistan*, Washington, DC: United States Institute of Peace, 2008, p. 83.

78. Kathy Gannon, "Pakistan militants focus on Afghanistan", *Associated Press*, 13 July 2008, http://www.msnbc.msn.com/id/25665381/ (last access: 12 Dec. 2008).

79. There are also reports claiming that the foreign fighters in Mata Khan and Kulalgo belong to the Mansur network.

80. "16 fighters under most wanted warlord killed in Afghan airstrikes", *Associated Press*, 8 Oct. 2007, http://www.wsvn.com/news/articles/world/MI64071/ (last access: 12 Dec. 2008).

81. "Taliban release video of German who targeted US Afghan base", Deutsche Presse-Agentur (in English), 20 March 2008, *www.earthtimes.org/articles/show/193640,taliban-release-video-of-german-who-targeted-us-afghan-base.html* (last access: 12 Dec. 2008). According to one source, it "appears that the IJU is an umbrella term used to link a network of affiliated Jamoat [Tajik/Uzbek form of Jamaat—the author] groups from Central Asia, comprised of Kyrgyz, Uzbek and Kazakh radicals, linked to, but not formerly associated with, the IMU". Another source describes it as an "offshoot" of the IMU" and as "dominated by Turkish Jihadists", at least members of the German Turkish community. See: Cerwyn Moore, "Uzbek Terror Networks: Germany, Jamoat and the IJU", *The Jamestown Foundation: Terrorism Monitor*, Vol. 5, Issue 21, 8 Nov. 2007, http://www.jamestown.org/terrorism/news/article.php?articleid=2373778 (last access: 12 Dec. 2008); Guido Steinberg, "A Turkish al-Qaeda: The Islamic Jihad Union and the Internationalization of Uzbek Jihadism", *Strategic Insights*, Monterey: Center for Contemporary Conflict, Naval Postgraduate School, http://www.ccc.nps.navy.mil/si/2008/Jul/steinbergJul08.asp (last access: 12 Dec. 2008). The former British Ambassador to Uzbekistan, however, believes that the IJU is a creation of the Uzbek secret service. See: "German Bomb Plot: Islamic Jihad Union", http://www.craigmurray.org.uk/archives/2007/09/islamic_jihad_u.html (last access: 12 Dec. 2008).

82. Not all these groups are linked to the Mansur network. Some are part of the Haqqani network.

83. Kathy Gannon, "Hundreds of fighters mass at front line for final push on al-Qaida caves", *Associated Press*, 13 Feb. 2002, http://staugustine.com/stories/031302/new_570286.shtml (last access: 17 Sept. 2008).

84. The following paragraphs are based on various interviews with protagonists of these events, held in Afghanistan between 2002 and 2008.

85. Edwards, *Before Taliban...*, cit., p. 255. Dorronsoro writes that it emerged in the 1950s in Herat under Faizani and only later moved closer to the Mojaddedi family. This seems to be incorrect. Faizani, instead, kept links to Jawanan-i Muslimin. Gilles Dorronsoro, *Revolution Unending: Afghanistan: 1979 to the Present*, London: Hurst & Co., 2005, p. 69.
86. His family had been resettled to the US-run Helmand and Arghandab Valley Authority irrigation project there.
87. This is the same tribe that the Hizb-i Islami leader Hekmatyar belongs to.
88. Zahid Hussain, *Frontline Pakistan...*, cit., p. 73; Mohammad Amir Rana, *A to Z of Jehadi Organizations in Pakistan*, Lahore: Mashal Books, 2004, pp. 251, 263–4, 271–2.
89. According to another version, Mansur was killed by members of the Eastern Shinwari in revenge for atrocities committed against this tribe by Andar earlier in the conflict.
90. Interviews with members of the Paktia provincial administration, Gardez, Oct. 2007.
91. Hamim Jalalzai, "Taliban commander killed in Parachinar, claims official", *Pajhwok Afghan News* (Kabul), 12 Jan. 2008, http://www.afgha.com/?q=node/5678 (last access: 12 Dec. 2008).
92. He was also said to have been instrumental in an exchange of secret messages between President Karzai and the Hizb leader Hekmatyar in 2008.
93. According to some reports, has also has moved north, taking up responsibilty for areas in Logar.
94. Abbas Khan Sabarai seems to have worked with the Karzai administration first but then was alienated by arrests in his areas.
95. Their *jirga's* public announcement that the whole tribe had to vote for Karzai, and that the houses of families acting against this decision, would be burnt down was widely reported in 2004. See: Scott Baldauf, "Afghans vote, ready or not", *Christian Science Monitor*, 8 Oct. 2004, http://www.csmonitor.com/2004/1008/p01s04–wosc.html (last access: 2 Oct. 2008).
96. For the discussion of the relation between tribal structures and religious/Jihadi networks, see Sébastien Trives' chapter following the present one.
97. As did the Zadran Unity Meeting with 2000 participants in the spring of 2007 in Dwamanda, Khost.
98. Ann Marlowe, "A Counterinsurgency Grows in Khost", *The Weekly Standard*, 19 May 2008, http://www.weeklystandard.com/Content/Public/Articles/000/000/015/080inxsb.asp (last access: 27 Nov. 2008).
99. Jon Hemming, "Longer tours, Afghan solution bring peace: U.S. troops", *Reuters*, 12 Feb. 2008, www.reuters.com/article/newsMaps/idUSISL23193520080212 (*last access: 12 Dec. 2008*).
100. Marlowe, "A Counterinsurgency...", cit.
101. Author's interview, Khost, Oct. 2007.
102. Originally published in French in *Politique Etrangère*, 1, 2006, as part of a larger article.
103. The Ghilzai tribes (Ghazni and Western Paktika) were brought under direct government administration in 1887 by Amir Abd al-Rahman Khan after a long unsuccessful uprising.
104. One exception to this is the Zadran Arc Stabilization Initiative (ZASI), a UNAMA-inspired programme endorsed by the three governors of Greater Paktia in mid-2005, whose implementation started in three districts of Paktia in late 2005.

5

THE RETURN OF THE TALIBAN
IN ANDAR DISTRICT

GHAZNI

Christoph Reuter and Borhan Younus

How it all began—again

Mullah Mohammad Anwar Farooq was desperately looking for at least one friend in the whole Andar district of Ghazni province to take a gun and fight with him against the government forces. Met on a sunny November day at the end of 2002 in his vineyard, he continually expressed his wish to show that at least a tiny presence of the Taliban remained one year after they had been defeated. He had invited a former commander, Abdul-Ahad, a legend among the old Taliban. He wanted to persuade him to join a new force. "No", said Abdul-Ahad, "it's too early. We need time to re-organise. Nobody would follow us now. Not yet."

The Taliban were forgotten, and so was the war since it was officially declared over on 12 December 2001 by the USA. The main road linking Ghazni to the south-eastern Paktika province was looking quite calm from Mullah Farooq's vineyard, just some hundreds of metres from the road. Local police and high-ranking officials like governors and provincial police chiefs were travelling in their black-windowed jeeps on the bumpy road without any fear. And they had no reason to be afraid since nothing threatening had happened so far along the road. Local government institutions were well in control of the situation in terms of security. Everything looked normal. The only difference from the Taliban era was that the road previously patrolled by

101

Taliban 4 × 4 pickups now was patrolled by American Humvees and Afghan police cars. It was the time when the United States was proudly presenting its invasion of Afghanistan as a success story to build up for its war on Saddam Hussein's regime in Iraq.

But the impression was misleading. The people were not happy about the new situation. This was for various reasons, as an example shows. Soon after the Taliban were ousted in late 2001, Haji Abdul Karim had closed his business, a clothes shop, in Ghazni city. He says it was hard for him to see the "new shape" of the city and the "new guys" who harass people from the villages, whose dress resembles that of the Taliban. "I was going to the city in my car for a few days, but now there was disturbance everywhere in the city," Karim said. "From the strange gazes of the city people to the traffic police stopping every car that had came from the villages for bribes, all was unpleasant for me." But the decisive factor in leaving his shop was an argument he had with an intelligence officer, who came to his shop in plain clothes as a customer. "When we failed to agree on the price of a cloth he wanted, he started to tell me bad things. I replied humbly that it was up to him if he wanted to buy it or not. But he intensified the argument and immediately accused me of being with the Taliban in the past." Karim says he was arrested and his shop closed, and later he was beaten in detention. "I was freed only after I paid the officer, who was a new militia commander, 10,000 Pakistani rupees," said Karim. It took him more than a year to return to his business.

Instances of armed men and intelligence people mistreating everyone with turbans and beards extended beyond Ghazni city. Complaints about labelling ordinary people as "al Qaida" and "Taliban" were common wherever a man faced the police and army on the roads and cities. Abdul Wadood, 45, had a chronic illness and used to go often to Kabul for getting medicines. When he tried in March 2002, he was first stopped by the police at the entry to Kabul and later detained after arriving in the capital. "People told me in the village not to wear a turban when going to Kabul, but I did not agree. When I arrived at the Arghandi Police Checkpoint near Kabul, I was singled out from among all the passengers in the bus to get off. The bus was told to go and they kept me in the checkpoint to check my pockets for money and documents," said Wadood. He added that the policemen, mainly from Panjshir valley, did not leave him with a penny and took all the money he brought for treatment. "They later stopped a bus and ordered it to take me to Kabul for free and it did so. But when I arrived in Kabul, I had no money and had an appointment with a doctor. I went to a distant relative of mine living in Kabul and borrowed him money. The next day when I finished my business with the doctor, I was picked up from a restaurant at the bus station where I was staying for the night," added Wadood.

Residents of areas where the Taliban were raised and supported felt that they had no status or honour when they got out of their areas into those under the control of government forces. People from Andar were not necessarily Taliban. But they were Pashtun and they looked like Taliban. The new government agreed upon at the Bonn conference laid the foundation of a nominally Islamic, but still liberal government. The Taliban's long-standing enemies, the United Front, were given the upper hand.

A surprising but very important reason that impelled a new generation of the Taliban to take up arms was the "immorality" of the Kabul government and its international backers, which was wildly exaggerated as small incidents were spread as rumours and widely quoted. Extremely negative propaganda worked well in an area where people had almost cut off their relations with major cities, especially Kabul, both for security reasons and because they were "centres of immorality". When Gul Mohammad, who married a woman from Kabul during the Taliban era, went to take his wife to her father's home in late 2002, the stories he brought back for villagers struck a chord with the people, and were spread from one village to the other, everyone adding his own propaganda. Those stories were the favourites and many were narrated for several weeks in his area in Giro district. One of these stories went that a woman and a man were caught "doing some love affair" in the Kabul's narrow streets in Froshgah. The man and the woman were followed by a crowd of people until the police arrived and took them for investigation. This story was widely quoted as "a tip of an iceberg" of immorality quickly spreading under the new government in Kabul. When the mullah at the central mosque of the district stood to deliver his sermon the next week in the Friday Prayer, he said: "Do you know young boys and girls are making sex openly on streets of Kabul. Our beloved Kabul is now turned to a stronghold of immorality and a piece of Europe. It has never happened in Afghanistan's history, even in the era of King Zahir Shah when girls were wearing mini-skirts. If we don't raise up against them, such immorality can reach our homes," the mullah told his people, calling them to *jihad*.

Another man, Jalaluddin, from Andar district, who visited Kabul in mid-2003 told people of "bottles of alcohol lying everywhere on streets and ditches of footpaths in Kabul's downtown areas every morning". Also in 2003, a couple of farmers irrigating their farms at night in Pirzada village near Ghazni city were arrested after an American military convoy was ambushed nearby. What happened to them later is not clear, but the village people claimed the old "farmers were sexually abused in detention by the Americans". There are no independent confirmations for the different versions of this story, but the rumours quickly spread across the province with much exaggeration added. Everybody said, "Americans are sexually attacking even our old men." It caused a feeling of public harassment and fear in many people. In a village down in Qarabagh district, Matullah Jan was telling his 65–year-old father not to go to Ghazni city and other places where Americans were roaming, so as "not to be dishonoured". Real injustice and rumours were mixed, fuelling the resentment of the people. A first air strike by the US military on a village in Moqur district, which killed nine children in December 2003, sparked a public outcry. The US forces apparently targeted a suspected Taliban leader, but it is not known if anybody with links to the Taliban was killed in the strike, since all the victims were children, except for one man. This was also widely interpreted as a cruel act of the "liberators".

If in Ghazni there ever existed a "window of opportunity", it was closing now. Slowly, but surely. Nothing prevented it from closing. The locals saw no changes, their infrastructure remained as rotten as before, the government was considered hostile and the few enlightened voices among the mullahs had no chance against the more popular hate-preachers.

First actions and underground organisation

Thus Mullah Farooq, the former *madrasa* student who desperately looked for co-fighters in 2002, one year later started finding recruits: locals, but also Afghans who had returned from Pakistan, former refugees as well as *madrasa* students. Until today the recruitment follows personal lines of kinship or other personal relations: a friend, a classmate, a cousin, a village-neighbour normally "recruits" someone. At least in Andar there are no reports of "forced" recruitments, which would also not be practicable in view of the competition among various groups which require loyalty of the followers to stay in one group. Also, at least until 2006, the fighters would not be motivated by offers of wages to join the Taliban, but would be provided by relatives, friends, leaders of sympathetic village people with food, fuel and other necessities.

In August 2003, Ghazni saw the first attack by the Taliban. The first target hit by Mullah Farooq was a jeep carrying workers of the Afghan Red Crescent Society in Andar district. As this attack drew attention and condemnation by the UN special envoy to Afghanistan, more successful attacks followed slowly during the coming months. In November, two Taliban fighters entered Ghazni city and shot dead a female UN worker after following her car on a motorbike. The killing of the UNHCR's French aid worker Bettina Goislard, 29 years old, caused widespread condemnation around the world. The two young men who shot Bettina were arrested, beaten and handed over by local shopkeepers to police. But the outcome was still very important for the Taliban, who made international news headlines with this murder, while the local population did not react with overall hostility, but with indifference—despite the fact that in Afghan custom it has always been an evil crime to kill a woman, even though she is at war with you. The Taliban apparently deemed violation of the traditional rule worthwhile, considering the gain derived from hurting the morale of international targets with an attack in a hitherto calm city.

The Taliban were yet to get public support for their campaign. Nobody, even family members of the fighters, knew who were the ones carrying out the sporadic attacks. In the Andar attack in August 2003, when Farooq and another fighter attacked the ARSC jeep, he drove his motorcycle fast to the nearby village to seek refuge in people's homes, but nobody accepted them.

The idea of resisting the government and its foreign backers was accepted among most of the people, but the secretly moving, masked attackers were still a mysterious force and were therefore not supported publicly. The commanders in the field seemed reluctant to appear and carry out attacks in places where their identity could be known. They argued that since launching the attacks after about two years of idleness went according to their plan, the public comeback would also follow according to a plan. When Mullah Farooq's chief of intelligence in 2005, Shah Mahmood, was asked why there were no significant Taliban operations before the summer of 2003, he replied: "For two reasons. The first is because we needed time to recover and re-supply ourselves. The second, we gave a pretty long time to the public who expected the country will turn to a 51st state of the United States in terms of development and prosperity. It was a good testing time. The very basic promises of the West proved false and people know now that the Western people are the big liars, and they turned against them after they got disappointed."

Throughout 2004, several bombs went off, targeting government forces in most cases and foreign troops in some incidents on the road linking Ghazni to Paktika, specifically in Andar district where Commander Farooq was slowly consolidating his hold. One of the bombs targeted an Afghan National Army convoy in Sanai village on the way from Andar to Ghazni city and killed two soldiers in June 2004. The soldiers started firing shots in every direction. Then they went to the nearby petrol station and a farm to take the station's two attendants and three farmers to Ghazni city. The detainees were beaten on the way as they argued about why they were being detained. The ANA soldiers probably knew well that the people they were holding were not the prime suspects, but they were the nearest and easy ones to be held responsible. "At least, they have sympathy with the attackers," an army commander told local elders who later visited the army base to complain to him about arresting of innocent people.

Four weeks later, there was an ambush against the security forces on the same road, close to the previous site. The Afghan forces called on more government troops for support after the attack. Scores of security forces made up of police, army and intelligence troops took the war to people's homes again in Sanai village. A "suspected Taliban" fighter was in a house. He was not Talib, but when he saw the government troops had struck his home with RPGs, he climbed to the roof and started firing at the forces. He was shot dead after an hour-long exchange of fire, but the village was under siege for two days. Villagers were forced to feed the soldiers and when leaving, five people were taken from their homes and farms as well as two passers-by, arrested for links with the Taliban. The detained people in this as well as in the previous case were handed over to the police and later to the intelligence services for interrogation. No evidence was found to prove any suspicions against them. Not all the detainees were freed; two of them were handed over to foreign troops. Those freed said they were tortured and beaten in custody by the army, the police and the intelligence service.

Taliban ambushes increased in the subsequent months and the government forces reacted in the usual way, capturing anyone they found near the attack site. A group of local elders from the area met the governor of Ghazni, Asadullah Khalid, complaining to him of the bad behaviour of his forces against the people. Khalid's response was nothing less than "salt in the wounds", as described by an elder who commented on the governor's remarks later in the meeting. "You are asking me to find a solution for this terrible situation. But I am asking you to stop your bastards (from attacking) if you want security. Otherwise, I will deal with you all the same way," the governor threatened them. When the Taliban attacks intensified in the spring of 2005, men of former ethnic Tajik militias from northern and north-eastern Afghanistan, now incorporated in the police and army, were sent into the area to curb the rising Taliban insurgency. This initiative curbed the insurgents' activities somewhat, but the public turned further against the government. The new troops gained notoriety quickly. When they went to Daleel village at night in August 2005, they searched every home. Haji Gul Rahim, a rich resident of the village, said: "They broke into our houses at midnight and searched everything from boxes where our women kept their clothes to basements and cupboards. They looted our money and other precious possessions, like the women's jewellery and even watches." In Mirai village, virtually the back yard of the district headquarters, where the militias-turned-security force were based, they sawed the people's grape vines. This was widely considered as a revenge action in the heart of Taliban land by former Northern militias, whose gardens and grape orchards were destroyed in the same way by the Taliban in the late 1990s (in Shamali).

The battle for the road

The Taliban were meanwhile getting stronger and more able to challenge the government forces as well as the people's traditional sources of power. In 2005 started the biggest development project, the building of the main road passing through Andar district and connecting Ghazni to Paktika province. As soon as the road crossed the environs of Ghazni city and reached the area under the Taliban's control, Mullah Farouq blocked the work by frequent attacks on the construction workers and the government forces in charge of protection, despite the fact that most villagers welcomed the road as opening up economic opportunities. Mullah Farouq declared that he would never allow the road to be built with the government's security forces patrolling their area: "After some attacks, the government paused the work, but again it sent more reinforcements to continue the work. Then I told the officials (through mediators) that if they want to have the road constructed, then don't send your security forces for its protection and we will not attack civilian road workers. They can go ahead with the work. But the problem is that the road is bringing our enemy to our land and we can't stop attacking them." This attitude reflected a compromise with the village elders, who still wanted the road to be built. The government however did not accept the deal. The former governor of Ghazni during the *mujahidin* period and in the early monhs of the Karzai era, Taj Mohammad Qari Baba, vowed he could do the security job after the government failed.

Qari Baba was the most influential local elder in Andar, still with vast support among other local elders. He had had the backing of the mullahs and tribal chieftains since the *mujahidin* era, when he had been a successful commander in the war against the Soviets and had later been appointed as governor. Qari Baba, seemingly under an agreement with the construction company and the government, took the job of protecting the road construction work in the entire Andar district, using his rearmed young loyalists as security guards. But Qari Baba's forces also failed and attacks continued. Both powers—the government's and the elders'—were defeated by the Taliban in the battle over the road. Ultimately, Mullah Farouq's condition was accepted unofficially, to make it possible for the work to go ahead. The road was constructed with no or only random presence of security forces.

Qari Baba was later killed in September 2006 by Mullah Farouq's men, in an ambush set for him on the road from Andar district centre to Ghazni city. Baba became the second governor to be killed in Andar district in 2006. In May a former governor of Paktika province and erstwhile adviser to President Hamid Karzai on tribal affairs, Mohammad Ali Jalali, was killed by Mullah Farouq's men after he was kidnapped from the road to Ghazni in Andar. He was shot dead after "documents" showed he had helped the US forces in war against the Taliban when he was the governor of Paktika. The reason for the Taliban to kill Qari Baba, an influential *mujahidin* commander even if he was not holding an official job, was his attempt to provide security for the road construction project. "He has told the governor last year that he will protect the road by his own force and will eliminate any Taliban fighter in Andar if they disturbed. Now, we showed that we are those who can eliminate, not him," said Farouq.

Peak time

The Taliban were getting stronger, taking roots among the people and launching major attacks on government workers and Afghan and international forces. The fighters developed the ability to threaten their armed enemies face-to-face. Qari Naeem, known for his boldness among the sub-commanders of the Taliban, threatened an intelligence officer in his own village among his bodyguards. He told him to get out of the government, otherwise "I will kill you here". In another incident, Qari Naeem's men took out an armed national army soldier from a wedding party and shot him dead in public. The Taliban were clever enough to thwart any new tactics used by the government to curb them. When the government ordered a ban on motorbikes (the

Taliban's favourite transport) in two districts that were Taliban strongholds, Andar and Giro, the Taliban responded by banning all vehicles in the two districts. The village people were told in their mosques and public sessions not to bring out their vehicles from their homes. To make their ban effective, the Taliban planted anti-tank mines on all main roads. The Taliban's ban was better implemented than the government's. Several ordinary people on donkeys and bicycles were also killed when the mines went off as they walked along the road. For several weeks, until the government allowed motorbikes again, people were travelling on donkeys and horseback. Even in wedding celebrations, a bride was taken to her husband's home by camel.

The Taliban finally won. The government was forced to lift the ban on motorcycles in return for the Taliban's ending of the ban on vehicles' movement. But the motorbike war was not over yet. There were other forms of confrontations, wherein too the Taliban were victorious. In August 2006, Mullah Farouq's squad clashed with the police on the Ghazni-Paktika highway. Farouq and his men were forced to retreat and hide themselves in the nearby village. They had parked their motorbikes on the side of the road. Escaping hurriedly, they could not get back to their motorcycles after 15 minutes' fighting. The police took the fighters' motorcycles with them to the district centre of Andar. The Taliban through a call warned the district chief to return their motorbikes to them, otherwise they would attack the district centre. The motorbikes were brought back the next day to the site of the fighting and left there by the deadline given by Mullah Farouq.

The Taliban became strong in the area as aid workers and journalists, who would know somebody in the local Taliban, had to check with the Taliban when they wanted to travel on the road. The Taliban were considered as the real ruling authorities who could tell you of security of the area and the road.

The year 2006 also marked the beginning of a campaign to clear the area of all suspected "spies". Warnings were issued to some former commanders, government officials and district chiefs, some of whom ultimately surrendered along with their weapons.. Juma Gul, aged 40, who had just quit leading a small group of pro-government militias, found himself and his family caught inside Taliban held land, and so he was forced to surrender. In September 2006, Mullah Farouq sent him a letter through a fighter to tell him "come to me to surrender and hand in your weapons to my group if you wish to live in this world, or be ready for the fight." Juma Gul called Mullah Farouq immediately after getting the letter, to give him a chance to sit together and talk on the issue. The next morning, Commander Juma Gul went along with three of his men to Mullah Farouq's home and had a long discussion during breakfast. Nothing would satisfy Farouq but a two-option solution: to join the Taliban along with his armed loyalists or to give in the weapons and stop making contact with the government. Juma Gul finally agreed to the second option.

At the same time, an active district chief was also forced to quit his job after frequent threats from the Taliban. Zabit Salih Gul, aged 55, had recently been appointed as district chief of Qarabagh. His big family was living in the neighbouring Andar district. The Taliban were on their guard against Salih Gul's ambitions to reach an official post after he stood, unsuccessfully, in the provincial council elections in 2005. Mullah Farouq's suspicion that Gul's family had close links with the government proved right when Salih Gul's son, Ridi Gul, joined the National Army. Ridi Gul was soon forced to leave his job after Farouq's men sent him night letters as the last warning. When Salih Gul assumed the job of district chief in Qarabagh, the Taliban attacked his home one night with rocket propelled grenades, damaging it. The Taliban sent letters to Gul, ordering him to quit the job or face the elimination of his sons. Eager to keep his government job, Salih Gul did not pay heed to the threatening letters. Mullah Farouq with his team moved to kidnap Gul's son, Ridi Gul. Salih Gul called Mullah Farouq to negotiate about freeing his son. The telephone negotiations continued for three days, with Salih Gul trying to find Mullah Farouq's location and trace his son. Ridi Gul was rescued by the Americans in an underground water canal, but his father found it hard to continue the job with his home located in the heartland of the Taliban. He left his job and returned home, assuring Mullah Farouq that he was no longer with the government if he and his family were guaranteed safety.

At the end of 2006 Andar's district chief, Lahoor Khan, miraculously survived several roadside bombings. Once, a remote-controlled bomb went off just in front of his car. Another time, a bomb merely hit a police jeep that followed the district chief. In another attempt, all the roads connecting the district centre to police stations in the district were planted with bombs. People in the nearby villages were told not to drive on those roads. But an outside civilian car stepped on a bomb and three people were killed, including a woman. When Lahoor learned that he would be soon dismissed from the job by the provincial government, he took the opportunity and went to Mullah Farouq to tell him of his intention to surrender. The Taliban commander welcomed him. By the secret surrender of a couple of AK-47s, the animosity was over and Lahoor was back safe in his home.

Abdul Hakim from Nazar Khan village was working with the police in Ghazni city. The Taliban tried several times to arrest him, but failed. He was only going home at weekends. His son Rahmatullah Khan was later recruited by the army in Gardez, Paktia province. When Rahmatullah returned after a month from Gardez on his first visit home from his job, he was caught by the Taliban some 200 metres away from his home. Mullah Farouq's men shot him dead and the Taliban spokesman later called to tell the media that they had killed "a big spy" in Andar. A month later Hakim's younger son, Ahmad Javid, was returning from Karachi, where he was working in a shop. He was also captured by the Taliban, in the farm just behind his home, before meeting his family. The 18–year-old boy was questioned for a short while to find if he was a spy; the "court" lasted for a few minutes and he was found to be a spy like his brother, according to the Taliban leaders in Andar. He was shot dead after a phone call to the Taliban governor for Ghazni, in Quetta in Pakistan, who approved the boy's execution. The farmers in the nearby farms knew the boy had no links to the government, but did not intervene because they were afraid of the Taliban.

Several similar executions occurred. One could easily come under suspicion of spying even from indirect indications, like treating the Taliban in an unfriendly or strange way. Even four mullahs, some of them imams, were killed for links with the government. The first, Mullah Abdul Bari, who had taught most of the neo-Taliban when they were students during the Taliban Emirate regime, was killed in September 2004. He was working with the provincial court in Ghazni and had been one of the most respected mullahs among the Taliban during their period in power; many continued to respect him even though he was working with the government. The second mullah was killed in late 2005; he had been a frontline Taliban commander in the late 1990s. Mullah Noor Mohammad had joined the Taliban in the early years when the movement emerged and was praised for his bravery in the fight against the Northern Alliance. But when the neo-Taliban fighters became suspicious of him, he was shot dead in his car close to his home. Another Mullah, Fazel Rahman, who once worked briefly with the UN-funded parliamentary elections, was killed when he was returning from a graduation ceremony for *madrasa* students. The fourth mullah killed in Andar was Abdul Hakim, formerly the Taliban's district court judge and a respected scholar who was preaching in the district's only Friday mosque. He was taken out of his home and shot dead for speaking in favour of the government. The Taliban suspected that he was passing information to the government against them. The "spies" and government workers were being taken out from mosques, from amid the people and from their homes and later killed. On the surface this showed the strength of the Taliban, but it also alienated the people from them.

Fear and sympathy

Fear of being called a spy, and the fact that the Taliban were resisting a foreign invader, contributed to public cooperation with the fighters, especially as they were emerging as the victorious force. As most of the areas where the Taliban operated were covered by the mobile phone companies, it became very easy for ordinary people to help the fighters, at least in passing intelligence quickly to them. "It became an easy link with the emerging heroes to be online with them through mobile phones and became something of a pride for many youths," says a local journalist, Hamim Hafizullah. These "volunteer intelligence officers" helped the Taliban to escape many attempts by the US forces to raid their positions and to set up ambushes. If a convoy of foreign or Afghan troops was passing on the road, all the Taliban commanders hiding next to the road would know in advance that their enemy was approaching.

As the Taliban were taking over control of the area, they appointed their own governor, district chiefs, somebody in charge of education and liaisons with the media. The extent of control varied, depending on the obedience of local commanders and their capabilities, whether they were "earning" enough ransom money and "taxes" from rich people, from poppy farmers and from smugglers to send money to the leadership or were dependent on support. All appointments came from Quetta, and the money also went to or came from Quetta. In some richer provinces such as Helmand or Kandahar, where people are earning vast amounts from poppy cultivation, a large sum in "*zakat*" is paid to the Taliban. In Ghazni, where farmers are poorer, the overall sums are smaller and the motivation is more ambiguous: some people pay out of sympathy for the Taliban, others pay because they are afraid.

The Taliban leadership in Quetta also set up mobile courts for solving the people's legal disputes. One example was an adultery case in Mullah Asadullah's village. Asadullah himself acted as a judge in that case. He was a close friend of one side of the case: the man who had sex with his neighbour's daughter, who then bore a child, a major dishonour in Afghan tradition. Farouq's rival group wanted to stone the adulterer to death because it was now clear that he committed the sin. The father of the girl also wanted the man to be killed, and according to Sharia that should have been the sentence. But Mullah Asadullah convinced the father of the girl to accept money or get two girls from the adulterer's home and marry them to his relatives as compensation. It was unusual to have the military commander act as a judge, but in this case Mullah Asadullah was afraid that if the other groups intervened he would lose his friend—the adulterer, who had for long been feeding the Asadullah group. Finally, after some attempts at other options by the father of the girl, the two sides accepted Asadullah's judgement. The court in this case was held in the home of the adulterer's uncle.

In setting up these courts, the Taliban banned people from going to the governmental courts, which were already partly deserted on account of widespread corruption and incompetence. Various issues from getting divorce to land disputes were being presented to the Taliban's courts. The judges, pro-Taliban mullahs, were announced to villagers in their mosques in leaflets signed by the local Taliban commander. The leaflets also named an influential elder in every village as the village representative to be accountable for the Taliban if something went wrong in his area.

The Taliban's campaigns to return to power were largely successful in every sector. Their power and comeback reached a peak in the summer of 2006. Apart from the highways and district centres, all the area was virtually under Taliban control. In most areas in Andar and the neighbouring districts, the government and foreign troops could not even enter, although they were wide flat areas with no mountains and slopes. The Taliban fighters acted as police patrolling the area. They also netted an armed gang of notorious robbers and executed its ringleader, Bismillah Khan, an action which attracted wide praise from the public. They were also judges with mobile courts operating in every area. The Taliban again became the religious police who banned public music parties, even at weddings, and those who had been shaving their beards started letting them grow again.

Finally the US military ran out of patience with the fact that the Taliban could hit their main base in Ghazni city with rockets launched from a stronghold a few kilometres away. The US forces launched an offensive to sweep the Taliban from the whole southern region, with special focus on Andar, in September 2006. Operation Mountain Fury, with heavy air support and ground patrols and raids, managed to restrict the Taliban from roaming freely. The US military for the first time entered areas where the Taliban hat set up their strongholds. But for the Taliban it was just a tactical retreat. US troops deployed forces in several key locations in Andar, while Taliban leaders and most of the ordinary fighters stayed hidden in their homes and in nearby villages. Some others went to Ghazni and Kabul cities, hiring rooms in hotels until the operation was over; nobody could recognise them there as Taliban commanders. A small number of the fighters remained armed and carefully prepared ambushes to attack the large convoys of US Humvees. Few confrontations took place, but the sporadic attacks disturbed the US operation. The Taliban acknowledged only the killing of three Taliban fighters in bombing by US fighters. On the other hand the US forces claimed to have killed large numbers of insurgents, but the Taliban and some local people claim that the Americans had in fact killed several civilians by bombing, causing hatred among the people and increasing their resentment against the presence of US forces in Afghanistan in general.

The Taliban returned to their areas and back to normal operations in mid-November, but they were still being chased by US planes, flying overhead mostly at night. After-effects of the operation remained until the following winter. But despite the contempt among the people for the brutal US military operations, the peak of power for the Taliban was over in late 2006, not because of the US troops, but because of internal dynamics.

A crisis of growth

The winter lull of 2006–7, like the previous winters, was a good opportunity for the victorious and tired Taliban commanders to go on "R & R" alongside their leaders in Quetta and Peshawar. Some of them, like Mullah Farouq, took their families with them to Pakistan. Some training and mind-refreshment programmes were also included in the field commanders' activities in the winter. The winter pause was also used for accountability sessions with some commanders or fighters who had made mistakes. The big successes of 2006 had however created rivalries among some of the commanders. Andar district was divided into two separate fiefdoms, with both leaders living in Quetta. A third group of young fighters loyal to Hizb-i Islami of Gulbuddin Hekmatyar had also emerged. They were more ideological and more intellectual than the Taliban, with some speaking English and Urdu fluently. Field commanders complained to the leaders in Pakistan about the need to reform the failing commanders, but only recommendations to unite and not to criticise each other were given. The following spring, when returning to Afghanistan, both the groups had their separate plans and strategies. One group ruling the central Andar left schools open, while the other in the east and south closed schools and warned teachers not to return to work. However, in enforcing other regulations, the Taliban in central Andar were more aggressive in 2007.

Generally, all the groups became tougher and more aggressive in 2007 than they were in 2006. They were burning aid material donated to people by the US forces. When a two-vehicle convoy of US troops left Badwan village after they distributed aid material, Mullah Farouq first planted a bomb on the convoy's road to blast one of the vehicles, and later moved into the village to burn the donated material. The villagers watched powerless, as Mullah Farouq collected the material in the centre of the village to burn. A water-handpump built by a Swedish non-governmental organisation was sawn apart by a former *Mujahidin* commander, now a sympathiser with the Taliban, who argued that nobody could take water from the pump since it was built by the money of *kafirs*, the infidels. In another incident ordered by Mullah Farouq, the Taliban burned a tractor of a private construction company hired by an NGO for work on water supply for pupils in Nazar Khan village. The schools were kept closed until the end of the year.

In central areas, the courts were gaining momentum. But sentences were applied to people in the form of torture and beating. People were forced to feed the Taliban and pay for filling their motorbikes' tanks. Bribery also started to operate among an influential part of the Central Taliban group which was receiving the most disputed cases. Abductions that ended up in ransom payments also started targeting suspected opponents of the fighters. Abdul Naser in Deh Yak district came under suspicion of having links with the government since he was frequently visiting Ghazni city and sometimes Kabul without any private business. He was arrested at his home in a night-time raid in August. The Taliban finally released him after he handed over a Kalashnikov and 10,000 Pakistani rupees (the common currency in eastern Afghanistan). Abductions of government workers, NGO staff and foreign nationals intensified, making Ghazni one of the most dangerous kidnapping scenes in Afghanistan. Five engineers from the Ministry for Rural Rehabilitation and Development (MRDD), kidnapped on the road from Paktika province to Ghazni, were kept in the Taliban's remote detention centres. When the government did not meet the Taliban demands, one of the engineers was killed in January. The government and US forces launched a house-search operation in the villages close to the Kabul-Kandahar highway where the abducted people were thought to be held. Two of the engineers later managed to escape, but the two others were killed after the government refused to strike a deal. The government had already been criticised for releasing Taliban prisoners in exchange for abducted foreign nationals; this encouraged them to resort to further kidnappings.

The most spectacular incident of kidnapping was in July 2007 when 23 South Korean missionaries were taken hostage from the Kabul-Kandahar highway in Qarabagh district, Ghazni. Mullah Abdullah Jan, the commander who kidnapped them and was later killed in a bombing raid, had good relations with the "South-Easterners", one group of whom was now operating close to the same road from which the Koreans were taken. In time of operations or other hardships in areas of the South-Easterners, they would go to the area of Mullah Abdullah Jan in Qarabagh, where they would carry out joint operations. Therefore, when the Koreans were divided into several groups to be kept separately, one group was handed over to Mullah Farouq's men to be kept in Andar and its vicinities. The whole ordeal lasted more than a month. Two hostages were killed as the government did not heed demands to release one Taliban prisoner in exchange for one hostage. The South Korean government sent a delegation to hold talks with the Taliban to reach an agreement. The government in Ghazni allowed two Taliban representatives to come to the city and ensured their security. The two Taliban envoys talked to South Korean officials in face-to-face meetings at the office of the Afghan Red Crescent Committee in Ghazni, along with four members of the International Committee of the Red Cross. They later appeared to journalists to give the first open press conference of the Neo-Taliban to the media. All the hostages were freed by the end of August. The Taliban, according to a local spokesman, said they received up to $20 million in the deal, of which most was transferred to Quetta.

In a series of abductions, four judges working in the provincial court in Paktika were kidnapped at the same time when the Koreans were being kept in August. The judges were travelling from Paktika to Ghazni city when they were stopped in Andar district by the Taliban. Their bullet-ridden bodies were found ten days after their kidnapping. Later in the summer, 18 workers of an Afghan mine clearance organisation were abducted, questioned and released. The Taliban stopped the OMAR deminers' bus in Urzu village, 7 kilometres south of Ghazni city. They killed the mine detecting dog and took the workers to a village for questions. The Taliban said the deminers were innocent, and therefore released them. Except for the dog.

The US military in 2007 continued sporadically to penetrate Taliban heartlands in Ghazni, but their raids did not hamper insurgent activities. The Taliban were still getting stronger militarily and expanding their power in the area. Soft targets, mainly "spies" and convoys of food and oil tankers, were increasingly targeted. Some of the fighters were taking out parts of the trucks and tankers for sale in the bazaar. The three groups—the Central and more aggressive Taliban, the South and Eastern Taliban group and the Hizb-e-Islami fighters—whose relations started turning bitter in 2006, entered into practical rivalries in 2007, and some clashes even occurred. Asadullah's group was disarmed after consecutive reports sent to the leaders in Quetta showed that he was turning corrupt and arrogant, under pressure from the South-East Andar Taliban. But the leader, the deputy governor of the Taliban for Ghazni, had influence over the Central Taliban where Asadullah was operating and was in full control of the other areas. Thus Asadullah's group was soon afterwards rearmed by the Central sub-commanders. This further intensified the rifts. Hizb-i Islami fighters, in their turn, were hated by both groups because of their order and their intellectual resources—most of them could read and write, which was not true of the Taliban. When Hizbi fighters carried out an attack and claimed credit for it in the media, the Taliban would quickly call the journalists and claim it for themselves, denying any Hizbi presence.

A Hizb-e-Islami man, a well-educated activist, was even killed by the Taliban. Qazi Abdul Rahman was once working in the district as deputy court judge, but was in contact with the Taliban too. The Taliban were counting on him and had provided a motorbike for him. But when they knew that he was a strong ideological Hizb-i Islami follower, they accused him of links with the government. One day, he was taken from his home by two fighters on a motorbike and was told that he would be questioned regarding some matters. Abdul Rahman knew that he would be killed, jumped off the motorbike and started running. The Taliban fighters opened fire at him from the back and killed him. The Taliban had been at odds with Hizb-i Islami even before it had set up its military wing. Kafeel Sharafuddin, an influential local elder, was attacked by the Taliban for no other reason than being loyal to Hizb. A well-supplied hospital was built thanks to his efforts and influence in NGOs, and a school was also built thanks to him. He also brought aid materials, like wheat and flour, when the area was once struck by floods in 2004. He had not worked with the government, but he was a candidate for the Constitutional Loya Jirga. The Taliban planted a bomb at the gate to his home the night-time explosion did not kill anybody, but it certainly scared Sharafuddin.

Although very powerful in 2007, the Taliban suffered a high number of casualties and some of the leading field commanders were arrested by the US troops in sudden raids. Mullah Kakar, one of the first and best commanders, considered as the right-hand man of Mullah Farouq, was arrested when a helicopter suddenly landed and US and Afghan troops surrounded him on a small hill in Waghaz district. He was out there unarmed and therefore was captured without any resistance. It was he who had kidnapped the MRRD engineers. Mullah Baraan, another important Taliban commander, was captured in a similar operation. Mullah Ahmad Jan, a sub-commander in Andar, was arrested in a night-time raid by the US military. Earlier, a frontline commander of the central Andar area, Mullah Momin, had been killed in US bombing. Some others were wounded.

The Taliban's harsh rules when they overran the area had exhausted the patience of many people, who were left with no schools. Ordinary people, and even the influential religious clerics, were being killed on simple suspicion. Possessions were sometimes taken and villagers were forced to feed the fighters. The Taliban's courts were turning as corrupt as the government's and on top of that they were also torturing people. Mines planted to harm foreign and Afghan troops often killed civilians. No development work was allowed. Nobody was allowed to take an official job, or a job in any NGO. The Taliban became more aggressive in their rule over the people. Mullah Basir, a local

Taliban spiritual leader, was preaching against whatever could benefit the government. He told a big session in Andar that whoever said that it was acceptable to travel on the road built by the foreigners and the government was *kafir* and must be questioned if he was against the Taliban.

In one incident, Mullah Asadullah, the notorious and powerful commander of Central Andar, wanted to plant a bomb near Sarfaraz village. He had been informed that US forces were on their way. Just one week earlier, a similar bomb planted by Asadullah near Zarin village had killed a large part of a sheep herd instead of the guards of a road construction project. Residents of Sarfazraz village wanted to stop Asadullah from planting a bomb in their area because it would again take lives of civilians or livestock. The Taliban threatened the villagers and arrested two villagers from among those who opposed the bomb-planting. The bomb was removed by the villagers soon after Asadullah left and just before the US forces arrived. The next day the villagers went collectively to Mullah Asadullah's home on their bicycles. They surrounded his home to demand that he release the two arrested villagers and promise never to plant any bombs in their area in the future, and Asadullah had to give way.

The Taliban in 2008 emerged with cautious steps, some of them more aggressive but others reformative. As they suffered losses at the military leadership level in 2008 in southern Afghanistan, they thought that the mobile phones were the prime factor in the leaders' locations being discovered and bombed. On the basis of this perception, the Taliban through their spokesman announced that mobile operator companies must shut down their towers during the night from 5 pm to 7 am. They said the commanders killed recently were intercepted through their mobile phones—which was probably true, since the initial sympathy among the villagers, who had created a large network of part-time intelligence gatherers, had vanished. Instead of assisting the Taliban with information, the people would now use their phones to leak the precise localities of Taliban hideouts to the government or the foreign forces. Nearly all of the mobile companies obeyed the order after some of the towers were blasted in southern Afghanistan. Instead of mobile phones, most Taliban, especially the commanders, are using Walkie Talkies again, claiming that they cannot be listened to and identified easily.

Stalemate

Making some changes, the Taliban who returned from the winter holidays to Andar in early 2008 were allowing schools to be run. They have also dismissed and disarmed Mullah Asadullah's squad once again and they say they are more cautious this year about dealing with suspected spies. Recently, however, something changed the more lenient course of Mullah Farouq. The Polish-led Public Recontruction Team (PRT), i.e. the military camp, in Ghazni opened a local radio in the Andar district centre, Mirai city. The district chief, Abdul Rahim Disiwal, is quite smart propaganda-wise and in provoking the anger of the Taliban through his evening radio broadcasts. He names the Taliban leaders on air and tells the audience of their atrocities. He even announces, for example, where Mullah Farouq stayed last night; and threatens on air the person who fed and kept Farouq then. He tells the audience of his background, his father and their poor living. An increase in these provocative radio speeches against Farouq and his friends made the latter again threaten to close schools, recognising this weak point. Farouq demanded the radio be closed down and the on-air threats and propaganda stopped. He issued a deadline, and after it passed, the main school in the district centre was closed after Farouq called the headmaster. The headmaster brought together the students at 10 am and told them that the "Respectable Mullah Farouq has called us to go home and close the schools. So, we will be off until he allows us again." More schools were closed after the district chief said he would not submit to the Taliban and would go ahead with telling the truth about the Taliban to the people of Andar. But the school administrators easily submitted to the Taliban threat, knowing that neither the police nor the foreign forces would be able or willing to protect the schools, the teachers and the students.

Farouq was throughout 2008 busy strengthening his force so as to fill the vacuum left by the commanders detained or killed in the previous year. But until late summer his achievements were modest. He was able to ambush the district chief, but failed to kill him; as a result the district chief was prompted to step up his propaganda. A convoy of tankers was set on fire and a convoy of Afghan security forces was attacked. No big achievements yet, from Mullah Farouq's perspective. But then, around September, Mullah Farouq disappeared. First, everybody thought he might have moved over to Pakistan, but when no news came from there, rumours about his death started circulating. Since there has been no sign from him since, it is to be believed that he died during one of the raids by Polish soldiers in the area. In early December, the district chief Abdul Rahim Disiwal was killed in the centre of Ghazni City: several Taliban on motorcycles attacked his convoy, shot and injured Disiwal's bodyguard and killed the district chief. But even though both those bitter opponents are, or seem to be, dead, schools have remained closed.

There are two other developments. The Taliban's weaponry has increased in quantity, but also, in the summer of 2008, in quality: from Pakistan (although it is unclear who paid for them) they have obtained several Russian sniper rifles. In the summer, only the commanders and very few fighters would have one. It is not clear who assists the Taliban with military equipment directly, but most of it is bought by the Taliban themselves, sometimes on the black market in Afghanistan as well. The material (weapons, explosives, bombs) is carried in private cars but also frequently in vehicles which have been confiscated from the Afghan police and army.

For years, the number of foreign fighters has remained rather stable: mostly Pakistanis from the Pashtun tribal areas would come, some Arabs, some Uzbeks. But 2008 saw a sharp increase in Pakistani fighters. With this, conflicts have increased sharply between local Afghan Taliban, whose main interest is to regain power, and the Pakistani fighters who take their *jihad* literally, aiming to kill indiscriminately Afghan government officials, aid workers, foreigners. According to local sources (but without absolute confirmation), this rift even led to a shoot-out between an Afghan commander and some Pakistani fighters in the early autumn of 2008, after a dispute about whether to kill a kidnapped government engineer or not. He survived, but the Afghan commander, whose name is not known, had to leave Ghazni.

6

THE TALIBAN IN HELMAND

AN ORAL HISTORY

Tom Coghlan

Prologue

On 18 June 2006 a car set out from Ghorak District in Kandahar Province, heading for the town of Sangin in neighbouring Helmand. Among the tracks that border the heavily irrigated land of the Sangin Valley the car was ambushed and its five occupants shot dead. The dead men were members of the family of Dad Mohammad Khan, known locally as "Amir Dado", the most prominent government figure in the Sangin area. "Amir Dado" was the tribal leader of the Alokozai tribe in Helmand, an Afghan MP and the Helmand Intelligence Chief in the years between 2001 and 2005. One of the dead men was his brother, a former District Governor of Sangin named Juma Gul.

In the hours after the first attack there were further ambushes and firefights targeting Dad Mohammad's family and supporters. By the end of the day more than 40 relatives and followers were dead. From his home in Kabul, Dad Mohammad blamed the Taliban. Later a known spokesman representing the Taliban, Qari Yousaf Ahmadi, contacted news agencies to claim responsibility. The Taliban had good reason to hate Dad Mohammad. As the provincial head of the NDS, the Afghan intelligence service, he had a reputation for torturing and executing those he accused of being Taliban. As Dad Mohammad was fond of pointing out, a deep scar on his own head was a gift he had received from the Taliban some years earlier.

The Alokozai leader was one of four anti-Taliban 'jihadi' commanders who seized power after the overthrow of the Taliban in 2001 and set themselves up as Karzai government allies in the province. They were rewarded with government positions by the grateful president. But the killings in Sangin were more than a simple blow in Taliban versus Afghan government struggle, even with Dad Mohammad's anti-Taliban credentials. Sangin sat on a fault line in the fractious politics of Helmand. It was an area of increasing friction between competing local interests, the Alokozai and Ishaqzai tribes particularly, with Helmand's burgeoning drugs trade the biggest driver for that competition. Dad Mohammad's Alokozai were part of the trio of dominant Durrani Pashtun tribes (Popolzai, Barakzai and Alokozai, known collectively as *Zirak*), favoured since 2001 by the Karzai government (Karzai is himself a Popolzai). The Ishaqzai were not included in the carve-up of power in the province, indeed they were widely marginalised dismissed as a tribe of "thieves".

The regime of Dad Mohammad and his brother, the district governor Juma Gul, was notably predatory and local Ishaqzai complained bitterly that they were persecuted by the more dominant Alokozai. In October 2007 Ishaqzai tribal elders in a village north of Sangin told British soldiers and this writer: "People round here don't like the government. We don't like Dad Mohammad Khan and we didn't like his brother either." South of the town a young Ishaqzai boy described Dad Mohammad as simply "a very bad man". If Ishaqzai marginalisation made them fairly obvious targets for Taliban recruiters, the process was helped by the presence of Ishaqzai figures in the highest echelons of the Taliban leadership. Mawlawi Aktar Mohammad Osmani, second only to Mullah Omar in the entire Taliban leadership, was an Ishaqzai from the village of Josh Ali, near Sangin, where he also ran a *madrasa*. He was to die in Helmand in December 2006 in an air strike. And the Taliban were astute in placing figures from the Ishaqzai in key positions in the shadow government structures they sought to build in Helmand after 2001. Taliban's Helmand Provincial Governor since 2001 is an Ishaqzai, Mullah Mohammad Rahim.

So when the attack on Dad Mohammad's clan came in June 2006 it was, in one sense, a Taliban attack on the Afghan government. But it was also, to a greater or lesser degree, an Ishaqzai tribal vendetta, a drugs war hit and a popular uprising against a notably unpleasant local regime. This episode is worth noting because it demonstrates the way in which the Taliban insurgency in Helmand sits within and overlaps with other tensions and drivers for instability within the province and in the south of Afghanistan as a whole.

Geographic, political, economic and tribal setting

Helmand was the last province to fall when the Taliban were overthrown in 2001. It lies within the orbit of what was once known as Greater Kandahar and is therefore subject to the political influence of events within Greater Kandahar.

Geographically the province is defined by the presence of the Helmand River, which is fed by snowmelt from the mountains of Uruzgan and Ghor lying to the north. It is the Helmand River that makes Helmand one of the most fertile areas of Afghanistan, and differentiates it from the featureless desert of neighbouring Farah Province to the west.

The Helmand River flows north to south, before bending westward to dissipate eventually in the Sistan wetlands on the border with Iran. The land on either side of the Helmand River has been heavily irrigated, much of it thanks to the US-funded Helmand River Project of the 1950s–70s period. The legacy of this overseas aid is a system of irrigation channels through the central areas of the province around Lashkargar, the provincial capital, and Nad Ali, Marja and southward to Garmser. It is this heavily populated land with its high walled compounds, narrow tracks and country perfect for ambush that now forms key logistical lines for Taliban fighters and supplies moving through the province from the southern border with Baluchistan.

The province's population is overwhelmingly Pashtun (approximately 95 per cent) and very conservative. There are significant numbers of Tajiks, Hazaras and Uzbeks, as well as a small Sikh population, concentrated in Lashkargar and southwards towards Garmser. Many of these minorities arrived either as a result of work opportunities afforded by the Helmand River Project or during the Soviet occupation of the province in the 1980s. Pashtuns from eastern Ghilzai tribes have also migrated to the area. A survey by Danish forces in the summer of 2007 of the area between Gereshk and Sangin, an area of historic settlement by the Barakzai tribe, found some 20 different tribal identities (Barakzai 62 per cent, Asakzai 8 per cent, Khugiani 7 per cent, Khundi 6 per cent, Kakar 5 per cent, etc.)

A significant Pashtun population of internally displaced people from the north of Afghanistan, notably Faryab Province, also ended up in Helmand during the civil war period as a result of Uzbek land-grabbing in the north. There are refugee camps around Lashkargar which have taken on the appearance of permanent settlements and have been in existence since the 1980s. The Faryabi Pashuns in particular have been prominent supporters of the Taliban in Helmand, driven by the particular sense of grievance at the failure of the central government to address their suffering.

As tribal dynamics matter in Helmand, it worth looking at them more closely. The central areas of the province are more ethnically and tribally mixed and generally more educated (though this is relative as literacy rates in Helmand are just 8 per cent for men and 1 per cent for women). A number of leftist militias flourished in the central areas of the province under the Najibullah government, until the early 1990s. The north is less educated, with stronger tribal dynamics.

Most of the Pashtun population is from the Durrani Pashtun tribes. The north is primarily Alizai, a Durrani tribe of the Panjpai (Five Fingers), the five lesser Durrani tribes (though the Panjpai sometimes claim descent from the Ghilzai branch of the Pashtuns when it is politically advantageous to do so).

The Barakzai tribe, one of the big three Durrani tribes known as the Zirak Durrani, dominates the area between Gereshk and Sangin. To the north of Sangin are concentrations of Alokozai, another Zirak Durrani tribe, and Ishaqzai who come from the Panjpai. There are also significant concentrations of Noorzai, a Panjpai tribe, in Nawa and Nad Ali. The southern part of Helmand has concentrations of Alizai, Ishaqzai and Kakar and a significant Baluch population which straddles the border and has historically been heavily involved in smuggling.

The tribal society of the southern provinces has grown increasingly unstable since the 1980s. "All the tribes in the south have enmities, a long history, over money and resources," said Professor Habibullah Rafi of Kabul University, interviewed in December 2007. Government attempts at redistribution of land during the Soviet period saw the erosion of the old Malik and Khan system of landlords and tribal elders, who historically acted as the negotiators between the government and the populace in the south. In Helmand the 1980s and 1990s saw the rise of a number of warlords, which despite grouping round particular families were rooted in the tribal society of the south. Interviewed in Gereshk at a *shura* in May 2007 a Barakzai Tribal Elder, who would not give his name, lamented: "The local people used to support the elders. But nowadays the elders have lost their trust and the government does not listen to the elders." Commenting on the tribal dynamics of the province a Mr Tadabir from the Tribal Liaison Office in Kabul said: "The tribal issues remain but it is families who fight for influence." Hafiz Mansur, an Islamist intellectual from Panjshir interviewed in October 2007, noted: "The tribal element exists in these areas (Helmand). One part of the fight is tribal. Administrative corruption, drug trafficking, opposition of tribes, these things exist."

The Helmand warlords were mostly ejected during the Taliban period, but re-emerged as allies of the Karzai government after 2001. Several were rewarded with senior provincial government positions; Sher Mohammad Akhundzada from the Hassanzai sub-tribe of the Alizai tribe was made provincial governor, Abdul Rahman Jan from the Noorzai was made police chief, Dad Mohammad Khan ("Amir Dado") from the Alokozai was made Intelligence Chief, the militia of Mir Wali from the Barakzai tribe was incorporated into the Ministry of Defence (Afghan Military Forces). Today Dad Mohammad Khan and Mir Wali are MPs, Sher Mohammad Akhundzada is a Senator while Abdul Rahman Jan's son is also an MP.

The infrastructure of Helmand, like that of many parts of the country, was devastated by warfare prior to 2001. However, the province has become the centre of the most widespread cultivation of opium poppy anywhere in the world, producing on its own around 50 per cent of the world's heroin by 2007. This drives the local economy and generates income in hundreds of millions of dollars for local farmers and income worth billions of dollars for smuggling mafias. It is hard to overstate the importance of the opium industry as a driver for rampant corruption, instability and violent competition within

Map 3: Tribes of Helmand

Helmand Province and the south as a whole. An Alokozai tribal leader, interviewed in April 2007, explained: "In Helmand the biggest tribes competing for the drugs trade are the Ishaqzai and Noorzai and the Alizai are the next biggest. The Alizai are the largest tribe in the province. The Ishaqzai are the greatest Taliban supporting tribe."

Antonio Giustozzi defines these Helmand strong men as "tribal warlords",[1] as distinct from the term "warlord" which is applied to the figures who gained dominance in the north and west of Afghanistan during the 1990s, such as Ishmail Khan or Rashid Dostum, and who continue to exert considerable influence at a central government level. Within the more fractured, patronage based system that has survived the upheavals of the 1980s and 90s in Durrani-dominated Helmand the "tribal warlords" emerged as feudal robber barons rooted in the dysfunctional remnants of the tribal structure. Figures like the Akhundzadas have proved themselves an acquisitive and tenacious presence. The foundation of their power continues to be their own tribe and it is this that gives them their durability and at the same time limits their ability to build lasting alliances across tribal lines. The result is endless factionalism, and it is onto this complex backdrop that the Taliban insurgency is overlaid.

Historical background 1994–2001

In 1994 the Taliban were welcomed into Helmand, which like neighbouring Kandahar was at that time beset by anarchy and the depredations of numerous warlord militias, most of them loosely allied to the old *mujahidin* parties of the anti-Soviet war. "In 1994 when they entered Helmand I joined them, till now," said one Taliban commander interviewed in Lashkargar in September 2008. "The *mujahidin* had been robbers. They were appalling in their behaviour to people. In the beginning the Taliban were good and holy people." Much of the rural populace shared the same ethnicity and basic cultural values as the Taliban, who originated in rural Kandahar. After the local experience of the *mujahidin* since the Soviet withdrawal the Taliban's promise to impose Sharia law and bring security was widely supported, particularly in the illiterate, ultra-conservative rural backwaters of the province.

An instinctive empathy with the straightforward religious ideals of the Taliban gained deep roots in Helmand. However, the excessive harshness of Taliban rule, particularly the impact of Taliban social edicts banning music, television, kite flying, dog fighting and other local sports; the forced attendance at prayers, the bans on secular education, and above all the Taliban's self-evident incapacity to deliver economic and infrastructural improvement; all this was increasingly resented by the late 1990s, particularly among the urban populace which had more aspirations. "Honestly, pre-2001 even in the Taliban itself there were people trying to make the regime collapse," said Helmand Parliamentary Senator Haji Mahboob Khan in an interview typical of many. "There was no hope for the people." In the latter years of the Taliban regime there was also widespread unhappiness over its conscription of young men from Helmand to fight in incompetently managed and bloody frontal assaults against the Northern Alliance in the north of the country. In the Garmser area of Helmand, one local police commander claimed in June 2008: "The Taliban were forcing people to fight with them from this area in 1997 in the Panjshir Valley. That is why only 10 per cent of local people are supporting them as fighters today."

The Taliban in Helmand 2001–2008

In the months after the overthrow of the Taliban the Karzai administration divided power in the province between the various anti-Taliban commanders who had returned from exile as Western forces and the Northern Alliance advanced southward into the country. The US military footprint in Helmand remained light with small numbers of US Special Forces and a US Provincial Reconstruction Team established in October 2004, never numbering more than a 300–man manoeuvre force in total. The PRT began fairly limited reconstruction work, amounting to $9.5 million in two years while a USAID contractor, Chemonics International, was given $130 million to implement agricultural redevelopment in Helmand. Their projects were largely suspended in 2005 because the US forces in the province were insufficient to provide security after an attack that killed five Chemonics employees.[2] Helmand, like much of the rest of the south of the country, remained a near void for US intelligence and was left more or less to its own devices save for aggressive counter-terrorism operations by US Special Forces units. In particular there was no satellite cover for Helmand, with all such assets switched to Iraq.

The leadership of the Taliban fled to Pakistan and began to reorganise. According to two Taliban commanders interviewed in Lashkargar in September 2008, the first emissaries from the Taliban in exile returned to Helmand within six months of the US invasion. "Three months after the invasion Toor (Black) Mullah Ghani and Mullah Mohammad Rahim (the current Taliban Helmand Governor) came to Spin Boldak with Haji Hafiz Abdul Rahim from the Noorzai tribe. Haji Hafiz became the first martyr for the Taliban. Mullah Ghani was also killed later and both of their sons are now fighting. First they went to Zabul. They set up the first Taliban strongholds in Shin Kay and Daichopan. Then they came to Helmand." The commanders said that the Taliban began to approach supporters who had simply hung up their weapons and gone home after the US invasion, appealing to commanders to reactivate their *Andiwali* (their networks of old comrades) and using preachers to propagate anti-Western feeling. "They were using loudspeakers and going into the villages, talking to the community. They said: 'You will not be free. Your wives and your children will not have rights. Your country is under the occupation of infidels'," said one Taliban Commander. This process continued between 2001 and 2005. Many Helmandis claim it was helped by the predatory behaviour of the former Jihadi leaders. Many interviewees also say support for the

Taliban was increased by the failure of the government and international community to provide expected economic improvements, and by aggressive search operations and aerial bombing by Western Special Forces on counter-terrorism missions.

Interviewed in April 2006 in the Lashkargar bazaar, Abdul Raouf, aged 42, was typical of interviewees who named the former Jihadi leaders as a malign influence exploited by Taliban propagandists: "Abdul Rahman Jan much increased the support for the Taliban. He was an example the Taliban could use to question the strength of the government. The Taliban come to the village and preach in the mosques. They always name Abdul Rahman Jan. I support Taliban. In Sangin, if one man is guilty they come to your village and they bomb the whole area. 20 innocents are hurt." Interviewed in July 2006 a young Taliban fighter, Mullah Qudratullah, who had been fighting US forces in north Helmand and was recovering from an injury to his leg in Kabul, gave a detailed account of how his initial enthusiasm for the West dissipated in outrage over what he perceived to be atrocities by Western forces:

"When the Taliban governed we were not happy. They were too harsh and they oppressed people. When the Americans came we thought they would bring prosperity and be good for the country. But after they started injuring and killing and oppressing people we realised that the Americans were not here to help, but to help themselves and impose their will on us. Right now we don't have a problem with the Taliban. It is clear what the US and the Karzai government are doing. What reservations we have with the Taliban are overshadowed. We will sort them out when we have kicked out the Americans. This is the view of the majority of Afghans. When I spoke with my commander about speaking to you he said 'speak to the journalists, tell them about our righteousness and our victimhood.'"

Mullah Qudratullah said that his father died under Afghan police interrogation and his mother was dishonoured by a US army search operation that went through their property. Of eight young men from his village who joined the Taliban around 2004, he said three were already dead. By the time of the interview he appeared to have become heavily radicalised. He is believed to have died himself conducting a suicide bomb attack on Canadian forces in Panjwayi in late 2006.[3] A tribal leader from the Alokozai tribe interviewed in October 2007 said: "The government's failure of 2003 to 2005 explained all the coming dangers."[4]

The incidence of Taliban violence was limited until 2005; Westerners working for aid agencies in the province reported that they were still able to reach remote areas such as Baghran district on the Uruzgan border without being attacked. It seems likely that in this period the Taliban concentrated on building their structure and their supplies (though it is clear that there were already huge weapons stockpiles in Helmand). The influence of the warlords does not appear to have extended into the remoter areas, particularly in parts of the north of the province. Major Dirk Ringennburg, who led the US army reconnaissance force from the 173rd Airborne division that was the principal US manoeuvre force in Helmand in 2005, said: "The jihadi commanders helped out a fair bit and were as active as they could be, but their militias were not that big." The militias were fighting without uniforms and the US commander began tying white mine tape around their arms to identify them in combat and prevent fratricide; they also issued militiamen with orange baseball caps. Large parts of the province, particularly in the north, were left very much to their own devices. Sher Mohammad Akhundzada, for instance, left Rais-e Baghran, the warlord controlling Baghran, who was still aligned with the Taliban, to rule the northern Baghran district while engaging in periodic negotiations with him about joining the government. Rais-e Baghran was alleged to have sheltered Mullah Omar in late 2001.

However, the violence levels began to rise in 2005. Major Ringennburg's force began running into large Taliban formations in Helmand and north Kandahar. On 21 June 2005 his unit was briefly surrounded by around 300 Taliban in north Kandahar. He estimated that given a couple of days' preparation, they could concentrate as many as 500 fighters. Ringennburg felt at that time that the Taliban had achieved little penetration in areas far north of Sangin, but that the Ishaqzai around Sangin, under the leadership of Mullah Mamuk, were already allied with the Taliban because of local tribal issues. In other areas the US commander felt that local tribes were undecided. In Nawzad Ringennburg claims that the Taliban were present, but gaining very limited support from the local populace. In other areas, with the exception of Sangin where the die was already cast, the populace was often disillusioned with the government, but as yet uncommitted. "We never bombed a single village in Helmand," said Ringennburg in a telephone interview conducted in October 2008. "The people in Helmand, except around Sangin, were eventually going to go with the government or go all in with the Taliban. We were very careful not to tip the scale. In 2006 there were delicate tribal alliances but a little heavy handedness made them more anti-government. They were not necessarily pro-Taliban but there was agreement being made with the drug dealers. The very wealthy drug dealers came to a mutual agreement with the Taliban in 2006. We tried to use the Afghan National Army to deal with the tribal issues, but they were very deeply rooted."

US forces operating in the northern areas up past Musa Qala felt that they were meeting explicitly drug-business militias rather than Taliban fighters in those areas. "The drug militias were the finest fighting organisation we ever faced, and I've faced a few. Not a lot of Taliban tangled with those guys either. They were professional fighters and they weren't from the area. There were things they were doing that didn't fit. They would hold terrain against us, they didn't want us to go down a specific road for instance. We knew that if we got embroiled with these guys way up in the Baghran Valley, this was nothing to do with the Taliban, and we would be dissipating our force to no purpose."

Thus large tracts of the province remained untouched by any government or international military structure, as had been the case for much of their previous history. Major Ringennburg's brief was specifically to facilitate the 2005 elections. His unit was, he was told, "an economy of force operation" because of the movement of combat assets to Iraq. "NATO made mistakes," claimed Sher Mohammad Akhundzada, who was sacked at British insistence because of his narcotics links in December 2005 and replaced by Mohammad Daoud as governor. "The powerful people in the province were kicked out of government and people unknown by the community were brought in,", he claimed He also blamed the UN-backed policy of disarming local armed groups, many of which, in the south, were anti-Taliban militias controlled by the warlords.[5] Akhundzada claims that his own forces lost 1,000 weapons, though commanders are known to have routinely handed in old and defunct weaponry and stashed their best arms.

While the control of the province by the former Jihadi leaders appears to have been often divisive and their control far from comprehensive, their abrupt removal in the absence of significant government or foreign forces to fill the void seems to have been a still larger error of judgement. Naseema Niazi, one of Helmand's two female MPs, also blamed a vacuum in Helmand's power structures for providing the Taliban with an opportunity to dramatically expand their influence in early 2006. "The government of the ex-mujahidin was strong for security at that time. The local administration and the US forces were effective in building links to local communities, going to the districts. Then when the command went to another country there was a vacuum. They had to start rebuilding the links. Everything changed. The British did not know friend from enemy. The old administration was also changed. A space opened in both. They brought a force with no knowledge on the ground. This was the chance for the Taliban."

Taliban fighters began to appear in southern areas of the province such as Garmser from across the border in Baluchistan in early 2006, in what was part of the wider offensive unleashed by the Taliban leadership based in Quetta that year and pursued with vigour in Helmand by the charismatic Taliban leader Mullah Dadullah Akhund. "There was not a Taliban presence in my district," said Garmser parliamentary Senator Haji Mahboob Khan; "then in 2006, before the British arrived 20 Taliban arrived. People informed the government. The ANP (Afghan National Police) came and cleared the area. Then they (the ANP) looted people's houses and insulted people. They angered people. The Taliban never insulted and robbed people. They were disciplined. People went to the Taliban and asked them to come back. The Taliban retook the district."

The arrival of British forces began in April, but there was little British presence in the districts before June and US officers claim there was no exchange of intelligence or working-up period with British forces, as there was for over three months with Canadian forces in neighbouring Kandahar.[6]

The British plan, as outlined at the time of their deployment, envisaged focusing UK forces around Lashkargar and Gereshk in what was going to be termed an "Afghan Development Zone". This was to be deluged with reconstruction aid, creating economic improvement which would win local support. UK forces would contain any signs of Taliban threat in outlying parts of the province but remain focused on the centre. Gradually other "ink spots" of progress would be established and begin to join up with the centre. However, in June Taliban groups began concerted attacks on a number of district centres in the north of Helmand, specifically Sangin, Musa Qala, Nawzad and the hydroelectric dam at Kajaki. In response British forces were deployed to what were termed "Platoon Houses" in the towns to prevent them falling. Owing to the small size of the British force, which at that stage only included around 1,000 fighting troops, the units were small, usually around company strength (approximately 100 men and in some cases less). British commanders subsequently claimed their forces were deployed to these areas at the insistence of the Helmand Governor, Mohammad Daoud. Daoud denies this, insisting it was a consensus decision made with British commander, Brigadier Ed Butler.[7]

The Taliban were in far greater numbers than UK forces appear to have anticipated; parliamentary questions filed by the Liberal Democrat party in the British parliament in early 2006 on the UK intelligence assessment of the Taliban produced a countrywide estimate of just 1,000 active fighters. That assessment was clearly wildly off. Taliban numbers appear to have been boosted by the heavy influx of fighters from Pakistani *madrasas*. But a further factor also appears to have recruited large numbers of local villagers as fighters to attack the British bases. While Pashtuns tedm to be hostile to foreign armed presence, some antipathy appears to have been specifically linked to the presence of British forces in Helmand and a belief that British forces were historic enemies bent on revenge. "There is long animosity to the British here and history means much here," warned a US Official in Lashkargar interviewed in April 2006. "Afghans have long memories." In December 2007 Professor Habibullah Rafi of Kabul University claimed: "There is a belief that the British have not forgotten the Battle of Maiwand in 1880 and that they have come to claim revenge."[8]

That view is echoed by Wali Jan MP, the son of Abdul Rahman Jan, in 2008: "Why did the British go to Musa Qala and those other places? From the start the Taliban preached that the British are old enemies coming back, so then people thought it is happening. So initially a lot of people joined the Taliban in places like Musa Qala, but later the harshness of the Taliban affected them and the Taliban attacks attracted aerial bombing in response."[9] During the summer of 2006 Taliban attacks on the "Platoon Houses" in Musa Qala, Sangin, Nawzad, Garmser and Kajaki saw concentrations of Taliban sometimes numbering several hundred fighters. Western forces compensated for their small numbers in poorly sited defensive positions by resorting to massive firepower, destroying whole tracts of the district centres they were supposedly defending. There was heavy displacement of the local population and allegations of collateral damage were frequent.[10] Interviewed in a British newspaper in September 2006, British army Captain Leo Docherty claimed: "Having a big old fight is pointless and just making things worse. All those people whose homes have been destroyed and sons killed are going to turn against the British. It's a pretty clear equation—if people are losing homes and poppy fields, they will go and fight. I certainly would." "We've been grotesquely clumsy—we've said we'll be different to the Americans who were bombing and strafing villages, then behaved exactly like them. We're now scattered in a shallow meaningless way across northern towns where the only way for the troops to survive is to increase the level of violence so more people get killed. It's pretty shocking and not something I want to be part of."[11] Captain Docherty resigned from the army in September 2006.

"In 2006 people joined in great numbers," said one Taliban commander in September 2008. "Since then every month more people have joined." British commanders estimated that approximately 1,000 Taliban died during 2006. By one estimate leaked to UK newspapers in April 2008, some 7,000 Taliban were killed by British forces in Helmand from June 2006 to April 2008. These figures are impossible to verify and seem improbably high. As one senior British officer pointed out in November 2007: "Claims were made in 2007 that 2,500 to 5,000 Taliban were killed (in Helmand), that would mean 15,000 wounded. Are there graveyards? Are there clogged hospitals? No."

In September of 2006, with British forces cut off in Musa Qala and under intense pressure, particularly due to the threat to resupply helicopters, British commanders with the Afghan provincial government negotiated a ceasefire in Musa Qala under which tribal leaders in the town undertook to exclude the Taliban and police the town with local men. After the ceasefire had held for a month, British forces were withdrawn. The Musa Qala deal held officially until February 2007 and there were discussions of extending a similar deal to other towns. However, the deal was opposed by the US government and by senior figures within the Karzai administration, though it was popular with Helmandis. In February Taliban fighters openly took control of the town, citing a British bomb attack directed at Mullah Ghafoor, a leading Taliban commander from the area, as breaking the deal; Ghafoor survived the attack, but his brother was killed. The fall of Musa Qala to the Taliban was a huge propaganda coup for the insurgents. For the next ten months, until its recapture, it was the only significant urban area that the Taliban held in Afghanistan.

Sher Mohammad Akhundzada complains that the Taliban and "ISI backers" used claims of repressive behaviour by the Jihadi leaders as an excuse to expand Taliban influence and seize control of Musa Qala:

"The Taliban had the excuse that 'we are angry with Sher Mohammad, it is because of Sher Mohammad's men that we are fighting, but if they leave we won't fight them'. They were saying 'we are not real Taliban, this is just a personal enmity'. The ISI were just trying to get rid of all the anti-Taliban forces. They tried it in Sangin, Nawzad and Garmser. The Taliban were suddenly in trucks in Garmser and Baghran. There was a big increase, though they were still local Taliban. They were contacting governor Daoud and saying we are a tribal government, not Taliban, and we are angry with the Jihadis."

Tactical adaptation

Following the six-month rotation of British units in the winter of 2006–7 British forces, while continuing to defend the "platoon houses", began using mobile columns resupplied from the air to push into Taliban-held districts of the province. The siege of the Sangin district centre was relieved in April 2007. The arrival of the third rotation of British forces that month saw a switch to conventional battalion-strength sweep operations between Gereshk and Sangin during the summer months. In response to these developments the Taliban appeared to adapt to the use of progressively smaller mobile units, usually of around 15 men. In September 2008 a British commander described "formed bodies of 6 to 20 fighters". They also proved adept in reinfiltrating areas behind sweep operations conducted by British forces.

In June 2007 Danish CIMIC teams moving behind British troops during Operation Chakush (Hammer) found civilians receptive to their presence and enthusiastic about the promise of reconstruction. However, the Taliban then reinfiltrated the area. A further sweep operation to retake the area was launched in August. This time the locals were unfriendly. "After Chakush those who had engaged with NATO forces were killed or at the least hassled by the Taliban (when they reinfiltrated the area)," admitted one CIMIC officer interviewed in October 2007.

During the summer of 2007 British forces fought protracted battles with Taliban fighters who tended to stand off and fire at a distance and dropped an average of 22 tons per month of aerial munitions in Helmand, almost half the munitions being dropped in Afghanistan per month. The use of artillery, mortars and other heavy munitions was also widespread. The arrival of the fourth rotation of British forces in September 2007 saw a switch to the building of more numerous small bases in the area between Gereshk and Sangin with the intention of establishing local stability. In December 2007 the Taliban were pushed with relative ease out of the town of Musa Qala, which they had held since February, in a large combined operation by British, US and Afghan forces.

During 2007–8 UK forces noted an increase in the Taliban's use of roadside bombs in Helmand. The summer of 2008 also saw the heaviest month of losses for British forces in June, with 12 British soldiers killed. Firefights in 2008 remained numerous but were more intense and shorter, according to British soldiers who had previously fought in Helmand in 2006, with Taliban fighters usually breaking contact within 10 to 30 minutes, usually before air support could arrive. Towards the end of the year the levels, even accounting for natural drop off in the winter, appeared to fall as the Taliban switched more to the use of "assymetric tactics" of roadside and suicide bombs. A British bomb disposal expert interviewed in November 2007 reported a fourfold increase in IED attacks during the summer of that year. He also described the influx of more sophisticated bomb detonators, typically "Spider" detonators activated by mobile phone. However, he also noted that most Taliban devices were constructed from old ordnance, particularly mortar and artillery shells and unexploded Western ordnance.[12] "There are a few people with a lot of knowledge (of bomb making) and a lot with a bit of knowledge," he said.

The Taliban's use of multiple devices, follow-up bombs and more sophisticated methods of detonation progressed through 2008. More than 80 per cent of the UK soldiers killed in Helmand in the year to mid-September 2008 died as a result of roadside bombs. In May 2008 some 800 US Marines backed by aircraft and artillery from a 2,300 strong force deployed to Helmand dislodged around 500 Taliban fighters from fixed positions they had held since 2006 south of the town of Garmser. The Taliban had faced a force of around 200 British soldiers in a static stalemate. Large numbers of Taliban were killed in more than 100 separate firefights: "For a whole month they died in large numbers, 20 men were running across open ground in flip-flops with small arms against 60-man US Marine positions," said Colonel Nick Borton, a British officer in Garmser in June 2008, his voice betraying both bemusement and admiration. The removal of the Taliban from Garmser seriously affected the Taliban lines of communication and logistical supply through the summer months until new lines of communication were opened through Washer and Nawzad districts by the Taliban.

Who are the Taliban in Helmand?

Broadly speaking, the Taliban represent a coalition comprising mostly networks of individuals who are opposed to the government of Afghanistan, to the presence of foreign troops in Afghanistan, to the establishment of the law and order that the Western backed government seeks to impose. They do so for varying reasons.

At one end of the scale are what many locals call the "real Taliban": the religious students trained in *madrasas* in Pakistan or Afghanistan. A 23-year-old sub-commander interviewed near Lashkargar in March 2008 was typical of the most radicalised, Al Qaida influenced strain of the Taliban. "The first priority is to free the country. But the Jihad will not end. Then we go to America and make trouble there. In Pakistan we will give them a choice to lay down their weapons and accept Sharia. We pray that the Iraqis will defeat the infidels. My message to the British is leave the country. Bring as many troops as you can, it won't make a difference. Don't destroy my country. There can be no negotiation. This is global *jihad*."

Interviewed in September 2008, a more pragmatic, semi-retired, Helmand Taliban commander in his forties divided the motivation of the Taliban into three categories: "There are people who have problems with the government like me, there are Taliban who joined just for power and the real Jihadis (*madrasa* students) who just want to become martyrs. The real Jihadis are about 50 per cent of the Taliban in Helmand."

There are other motives cited in interviews with Helmandi people, politicians, or the Taliban themselves. Some mention general xenophobia, revenge for Western or Afghan government actions that affected the individual, his family, his tribe or Pashtuns in general; some allude to oppression along tribal lines or exclusion from power or resources. Broadly speaking, with the exception of a relatively small, though possibly growing, minority whose sole motivation is a mission of global *jihad*, the majority are motivated by a spectrum of localised grievances or issues of self-interest. As the respected Western analyst Michael Semple puts it: "They are the dispossessed of the post-2001 Afghan settlement."[13]

By most estimates the proportion of the Helmand population that actively supports the Taliban remains small. Common estimates would be in the range of 10–20 per cent. Michael Semple suggests that around 15 per cent actively support the insurgency, 10 per cent are active government supporters in Helmand and some 75 per cent are fence-sitters acquiescing with whichever force is most active locally. The same source suggests that a significantly higher proportion in rural areas "emotionally support or identify with the Taliban but do not actively support the insurgency." Again, those figures are broadly supported by other sources. A tribal elder from the Barakzai tribe interviewed in Gereshk in May 2007 claimed: "About 20–30 per cent of people are now supporting the Taliban, about 25 per cent are for the government and 60 per cent support no one." A Taliban commander interviewed in September 2008 claimed that the government enjoyed around 30 per cent support in the province.

According to a senior British officer interviewed in September 2008, "We don't get a sense of a civilian population in Helmand that is being radicalised." But on the ground in Helmand there is certainly a striking antipathy to the foreign forces operating in the province. When interviewed privately and beyond the hearing of their neighbours, many Helmandis' view of the struggle going on around them could be summarised as: "A pox on all their houses. We just want to be left alone but we will support anyone who can bring security." A Taliban commander from Helmand, interviewed in Kabul in October 2008, put it this way: "The overall majority of the Helmand Taliban are the old Taliban (from the pre-2001 period), the ex-power people. The minority are the people who hated the government of the warlords (2001–2006) or people who are anti-British. The new young Jihadis, the crazy guys, are also a small number compared to the old Taliban."

However, there is some evidence that the level of radicalisation within the Taliban itself has increased, and that this has created friction with the local populace in some areas of Helmand. A Taliban cleric from Garmser, who was interviewed near Lashkargar in March 2008, expressed unease over the extremism of younger commanders, who were emerging to replace the pre-2001 leadership as they were killed off by Western military operations. "These new crazy guys are really emotional, they are war addicted," he said. "If they get a word about someone (who is a spy) they just kill them. They are very impulsive. Some Taliban have been treating the people too harshly. We told them if you are intimidating the people too much there won't be space for you guys." The same commander went on: "In Zabul there are 5 per cent of these new (radicalised) Taliban and 95 per cent normal Taliban. In Helmand about 40 per cent are these new Taliban." A Taliban cleric from the area estimated that 40 per cent of fighters were foreign in Garmser in March 2008. A senior British commander suggested an overall figure of 25–33 per cent foreign fighters in Helmand in October 2007.

Helmand's lady MP Naseema Niazi also argues that there is indeed a more radicalised and more international outlook to the post-2001 Taliban. "The Taliban are now an international threat," she said in July 2008. "They have plans and strong command and they are redeveloped and equipped. They are brave and they are not simple people now."

The more radicalised element seems to have been concentrated in the Garmser area, which because of its location near the Pakistan border, and the static nature of the fighting there between 2006 and 2008, had a higher proportion of foreign fighters. "Most Taliban in Garmser were outsiders," said Haji Mahboob Khan. "Mainly they were foreign Taliban, they had no interference in the local community at all. They just went to the frontline." The foreign fighters appear to be often admired by the Taliban for their fervour, but they are also viewed with fairly deep suspicion. "Helmandis accept Waziris joining them as willingly as Afghan National Police accept foreign mentors," claims Michael Semple. The tensions that arose between Afghans and Arabs in particular during the Jihad period, notably over peculiarities of Afghan religious practise, are well documented. Interviewed in July 2008, the recognised Taliban spokesman Zabiullah Mujahid explained:

"All *mujahidin* who come to Afghanistan to fight have to accept the principles and rules and regulations of the Emirate. They can fight on the part of Taliban but they cannot give orders. They have to receive orders. Mullah Omar is Emir al-Moomineen. He is the leader of the Muslims worldwide. None of the foreign fighters are allowed to be the commanders. They are allowed to join the frontline."

The particular importance of foreign fighters to particular Taliban commanders is as a source of funding and possibly military skills and equipment. They are often tolerated rather than embraced for this reason. By early 2009 Taliban fighters in Helmand were claiming that the majority of foreign fighters. One Western diplomat described many of the Arab fighters arriving in Afghanistan during 2008 as "Saudi kids on their Gap Years" with little military value.[14] Overall estimates of the total number of active Taliban fighters in Helmand are put "in the hundreds not thousands" by senior British commanders. The total strength appears to have fluctuated considerably depending on the season and Taliban intentions. Overall, though, the Helmand Taliban appear to have been Helmandis and the insurgency seems to have retained its local flavour, for practical reasons of knowledge and contacts as much as anything else.

"We move from district to district of Helmand," said a Taliban commander interviewed in September 2008, "but a group that comes from another province won't know the terrain. We move in the province but not between provinces." However, commanders are clearly ordered into areas they are unfamiliar with when the Taliban tries, periodically, to concentrate forces and fight conventional engagements. The same commander, in a previous interview, described fighting in both Zabul and Kandahar, the latter during the big 2006 build-up of Taliban fighters around Panjwayi District, where the Taliban were heavily defeated ("in war sometimes you win and sometimes you lose," he said, admitting that large numbers of Taliban were killed in Panjwayi in 2006). However, with the exception of large operations such as the Panjwayi build-up and a similar attempt to concentrate force in Arghandab district of Kandahar in June 2008, it seems generally true that the insurgency remains a local phenomenon. In most cases where the Taliban have attempted to mass forces and fight conventionally they have suffered defeat with heavy losses to Western air power.

A senior British officer interviewed in September 2008 said: "The bulk of the problem is significantly of local Taliban and of tribes and therefore community. There are a number of different motivations, economic, ideological, religious, the disenchanted and the disenfranchised. There are also the Jihadis, with whom there can be no reconciliation or compromise. They are a minority, but a very influential one." An Afghan interpreter working for a British eavesdropping unit for Taliban communications claimed in June 2008: "Most of the Taliban (in Helmand) are talking with Helmand and Kandahar accents, there are other accents, maybe eastern region accents. There are also foreign languages. In Garmser they are mostly talking in Urdu. I heard Arabic 11 months ago. A few days ago I heard a strange language, probably Chechen."

There is considerable focus on which particular sections of Helmand society may have greater links to the Taliban, and especially which tribes may have greater links to the insurgency. In interviews, members of the Taliban usually refute any suggestion that the Taliban is an organisation with a tribal profile. It was, after all, founded on a pan-Islamic platform that explicitly rejects both tribe and nation state and aspires only to the establishment of a caliphate, representing the faithful, the Umma, under the Mullah Omar who claims the title *Amir al-Momenin* (leader of all Muslims).

The structure of social relations in Helmand is founded on the basic notion of *qawm*: kinship based solidarity. The south is a vast web of such overlapping networks, based on shared tribe, family, village, district, ethnicity, *madrasa* etc. In the case of the Taliban the most profound expression of this instinct is the bond between *Andiwali* comrades in arms and that, historically, has been a bond that was unrelated to the solidarity within a tribe.

However, as suggested above, the Taliban were able to make greater inroads with some tribes than with others, and their tribal profile seems to have become more pronounced since 2001. "In the Taliban government time the Taliban had no tribal profile," said Wali Jan, MP in 2008. "Now the Taliban has a tribal and political base." It is a broadly supportable claim to suggest that the Zirak Durrani tribes have contributed less to the insurgency because they have more to gain from the Karzai government, which has favoured them with power and position. Shortly before a British patrol was ambushed south of Sangin by Taliban on Christmas morning in 2007, a tribal elder of the Barakzai tribe explained to the British patrol commander: "There are about 300 people in this village. We are Barakzai. A lot of our tribe work for the government, the ANA and ANP. People say our tribe are British spies. The Taliban fire from this area at your base because they want you to fire back and for us to be killed."

Ishaqzai support for the Taliban is widely suspected, partly because of the tribe's exclusion from power, partly perhaps because of links with the drugs trade, and partly because of the presence of Ishaqzai in the upper-echelons of the Taliban,. "The Ishaqzai are at the core of the insurgency in Helmand," said one Western analyst in Kabul in October 2007. A leader of the Alokozai tribe interviewed in late 2007 said simply: "The Ishaqzai had no choice but to fight." The carve-up of power in Helmand after 2001 was one that systematically excluded the Ishaqzai and some of the smaller tribes. The Alizai, for instance, were given most of the district governor positions and the Education and Finance departments, while the Noorzai predictably secured the police chief posts during Abdul Rahman Jan's tenure as police chief of the province. The Alokozai held the Intelligence Service, the Hazara minority the Health department, and the Ghilzais briefly held the Culture and Information department. According to British officials who worked alongside the Helmand provincial government, after 2006 the line ministries had no history of delivering services, but were run as the private fiefdoms of whichever group controlled them, a means of strengthening patronage groups by dispensing such government or international funds as they could extract from the centre.

The Hotak, a Ghilzai tribe that includes Mullah Omar in its number, are also prominent in the Helmand Taliban, as are the Kakar, the tribe of Mullah Dadullah Akhund, the charismatic Helmand Taliban commander who was killed in May 2007 by British Special Forces. However, that influence is constrained by their relatively small numbers in Helmand, around 500 Kakar families according to Sher Mohammad Akhundzada, though there is a concentration of Kakar round Garmser which appears significant.

A Barakzai elder said of the local makeup of the Taliban south of Sangin: "The Taliban are from different tribes. Most are Ishaqzai, Kakar, Noorzai or Khugiani. There are also a group from the Barakzai." Colonel Hadood Wadood, commander of Afghan Army foces around Sangin claimed in November 2007: "There are tribal tensions around Sangin. The Alokozai are mostly pro-government. The Barakzai are about 50/50 and the Alizai situation is very complex." Both analyses sound plausible. The Taliban in Helmand welcome support from all tribes, but certain tribes have taken a more dominant role. Because of their fairly fractured and degraded nature there are those who feel disfranchised even within those tribes that might be deemed to have gained most from the Karzai administration; and of course people also join the Taliban for reasons of ideology, anti-Western sentiment and much else.

Where Taliban groups have a particular tribal makeup, that makeup is retained and if anything reinforced by the Taliban system of replacing commanders killed in battle with their nearest available relatives. This is designed to retain the loyalty of the commander's *andiwal*, "comrades in arms", and therefore the cohesion of the group. "If a commander is killed then by law his brother or cousin or the strongest person takes over," said a young Taliban commander interviewed in September 2008. Sher Mohammad Akhundzada names a large number of prominent commanders killed by Western forces in Musa Qala and replaced by a relative: "Mullah Matin was killed and his brother Mullah Wassee replaced him. Mullah Ghafoor was killed and his brother replaced him, Mullah Toor Jan was killed and his brother replaced him."

Since 2006 the Taliban in Helmand have become increasingly paranoid about their internal security and the threat from spies tipping off Western Special Forces, a threat increased by the prevalence of mobile phone possession among the local populace. This has helped to make more reliable ties, such as family and tribal loyalty, increasingly important to the Taliban, and appears to have been a factor in the partial undermining of the Taliban's tribeless aspirations. Helmand Taliban fighters also claim that standing within the organisation is partly dependent on local tribal respect and family influence, as well as the men that you can bring with you. "The first importance is the experience that someone had from the Taliban government time," said one source with close links to the Helmand Taliban. "What was his reputation, was he a brave fighter, a holy person or a robber? Second is the size of his Mahaz (his front). How many people you have, what are the number of your *andiwal* (followers)? Then third is how brave you are. You must be a brave commander or Taliban are not so interested in you. And then you must be well respected in the community. Generally people must come from the local community and be from a family and a tribe that is respected in that community. If you are from a different district then people will not know you and you don't have the contacts in the community." The same source gives an example of a particular figure in the Helmand Taliban who, despite good religious education and a reputation for valour, had struggled to rise within the Taliban locally. The reason was that his family had arrived relatively recently in the province from the east of the country and came from a relatively obscure Ghilzai tribe which had little base in Helmand. This limited his prospects.

The particular network (be it a family, clan, village, tribe, *madrasa* etc) that was the basis for a given Taliban group would be expected to provide replacements in the event of the group suffering casualties. If that were impossible, then the source claimed that the Taliban leadership in Quetta often provided a rough top-up system of fighters from Pakistani *madrasas*. When a Taliban group suffers a heavy defeat that causes it to lose its leadership and overall identity, the surviving fighters would typically be incorporated into an existing commander's group and become his *andiwal*.

The Taliban leadership

The success of Western Special Forces in targeting the command structure of the Taliban in Helmand since 2006 has meant that Taliban commanders who built a significant profile for themselves have tended to be killed very quickly. The Taliban commit very few of their senior figures to the risk of crossing into Helmand these days. "We are still very well organised. But we decided not to send the leaders to the frontline any more. The leaders send the orders to the small commanders," said a commander interviewed in Lashkargar in March 2008. The Taliban governor for Helmand, Mullah Mohammad Rahim, has survived since 2001, but was reported to have been arrested by, or possibly to have given himself up to, Pakistani security forces in the summer of 2008. His whereabouts is unknown, though a newspaper report in early 2009 suggested that he might have been released in a prisoner exchange for the kidnapped Pakistan Ambassador to Afghanistan in late 2008. A large number of prominent figures within the Helmand Taliban have been killed. In some instances, however, there are claims that leaders have been killed as the result of betrayal by competing elements within the leadership structure.

The most prominent Helmandi figure within the Quetta Shura, the overall leadership structure of the Taliban, was Mawlawi Akhtar Mohammad Osmani. He was killed in an air strike in Helmand in December 2006, but there were claims, not wholly far-fetched, that he might have been betrayed by the other prominent military leader of the Helmand Taliban, Mullah Dadullah Akhund. Dadullah, a member of the Kakar tribe, had a reputation for extreme behaviour and insubordination during the Emirate period. Indeed, Taliban folklore has it that he was stripped of his command on at least two occasions by Mullah Omar. He was also widely reputed by Taliban commanders to have had a difficult relationship with Osmani and on one occasion in 2006 to have had a fist-fight and beaten Mullah Osmani. "Dadullah was an indescribable person," claimed one awed Helmand Taliban commander in October 2008. "He was known as 'The Butcher' because he was cutting men's heads off. Even within other Taliban groups people were afraid of him. I remember when he laid down his weapons to Mullah Omar in the Emirate time. He threw away his plastic leg as well and said 'the (Taliban) government can take this too'."

Dadullah built up a large semi-autonomous network of several hundred commanders both inside and outside Helmand and his charisma and ferocity briefly gave him a media profile akin to that of the extreme Al Qaida in Iraq commander Abu Musab Al-Zarqawi, whose behaviour he appeared to ape. He also claimed support for Al Qaida in a number of media interviews he gave. This independence appears to have alarmed the Quetta leadership. There are claims that Dadullah provided intelligence that led to the death of Mullah Osmani in a British bomb strike in December 2006. There were equally claims from Dadullah supporters that figures within the Taliban leadership betrayed Dadullah, leading to his death at the hands of British Special Forces in Helmand in May 2007. His successor was his brother, Mansur, and it appears that the Quetta Shura made a concerted effort to rein in the Dadullah network after the elder Dadullah's death. Commanders loyal to Mansur Dadullah claim that he was always loyal to Mullah Omar's leadership: "Mansur Dadullah comes from a holy family," said a Taliban commander interviewed in March 2008. "There was a meeting in Quetta talking about the leadership. Some people in the meeting were saying Mullah Omar is weak. They were saying he is not strong enough to be the leader. Mansur Dadullah was silent. Then he pulled out a pistol and pointed it around the room. He shouted 'who doesn't like the Emir Al-Momineen Mullah Omar.' He was very, very angry."

However, it is widely suggested that Mullah Baradar, who became the most senior Quetta Shura figure in southern Afghanistan after the death of Mawlawi Osmani, sought to take greater control of the Dadullah network. In January 2008 it was reported by Taliban spokesmen that Mansur Dadullah had been relieved of his command by Mullah Omar for insubordination and because his commanders had gained a reputation for criminality. Mansur Dadullah responded angrily through the media denying the charges, in what was a clear fracture in the Taliban command structure in the province. Mansur Dadullah was injured and captured by Pakistani forces in February 2008. Helmandi Taliban commanders allege that his capture was also the result of a tip-off from figures opposed to him in the Taliban leadership. "Mansur Dadullah created his own government away from the Taliban," alleged two Helmand commanders interviewed in Kabul in October 2008. "It was the Quetta Shura who passed him (to the Pakistanis)."

The death of Mullah Baradar was reported by NATO in late August 2007 in Sangin. However, as with many such reports its veracity is doubtful. Taliban commanders joke about the frequency with which Mullah Toor Jan, a senior figure in the Taliban in Musa Qala, has been reported killed by NATO. They insist he is still alive despite at least three separate reports of his death. Following the deaths of Osmani and Dadullah, and the capture of Mansur Dadullah and Mullah Rahim, there are no personalities to match their stature within the Taliban structure in Helmand. "There are others like Dadullah. But now no one wants to be a big name because then they become a target," said one senior Taliban commander from the Garmser area in March 2008.

The effectiveness of Western Special Forces attacks on Taliban commanders is a source of constant concern for the latter. The Taliban suspect that many of these attacks are due to Western surveillance of phone networks: "Our leaders who are using the phones are also getting killed by the air strikes. Especially the satellite phones," said a Helmand commander interviewed in March 2008. "We have a rule that anyone in the villages with a Thuraya phone has to be authorised to carry it by Taliban." Another commander interviewed in March said: "We have a lot of problems with using Thuraya from the British, though we have not noticed any problem with the local mobile networks. We lost one of our big commanders last week with seven bodyguards. He was using a satellite phone. The same night the British came down from helicopters and killed him. I don't want to say his name."

Relations with elders, the population and local authorities

It is clear that the Taliban enjoy active support from a minority, and the sympathy of a larger minority and the acquiescence of a majority of the population. The Taliban presence tends to be highly mobile and it is common for Helmandis to claim that their usual interaction with the Taliban is when fighters move through areas and stay in villages. This is an imposition that they have little choice but to tolerate, but many people complain about the danger from Western aircraft or ground attacks when Taliban are in the area. For the majority of Helmandis the Taliban represent a problem, an irritant and a potential source of danger. However, Western forces in Helmand are perceived in much the same way, and in those areas that are effectively held by the Taliban there is a widespread respect for the Taliban's ability to deliver security, which is often contrasted with the insecurity and predatory behaviour of the local police in government-held areas. Local people also contrast the efficiency and impartiality of Taliban enforced Sharia with the government legal system. "Security is 100 per cent under Taliban," said Senator Haji Mahboob Khan, "there are no robbers in the whole district. Justice is very effective."

The particular interpretation of Sharia and Taliban social edicts appears to have been devolved to the discretion of high-level commanders at a provincial level by Mullah Omar in 2007, according to sources in the Taliban. In Helmand this has resulted in some more relaxed interpretations in areas such as Garmser and, during summer 2008, in Nad Ali and Marja. "They are quite different from the first period (1996–2001), they do not care about people wearing the turban or the cap, there has been some amendment," said Haji Mahboob of Garmser. "They are not opposed to NGOs if it is in the national interest. They allow cleaning of the Karezes (underground water channels) under the National Solidarity Programme. They would not allow a government representative, but would allow a supervisor not linked to the government. The majority of people were happy with peace and security. But the educated suffered. There were no roads or schools, people want clinics and doctors, they want reconstruction, telephone was banned. When they do not have the whole country, the Taliban are not so tough on the people." People in Lashkargar in September 2008 reported a strikingly less repressive interpretation of the Taliban's social edicts after the Taliban incursions into Marja and Nad Ali. "These are not like the old Taliban who destroyed your cassettes, shouted at you and beat you. When they were in government they were harsh," said one Lashkargari man, Mohammad Zahir. Many other local people reported similar changes with bans on television, music, dog-fighting, kite flying and other pastimes all relaxed as well as the demand for turbans and a fist length of beard. It was also reported by local people that the Taliban were offering amnesty to police and government officials who defected.

Mr Zahir's own explanation for the change was: "Now they need food and shelter so they are nice. If they get to government again then they will be harsh again. I don't trust them." Others, however, appeared more convinced. "Support for the Taliban has gone up a lot," said one man among a group of shopkeepers interviewed in September 2008, expressing a view that appeared to be widely shared. While the Taliban may now be adopting a more flexible approach to the local populace, they have historically adopted an extremely harsh approach to government officials, almost always executing them, and a generally repressive attitude to both tribal elders and clerics who have shown any pro-government sentiment. The assassination of government officials appears to have been almost metronomically efficient as the Taliban pushed government influence out of outlying districts of the province in 2006 and 2007.[15]

The role of tribal elders has historically been one that the Taliban has sought to usurp with their own structure of religious networking. However, though they are often harassed, it seems that the Taliban are judicious in the instances where they kill tribal elders. This is likely to be because of the Taliban's need to retain support levels within local communities, the danger of sparking concerted anti-Taliban action by the community, and the fact that in many instances they come from those communities themselves. In Musa Qala, for instance, the Taliban did not kill the elders of the Alizai dominated *shura* in the town, even when they took the town in February 2007. Instead they gave beatings to the tribal elders, which caused most to flee to Lashkargar. In 2008 there was further intimidation when they kidnapped eight members of the Alizai *shura*, but again they stopped short of killing them. "The Taliban got the signature of each that they would not support the government further," said Haji Salim Khan, a member of the *shura*.

Like many other Helmandis, the Alizai Shura members argue that the Taliban are not hugely strong, particularly not if the populace is united and aggressive against them. "The thing is that the people have no confidence in the government," said one member, interviewed in September 2008. "The Taliban are stronger, but it is because of the weakness of the government." However, they say that the Taliban appeared to become more confident in killing local people in 2008 around Musa Qala. Generally the pattern across the province appears uneven, emphasising the localised nature of the struggle and looseness and devolution of the Taliban's command structure. "The tactic of the Taliban is when they first arrive they are so nice to find who their friends are and who their enemy. Then they change and implement their law," said one *shura* member. Instances of open defiance against the Taliban in Helmand are few but not unknown. In May 2007 a school teacher in Sarwan Kala, an Alokozai area, assassinated a Taliban commander operating in the area, named Haji Wali Mohammad, and two of his bodyguards. The attack was reported to British intelligence sources and corroborated by Alokozai tribal leaders. The cause was the Taliban commander's refusal to leave the area with a band of up to 50 fighters and the fear of NATO bombing of the area among local people.[16] The Taliban commander was killed after he left a meeting with local people. According to Alokozai sources in the area, the teacher then sought refuge at the main British base in Sangin but was turned away with his family. En route for Kandahar they were caught and the man beheaded. One Alokozai leader from the area said that local opposition to the Taliban was badly affected by the failure of Western forces to offer support to the man.

Open defiance of the Taliban remains relatively uncommon. However, in November 2007 British military commanders reported that a village in the Upper Sangin Valley had made an offer to raise an anti-Taliban militia if British forces would supply weapons and logistical support. British intelligence also reported that the inhabitants of Sarwan Kala banned the Taliban from the bazaar. The Taliban then established an alternative bazaar nearby.

Spying on behalf of the government appears to be relatively widespread among the populace in some areas, taking advantage of the mobile phone network established since 2001 in the province. In October 2007 this author was with British officers and Afghan translators on the roof of the District Centre in Sangin as they took up to a dozen calls a night from local sources informing on Taliban movements in the area. Taliban paranoia over spying is acute. "Last Friday we got two spies, I shot them in the head with 16 bullets each," said a commander interviewed in Lashkargar in September 2008. "The spy problem has been stopped for now. We had another spy in Garmser. His wife was a good Muslim. He had a machine for contacting the foreigners. He told his wife it was a free radio but she told the *mujahidin*. They killed him. The British give a special coat to their spies. It has mirrors to show the planes where to go. The spies drop a tiny piece of metal on the roof of a house, it sends a signal so the British can bomb it." The same commander explained that the Taliban maintained a network of contacts in villages to identify potential spies to them. "We have our own secret police to tell us who is good," he claimed. "We have a trustworthy person in each village to tell us who is good."

As in other Taliban-influenced areas of the country, phone companies have been periodically ordered to turn off their phone masts or face Taliban attacks since March 2008. "In the night we stay in a village and immediately they come with an air strike," complained a commander interviewed that month. "The reason we turn off the towers is that when we go to the villages there may be spies who will call the government or the infidels."

How the Taliban are organised: military, administration and judiciary

The Taliban's structure in Helmand is a loose one in which the pyramid of command has been flattened by the ability of Western forces to target senior figures within the organisation. As described above, the overarching leadership of the organisation resides in Quetta, the seat of the 23–man Taliban Shura. Taliban fighters generally report that they serve rotations of frontline services inside Helmand before withdrawing for rest and refit in Baluchistan. The time frame for these is not exact. In March 2008 one commander from the Garmser area claimed that he had served alongside Turkish Jihadists in Helmand who were "very tough" and fought a six month on and six month off rotation. "It depends on your strength of belief how long you spend in the frontline," he said. "Some even spend 12 months in the frontline." The same commander claimed that his unit was serving three-month rotations followed by 15 days of rest. "But we are *jihad* addicted," he added, "so we come back after only 10 days."

The basic military formation of the Taliban is the *mahaz* (front). This is a far from exact term. Typically it would describe a very basic formation of fighters, approximately 20 in number, grouped around a single charismatic leader. The formation would typically arrive in the Taliban as a formed band, with its own weapons, and generally maintain a man in Quetta to organise funding from the leadership structure. However, the term *mahaz* can be expanded to include multiples of that unit size banded together and acting in coordination under a more senior commander. There is every indication that the personnel within a *mahaz* are usually fixed and personally linked to their commander. They are his *andiwal* ("comrades in arms"). They are likely, though in a far from exact way, to share network ties which could come from blood relations, tribe, ties of village or locality, attendance at the same *madrasa* or ties going back to the Taliban period of government. Certainly, they would usually have a bond predating their joining the particular *mahaz*.

If the commander is killed his successor is usually his brother, nearest relative or the strongest lieutenant in the group. The strength of the unit appears to derive principally from the strength and charisma of the leader and the ties that bind them. The particular focus on the commander's role appears to produce a culture of elevated self-sacrifice on the part of fighters, often heavily indoctrinated *madrasa* students, in defence of their leaders. "The lower levels will sacrifice their lives to save the leadership," said Major Dirk Ringennburg. "When they charged my machine guns it would be to sneak a commander away. We learned they are doing something so crazy to protect a commander. These younger *madrasa* kids, they were very brave. The Taliban are a very good army, but not a professional army. They would all get fixated on the fight that is happening. We would flank the enemy and every time we caught them by surprise. But the dudes in Iraq have not got shit on the Taliban—the Madhi Army, the Baathists etc.—they are not very brave. We caught *madrasa* trained kids from Pakistan who had no idea about the outside world, no idea of what it is to surrender. They were a very dangerous enemy—you could see it in their eyes."

While the *mahaz* unit is the basis of the Taliban fighting structure, it is important to note that the commander of Taliban band of fighters is not necessarily given the status of a full *mahaz* commander. This is how the structure works, as explained by a 23-year-old commander in Helmand in early 2008 with four years fighting experience:

"You have to be wise and brave to get a *mahaz*. In two weeks I am hoping to receive my own *mahaz* (a decision made in Quetta). Some people get it after only one year, but for some people it takes ages. One *mahaz* is a minimum of 20 fighters. The *mahaz* means you are an independent commander. You don't receive orders, you give orders. Otherwise you are a sub-commander. The average age to get a *mahaz* is 25 now. The next level up, you have a big commander who has many *mahaz* under him, maybe as many as 10 *mahaz*."

The number of different *mahaz* operating in Helmand is very hard to estimate. The British estimate that approximate regular Taliban fighter numbers do not exceed 1,000 suggests that no more than perhaps 50 individual *mahaz* should be operating in Helmand. But a commander from the Nawa district of Helmand claimed in an interview conducted in September of 2008 that there were 25 *mahaz* operating in Nawa District alone. Simply extrapolating from this figure and guessing at 25 *mahaz* of perhaps 20 fighters in all 13 districts of Helmand produces an overall strength of 6,500 fighters. This is clearly wildly inflated. I would suspect that the original 25 *mahaz* estimate for Nawa is exaggerated; in my experience inflation of 100 per cent is not uncommon in the numerical estimates I have heard in Helmand. In addition the number of districts with a sizeable Taliban presence would be limited to approximately seven districts, with the others either largely in government hands or sparsely populated desert areas. That might produce a figure of up to 3,000 fighters, but with variation for forces rotated out of the province for rest, and with a measure of possible exaggeration in the original figure, perhaps 1,000 to 2,000 fighters seems a reasonable estimate. Inevitably this figure is only just better than guesswork, and the true figure must also fluctuate with the season and with the scale of operations being planned by Taliban commanders in Quetta. In early 2008 NATO and the Taliban both offered estimates of around 500 fighters in the fixed frontline positions held in Garmser.

The level to which full-time fighters are supplemented with so called "$10 Taliban" pulled in for particular operations is a moot point. Among the Taliban the idea provokes outrage: "It is a great insult to Taliban that the foreigners are saying that Taliban are getting paid. It is not true. We get no salaries," claimed a Taliban commander interviewed in March 2008. Certainly the regular commanders and fighters I have met have not given off signs of wealth. But it does seem plausible that, whether because of money, pressure to join, or peculiar sets of circumstances, Taliban numbers are quite often supplemented by temporary local additions. This happened particularly during the large-scale fighting around the district centres in 2006. It also appears to have been the case during Taliban lead attacks on the government Poppy Eradication Force in Nad Ali in early 2009.

On the ground, though, Taliban fighters are not typically encountered in concentrations of more than a few dozen, and frequently engage Western forces of platoon strength or greater with as few as half a dozen fighters. A British officer based in Forward Operating Base Gibraltar in the upper Gereshk Valley in December 2007 estimated local Taliban numerical strength at 30 to 40 regular fighters operating out of the town of Hyderabad a few miles to his north and a further 30–40 regular fighters moving southward, sometimes into his area, from further north. Ambushes on his patrols were regular but typically conducted by around a dozen Taliban fighters, sometimes by half a dozen. The weather was cold at the time, which probably suppressed Taliban activity somewhat, but the numbers were seen by the British as typical of the sort of formations they were meeting on their tour. In Sangin in October 2007 British officers estimated the presence of three separate *mahaz* operating around the town. To the north near Ju Salay was Faizal Rahman's *mahaz*, which was using small arms and rocket propelled grenades to mount attacks. In the centre were Sher Agha's forces which used small arms, mortars and occasional suicide bombers. To the south of the town Haji Adam was operating a further front which also ran supplies to the north. Attacks on ANA and British bases south of Sangin involved, at that time, small arms and air-burst Rocket Propelled Grenades with forces numbers of typically around 15 fighters. But British officers still estimated in September 2008 that the Taliban were able to concentrate 150 fighters at one time if required. In late September NATO estimated that around 170 fighters were massed around Lashkargar to attack the city. As so often with Taliban attempts to coordinate and concentrate force, the attacking force was destroyed by Afghan ground troops and NATO attack helicopters. However, Western officials later admitted that it had come close to successfully penetrating the city defences. An additional 300 British troops were subsequently sent to Afghanistan to bolster defences around Lashkargar.

The targeting of Taliban commanders appears to be a major problem for the Taliban, and to have contributed to the increasingly loose formation of the organisation. "Now, after Dadullah's death we have a motto that everyone is a Dadullah. There are many smaller commanders now," said a commander interviewed in March of 2008 in Lashkargar. "Whoever is called a leader, we listen to them." The commander of British forces during the summer of 2008, Brigadier Mark Carleton-Smith, assessed that the Taliban were a battered but durable opponent:

"The Taliban is now not monolithic or homogenous. It is riven with deep fissures and fractures. It is still tactically reasonable resilient and certainly quite dangerous. It is an amoeba, impervious to losses. Its ability to join tactical actions to achieve strategic intent is very limited. Its potency lies as a force for influence."

The competence and enthusiasm of the Taliban are uneven and there are certainly reports of Taliban units that are of very limited military value. An Afghan interpreter employed by the British to listen to Taliban radio exchanges around Kajaki described almost comical attempts by different commanders to shirk combat and foist the responsibility on other commanders. "The Taliban are getting weaker and no longer do the face to face fights," he claimed. "They are always saying 'the tanks are coming, get ready, move to the ambush position'. But when the ISAF forces get close one commander will say 'you attack, I am too far away'. The other commanders will say 'no, you attack'."

The question of logistics is one that receives a great deal of attention from Western military commanders. The Taliban's logistical lines to Quetta and even to the Pakistan border are quite long in Helmand. Thus supplying the insurgency with arms, ammunition and fighters with food represents a challenge. It is clear that the Taliban's campaign is a relatively economical affair, at least by comparison with their opponents. Some supplies of ammunition are transported in from Pakistan or Iran by Land Cruiser, in what appears to be a trade that utilises the already existing flow of drugs out of the country by the same route. "We do not carry it in by hand. We have vehicles," said a commander interviewed in March 2008. "The Iranian Land Cruisers bring it in. They are the smuggling vehicles for the drugs. They are six cylinder vehicles, very powerful. There is just one driver, the rest is ammunition. They come in across the desert. When we are moving around we carry 10 days of ammunition on our bodies in a parcel and at least ten grenades to throw." The supply of weapons from outside Afghanistan appears, though, to be a relatively minor part of the Taliban's logistical chain. More significant are huge existing stockpiles of weaponry left in the country by 30 years of war and supplies that are either smuggled from other areas of the country or bought from corrupt government police and army personnel. "There was more RPG and machinegun ammo out there in Helmand than we will ever find—local police, everyone said so," claimed Major Dirk Rigennberg, who served in Helmand in 2005. "We would rarely catch a Talib carrying a weapon—they were always cached. We were finding caches of RPG rounds. We would find 1,000 of them and it wasn't even the tip of the spear."

These stocks are clearly still extant. The dry climate in southern Afghanistan helps to preserve them, but nonetheless there is corrosion of explosive material, combined with poor maintenance of weaponry by Taliban fighters, which means that misfire and failure to detonate rates are high particularly for RPG and mortar rounds. Taliban fighters have economised by making much use of old artillery shells, mortar rounds and RPG warheads as the explosive component in roadside bombs. "We enjoy finding UK bombs unexploded," said a commander interviewed in September 2008. "We have people, not Afghans, who come and use it back against the British. Bomb making is a profession for us all now." A commander interviewed in March 2008 also claimed to be outfitting his group with ammunition bought from corrupt Afghan police in Lashkargar, paying 10 Pakistani rupees per bullet. Two commanders interviewed in September 2008 were adamant that no shortages would be felt by the Taliban and that there was an increasingly effective supply route for arms and ammunition running through Ghor to the provinces of Faryab and Badghis in the north of the country. "I bet that for more than 20 years there will be no need to go to another country for help with ammunition or weapons. There was no DDR of the huge depots. Commanders are buying from the police and the ANA. There is ammunition coming from Ghor. The Land Cruisers of the smugglers go from Musa Qala to Maimana (in Faryab) with guarantees to deliver. We call the route the Siaband: Faryab, Badghis, Ghor and Helmand."

Indeed the role of the Taliban High Command in Quetta in supplying the fighters on the ground seems to be limited to relatively small amounts of high value weaponry, such as occasional stocks of specialist mines or bomb detonators, centrally allocated suicide bombers trained inside Pakistan and periodic injections of cash. "We have magnetic bombs. They make the bomb in Pakistan and we receive it through Spin Boldak," said a commander interviewed in September 2008. "It is a green bomb that is about 40cm across." The same commander also claimed that high tech bombs to be operated by computer were delivered to them and operated by foreigners, whom he would not identify.

The role of outside forces linked to foreign governments remains a subject on which clearcut evidence is rarely available to back up widespread claims. However, there is enough corroboration to support claims of some highly calibrated assistance apparently coming to the Taliban from Pakistani ISI advisers and elements that are at least Iran based, if not Iranian government organised. In late 2006 a well connected Alokozai tribal source in Helmand named an Iranian intelligence agent, Sardar Baghrani, as having visited Helmand during the summer months and met insurgent figures in the Nad Ali and Marja areas. His presence has been reported on several subsequent occasions by tribal sources in Helmand. The US commander in Afghanistan, General Dan McNeill, alleged that on 5 September 2007 that two trucks from a convoy of four trucks were intercepted after crossing the Iranian border into Nimruz and found to be containing well-constructed Explosively Formed Projectile (EFP) devices. EFPs significantly increased the capability of Iranian backed militants in Iraq, producing devastating roadside bombs which succeeded in defeating the armour of main battle tanks on a number of occasions. There have, though, been no reports of EFP attacks in Afghanistan since the alleged finds.

Western diplomats have said they believe that elements linked to the Al Quds force of Iran's Revolutionary Guard are supplying weaponry to the Taliban, or at least to some individual commanders. Senior Western military figures confirm that a meeting took place in Peshawar in late 2007 between Iranian intelligence agents and members of the Taliban and Hizb-e-Islami. Clearly weaponry is flowing across the Iranian border But is unclear what proportion of this is coming from ethnic Baluch supporters of the Taliban who live in Afghanistan, Pakistan and the Sistan-Baluchistan region of Iran. They are Sunni, have a history of involvement in smuggling, and have established sympathies with the Taliban. Interviewed in September 2008, the police chief of Helmand, Assadullah Khan, specified Mawlawi Abdul Hamid, a cleric from Zahedan, as a figure organising the supply of weapons from Baluch sympathisers to the Taliban. Interestingly the Iranian government has alleged that a Sunni militant Baluch group called Jundallah, operating in Sistan-Baluchistan, is covertly supported by the British and American governments, suggesting a highly complex dynamic in that region.

Pakistani ISI links to Taliban commanders are widely alleged by Western diplomats and military commanders, though British policy in particular is to constrain public criticism because of the assistance the ISI gives to British domestic intelligence gathering on British citizens of Pakistani origin. British military officers have claimed that a Pakistani found dead on the battlefield near Sangin during the summer of 2007 had papers identifying him as an ISI officer. Pakistani authorities averred that the man was "on leave" at the time of his death. A senior British officer interviewed in 2008 mentioned several insurgent commanders with ISI links, naming two commanders in the Garmser area, Mullah Naeem and Mullah Mahboob, in particular. Pakistani officials claim that any such links are historic and date to the period when Pakistan openly supported the Taliban prior to 2001. If such links persist, it is claimed that they are the work of "rogue elements" within the Pakistani security apparatus. Western and Afghan officials suggest otherwise.

Civil and judicial administration

The area where the Taliban are seen to be a force for good is their ability to deliver a particularly tough brand of justice and security. Here they are often contrasted with the ineffectuality and indeed malign influence of Afghan government structures, most notably the police force. Interviewed in March 2008 the then Helmand Police Chief, Mohammad Andiwal, was candid enough to admit that he had arrested 37 of his own officers for offences ranging from corruption to kidnapping in the first month he was in office. "In government held areas the police arrest the criminals for a couple of days, then the criminals pay a bribe and are released," said a local man named Mohammad Illyas in March 2008. "When you go to the Taliban held areas there is justice. The Taliban are chopping off hands." A 25–year-old small time opium smuggler, Abdul Wali, interviewed in Lashkargar in early 2008, claimed: "There is no security in this area, but the Taliban areas have security. You can move money, do your business openly. We give money to the Taliban by the name of God and charity, but you volunteer this and you aren't forced. That is the reason the people support Taliban. Here (government held areas) you must pay money for everything. The Taliban act on the criminals and there is no bakshish (bribes)." At a refugee camp on the Lashkargar in March 2008, interviewees told a similar tale: "The Taliban hate criminals," said a man named Rahmattulah. "In the Taliban areas you have money and you are safe. Here the police take your last Afghani note."

The administration in Taliban held areas seems to be very basic, but effective in its delivery of a basic level of security and harsh but impartial justice. The exact model of governance that is adopted appears to be devolved to local Taliban commanders by order of Mullah Omar in last 2007. A Taliban cleric from Helmand, interviewed in March 2008, explained:

"Mullah Omar made a declaration (apparently in late 2007) that the commanders' responsibility is to introduce Sharia to the local law, but not to be too harsh. Commanders are responsible to Mullah Omar, but they have to respond to the public. That is according to Mullah Omar's wish. We don't have to break the borders of the Emirate Law. Shaving is not a crime now; if you want to wear a turban or not, this is up to you. But if you have a single complaint about commanders you can say it to the Shura."

In Garmser, an area the Taliban were able to hold for a protracted period, the Taliban government apparatus appears to have developed several layers. Haji Mahboob Khan, a senator from Garmser interviewed in July 2008, said: "Justice is very effective. The Taliban built up the *shura* system. They had a central *shura* and a sub-*shura* made up of Taliban alongside tribal leaders to settle disputes over water and other matters. Or the issue was referred to the Taliban court system of three judges."

This was simply the re-establishment of the existing tribal *jirga* system rooted in Pashtunwali rather than Sharia law, with an option to refer matters up to the more punitive Sharia system. According to the Taliban cleric from the area:

"We are running the courts—for complaints. We are 4 or 5 judges in the courts. Often as a judge we are doing negotiation between two sides. If the meeting is on Tuesday and one side has not got any evidence prepared then we are delaying until Wednesday. Ours are the permanent courts. The sentence is often to chop the hand. People mostly try to sort things out themselves rather than bringing the case before Taliban."

In Garmser the cleric claimed that NGOs were allowed to operate and, despite internal opposition from more hardline Taliban commanders, a school was allowed to operate within certain restrictions. "We allow all the NGOs to work there around Garmser," said the cleric. "They are cleaning the canals there. They are local NGOs that are sub-contracted to the internationals. We allowed the school to reopen with 300 pupils. There are 12 teachers and the deal that we have with the community is that six must be *Ulema* (clerics). One teacher has the responsibility to report on the school to the Taliban; to make sure that they are not teaching Christianity and not spying for the British." Senator Mahboob Khan only partially corroborates this claim: "They were not opposed to NGOs in the national interest," he claimed. "The majority were happy with peace and security. But the educated suffered. There were no roads or schools. People want doctors and clinics. They want reconstruction. Telephone was banned." The Senator also complained about the Taliban's internal security component, known as The Commission. "The Commission were chopping off the heads of those they accused of spying. Four people were killed who were completely innocent."

Assessing the overall quality of life in Taliban held areas, Senator Mahboob Khan said:

"When they occupied the area they immediately made structures. They are much better now than they were in the time of the regime. But it is only a temporary system, not a permanent system. The Taliban did not help with reconstruction, but then they never did before either. The Taliban do not care about people. I advise my people to do deals with the Taliban because who guarantees that the foreigners will stay? They are not trustworthy."

The Taliban's ability to deliver a basic level of justice is widely acknowledged and indeed admired. The Taliban were able to score an effective public relations coup in September 2008 by simply imposing a very basic order on the Marja district bazaar after displacing government militias from the area. "When the government was in charge, the police were beating people and stealing from them," said Maleeq Khan, a Lashkargari. But he explained that at the first bazaar after the Taliban took control of Marja there was no stealing by the Taliban and the only beating was of a thief the Taliban caught stealing a motorbike. "The Taliban covered his face and clothes in the black oil," said Mr Khan. "Then they paraded him through the bazaar. The children were throwing things at him and they made the thief stand on a platform and state his name, his father's name and his crime to the people. Then they beat him and threw him out. He won't do it again." The impact this small incident had was considerable in Lashkargar and was widely mentioned in interviews conducted with local people at the time.

In spite of their generally effective reputation as dispensers of justice and security, the increasingly anarchic situation in Helmand has seen this reputation damaged by accusations that Taliban sometimes engage in criminal behaviour. This appears to have been linked to some degree with the erosion of the Taliban's leadership structure and internal cohesion. "Everyone feels like they can give orders now," said Abdul Ahmad Rohani, a local reporter based in Lashkargar in March 2008. "Day by day there is greater distance between the people and the Taliban. They have their private interest and people are realising this. If you are a bandit or a thief you wear a black turban, do what you want, and say that you are a *mujahid*. To be honest in the Taliban held areas there are no thieves, but in the disputed areas the thieves proliferate." Rohani was abducted and killed in July 2008.

The view of a Taliban commander, an older man, interviewed in September 2008, was that:

"In the beginning the Taliban were holy and good people. There are still good people. 50 per cent of the Taliban are still people who believe in God, country, who are respectable. But 50 per cent are people who are robbers or bring personal enmities. There are many robbers in Taliban, but it is now an emergency situation in the country. The Taliban are trying to purge these people, but their first priority is to weaken the government."

This was also acknowledged by a commander operating in Garmser in an interview in March 2008. "A lot of local criminals were using the name of Taliban for their own interest," he said. "A lot of them were sacked. Some people in Taliban were taking people, killing them and taking their money." The commander also claimed that a new edict had been issued to Taliban forbidding them to take food from the populace "unless they are given permission".

In late 2008 Western military commanders anticipated that expected food shortages and price rises would put an increasing strain on the Taliban's preferred method of moving across territory and demanding food and lodging in local villages. In early 2008 a number of Taliban commanders contacted by phone in Helmand and other areas of the country spoke of a concerted attempt by the Taliban to conduct an "internal audit" of Taliban commanders and men, with a view to rooting out criminal elements that had attached themselves to the organisation. However, this clearly did not extend to the drugs trade, which has become increasingly central to the Taliban's development in Helmand.

The proportion of funding that the Taliban receive from the drugs mafia, as opposed to the Quetta command structure, seems to have shifted significantly over time. By some estimates it may be more than 50 per cent of the total that comes from the drugs mafia now. "Over 50% of the money for the *jihad* now comes from the Zakat (charitable donations) from the smugglers," said one commander interviewed in Lashkargar in early 2008. That estimate is supported by one Western analyst in Kabul who estimates that an original 80–20 per cent split in funding between Quetta and local sources of income has now shifted to around 50–50. US Defence Secretary Robert Gates estimated that the Taliban was making between $60–80million dollars from drugs in October 2008; the majority of that would come from Helmand. One can speculate that this would reduce the effective control that the central command structure is able to impose and, together with the ever more loosely controlled internal command structure within the province, makes the Taliban in Helmand an organisation that is increasingly fractured and prone to the breakdown of internal discipline.

Conclusion

If Kandahar is the spiritual home of the Taliban movement, then rural Helmand is where its simple ideology found its strongest support base in the 1990s and where the insurgency since 2001 has been fiercest. However, the fighting in Helmand is more than simply an ideologically driven war against weak and corrupt central government and an 'infidel' military occupation. It must be viewed through the prism of Helmandi local politics, of inter and intra tribal friction and competition between criminal networks for resources, through the economics of the narcotics trade, through the wrecked and dysfunctional social and tribal structures left by 30 years of conflict and the rise of feudal warlords.

Since 2001 the conflict and the Taliban have gone through a process of evolution. As of early 2009 it appears that the old structure of the Taliban in Helmand is breaking down and the influence of the Quetta based leadership is being eroded. Partly this is the result of Western military pressure, particularly the technological advantage of Western forces that allows them to relentlessly pick off Taliban leaders dependent on phone communications networks. But it is also due to the enormous financial temptations presented by the drugs trade and a gradual fusing of the insurgency with the narco mafias; a marriage based partly on shared interest in instability and partly on greed. The access to drugs money has made the Taliban in Helmand a more or less self-financing enterprise and given figures within the lower structures of the leadership access to large amounts of money. This has helped to mutate the insurgency into something that appears increasingly anarchic, criminally driven and tribally based. The Taliban do not enjoy very high levels of public support in Helmand, but Western forces and the Afghan government do not either. Ironically this leaves a lawless scenario not unlike that which inspired

151

the original Taliban to emerge as a response to the chaos and corruption of the Mujaheddin government of the early 1990s.

Notes

1. A. Giustozzi and N. Ullah, "'Tribes' and Warlords in Southern Afghanistan 1980–2005", Working Paper, Crisis States Research Centre, London School of Economics.
2. Ahmed Rashid, *Descent Into Chaos*, New York: Viking, 2008, p. 323.
3. The casualty rates apparent in Mullah Qudratullah's account are not untypical. Another commander who joined in 2004 from Nawa District of Helmand said that he joined with three other boys from his village. As of March 2008 one is dead, one is disabled by injury, one is in prison and the commander is still fighting, though he suffered shrapnel injuries to his shoulder.
4. The consensus among Helmandis that the 2001–5 period saw a disastrous loss of faith in the new government and its Western backers is extremely consistent. A Taliban commander interviewed in September 2008 said: "Generally Dad Mohammad Khan and those others were offensive to everyone. The main cause of making the Taliban problem was these gunmen." A Helmand tribal leader interviewed in September 2008 said: "There was huge hope for the new government. People waited three or four years, but nothing happened. Instead the cruel leaders were redeployed and supported by the government. They brought back the jihadi leaders. We thought King Zahir Shah would return and the people would be educated and prosperous."
5. Sher Mohammad Akhundzada complained: "The DDR programme did not take place at the right time. After the ANA was strong enough to take over it should have happened." Despite his considerable self-interest it is a valid point.
6. "We left by April," said Major Dirk Ringennburg. "I would like to have been a liaison to the British but that did not happen. When the Canadians came in, we spent several months with them. We showed them the tactics we had developed, we drove them to every corner of the battlespace. We got into some fights alongside them. They really absorbed a lot of the operations we had been doing."
7. When I interviewed him in December 2006, Governor Daoud categorically denied British military claims that he forced British commanders to deploy to the Platoon Houses. "The ISAF mandate was to support Afghan security institutions. When we felt there was an enemy threat, we asked for help. To a large extent they replied positively. Every decision we made together. This was not a governor's decision, but a governor, Security Council decision involving NDS (Afghan intelligence service), police, army, NATO, PRT, FCO (British foreign office) decision. It is true that the governor chaired these meetings, and therefore my position was stronger, but we decided on these matters together. The minutes of the meetings are there. If (Brigadier) Ed Butler, who I consider a close friend, if he chose to accept these instructions, there were many times he did not accept other instructions. The British were not under our control. ISAF's job was to implement as a joint effort, as partners. If he wanted he could have not put his forces into these places (the platoon houses)."
8. Maiwand lies a few miles to the east of the border between Kandahar and Helmand. It was the scene of the most famous Afghan defeat of British forces in Afghan

history. The battle contains one of the most celebrated incidents in Afghan history when Malalai, the bride of an Afghan soldier, ran onto the field as the Afghan army began to give way, raised her bridal veil as a flag and exhorted her husband to greater efforts with the words: "Young love, if you do not fall in the Battle of Maiwand, By God someone is saving you as a symbol of shame!" According to legend the Afghan army was galvanised and the British suffered a comprehensive defeat with the 66th Regiment of Foot, making a last stand around their regimental colours on the edge of the town to cover the British retreat.

9. Many Helmandis concur that they reserve a particular hostility for British soldiers. At a refugee camp on the edge of Lashkargar in February 2008, a man from Garmser named Rahmatullah claimed: "The British are old enemies. They want to kill us and our children. Whatever they want to bomb they bomb, whatever they want to kill, they kill." There is also more general xenophobia present among the Pashtuns of the south. Haji Matoor Khan, a Noorzai tribal elder interviewed in June 2008, said: "Afghans are village people. They do not like foreigners. They like people who speak their language, understand their people, have the respect for the community."

10. Some of the fighting in Helmand in 2006 seemed to echo the infamous words of a US army major in Vietnam in 1968: "It became necessary to destroy the village (of Ben Tre) in order to save it."

11. Christina Lamb, "Top soldier quits as blundering campaign turns into 'pointless' war", *The Sunday Times*, 10 September 2006 http://www.timesonline.co.uk/tol/news/uk/article634344.ece

12. A Taliban bombmaker interviewed in September 2008 described his particular pleasure in using British-dropped unexploded aerial ordnance against UK forces. Though he also described Pakistani made magnetic mines and more sophisticated remote controlled devices, most of the IEDs were being made using old ordnance, often in combination with non-military improvised equipment such as gas canisters.

13. Personal communication.

14. Personal communication.

15. "From the Ulema (clerics) they killed Mawlawi Salim Mohammad and Mawlawi Amanullah Mufti," said Wali Jan, MP, interviewed in 2008. "In 2006–7 they killed Kohim Jan, the Dishu police chief, Amanullah Khan, his successor, Shadi Khan, his successor, Abdul Khaliq, a jihadi leader in Marja and Haji Kabir Khan, a jihadi leader. These commanders fought the Taliban and after collapse of Taliban they had positions in the government. Then they were DDRed. The Taliban went and killed them." Sher Mohammad Akhundzada lists a number of Jihadi commanders and tribal leaders killed in the 2005–6 period: "Mawlawi Salim Mohammad, Mawlawi Sayed Gul, Amir Akhund from Gereshk. When the DDR started the commanders were not ready to help. People started not supporting the government and recontacting the Taliban."

16. The incident coincided with a collateral damage incident near Sangin involving US Special Forces in which 20 local people were killed.

7

UNRULY COMMANDERS
AND VIOLENT POWER STRUGGLES

TALIBAN NETWORKS IN URUZGAN[1]

Martine van Bijlert

Uruzgan, an unruly province

Uruzgan was established as a separate province in 1964, but it is still very much seen as part of "greater Kandahar" (which includes Kandahar, Helmand, Zabul and Uruzgan), with the main tribal, political and economic networks transcending the current administrative boundaries. Uruzgan's population is estimated at 395,000, with the overwhelming majority of the population (97.6 per cent) living in rural areas.[2] The province's original inhabitants, the Hazaras, were forcibly expelled from western Uruzgan by King Ahmad Shah Baba in the mid-18th century and from eastern Uruzgan by Amir Abdul Rahman Khan in the 1890s. Their lands were given to the Pashtun tribes that had helped quell the uprisings. As a result the province is now populated by a wide variety of Pashtun tribes and sub-tribes. Around 40–45 per cent of the population are Durrani Zirak (Popolzai, Barakzai, Achekzai, Mohammadzai and Alokozai), about 30 per cent are Panjpai (mainly Noorzai and Khugiani), about 15–20 per cent belong to the Ghilzai tribes (Tokhi, Hotak, as well as Niazi, Kakar, Taraki, Wardak, Suleimankhel and Mullahkheil). There is a sizeable Hazara minority (around 10 per cent), mainly concentrated in pockets in the districts of Khas Uruzgan and Gizab.[3]

Being remote, mountainous and poor, Uruzgan has traditionally had low levels of education, a limited government presence and high levels of conservatism and violence, even by Afghan standards. Uruzgan has no great strategic importance, but gained symbolic significance as the province where many of the Taliban's original leaders come from (or spent considerable time) and as the place where President Karzai started his uprising against the Taliban in late 2001. This has however not translated into any particular attention to the province from either side, and the area is largely left to local power play and infighting, both by the central government and by the central Taliban command, with both sides seeking to use rather than control or mitigate existing conflicts.

Although the tribal system in Uruzgan has never been as strong as in the east and southeast, tribal affiliations continue to be the dominant factor shaping political and social loyalties. In particular the sub-tribe remains the main solidarity group, defining patterns of loyalty, conflict and obligations of patronage. The importance of these affiliations and divisions has increased since the Taliban's collapse, owing to the absence of functioning and credible government institutions and local governmental policies that have encouraged tribal polarisation. The (potentially) armed group remains the main organisational unit, despite disarmament drives under the various regimes.[4]

Earlier attempts to govern

Government presence in Uruzgan has been limited under all regimes. In pre-revolutionary times, the government largely depended on feudal land-owning elites to deliver the loyalty of their subjects. The Communist government tried to establish a new bureaucracy, but lost control of the entire province, with the exception of the bazaars of Dehrawud and Tirin Kot, within a year of coming to power—after having detained and executed a large number of local leaders. The continued presence of the Communist government in Dehrawud and Tirin Kot suited all sides, as it justified continued requests to their backers for additional resources. While the main *mujahidin* commanders kept up an appearance of fighting the Communist administration, the government's policy of "national reconciliation" proved quite successful; almost all commanders are said to have entered into some form of agreement with the local government (only two commanders were mentioned as having been "irreconcilable").[5]

The main *mujahidin* parties in Uruzgan were Hizb-e Islami (both Hekmatyar and Khalis), Harakat-i Enqelab-e Islami (Mohammad Nabi), Mahaz-e Melli (Pir Gailani), Jami'at-i Islami (Ahmad Shàh Massud) and Ittehad-e Islami (Sayyaf). Loyalties were however somewhat blurred, with local commanders often linking themselves to multiple parties depending on which one could provide weapons and resources at any given time. Among the Hazaras the main parties were Sipah-i Pasdaran (Kazemi), Nasr (Khalili) and Harakat-i Islami (Mohseni), although there were also a few Hizb-e Islami commanders. *Tanzim* affiliation among the Hazaras seems to have been more clear-cut and remains very much relevant to current-day relations.

As in most areas, much of the combat activities concerned inter-factional fighting, although there were attempts to solve the worst feuds through tribal mediation. There were bloody conflicts between Hazara and Pashtun commanders in Gizab and Khas Uruzgan, which were mediated by among others Pir Gailani; there was a re-run of the longstanding Popolzai-Barakzai conflict (during which Jan Mohammad, who was governor at the time, saved Hamid Karzai from a Barakzai assassination attempt in the early 1980s); and there was a multitude of bloody clashes between rival commanders, usually over resources or over prominence within their sub-tribe. Examples of such fights include the power struggles between Mullah Khudainazar and Haji Ikhlas in Dehrawud (both from the Sultanzai sub-tribe), the fight between Haji Gholam Nabi and Khalifa Saadat in Dehrawud over prominence within the Babozai, and the fight between Haji Hodud and Haji Hashem Khan (both Tokhi) in Darafshan, which was reported to have started as a conflict over an RPG and escalated from there.[6] Such conflicts are of course not between individuals, but between their extended families and supporters, and often start with one of the relatives or supporters killing or humiliating someone from the other family or sub-tribe.

A few commanders managed to achieve a degree of prominence within their tribal group and controlled larger areas, but in general power was dispersed among a multitude of small commanders, whose support networks and areas of activity were largely arranged along sub-tribal lines. This continues to be the case.

The Taliban regime and its fall

After the Taliban took Kandahar in 1994, they marched on to Uruzgan province almost without a fight. As in most places, people were tired of the infighting and lawlessness under *mujahidin* commander rule and welcomed the new order in the province. Many of the top figures in the Taliban military hierarchy were from Uruzgan and several local commanders landed positions in the Taliban administration. Prominent local figures who were from the "wrong" tribe or *mujahidin* party were marginalised and harassed (there are the usual reports of forced disarmament and extortion), but were otherwise largely left in peace. There were no reports of large-scale armed resistance and it seems that practically all commanders and leaders entered into some form of accommodation with the Taliban regime. This may explain why it was initially so difficult for Hamid Karzai to mobilise the province's tribal leaders for his armed uprising against the Taliban in October 2001. It was only after it was clear that he had the backing of US Special Forces that he managed to mobilise a significant following.[7]

After the fall of the Taliban regime, many of the Taliban leaders and commanders sought guarantees from the new administration that they would be left alone if they laid down their arms—as is customary—and went home. However, the ongoing American "war on terror" and traditional predatory behaviour, carried out by those who had been deposed by the Taliban and were now reinstated, resulted in the targeting of a wide range of tribal leaders and commanders, including many of the Taliban leaders who had surrendered. The targeting had a strong tribal dimension, with the Popolzai-dominated local administration seeking to marginalise the weak (the Ghilzai and Panjpai Durrani) and to divide the strong (Barakzai and Achekzai).[8] Tribal grievances and the alienation of former Taliban commanders thus strengthened the re-emerging insurgency and ensured a base level of popular support higher than in other Pashtun regions.

The return of the Taliban[9]

The resurgence of the Taliban movement in Uruzgan has been closely linked to the behaviour of the province's local powerbrokers, in particular that of Jan Mohammad, the first governor after the fall of the Taliban, and the commanders linked to him. Jan Mohammad, who had been close to President Karzai's family since the 1980s, used his relations with US Special Forces and his reputation as an effective Taliban hunter to target a wide range of tribal leaders and former Taliban officials, particularly from the Ghilzai and Panjpai tribes. Leaders who were targeted during the early years, mainly in counter-insurgency and counter-narcotics operations, and who have since then gained prominence in the armed insurgency include Mullah Shafiq from Mirabad, Haji Nassim and his brothers from Charchena, Dr Anwar from Khas Uruzgan, Kheirullah Akhundzada and Mullah Amanullah from Darafshan, Mullah Gul Badu from Tirin Kot district, and Mullah Abdul Wali from Dehrawud (killed in August 2008).

The areas in which the insurgency first resurfaced were, unsurprisingly, the Ghilzai areas of Mirabad and Darafshan in Tirin Kot district and the Panjpai areas of Charchena and Dehrawud. The insurgency in the Achekzai and Barakzai areas of Khas Uruzgan, Gizab and Chora started later and is to a larger extent shaped by internal sub-tribal rifts and power struggles (which have in some cases been intentionally provoked and escalated). Currently the insurgency is at its most virulent in Mirabad, while most of Charchena and Khas Uruzgan remain no-go areas for anyone openly linked to the government, with the local administration in these districts essentially under siege. Gizab has been totally in Taliban hands since the district governor vacated the area in 2006. Military operations in Darafshan in September 2007 and in Dehrawud in January 2008 have, for the moment, considerably limited the insurgents' freedom of movement in these areas (the effect of the October 2008 operation in Mirabad could not yet be assessed at the time of writing).[10]

The re-emergence of the Taliban in Uruzgan was greatly facilitated by the fact that many prominent figures within the Taliban leadership hailed from the province. Such leaders included Mullah Omar himself, but also Mullah Baradar and Mullah Dadullah "Lang" (killed in 2007), Taliban ministers Mullah Noorudin Torabi (Minister of Justice) and Mullah Abbas Akhund (Minister of Health), as well as Mullah Mir Hamza and Haji Gholam Nabi (both reported to be members of the Supreme Council) and several Taliban governors. These figures had gathered around them lower-level commanders and officials, largely on a tribal and factional basis, so that when the targeting of the former Taliban started there was a strong network of commanders who had worked and fought together, which was easy to revive. Several of the current Taliban commanders in the Darafshan and Mirabad regions, for instance, served together in the east (Khost, Paktia and Ghazni) and the north (Mazar, Kunduz and Maimana) under the Taliban regime, often as each others' deputies or group commanders. This included a generation of younger men who had not participated in the armed resistance against the Soviets, but were linked to these old networks through the commanders they were working for. This greatly facilitated the revival of the Taliban as an armed insurgent movement.

The core of the Taliban movement in Uruzgan is stable and is being fed by a pool of potential commanders, occasionally shifting allegiances from the government to the Taliban and vice versa. These commanders are a combination of the old *mujahidin* fighters and the younger generation who were given positions under the Taliban regime. So far there seem to have been practically no commanders without a history in either the *mujahidin* or the old Taliban networks rising to prominence within the current movement (with the exception, possibly, of the relatives of prominent commanders killed in battle, who are then expected to fill the gap, as happened with the brothers of Mullah Dadullah and Mullah Mutaleb).

The lengthy detention of former Taliban officials in the Guantánamo Bay prison has led to the emergence of a new class of Taliban "notables": the Guantánamo returnees. Although many of them were not involved in combat activities when they were arrested and have not joined the armed insurgency since they were released, they gained a certain increased "moral standing" and are now seen as potentially very influential within the Taliban movement, both by the fighters on the ground and by those who seek to influence the movement or to lobby certain leaders.

The Taliban in Uruzgan thus seem to roughly follow the model suggested by Ruttig (2007) when discussing the Taliban structure: a series of concentric rings with at its core a Taliban leadership of "fighting mullahs", an inner circle of indoctrinated and highly ideological *madrasa* students, and an outer ring of local fighters who have joined the movement for a variety of non-ideological reasons—often because of tribally based grievances, or for economic gain.[11] However Ruttig's suggestion that the core and the inner ring represent continuity between the old and the new Taliban and that the outer ring is new does not correspond with the situation in Uruzgan. In Uruzgan many of the non-ideological Taliban commanders who fight because of local grievances, and who in this model would be part of the outer ring, were also linked to the former Taliban regime (they were not necessarily ideologically motivated at that time either, apart from possibly hoping for the return of the king and some form of Islamic government). These commanders are locally prominent, but are too distant from Quetta to be considered part of the local leadership. However, they cannot be considered a new generation of fighters either.

The Taliban 'caravan'

Bernt Glatzer has described the original Taliban movement as a "caravan, to which different people attached themselves for various reasons".[12] This continues to be a valid description. Over the years it has become clear that Afghans themselves use the term "Taliban" loosely for a wide range of people and use various criteria to distinguish between the different categories of Taliban. Such distinctions include:

- the *Taliban-e jangi* or *Taliban-e shuri* (fighting or insurgent Taliban) as opposed to the *Taliban-e darsi* (the *madrasa* students) or those who are labelled as being Taliban without being involved in active combat
- the *Taliban-e asli* (the real Taliban) or *Taliban-e pak* (the clean Taliban), which usually refers to the "non-corrupted" Taliban committed to Islamic principles of justice and purity, as opposed to the more opportunistic and violent parts of the movement; sometimes also as opposed to the *Taliban-e Pakistani*, i.e. the Taliban who are described as doing Pakistan's bidding and who are considered to be working to undermine the country's welfare[13]
- the *Taliban-e duzd* (the thief-Taliban), which is used to describe local bandits and thugs who use the cover of the movement to prey on the population
- the *Taliban-e mahali* (local Taliban), as opposed to the Taliban from outside who are generally considered to be more violent and indifferent to the population's interests; however not all *Taliban-e mahali* have a "softer touch" and some of them are known to be *zalem* (cruel) and *badmash* ("good-for-nothing")—usually even before they joined the Taliban
- the *Taliban-e khana-neshin* (the Taliban sitting at home), which is generally used to refer to those who held positions during the Taliban regime, but have not been actively involved in the movement since its fall; they may be residing in their areas of origin or may have taken refuge in places such as Quetta, Kandahar or Helmand.

These descriptions eloquently convey the message that not everyone who is called a Talib is considered an enemy. This message is reinforced by the frequent use of the concepts of *majbur* (forced) and *naraz* (dissatisfied) to explain the behaviour of leaders who have linked themselves to the Taliban. *Majbur* is used to describe those who were forced to leave their area after they were, often unjustly, targeted by local authorities or international forces for their alleged or former affiliation with the Taliban. Such targeting usually involved public humiliation (for instance arrest—hooding and shackling—in front of their families or searches of their houses, including the women's quarters, and looting of their property). In a culture where honour and revenge are central to a man's stature, many saw no other option than to join the resistance or, if they did not wish to do so, were unable to stop the young men from their tribe from joining. *Majbur* is closely related to the concept of *zalem* (cruel), which is used for commanders, whether linked to the government or the Taliban or operating independently, who are exceptionally violent and predatory.

Naraz is a term generally used for local leaders who, over a considerable period of time, have not been treated in accordance with their social standing. They are disgruntled that they have been offered no government positions or privileges and are not being consulted on important security or community matters. The key concept in both instances is the loss of face and prestige in front of the tribe or constituency, which forces the local leader or head of the family to act, either by leaving or by hitting back. The twin push factors of *majbur* and *naraz* have been crucial to the rise of the Taliban in Uruzgan, and the fact that they are regularly invoked illustrates the widespread view that many fighters would want to return, provided that the main push factors of predation and humiliation were removed.

The variety within the Taliban movement also illustrates that the movement has a spectrum of enemies, and that not all Taliban fighters will attack the whole range. There are countless links between the local population (including the authorities) and the local Taliban, and the way the people think of individual Taliban commanders, and are seen by them, tends to depend on tribal and factional proximity. Even those who are known to be ardent Taliban opponents are linked to individual Taliban commanders through tribal ties, marriage or shared history (as former classmates, neighbours or brothers in arms) and will use these links when necessary.[14] Many families in the meantime seek to maximise their collective patronage networks by having family members in all relevant power structures, as has been the pattern under all regimes.[15]

Some commentators have sought to portray the Taliban insurgency as a Ghilzai uprising against a Durrani government, implying that the Ghilzai have to be defeated for the government to survive.[16] This analysis however disregards the Durrani strands within the Taliban (for instance, the strong Taliban presence in the Achekzai areas of Khas Uruzgan and Gizab and the Popolzai strand which is linked to Mullah Baradar—the movement's number two—in the areas of Dehrawud and Nesh) and implies possible exacerbation of tribal tensions. Many Afghans from Uruzgan, from all tribes, have argued that the way forward is rather to end the marginalisation of the Ghilzai and the Panjpai and to reconcile with those who are willing to accept reconciliation.

Relations between the Taliban and the local population

There are different ways in which the Taliban movement seeks to assert its control over the local population—through threats, intimidation and harassment; taxation and forced disarmament; enforced guarantees of safe passage; the provision of justice; and limiting the freedom of movement of people whose loyalties are considered dubious. In some cases this takes the form of actual house arrest, while in other cases local leaders' freedom of movement is curtailed because all routes out of the area pass through hostile territory. Leaders in outlying districts, who wish to keep a certain distance from the Taliban, have to tread very carefully. They need to limit visits to administrative centres and other "suspicious" places, and are often ultimately forced to leave their areas of origin. A large number of leaders have been killed, while even more have been beaten or otherwise targeted (however, not all were killed by insurgents, as government-linked commanders have also used their positions and the ambiguity provided by the prevalent insecurity to target rivals and to settle old scores). Even leaders who have openly aligned themselves with the government and who live in relatively safe areas are regularly contacted by Taliban commanders, who try to persuade them—through threats or appeals to Islam—to change sides. In the meantime, arrests and raids by international military forces have also prompted the departure of a large number of influential elders (who are influential precisely because they have links on both sides), thus further weakening the social fabric of the communities.

It is difficult to gauge the level of popular support for the Taliban as a movement; relations between the Taliban and the population can best be described as ambiguous. Local commanders and fighters can count on the population for shelter, food and sometimes weapons and money in large parts of the province, but this does not necessarily imply heartfelt support for the movement. Local Taliban commanders know how to use the existing ties of loyalty and obligation (tribe, kinship, a shared *jihad*), as well as the fear that they can instil. The fact that areas which fall into insurgent hands often turn into war zones from which the population is forced to flee has in several cases prompted communities to ask fighters to leave, or to at least refrain from launching attacks from residential areas—with varying success. The recent rise in food prices is reported to have affected the willingness of populations to feed groups of fighters that are passing through. At the same time, many Afghans feel alienated and betrayed by the predatory behaviour of government and security officials, the civilian casualties due to aerial bombing and what is perceived as heavy-handed and misguided search operations by international military forces. It is clear from many conversations that large parts of the civilian population feel caught between several forces—Taliban, international military, local government, violent commanders—none of them able to provide the security that would allow people to live in their villages in peace and with dignity.

Local leaders and populations often seek to negotiate with the Taliban— and vice versa—either directly or through messengers and written letters (depending on the level of presence). Such negotiations can involve requests for safe passage, permission for NGO activities, punishment of criminals or the reining in of oppressive strongmen, mediation in conflicts, or the removal of fighters from residential areas. Some leaders seek to enter into protocols with Taliban commanders, according to which both sides agree to leave each other alone. This usually means that the Taliban agree not to enter the area or

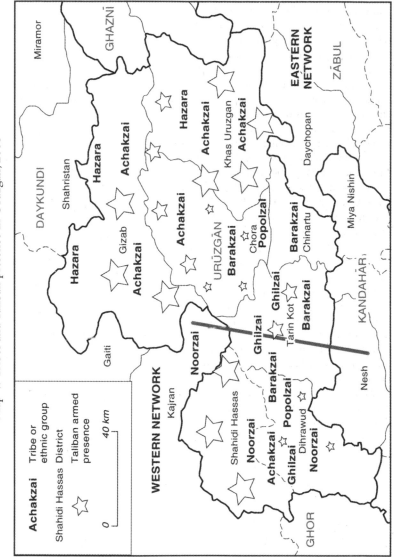

Map 4: Tribes and Taliban presence in Uruzgan, 2008

harass its residents, and not to take from its resources, on the condition that the community agrees not to work with the government (or NGOs) and not to establish an armed presence. Such agreements however do not necessarily lead to a sustained relaxing of restrictions, as Taliban district governors and commanders who are considered too accommodating are sometimes success-fully replaced by the Quetta leadership, in an attempt to retain control of what happens on the ground.[17]

Local populations have also tried to stand up against the Taliban, for instance when they sense a build-up of forces and fear that these will enter their area, or when the behaviour of certain commanders is considered unac-ceptable. There have been reports of Taliban commanders being beaten or chased out of certain areas (for instance in Darafshan and Gizab), but their removal tends to be temporary. Other interventions include the negotiated or enforced release of tribal leaders who have been detained or taken hostage, such as the release of Mullah Khodainazar in Dehrawud in late 2007 (he was later killed in May 2008, after he had reconciled with the local government, most probably by government-linked commanders) and Haji Naqibullah in Khas Uruzgan in January 2008. Both had been detained by Taliban com-manders from rival sub-tribes who intended to kill them, and both were released after their own sub-tribe mobilised and threatened to violently inter-vene. A commander in Gizab recounted how in 2007 he had closed a road that was used by the local Taliban (i.e. rival commanders) and did not allow them to pass until they had released a captured relative (whom they had wanted to trade for weapons and ammunition).

The Hazaras of Khas Uruzgan have reportedly started threatening their Pashtun neighbours with a repetition of the bloody Hazara-Pashtun wars in the 1980s, if they do not restrain the increasing harassment and targeting of Hazara leaders by local commanders linked to the Taliban. In the outlying areas, however, Hazaras tend towards "negotiated submission", as there is nobody who will come to their rescue if the conflict should escalate.[18] The relationship between Hazaras and Pashtuns in Uruzgan is further compli-cated by the use of Hazara militias by American Special Forces, as will be illustrated below.

The theft of NGO project money by local Taliban commanders from Gizab in late 2007 sparked a traditional tribal lobby. The elders not only petitioned the local government to intervene, but also sent representatives to Quetta to complain to the Taliban leadership. Although this did not lead to the money being returned (even though according to the local population the com-manders had been ordered to do so) the incident illustrates the dynamic relationship between communities and the Taliban network.[19]

The Taliban structure in Uruzgan: a movement with many faces[20]

Western and eastern networks. The Taliban fighters in Uruzgan are roughly divided into two geographically separate networks, one in the west and one in the east. The western zone, which roughly covers Dehrawud and Charchena, is directly linked to Mullah Baradar (Popolzai from Dehrawud, whose influence is strongest in the southern part of the network) and Mansour Dadullah (Kakar from Charchena, brother of the slain Mullah Dadullah "Lang", with more influence in Charchena and among the Noorzai). There have however been indications of rifts between Baradar and Dadullah, for instance during the Taliban offensive in Dehrawud in late 2007, when there almost seemed to be two separate operations going on: one dominated by Noorzai commanders aimed at localised revenge and one directed by Mullah Baradar as part of his announced "Nusrat" offensive. Taliban commanders in the western area include Tor Mullah Zeinullah (a Babozai from Dehrawud in the Baradar network), Mullah Abdul Wali and Haji Nassim (both Noorzai, respectively from Charchena and Dehrawud) and "Sur Tekai" (red-spotted) Mullah Ismail (Taraki from Dehrawud). Gholam Nabi Aka, the main Babozai leader from Dehrawud, is also said to have joined the Taliban, after having been consistently marginalised and accused of collaboration—which may or may not be true. The western network is linked into northern Helmand (particularly the Zamindawar valley), north-western Kandahar (Nesh, Ghorak) and southern Daikondi (Kijran) and covers important drug trading routes. Military operations in northern Helmand have a direct impact on the situation in western Uruzgan.

The eastern zone covers Gizab, Khas Uruzgan, Chora, the newly established district of Chinartu (although Taliban influence is limited here) and the north-eastern part of Tirin Kot district (Mirabad and Darafshan). Commanders in the Mirabad and Darafshan area are linked to Mullah Yunus and Mullah Shafiq, who are both in Pakistan, with Mullah Qaher acting as the main local commander (respectively Tokhi and Hotak from Mirabad). Mullah Yunus is said to be responsible for operational matters in Zabul, Uruzgan and Ghazni. The main Taliban commanders in Khas Uruzgan hail from two different Achekzai sub-tribes and are involved in an internal power struggle. Those involved include Qari Abdul Aziz, Mullah Azizullah, Mullah Hamidullah (all three Matakzai, some of them related to Senator Hanifi), and Mullah Hamdullah and Mullah Abdul Razeq (both Alizai). Non-Achekzai commanders include Qari Qodratullah (Suleimankhel) and Dr Anwar (Mullahkheil originally from Ajiristan). The main Taliban commanders in Gizab include Mullah Assadullah, Mullah Kheirullah, Mullah Abdul Hakim and Mullah Salam, while the main Chora commander "Sur Stergai" (red-eyed) Mullah Akhtar Mohammad was recently reported killed.[21] He is said to have been succeeded by another Achekzai, Mullah Shah Mohammad. The eastern network is linked into Kandahar (Shah Wali Kot, Mianeshin), Zabul (Meizan, Arghandab and Daichopan, which is a major supply base for the Uruzgan Taliban) and Ghazni (Ajiristan, locally referred to as Daya).[22]

The divide between the two networks is largely based on the tribal and geographical characteristics of the area, with the eastern zone roughly covering the Ghilzai and Barakzai/Achekzai areas of the province and the western zone covering the Noorzai, Babozai and Popolzai areas. The zones are sepa-rated by mountain ranges with only a few passes connecting them. The divide also coincides somewhat with the pre-1964 administrative boundaries, when Khas Uruzgan belonged to Ghazni (forming the *loy woleswali* Uruzgan, together with current-day Ajiristan and Daichopan) and the rest belonged to Kandahar province.[23] Gizab is where the two networks meet. The area is connected to the eastern network through its Achekzai Pashtun popula-tion and the routes into Chora and Khas Uruzgan, and to the western net-work through the routes into northern Helmand, via Kijran and Charchena, while commanders from Charchena play an important role in the district's power play.

Mobility between the two networks is limited. Commanders from one side seem only rarely to cross over to the other side for operations or consultation, which suggests that there is little direct coordination or cooperation between the networks. They rather seem to operate in parallel, both reporting to the Taliban shadow governor (who in turn reports to the Quetta leadership for operational matters) or directly to the Quetta leadership. The few foreign fighters in the province are mainly concentrated in a number of bases in out-lying areas (Charchena, Gizab, and a valley in the far north of Chora). During military operations their numbers and spread tend to increase. There have been reports of a kind of mentoring system, where international jihadist fighters are "seconded" to mobile Afghan combat groups to increase their effectiveness.[24]

Establishing a shadow administration.[25] Uruzgan has a rudimentary "Taliban administration", which is appointed or confirmed by the Quetta *shura*. The main leaders of this administration seem to spend much of their time in Quetta. The Taliban shadow governor at the end of 2008 was Baz Moham-mad, a Popolzai from Nesh district and a close confidant of Mullah Baradar. He was appointed in September 2007 after his predecessor, an Achekzai from Khas Uruzgan, was killed in a Coalition air attack. His appointment was probably in support of the September 2007 Taliban operations in Dehrawud. There was some confusion over whether he remained governor after he was wounded in June 2008 (during that time his position was temporarily filled by either his deputy Kheirullah Akhundzadah or Mullah Bari Gul), but he is believed to have taken up his position again since then.[26] His authority should, in principle, have covered the whole province, but there are indica-tions that his authority over commanders in the eastern network was limited. He was for instance said to have been slapped by Mullah Qaher, who did not appreciate being summoned to Quetta over his role in the killing of a spir-itual leader.[27] The deputy governor, Kheirullah Akhundzadah, a Taraki from Darafshan, was said to have rejoined the insurgency only after several of his family members were killed and he himself was arrested and beaten by local authorities—even though he had been promised a dignified surrender after the collapse of the Taliban regime.[28]

The rest of the Taliban administration is more fluid than reports mapping Taliban structures often suggest. Local sources tend to disagree on who the "officials" are at any given time and what their exact positions and responsibilities are. In practice, several key commanders are interchangeably described as security commander (*qomandan-e amniya*) or front commander (*qomandan-e mahaz*) or as responsible for operations (*massoul-e amaliyat*), guerrilla warfare (*massoul-e amaliyat-e cheriki*) or military matters (*massoul-e umur-e nezami*), leaving analysts and observers with diverging lists of who is who. This fluidity of the "administration" seems to reflect the fact that the Taliban in Uruzgan remain, in the first place, an armed insurgency. The "officials" tend to be military commanders, whose main importance remains their role on the battlefield (with the exception of the judges), as in the days of the Taliban regime when officials up to minister level were sent to the front lines to fight. Names often mentioned as having provincial security responsibilities include Mullah Qaher and Mullah Yunus (respectively Hotak and Tokhi from Mirabad), Mullah Hamdullah (Achekzai from Khas Uruzgan), Mullah Janan Agha (Seyyed from Darafshan) and Mullah Bari Gul (Taimani from Darafshan, reported to have been arrested in August 2008).[29]

There is a similar confusion at the district level, with a limited number of names—sprinkled with occasional new contenders—interchangeably being put forward as shadow district governor (*woleswal*) or security commander (*qomandan-e amniya*).[30] The confusion is compounded by the fact that the positions can be hotly contested, particularly in areas with no effective government presence, which results in multiple claims and counterclaims. The various candidates tend to be local, in most cases from the district itself (or in the case of Dehrawud and Charchena from the neighbouring district, which socially and tribally is considered part of the same area), with the exception of Gizab where some of the contenders came from Dehrawud or Charchena, probably illustrating the importance of the district for the route into Helmand. The hottest contest is in Khas Uruzgan, where two Achekzai sub-tribes (Alizai and Matakzai) are vying for the positions of Taliban district governor and security commander. This competition has, in essence, very little to do with popular support for the anti-government insurgency; instead elders and leaders on both sides of the Taliban-government divide employ their influence to seek the "appointment" of their tribesman, in order to strengthen the hand of their sub-tribe and to provide opportunities for negotiations and favours when the need arises. For instance, the Senator from Khas Uruzgan (a Matakzai), who is considered a government supporter, is said to support his sub-tribe's bid for power in the local Taliban administration. There has as a result been a long string of changes and rumoured changes in the Khas Uruzgan administration over the last year.[31] This dynamic is, incidentally, very similar to the rumour mill surrounding government appointments, which is fed by the process of lobbying and the fact that a prospective candidate often tries to help the process along by prematurely announcing his appointment.

All of this suggests the superimposing of an "administrative structure" on existing power relations and power struggles, rather than a rigid system of top-down appointments. The Quetta leadership does however seek to influence the composition and behaviour of the local administration, and there have been multiple reports of local district governors being replaced over allegations of cooperating with the government or being "too soft" on NGO activities. The situation seems similar to the government administration under the *mujahidin* regime or in the early Karzai years, with administrative positions and changes being determined by a complex interplay of local dynamics and attempts to enforce centralised appointments or confirmations.

Appointments and replacements of Taliban district administrators are followed with great interest by the local population, particularly in areas where there is no effective government presence, as the differing opinions of the contenders on issues such as taxation, education or NGO activities are likely to have a direct impact on daily lives. News about appointments and changes tends to be passed around by word of mouth and is thus often inaccurate. Though there has been some mention of letters being sent from Quetta, announcing or affirming positions, this does not seem to be the norm and there is certainly no centralised and unambiguous system of announcements or appointments. New appointees usually try to establish their authority by a combination of threats, instructions and offers to mediate, communicated to the elders of the various communities. One of the many newly appointed district governors of Khas Uruzgan was for instance reported to have sent letters to the Hazara communities in early 2008, presumably in an effort to establish his credentials in the face of other contenders.[32]

Running a court system. There does not seem to be a coherent Taliban court system in Uruzgan, although there are attempts to establish at least the perception of some form of centralised rule of law. Mullah Gul Badu is said to be the chief judge for the province, residing in Pakistan and declaring *fatwa*s and rulings from there. The area where the Taliban are most likely to be able to establish a court system of their own is in Gizab, as there is no rival government presence and international forces rarely venture into the area. However, the relative strength of the local commanders and religious leaders, and the limited strategic importance of the area (other than as a safe haven), seem to have precluded the emergence of an organised Taliban-controlled local judiciary. Local religious leaders continue to deal with the local cases and although some of them may be linked to the Taliban, they seem to largely operate independently.[33]

There have been reported cases of locals petitioning Taliban judges, sometimes after tribal mediation or government justice did not produce the desired result. Local Taliban courts have also aimed to administer justice and punishment. There have been "death sentences" for alleged spies and government collaborators, but this often seems linked to the occupation of new territory and tends to take the shape of summary executions, as happened in Dehrawud in late 2007. Taliban judges do not seem to be able to effectively control the population or their own people and there have been instances where commanders who have been summoned to a Taliban court have apparently refused to appear (see below).[34]

Co-opting and controlling the commanders. The Taliban military structure in Uruzgan is a somewhat loose network of local commanders, who have been co-opted or intimidated into joining. Although these leaders and command- ers are given positions in the local command structure, which in turn answers to Quetta, many of them have sufficient local influence or fire power to allow them to act with a certain degree of independence. In some cases, the com- manders have been approached by Taliban leaders or tribesmen and asked to "establish a front", i.e. to gather their men and to be available for operations, in return for which they are equipped and possibly paid. Other commanders have "applied" to establish a front, explaining how many men they have and how much resources they need in order to be effective—in the same way that a commander may offer his services to governors, international military forces or road construction companies. To whom a commander chooses to link him- self usually depends on a combination of local circumstances (who is in con- trol, who are his tribesmen siding with), former contacts and networks (which people can he approach), local feuds (who does he want to take revenge on, or protect himself from) and opportunity (where will he get the best offer).[35]

A "front" (*mahaz* or *dilgay*) does not refer to a location or frontline, but is generally used for a group of sub-commanders commanded by a front com- mander. The front commanders in Uruzgan do not seem to be centrally appointed or assigned to a certain group of armed men, but rather become front commanders by proving themselves in battle. There are no indications that the Taliban leadership has the power to rotate commanders or determine their group sizes. Although they can instruct or request commanders to take their men elsewhere to fight, they do not seem to be in a position to interfere with the power base of the local commanders whom they have co-opted (just as the government is not really in a position to do so). There have been reported instances of local commanders refusing to fight in other places, after being requested to do so by visiting outside "delegations".[36]

The relationship between local Taliban commanders and the Taliban leader- ship is a highly dynamic one, in which the leadership seeks to increase its control, local commanders seek to retain their independence (while tapping into the resources that are on offer) and rivals seek to undermine each other through strategic affiliations. Local commanders are linked to the Quetta *shura*, in the sense that they receive arms and other forms of support and par- ticipate in centrally-led operations, but much of the day-to-day insurgency activities (attacks, ambushes, assassinations) is driven by local conflicts and grievances which long predate the current Taliban-government divide.[37] Big operations are usually led by commanders coming from outside (often Paki- stan, where they reside to avoid arrest and harassment of their families), although they may originally be local. The Dehrawud offensive in September 2007, for instance, was precipitated by the return of a large number of promi- nent commanders originally from Dehrawud and Charchena, most of whom had been living and/or fighting in Helmand and were being pushed out by the military operations in that area.[38] Local populations thus follow the move- ments of senior Taliban commanders very closely.

Local charismatic leaders who have joined the Taliban, bringing with them a large number of their followers, are usually not very mobile and commonly do not command a front. Their main aim seems to be the protection of their area, by allowing the Taliban nominal control and keeping out the "outside" Taliban—the foreigners and fighters from other areas who do not care about local relations and may spark cycles of revenge and feuding by their cruelty and harsh forms of justice. This has been most pronounced in Gizab district where, as there is no government to fight, there is less harm in allowing what is in essence a form of self-rule. This is a dynamic process in which the Quetta and provincial leadership seek to consolidate control over the co-opted leaders, who in turn seek to retain as much independence as possible. And although Quetta cannot move commanders around, it can seek to alter the balance of power by replacing district governors and other appointed office holders.[39]

The killings and arrests of key Taliban commanders can have unintended consequences.[40] The removal of key commanders often makes it more difficult for the leadership to control the many small commanders in the province, which in turn makes life more unpredictable for the population and for those trying to implement development projects in these areas, as the local Taliban structure is kept in continuous flux—without necessarily weakening it.[41] The removal of prominent local commanders can even result in an escalation of insurgent activities and influence, as illustrated by the June 2008 arrest of Mullah Assadullah by international military in Gizab. As a prominent local commander who had (nominally) rejoined the Taliban, Assadullah had facilitated and protected small-scale development activities and had managed to keep the more extreme forces—foreign fighters and outside Taliban commanders—from entering his area. His removal from the scene allowed other Taliban commanders to move in and facilitated the forced recruitment of a large number of local young men, many of whom died on the battlefield shortly afterwards (which in turn feeds local resentment).[42]

The fact that most commanders are deeply embedded in their own social and tribal networks makes the Taliban structure vulnerable to defection and double-dealing—as every regime and insurgency in Afghanistan will find. Even the most entrenched Taliban leaders are likely to be regularly sounded out by people they know, often acting as intermediaries. Prior contacts, deals and the calling in of favours may result in localised or individualised agreements to leave certain areas or individuals alone. The process, incidentally, goes both ways—government and security officials are contacted in the same way and may enter into similar agreements, leading them to disregard orders and turn a blind eye or to support certain insurgent activities.

Taliban actions in Uruzgan: revenge, rivalry and opportunity

The fact that the Taliban "caravan" in Uruzgan harbours a wide range of personalities, loyalties and enmities has resulted in a movement with many faces.

It is clear from reports on the ground that the Quetta leadership, which internally is not always in agreement on the way ahead, has trouble controlling the behaviour and activities of their local representatives. This unpredictability in terms of rulings and reactions is likely to remain one of the main obstacles to more widespread popular support, with recruitment remaining largely conditional on tribal or factional closeness to Taliban leaders. A closer look at some of the recent Taliban actions in the province will illustrate this point.

The killing of opponents. There have been a large number of assassinations and attempted assassinations in the province, which are generally attributed to the Taliban. On closer inspection, however, they are almost never that straightforward. There are usually multiple stories of victimisation and power play, while the killer, or the person ordering the assassination, and the victim almost invariably share a long history of rivalry, intrigue and pending revenge. This is illustrated in some of the more recent successful or attempted assassinations.

The killing of Kheirullah Jan Agha, a Barakzai *pir*, in April 2008, ordered by Mullah Qaher, was probably related to the fact that he was a rival spiritual influence whom the Taliban could not control (the killer, who was apprehended, apparently reported the existence of a "hit list" of influential leaders in the area). But there was also an old grievance—an unsolved water dispute between the Hotak and the Barakzai—in which the *pir* had played a pivotal role, among others by standing up to the local Taliban regime. It is unclear whether the killing had been sanctioned by the Taliban leadership, but the fall-out in terms of local anger and tribal mobilisation led the Quetta *shura* to distance itself from the act and to summon Mullah Qaher (who, as mentioned before, is rumoured to have slapped the shadow governor in response).[43]

The killing of two cousins from a Karimzai *khan* family in Gizab in May 2008 is believed to have been in revenge for the treatment of Mullah Hafez, a local Taliban commander who had recently been detained, beaten and humiliated (his beard had been cut off)—because, it was reported, he took too much money. One of the cousins, Mohammad Nader, in a bizarre twist, was killed by his own brother, who according to some reports had been detained and badly treated because Nader had ignored a Taliban summons to appear in court (over the treatment of Mullah Hafez). The other cousin, Mohammad Yunus, had been embroiled in a story of killings and counter-killings: he had shot dead Qodus Khan, the district governor of Khas Uruzgan in 2005, after he had been led to believe that Qodus was the killer of his brother Assadullah, whereas in reality his brother had most probably been killed by the local Taliban commander Dr Anwar in revenge for past mistreatment. While there are strong indications that Yunus was also targeted in relation to the mistreatment of Mullah Hafez, others believe that he was killed by the Qodus Khan family in revenge—an interpretation that is being actively propagated by local Matakzai leaders, who would welcome a further targeting of their (Alizai) rivals.[44]

Even the attack on the house of the Hazara security commander Shah Wali, in Khas Uruzgan in June 2007, is more complex than it seems. The attack was ordered (again by Mullah Qaher) after Shah Wali and his men had ignored repeated warnings to leave their jobs at the district's US military base. Shah Wali escaped but there were several casualties, including his mother and four attackers. The slain attackers were from the Mullahkheil and Sin tribes (one of the locals ominously described the latter as "a wild Sin with five brothers").[45] Their death led to the displacement of a large part of the village's population, who feared revenge—not necessarily by the Taliban, but by the Mullahkheil tribe from neighbouring Ajiristan, with whom they had been in war in the past, and by the local Sin population, who had long laid claims to the land on which they were sharecroppers. In the meantime, while Hazara elders decried the attack, some of them privately acknowledged that Shah Wali's militia had alienated the Pashtun population and endangered inter-ethnic relations by bragging about their anti-Taliban and anti-Pashtun exploits and by their alleged involvement in "false reporting".[46]

The killing of checkpoint commander Abdul Rahim in Dehrawud in November 2007 illustrates the risks involved in making deals with the Taliban (or anyone else for that matter). Abdul Rahim had surrendered to the Taliban, according to most accounts on the basis of a pre-existing deal. He however soon found out that the brokered reconciliation with one of his former enemies, Mullah Abdul Wali (with whom he had a long history of killings and counter-killings of relatives), was not going to hold. His tribesmen within the Taliban unsuccessfully tried to negotiate his release—they even lobbied the Quetta leadership—but he was ultimately killed, two months after his surrender; following a *fatwa* from Quetta.[47]

The killing in Helmand province of Amer Abdul Rahman Khan, one of the main Noorzai leaders from Charchena, in May 2008 is reported to have been ordered by the Helmand Taliban commander Mullah Khaksar, who considered him a government collaborator. Abdul Rahman had been forced out of Charchena after he fell out with Jan Mohammad (most probably over the division of drug spoils), but remained in regular contact with President Karzai. He was however accused of being a Talib, as many of his tribesmen had joined the insurgency and he himself was suspected of providing the Taliban with money and weapons. Other reports however suggest that Abdul Rahman's death was in revenge for one of many past killings (in this case from the Kakar tribe).[48]

In January 2008 the former PDPA-era governor and respected Popolzai elder Fazel Rabi was killed by a targeted IED. The family of Mullah Naeem, distant relatives with an existing grudge, was swiftly identified as probably being behind the killing (Mullah Naeem was killed months later in revenge, after he had joined the PTS reconciliation programme). Some believe that the killing of Fazel Rabi may have been encouraged by powerful Popolzai, who considered him a threat to their position.

Many of these killings are, at least in part, inspired by or embedded in pre-existing enmities. This should however not obscure the existence of a consolidated effort on the part of the insurgents to kill, terrorise and push out local leaders who refuse to be co-opted. In many cases, the wider policy of targeting leaders and the more narrow focus of private revenge have coincided, leading to a constant incidence of high profile killings.

Attacks on district centres and police checkpoints. The attacks on district centres and police checkpoints are often part of larger military strategies and should in principle be less prone to personal and tribal enmities and considerations. However, in many instances where checkpoints or district centres are overrun by Taliban forces, this is often based on a pre-negotiated deal between district authorities or post commanders and the attackers. For instance the abandonment of several police posts in Dehrawud in September 2007 was widely ascribed to a deal with the main post commanders, including the unfortunate Abdul Rahim mentioned above. The assault was probably meant as a visible sign of the "Nusrat" offensive announced by Mullah Baradar and aimed to establish a safe haven for Taliban fighters who were being pounded in northern Helmand. But it was also clear from local narratives that many of the commanders who returned to their areas as part of the offensive had revenge in mind and were looking for specific targets, in particular the local commanders who had linked themselves to the US Special Forces and who were considered *zalem*.[49]

The repeated aggressive attacks on the district centre of Khas Uruzgan in the late summer of 2007 were probably not meant to overrun the centre, as the proximity of a US military base with its promise of air support when needed made this very unlikely. The actions, according to the local population, were rather meant as a show of force, inspired by rage over the killing of the shadow governor, who was from Khas Uruzgan.[50]

In the summer of 2006 Chora fell to the Taliban, as a result, so it was reported, of a deal between the then district governor Haji Obaidullah and the local Taliban. Obaidullah had struck a similar deal the year before in Khas Uruzgan but was not prosecuted either time. Governor Hamdam tried to restore him as Chora district governor in 2008, but the population revolted. A second assault on Chora in the summer of 2007 was pushed back, but only after an ad hoc force headed by the former police chief Ruzi Khan, together with the Dutch ISAF forces, came to the aid of the besieged villages.[51] The government security forces had been nowhere to be found. There are strong indications that across the whole of southwestern Afghanistan such deals to temporarily allow a district centre to be overrun by Taliban forces are backed, if not ordered, by local strongmen who have been sidelined—in an attempt to illustrate (and increase) the weakness of the local government and to force their reappointment.[52]

As always, there are also the fights that start over small things. A case in point is the killing of Daro Khan in August 2007. Daro Khan, initially the mayor of Khas Uruzgan, joined the Taliban in early 2007. He was described by his opponents as a *badmash*, while his supporters say he left the government because he refused to become corrupt. Locals provided a detailed account of how he was killed after an attempted motorcycle theft had got out of hand: during the ensuing scuffle the Pashtun owners of the motorcycle had happened to flee to the house of Ibrahim, a known Hazara troublemaker (another *badmash*), after which Ibrahim and his brothers started a firefight with Daro Khan and his men. The escalating shoot-out was ended by several artillery rounds from the American military base, most probably called in by the Hazara side, killing Daro Khan. It should come as no surprise that Ibrahim has since then been killed by relatives of Daro Khan.[53]

Concluding remarks

The insurgency in Afghanistan is often interpreted as an ideological battle over who gets to govern and on the basis of which beliefs. In Uruzgan, however, it rather seems to be the continuation of what has become a very violent way of waging local power struggles. Many of the current mainstream counterinsurgency and governance interventions, unfortunately, do very little to strengthen the hand of local leaders who command the respect of their people and who pursue less violent means to solve conflicts. Although many of these leaders have been killed, terrorised or forced to leave their areas of origin, interventions that help consolidate their position can help transform the patterns of killings and counter-killings, which will otherwise persist long after the insurgency has been quelled or the regime has been changed. With this in mind, it is crucial that local reconciliation efforts do not focus only on the co-optation of formerly hostile commanders, but seek to de-escalate deadly conflicts and discourage *zalem* (cruel) behaviour on all sides. The worst of all worlds would be to not only employ violent and predatory commanders to wage the war on terror, but also welcome back—without conditions—the most violent Taliban commanders in order to "win the peace".

Notes

1. The analysis in this chapter is based on conversations over a period of several years with tribal leaders, commanders, villagers, government officials and NGO workers, who either are from Uruzgan or spent considerable time working in the province. Separate references to sources will only be made in relation to specific and detailed information.

2. Central Statistics Office's household listings of 2003–5 (*Afghanistan Socio-economic and Demographic National and Provincial Profiles*, UNFPA and Central Statistics Office, 2007). The estimates include the population living in Gizab district. Although Gizab was declared part of the newly established province of Daikondi in 2004, it was temporarily placed under Tirin Kot's responsibility again in 2006, after the district fell into Taliban hands. In terms of Taliban networks, Gizab is firmly part of Uruzgan.

3. There is confusion over whether the Babozai population in western Uruzgan (Dehrawud and Charchena) should be considered a sub-tribe of the Noorzai or the

Hotak. Originally a sub-tribe of the Hotak from Zabul, the Babozai are said to have joined the Noorzai under King Ahmad Shah Baba after being persecuted under King Nader Shah. Contacts were however reported to be maintained between Hotak elders in Zabul and the Dehrawud Babozai elders (interview with Babozai tribal elder in September 2007).

4. Shifts in power usually result in attempts by new power holders to disarm the parties that are no longer dominant, while strengthening and arming their own forces (although surrendering parties are usually allowed to retain some of their weapons—and honour). The local government under the Karzai regime has been no different. Formal DDR and DIAG disarmament programmes have thus not resulted in across-the-board demobilisation of factional groups, but were used to weaken opponents while keeping intact the system of armed groups based on tribal loyalties and shared economic interests.

5. Interviews with former *mujahidin* and former Communist government officials, June 2007 and April and May 2008.

6. Interview with tribal leaders from Khas Uruzgan, Tirin Kot and Kandahar in August and October 2007 and January 2008.

7. Interviews with tribal leaders from Chora and Dehrawud, a local security official from Dehrawud and an international analyst in May and September 2007 and June and August 2008.

8. Achekzai is a sub-tribe of the Barakzai, but as the sub-tribe takes precedence over the main tribe (Barakzai) in terms of loyalty, it is mentioned separately throughout the chapter.

9. This section is based on the analysis of information gathered over the last three years in interviews with tribal leaders from all districts. See also Antonio Giustozzi, *Koran, Kalashnikov and Laptop. The Neo-Taliban Insurgency in Afghanistan*, London: C. Hurst & Co., 2007, pp. 56–60.

10. However, the experience in Darafshan and Dehrawud suggests that if the operation is followed by the establishment of strategically placed security posts, it could lead to a reduced presence and freedom of movement of the fighters, provided that the security measures are complemented by measures that address the sense of grievance and exclusion, i.e. some form of reconstruction and political outreach and an end to predatory behaviour by local security commanders.

11. Thomas Ruttig, *Die Taleban nach Mullah Dadullah*, Berlin: Stiftung Wissenschaft und Politik, June 2007 (SWP-Aktuell 31/07), pp. 2–3.

12. Bernt Glatzer, as cited in Robert D. Crews, "Moderate Taliban?" in Robert D. Crews and Amin Tarzi (eds), *The Taliban and the Crisis of Afghanistan*. Cambridge, MA: Harvard University Press, 2008, p. 242.

13. Many people in the south have also commented on the existence of the *Taliban-e Amrikai* (American Taliban), expressing the widespread belief that international forces are, for reasons of their own, supporting and arming certain Taliban groups.

14. Even Jan Mohammad has intervened to secure the release of a Taliban commander. Mullah Amanullah from Sur Murghab, who is related to one of Jan Mohammad's wives, was arrested in Khakrez in October 2007, but was released by the district governor after intervention by Jan Mohammad: interviews with tribal leaders and local government officials in November 2007 and May and November 2008.

15. Descriptions of the situation under the Communist regime remain valid. See for instance Goodhand and Sedra (2006): "Afghans on both sides of the conflict

consistently subverted the bi-polar logic of their external backers; alliances in the field were constantly shifting back and forth between the mujahedin and pro-government militias. At the micro level Afghans would have family members in both the government forces and the mujahedin as part of a political risk spreading strategy."

16. See for instance Kenneth Katzman, *Afghanistan: Post-War Governance, Security and US Policy*, CRS report for Congress (updated 11 July 2008) and Thomas H. Johnson, "The Taliban Insurgency and an Analysis of *Shabnamah* (Night Letters)", *Small Wars and Insurgencies*, vol. 18, no. 3.

17. Interviews with tribal elders from Darafshan, Gizab and Khas Uruzgan.

18. Interviews with tribal leaders from Dehrawud, Khas Uruzgan and Gizab in September and November 2007 and January, April and May 2008. The term "negotiated submission" is from the Introduction in Robert D. Crews and Amin Tarzi, eds, *The Taliban and the Crisis of Afghanistan*. Cambridge, MA: Harvard University Press, 2008, p. 32.

19. Interviews with tribal elders from Gizab and Chora and with local NGO staff in January, February and May 2008.

20. This section is based on the analysis of information gathered over the last three years in interviews with tribal leaders from all districts.

21. ISAF press release, 16 August 2008, see http://oruzgan.web-log.nl/uruzgan_weblog/2008/08/isaf-air-strike.html (last accessed 5 Oct. 2008) and press release by the Australian Ministry of Defence, 19 August 2008, www.defence.gov.au/media/DepartmentalTpl.cfm?CurrentId=8130 (last accessed 5 Oct. 2008).

22. These links are illustrated by the fact that eye witnesses reported the delivery of a large number of dead bodies to Khas Uruzgan after the heavy fighting in Ajiristan in the late summer of 2008 (interviews with tribal elder from Zabul and Khas Uruzgan, May and August 2008), while fighters from Khas Uruzgan are also said to have participated in the 2007 assault on Chora (interview with elder from Khas Uruzgan in June 2007).

23. Interview with local government official, November 2008.

24. Interview with international analyst in May 2008.

25. Interviews with tribal elders from all districts over a period of several years.

26. Interviews with tribal leaders in September and November 2008. Baz Mohammad was replaced in the leadership reshuffle in January 2009.

27. Interview with local leaders from Tirin Kot and Khas Uruzgan in May and August 2008.

28. Interview with security official from Uruzgan in June 2008.

29. Press release by the Australian Ministry of Defence, 10 August 2008, www.defence.gov.au/media/DepartmentalTpl.cfm?CurrentId=8127 (last accessed 5 October 2008).

30. Others may translate this as Police Chief, since "*qomandan-e amniya*" is the title which is given to (government) heads of police. Such a translation however suggests the presence of a parallel Taliban "police force", of which I have seen no evidence, and for that reason I prefer the literal translation which is "security commander".

31. Interviews with a large number of local leaders from Khas Uruzgan, since May 2007.

32. Interview with tribal leader from Khas Uruzgan, March 2008.

33. Interview with tribal elders from Chora and Gizab and with the head of a local NGO in September 2007, April 2008 and September 2008.

34. Interview with tribal elder from Dehrawud in September 2007, with tribal elder from Gizab in June 2008 and with tribal elder from Tirin Kot in May 2008.

35. Afsar, Samples and Wood (2008) quite aptly describe the Taliban structure as a network of franchises, in which small militant groups start calling themselves the "local Taliban" in the hope of gaining recognition (and presumably resources) from the leadership, in return for support and cooperation. See: Major Shahid Afsar, Major Chris Samples and Major Thomas Wood, "The Taliban. An Organizational Analysis", *Military Review*, May-June 2008.

36. Interview with Afghan security official from the area in June 2008 and with tribal leader in January 2008.

37. There has also been a string of assassinations ordered by Quetta. Although these are part of a wider systematic targeting of influential local leaders, they tend to be fed or facilitated by pre-existing local enmities.

38. Interviews with local security officials and tribal elders from Dehrawud in September and November 2007.

39. Interviews with a local security official and tribal leaders from Khas Uruzgan and Gizab in November 2007, January and June 2008.

40. Senior Taliban commanders from Uruzgan who have been killed during the last year or so include Mullah Karim and Taliban governor of Uruzgan Mullah Qahor (not to be confused with Mirabad commander Mullah Qaher) in Khas Uruzgan in September 2007 (the Taliban district governor of Khak-e Afghan in Zabul was reported killed in the same attack); Mullah Rahim (a.k.a. Arab) in Baluchi in October 2007; Mullah Abdulhai and Mullah Sultan in March 2008; the notorious Mullah Abdul Wali in Dehrawud, Haji Feda Mohammad in Khas Uruzgan and "Sur Stergai" (Red Eyes) Mullah Akhtar Mohammad in August 2008; and Mullah Shaker and several of Senator Hanifi's relatives (including the father and uncle of local Taliban commander Qari Azizullah) in October 2008.

41. Interviews with, among others, a tribal elder in Dehrawud and the head of a local NGO in September and November 2007.

42. Interviews with tribal leaders fro Gizab and an international analyst in June and November 2008.

43. Interviews with tribal elders from Tirin Kot, Chora and Khas Uruzgan in May, August, September and November 2008.

44. Interviews with elders from Gizab, Khas Uruzgan and Chora and with the head of a local NGO in May, August, September and November 2008.

45. "Sin" is the local name for a tribal group that has been described to me as a Ghilzai (possibly Kakar) sub-tribe, originally from the Tirin Kot area (interviews in November 2007 and January 2008).

46. Interviews with Pashtun and Hazara elders from Khas Uruzgan in October and November 2007, January, March and May 2008. "False reporting" is a common trait of the counterinsurgency operation in Afghanistan, in which local security commanders and informants use their relations with the international military to orchestrate the targeting of local rivals.

47. Interviews with Dehrawud tribal elders in September 2007, November 2007 and November 2008. See also "Taliban execute five policemen in southern Afghanistan, officials say", Associated Press, 18 November 2007.

48. Interviews with tribal leaders from Chora, Dehrawud, Helmand and Daikondi in May, June and September 2008.

49. Interviews with local security officials and tribal leaders from Dehrawud, September and November 2007.

50. Interviews with tribal leader from Khas Uruzgan, August 2007.
51. Ruzi Khan was killed by Australian forces in September 2008 in what appears to have been a "friendly fire" incident, while responding to a call for help by a friend who mistakenly believed he was under attack from the Taliban.
52. Interviews with tribal leaders and local security officials in February, July and August 2007, and August 2008.
53. Interview with tribal leader from Khas Uruzgan, September 2007 and July 2008.

8

TALIBAN IN ZABUL: A WITNESS' ACCOUNT

Abdul Awwal Zabulwal[1]

An overview of Zabul province

Zabul province is located in south central Afghanistan, with an important strategic position on the highway that links Kabul with Herat via Kandahar. Zabul is part of the large South-Western region that also encompasses Kandahar, Uruzgan and Helmand provinces, with Kandahar city as its political and economic centre of gravity. Its area is 11,203 square kilometres, its population 295,000. The administrative centre is the town of Qalat with a population of 45,000, located about 140 km north-east of Kandahar. It shares borders with Kandahar in the south-west, with Uruzgan in the north, with Ghazni in the east and Pakistan in the south. Zabul's society is one of the most backward in the south of Afghanistan. The province is mainly inhabited by Pashtun Ghilzay tribes belonging to the Tokhi, Hotak, Naseri, Suleimankhel, Kakar, Kharoti, Andar, Alokozai, Wardak, Taraki, Michankhel, Basokhel, Dawi, Safi and Marani tribes (see map for the location of the main tribes). There is also a small Tajik minority.

Sources on the situation in Zabul are very limited. The author has relied on conversations with the local authorities and local notables, as well as his own personal experience, to gather the information used in this chapter. The insurgency practically controls all the districts of the province with the exception of Qalat centre. Although there is a government presence, including police, in all district centres but Khak-e Afghan which is completely under Taliban control, this is in fact mainly symbolic. Members of the administration cannot travel to most of the areas of their districts without the protection of the international military. Often, government representatives can only sur-

179

vive there by tacit agreements with the insurgents. The more mountainous districts in the west and north (Daichopan, Khak-e Afghan and Arghandab), as well as Nawbahar, are safe havens for the insurgents. Khak-e Afghan is particularly known for the high number of very hardline insurgents, including foreigners linked to al-Qaida and supported by a local Taliban commander, Mullah Mubin Akhundzada from the Kakar tribe, and the religious family of Abdullah Akhundzada, formerly linked to Harakat-i Inqilab-e Islami. There is a major supply base in Daichopan that also caters for neighbouring Uruzgan. Zabul province is also one of the main entry points for insurgents coming from Pakistan, with the traditional routes through Darwazagai (Shumulzai district). Shinkai district is particularly linked to the Taliban leader Mullah Mohammad Omar, a Hotak Pashtun, as it is his family's place of origin. From here, his forefathers migrated to Uruzgan where he was born.

The presence of Afghan security forces in Zabul is limited, though not insignificant. The ANA has 3,000 men deployed here, of which 1,500 are based in Qalat, up to 300 each in Shinkai and Shahjui district and 60 each in all the other district centres. The ANA soldiers have a good reputation among the people because of their discipline, bravery and good morale. Currently most of the soldiers are deployed along the main highway to secure public transport. The Qalat, Shinkai and Shahjui units act as reserve forces in case of need for the other districts, where the ANA supplements the very weak police. Out of the 1,500 ANP policemen in the official structure, only about 500 seem to exist in reality. The ANP is deployed mostly in Qalat and the district centres. Their main duty is to patrol the towns day and night, but they have a bad reputation among the people because of their corruption, abusive behaviour and bad discipline. There are also some 300 of the ANAP led by commander Gul, a brother of Haji Hashem, the head of the Provincial Council and a former Hizb-i Islami commander from the Alokozai of Shahr-e Safa district. They are stationed in Spina Ghbarga, 15 km east of Qalat town, on the main road. According to some reports, Gul has made an agreement with local Taliban under which they will not attack each other, and indeed until now no fighting between the two sides has been reported. The NDS has 50 officers and 150 lower rank personnel, mostly stationed in Qalat, with two to three staff in each district centre. On top of all this, there are around 1,000 NATO soldiers based in Zabul, mainly from the US and Romania. The local PRT in Qalat is led by the US. There are also Forward Bases in Qalat, Shinkai, Arghandab and Daichopan. Generally, the population has a positive attitude towards NATO troops, but search operations during the night and arrests based on wrong intelligence are resented and provide opportunities for the insurgents' propaganda.

History of the Taliban before 2001

Zabul is one of the poorest provinces of Afghanistan and has been ignored by all the central governments of the past. As a result, it has very few schools and a very small number of educated people. According to the province's head of education, around 30 schools are actively working in the whole province, attended by 16,000 students in total. Besides, there is a teacher's college (*dar-ul-ma'alemin*) that imparts two-year training to future teachers, and a teacher's training centre, whose task is to improve the skills of teachers who are already on the job. Both are located in the provincial centre Qalat. At the same time, the Taliban have already intimidated parents systematically all over the province not to send their children to any government schools. If the parents don't heed the warning, they are threatened with harsh penalties. These are not idle threats. Usually the Taliban beat parents or their children as a first warning and threaten to kill them if they continue to ignore the warnings. The threats seem to work and there has been no report of killings of parents or students in Zabul yet. However, in September 2008 a group of Taliban cut off the ears of a teacher in Syurai district because he had not accepted the rules set by them.

The lack of government-run education forces many parents to send their children to the mosques instead, to learn some basic principles of Islam and reading and writing. On the one hand, to become a mullah is an attractive profession. Traditionally, each village has one mullah, called the mullah-imam, who is employed by the decision of the majority of the elders of this village. His work is to call for prayer, to lead the prayers five times a day, to exercise all religious ceremonies like *nikah* (weddings), calling the first *azan* (call to prayer) for a newborn child and for burials, and teaching the children how to pray, how to read the Quran, about the religious rules and the difference between the lawful and the forbidden (*halal* and *haram*). It is relatively easy to be chosen as village mullah and to earn a relatively good income for the family. If registered with the government, mullahs are paid through the department of *hajj* and *awqaf*, but first of all mullahs are entitled to collect religious taxes from the population, like *ushr*, the traditional ten per cent harvest income tax paid by Muslims, *zakat*, the 2.5 per cent levy on profits from business, land, cattle and other belongings, and *sarsaya*, a tax paid after Ramadan for every head of the family. With the mullah also goes a certain amount of respect in the community and of political influence.

The result of all this is the very high number of *mullahs* and *taliban* (students at mosques and *madrasas*) in Zabul, by comparison with most other provinces in the country. Zabul was in fact the first province in country that had a "*taliban* front" during the time of the *jihad*. It was established immediately after the resistance against the PDPA regime started in 1979, initially led by Mullah Musa Kalim, who was killed only a year later, and Mullah Ghias-ul-Haq Tokhi, who joined the Hizb-i Islami (Khalis) party. Its most famous leader was Mullah Maddad, a member of the Taraki kuchi tribe, who was killed in a battle with Soviet troops in 1988 in Qalat. He had studied as a *talib* at different mosques, after which he joined the resistance and quickly proved himself to be an extremely brave fighter, well respected for his honesty and incorruptibility. His front survived his death. One of his various successors, Mullah

Maddad's brother Aziz Khan, was leading the group when it joined the Taliban movement in 1995. He was killed during fighting with troops of the Northern Alliance in the Shamali plain north of Kabul in 1997 and succeeded by another brother, Amir Khan Haqqani, who became a famous Taliban commander and led the Emirate's Northern Zone.

While many other Taliban fronts in Afghanistan played a relatively marginal role in the 1980s, Mullah Maddad's Taliban front was the strongest front in Zabul province during the *jihad*. He established a parallel court, led by Mullah Abdul Baqi, a Hotak from Syurai, which solved many disputes among the people of the province, who did not respect the courts of the leftist government and preferred an Islamic jurisprudence, according to Shariah law. This court even imposed death sentences. Three cases are reported, among them the one against commander Takar, who had killed a fighter of a rival commander, Mullah Abdul Salam known as Raketi (Rocketi), today a member of the Afghan parliament.

When the Taliban movement started in 1994, Zabul province provided a large number of armed men to the movement. Among its first leading personalities in Zabul were Mullah Abdul Salam (not to be confused with Mullah Abdul Salam Rockety), the imam of Khwazi, the largest village of Qalat ·district, who later became an adviser to Mullah Omar and is known today for his *fatwas* against "unbelievers"; Mullah Abdullah from Shahjoi district (today the Taliban's shadow governor of the same district); Mullah Abdul Nabi from Arghandab, who was killed in November 2001 by a US bomb in the area of Kandahar airport; and Mawlawi Abdul Qayyum and Mullah Abdul Rahman, a Hotak from Shinkay district, both of whom just had graduated from a Quetta *madrasa* and were suspected of strong ISI links.

In the movement's early days, the Taliban strictly excluded all former *mujahidin* commanders. But later, in 1996, when they faced strong resistance from the United Front in Shamali and were not able to overcome it, they turned towards the *mujahidin* and succeeded in absorbing a large number of former commanders such as Mullah Salam Rockety, formerly a commander of Sayyaf's Ittehad-e Islami, Amir Khan Haqqani, the brother of Mullah Maddad and a well-noted commander of the Zabul "*taliban* front" in the *jihad* period, and Noorullah Hotak, formerly a commander of Pir Gailani's Mahaz-e Milli. Because these commanders brought huge numbers of fighters into the Taliban movement, they were able to gain power and high positions inside the Taliban regime. Mullah Rockety became commander of the Nangarhar division, Amir Khan Haqani head of the Northern zone and Noorullah Hotak the commander of division No. 8 in Qargha, in the outskirts of Kabul. They enhanced the Taliban troops' fighting skills and capabilities and improved their tactics, leading to a series of military successes. For example, Mullah Rockety led the famous Taliban offensive in Shamali in 1999, which pushed the United Front troops back to Charikar, a front that still existed on 9/11. They all remained affiliated to the Taliban until the end of their regime. While Mullah Rockety now is a member of parliament, the other two are still with the Taliban.

The return of the Taliban after 2001

After the collapse of the Taliban regime and the establishment of the new Karzai government in 2001, Hamidullah Tokhi, formerly an important commander of Hizb-i Islami of Gulbudin Hekmatyar and then one of the President's close friends, was appointed the first governor of Zabul province. However, Tokhi was known for his corruption and for looting public property during the *mujahidin* rule between 1992 and the Taliban takeover, when he was the commander of the *mujahidin's* Qalat frontier troops regiment. For example, he had sold in Pakistan huge amounts of wrecked army equipment and machinery that officially belonged to the government and had also run checkpoints to collect "taxes" there. When the Taliban started taking over power in the southern regions in 1994, the people of Qalat welcomed them and helped them to get rid of the dreaded commander. Tokhi was arrested and humiliatingly paraded through the town with his arms tied. Elders of his tribe negotiated his release and he took refuge in Pakistan.

When he returned after the Taliban's collapse, he took his revenge. Despite Karzai's announcement of an amnesty for all Taliban who would lay down their weapons, the newly-appointed governor forced them to hand in arms, cars and money, threatening to send them to Guantánamo. This alienated the leading Taliban in Zabul, such as Amir Khan Haqqani, Mullah Nazir, Mawlawi Abdul Qayyum and Mullah Assadullah, who originally were ready to give up fighting and return to a normal life. Apart from Tokhi's behaviour, they also viewed the dominance of their old rivals of the United Front in Karzai's government as a hint that the Taliban had no place to stay in Afghanistan. Consequently most of them left for Quetta in Pakistan, where they regrouped with the assistance of ISI and Al Qaida. Some of them would later rise to high positions in the new Taliban set-up; for example, Mullah Nazir was at the time of writing a member of the Quetta Shura and Amir Khan Haqqani was the Taliban's shadow governor of Zabul, until he was—according to unconfirmed reports—arrested by Pakistani authorities in March 2007.

In 2003 the Taliban raised their heads again for the first time in Zabul. Their first action was to kidnap a Turkish engineer working on the highway between Kabul and Kandahar, close to Qalat; the victim was released later in exchange for $50,000. The commander of the abductors was Ruzi Khan from the Tokhi tribe, at this time the most important active Taliban commander in Zabul.[2] From this time onwards, the Taliban were steadily growing and obtained the support of some alienated tribal elements. Much of their support stemmed from the weakness of the government and the lack of a clear military strategy to eliminate the insurgency on the part of the international forces and the Afghan government.

The structure of the Taliban in Zabul

The structure of the Taliban is, as far as Zabul province is concerned, a three-layer hierarchy with a strong chain of command from top to bottom. At the top (in Pakistan) stands the Quetta Shura, mainly high-ranking Taliban from the Emirate time under the direct supervision of Mullah Omar. This *shura* is responsible for adopting the general strategies and for the appointment of governors, district governors (*wuluswals*) and group commanders. Under this *shura* there is a special commission responsible for all provincial affairs in Zabul, led by Mullah Nazir[3]. Mullah Nazir belongs to the Tokhi tribe (Babrai subtribe) and lived in Qalat before he joined the *mujahidin* as a young man in the 1980s, and then the Taliban. In the time of the Taliban Emirate, he was the police commander of Nangrahar province in Eastern Afghanistan. In mid-2002, he left Zabul again under the pressure of governor Tokhi's regime. In Pakistan, he rejoined the Taliban and became very close to Mullah Omar. He is in permanent contact with nearly all Taliban commanders of the province, except a few who report to a second Mullah Nazir (also a Tokhi from Qalat, but from the Miramzai subtribe) who belonged to late commander Dadullah's network. The people of Zabul call the former "Ghat (big) Mullah Nazir", while the latter is known as "Kuchnai (small) Mullah Nazir".

It is known that Taliban field commanders in Zabul call the "Big" Mullah Nazir for all important decisions. This includes the capture, possible punishment or even execution of captured people like policemen, ANA soldiers, alleged spies, construction company workers, the seizure of government or private company property, and mediation in larger disputes that cannot be solved locally. A recent story of a captured truck shows how far the arm of the Taliban commission for Zabul reaches. In early 2007 a Qalat resident's truck was seized by a local Taliban commander very close to the town. The commander sold the truck in Pakistan and pocketed the money. The victim of the theft decided to go to Quetta to seek the judgment of the Zabul commission. He was able to prove that the truck was his private property, not the government's. The commission forced the responsible commander to buy back the truck and hand it back to the rightful owner. Another example is the release of three Afghan employees of the Red Crescent of Afghanistan, who were abducted between Shahjui (Zabul) and Muqur (Ghazni) districts. It was ordered in the summer of 2008 by the Zabul commission. Finally, in the spring of 2008 the commission ordered the execution of former *mujahidin* commander Jannan from the Tokhi tribe, who was accused of spying for the US forces. Such orders are usually given by mobile phone or through messengers.

The second level of the Taliban hierarchy in Zabul is represented by the (shadow) provincial governor (currently Mullah Mohammad Yunus, a Tokhi from Kandahar province) and district governors for all ten districts and Qalat centre. Furthermore, there are so-called "heads of the zones" (*de zon amer*); the province is divided by the Taliban leadership into four zones (Qalat centre with Syurai and Shinkai districts; Mizan, Shahr-e Safa and Eastern Arghandab; Shahjui, Nawbahar and Shumulzai; Western Arghandab, Daichopan and Khak-e Afghan). These zonal heads act as advisers to the Zabul commission

Map 5: Taliban and tribes in Zabul, 2008

in Quetta. The governor is responsible for implementing the instructions issued by the Quetta Shura, to inform the *wuluswals* about any change in policies and to order operations. The zonal chiefs instruct the group commanders on behalf of Mullah Nazir's Zabul commission. Most of these positions, however, seem to be rather ceremonial, to boost the standing of the appointees and also to present something like a parallel government to the outside world; they might also be a plan for the future, as the Taliban's hold consolidates.

In practice, the Taliban of Zabul have not established permanent structures in any area of importance. Most of the Taliban groups roam through their respective areas of operation without any permanent base and take shelter in private houses where they are fed either by frightened villagers or by relatives or friends. Consequently, there cannot be a real, functioning administration run by them. They only have bases in peripheral areas of the province, like in Daichopan and Arghandab districts. A supply base in this area, which also cares for neighbouring Uruzgan province, is under the control of Mullah

Abdul Qahar from the Suleimankhel tribe, a former *mujahidin* commander of Harakat-i Enqelab. He is now the Taliban district governor of Daichopan and is reported to command a substantial number of fighters from among the residents of this district.

The third layer of the Taliban hierarchy is represented by the field units, called *dilgai* (front). They are led by a group commander or *dilgai meshr*, most of whom answer directly to Mullah Nazir and his Zabul commission. These *dilgai* comprise members of the *dilgai meshr*'s tribe as well as others drawn from socially marginalised people and unemployed locals, who want to take advantage of the unstable situation. The group commanders are often responsible for mobilising their own fighters on any opportunity to embarrass the government and the international forces. They and their rank and file mainly originate from the immediate area around which they are fighting. Recruitment is often based on personal relations with the respective commander, on tribal or regional affiliation. These groups are mobile and scattered over the whole province without establishing distinctive permanent fronts, to avoid being targeted by air strikes. Most of the larger attacks are carried out by 60 to 70 fighters. Sometimes, the group commanders gather for larger attacks on government or international troops. They use coded language for their communication through mobile phones or radio (over short distances). The Taliban group commanders of the province (see Map) are official registered with the Quetta Shura and receive a letter that allows them to carry out activities against Afghan government and international troops in the name of the Taliban (*rasmiyat*).

The insurgency in Zabul is overwhelmingly dominated by the Taliban. Other groups such as Hekmatyar's faction of Hizb-i Islami, the Haqqani network, Salafi and Wahabi groups, Khuddam-ul-Furqan and groups of bandits, active elsewhere in the country, do not exist in this province. The Taliban network in Zabul mainly consists of local Taliban or Taliban from neighbouring provinces like Kandahar, Uruzgan and Helmand. A number of local commanders are assisted by foreigners (mainly Arabs), who often act as advisers to suicide bombers. The exact number of full-time Taliban fighters is unknown. But it seems that the Taliban have an enormous supply of rank-and-file fighters from local residents, in particular from among the youth, badly affected by unemployment in this province. They are of significant value to the insurgents, because on one hand they are familiar with the terrain and, on the other hand, they can provide shelter and protection to Taliban from outside the province and even to foreign fighters. It is also difficult for Afghan and international forces to differentiate them from the local population.

Most Taliban fighters use Russian or Chinese-made Kalashnikovs, rocket-launchers and PK machine guns, the weapons used by *mujahidin* at the time of the Soviets. The Taliban also use old *mujahidin* tactics, such as hit-and-run attacks, but have added the use of remote-control mines, often used as roadside bombs. It is said that the Taliban are supplied from old weapons arsenals hidden during their defeat in 2001, but some reports allege that the ammunition which is used in the fighting is supplied by ISI or purchased in the Miramshah weapons market in Pakistan. Zabul has no weapons or drugs market of its own. But in some parts of the province such as Surkhgan, 40 kilometres east of Qalat, and Nawbahar, 70 kilometres east of Qalat, people in the local bazaars buy up trucks, pickups or small cars seized by the Taliban during their operations. Meanwhile, businessmen who bring new or second-hand cars from Herat to Kabul and Ghazni are often victims of Taliban mobile roadblocks. Those vehicles are sold at a very low price and dismantled into spare parts which, in turn, are transported to Pakistan and sold there. In Zabul the Taliban have developed no logistical support system for their fighters. They lean on local residents for accommodation and food, which is a heavy burden for the impoverished population. The latter cooperates under pressure, because anyone who refuses will be accused of being a government spy or an anti-Islamic element.

Judiciary and tax collection policy

Although its administrative structure is superficial (see above), the insurgency is setting up courts and tax collection committees. The courts have been reported established in remote areas such as Daichopan and Arghandab districts. Meanwhile, in other regions close to the main highway between Kabul and Kandahar or in other districts, which are easily reached by the international and Afghan troops, disputes or other relevant issues that require judgment are handed over to the nearest mullah-imam of a mosque. Normally, the decision of an imam is considered as conclusive to any dispute among the people. Such procedures have a legitimising impact and give the Taliban the upper hand against the government in winning the support of the people.

Recently the Taliban have been launching a new tax collection policy that, however, differs from one location to the other. In Daichopan, Shahjui and Arghandab districts, where the Taliban's dominance is stronger, tax is collected in the form of *zakat*. In other areas, Taliban ask local wealthy people and landowners for "donation" (*e'ana* or *mrasta*, both meaning "help"). Sometimes the amount is fixed and sometimes it is left to the decision of the contributor. This new taxation policy has advantages and disadvantages for the Taliban. It gives them an important source of income and enables them to recruit more rank-and-file fighters among the mass of unemployed young people who can now be paid regularly. The ability of local Taliban commanders to collect these taxes depends on their regional and tribal affiliation. Taliban commanders who operate outside their own tribes' territories will not be allowed to collect any tax by the local commanders. This was shown by a recent dispute between two Taliban commanders in Shahjui district: Mullah Abdullah, the Taliban's *wuluswal* belonging to the local Tokhi tribe and resident of Shahjui, and Mullah Mohammad Alam, a well-noted commander from the nomadic Andar tribe. According to reports both wanted to collect tax, but in the end

Mullah Abdullah told Mullah Alam that the latter had no right to collect any tax in his region; he was only allowed "to eat and fight against the government" there.

The parallel courts and the new tax policy are examples of the tendency for the Taliban to set up long-term strategies towards their ultimate aims. They assume that the international community will soon disengage from Afghanistan and that the Afghan government will not be able to survive without strong international support. Judging from the Zabul's perspective, their strategy seems to have three main objectives. First, they want to curb the government outreach by isolating the population from it. This is done through intensified propaganda, the targeting of government personnnel and infrastructure, and the creation of an atmosphere of fear within the communities, fuelled by intimidation as well as acts of violence and targeted killings of individuals seen to be pro-government. As a part of this objective, particular efforts have been made to create and widen the gap between the *Ulema* and the government. Secondly, the Taliban aim at winning over the population not just through propaganda, but also by creating parallel administrative structures, which would become stronger and better accepted then those of the government. Thirdly, they continue to target the international presence, both civilian and military, to embarrass the contributing countries and pressure public opinion there.

On the ground, the insurgency in Zabul was able to limit the operational space of the reconstruction actors and to ambush governmental and international forces on the main highway. The Taliban's propaganda efforts are not as successful as one might think, however. While nearly all mullahs in the villages promote *jihad* against the foreigners, and especially against the Americans, during Friday prayers or at any public ceremony, it appears that the population listens to them less and less. The reason might be that Afghans have already experienced one clerical regime in the past and do not have a good memory of that.

The factors mentioned above seem to prove that the Taliban have become an increasing threat to the Afghan government and the international community. But on the other hand, some elders and other inhabitants from the region believe that the Taliban too are very vulnerable. One elder, in the typical Pashtun way of using a parable, compared the current movement of the Taliban to a "castle of butter" which can survive during the cold and darkness of the night, but will disappear when the sun rises and heats up the earth. He explained that the Taliban have been tested when they held power in Afghanistan and failed. By the darkness and cold of the night he meant the poor governance and corruption of the Afghan government. The heat of the sun symbolises good governance and strategies for the eradication of the insurgency based on the trust of the local people. The belief is that the Taliban structures consist of socially marginal people who often have a dark past of robbery and looting, and would melt away if faced with serious challenges.

Notes

1. This is a pseudonym. The writer cannot reveal his real identity for security reasons. This chapter describes the situation as of end 2008.
2. He was killed by an airborne ambush some two years later, when he visited his mother-in-law's house in Bazogai village, 25 kilometres outside Qalat.
3. According to unconfirmed reports, Mullah Nazir has been arrested by Pakistani authorities in late 2008 and replaced by Mullah Sa'dullah.

9

WHAT KANDAHAR'S TALIBAN SAY

Graeme Smith

Kandahar has been a political crucible for centuries, so many residents are not surprised to find themselves at the molten heart of the latest war. They tell the story of the previous Taliban government's rise to power in Kandahar with a sense of inevitability: of course the 1994 revolt against the *mujahidin* started in the ancient capital of the Durrani empire; of course the Taliban's leader, Mullah Mohammad Omar, preached at a village mosque just 40 kilometres west of the shrine that holds one of Islam's most famous artifacts, the cloak that according to legend belonged to the Prophet Mohammad. By the mystical logic of Kandahar, there was something appropriate about such an important place making history again. As the Taliban seized control of the country, advancing into the capital in 1996, then continuing their fight against ethnic Tajik and Uzbek warlords in the north, the war became relatively popular among the Pashtuns in the south. Each victory gave prestige back to Kandahar, as the city became the new seat of power.

The rising insurgency after 2001 has once again given Kandahar a dubious sort of prominence as the worst trouble spot in the country. As of 9 September 2008, the security consultant Sami Kovanen had counted more Taliban attacks in Kandahar (753) from the beginning of the year than in any of the other provinces,[1] and hundreds of incidents separated Kandahar from the second- and third-most affected provinces. Kandahar also recorded the highest number of attacks in the previous year. A different picture emerges from other data, such a June 2008 report for the US Congress[2] that ranked Kandahar third behind Helmand and Kunar provinces when measuring the number of attacks, but those figures use a counting method that tends to give greater weight to operations by the international forces. Qualitative indicators also point to Kandahar as the focus for the southern insurgency: the worst bombing in Afghanistan's history happened on the outskirts of Kandahar city in February 2008, and arguably the most spectacular single achievement of the insurgency so far was the June 2008 jailbreak in Kandahar city, in which Taliban fighters broke free hundreds of inmates.

The Taliban also appear to have devoted significant resources to a more subtle effort in Kandahar. In 2006, a former Taliban official now working with the Afghan government told me the insurgents were operating two safe houses in Loy Wiyala, a ramshackle slum on Kandahar's north side, where insurgents were compiling lists of city residents who collaborate with the government and arranging to kill them. That campaign of targeted hits has unfolded with terrible efficiency, and usually without attracting much notice. The deaths of major pro-government figures—Mullah Naqibullah,[3] Bacha Khan, Malim Akbar Khakrezwal, Abdul Hakim Jan, Habibullah Jan, to name a few for the September 2007–September 2008 period—occasionally make news, and their deaths are sometimes the result of elaborate attacks. More often, however, the killings follow a more prosaic routine. Two insurgents on a small Honda motorbike ride up to a minor target, the man on the back of the bike pulls a Kalashnikov from the folds of his shawl, and he unleashes a short burst of gunfire. The victim could be a judge, a police officer, an English-speaking translator, a local Afghan aid worker, or maybe just an unlucky relative of somebody who holds one of those jobs. Nowhere in the province is entirely safe for Afghans who resist the insurgency.[4] The Taliban's intelligence network has considerable strength even at Kandahar Air Field, the sprawling military base outside the city. During a conversation with a Taliban spokesman in early 2007, he proudly showed that he knew the colour of a shopping bag I was holding as I had walked out the gates of the military base earlier that day.

Despite such displays of power, the Kandahar insurgency does not appear cohesively organized. Officially, the Taliban leadership in Quetta in Pakistan has appointed a provincial chain of command that could be drawn on an organizational chart.[5] A Taliban leader with responsibility for the entire province is sometimes called the "shadow governor". At last check, in August 2008, the shadow governor Mullah Mahmood had been recently killed in an air strike in Khakrez district and not yet replaced. But his absence did not slow the pace of the insurgency, as the number of Taliban attacks reached historic highs in the two months after his death. Other senior insurgents are delegated responsibility for individual districts, and important districts are sometimes carved up into zones of operation. For instance, the volatile district of Panjwayi, southwest of Kandahar city, was divided into three zones: a strongly Taliban-held western zone including the villages of Taloqan and Mushan; a Taliban-controlled eastern zone encompassing Nakhonay and Salawat; and a disputed central zone that includes Taliban-influenced villages such as Zangabad and Sperwan, but also two NATO military outposts and the district offices for the Kabul government's local representative. Each of the three zones has a mid-level Taliban commander nominally in charge of the insurgents in that part of the district, all of them serving under the district leader—at the time of writing, a commander named Mullah Hamdullah.

Other prominent insurgents in Kandahar province, as of mid-August 2008, were Mullah Ghafar in Sangisar; Haji Noor Mohammad in Maywand district; Haji Noor Mohammad in Ghorak district; Mullah Rahim in Mianeshin district; Mullah Bismillah in Dand district; Mullah Aminullah, whose influence extends over Zhari and Panjwayi districts; and Haji Lala, who is powerful in Khakrez, Shah Wali Kot, and parts of Zhari district. Supervising all these leaders was the Taliban's council, or *shura*, composed of senior insurgents widely assumed to be living across the border in Balochistan province of Pakistan. the three members of the council who probably exert the most influence over Kandahar's insurgents are Mullah Berader, of the Popolzai tribe, a top military strategist for the southern insurgency; Mullah Obaidullah, of the Alokozai tribe, a former Defence minister under the pre-2001 government who was rumoured to be procuring new weapons and ammunition for the insurgency; and Hafiz Majid, of the Noorzai tribe, who has at times served as a personal emissary for Mullah Omar.

Cataloguing this bewildering list of names and responsibilities is a favourite pastime for Afghan and foreign intelligence officers, but there is no evidence that the formal structure of the insurgency has any real importance. Several of the insurgent leaders use pseudonyms, and the Taliban further confuse matters by occasionally replacing a slain commander with a deputy who assumes the same names as his predecessor. Taliban leaders do not exercise command-and-control in a conventional military sense;[6] when an important Taliban figure wanted to organize a large ambush against Canadian troops west of Kandahar city in September 2008, he had to canvass individual groups of insurgents across the districts and persuade each of them to volunteer a few fighters and weapons for the mission—a process that requires more effort and charisma than merely ordering troops to attack. Often Taliban commanders are killed or lose favour in internal squabbles, so new names appear on the scene with dizzying frequency. Insurgent units also migrate within the southern region, which the Taliban sometimes describe as a method of giving their foot-soldiers a rest if they have experienced hard fighting. It is fair to assume most of the Taliban commanders listed here will have changed by the time you read this chapter, with the possible exception of Mullah Baradar, Mullah Obaidullah, and Hafiz Majid, who have wielded influence over the Kandahar insurgency for years.

Beneath the level of such masterminds, the Afghan and international military forces usually overestimate the importance of the Taliban leadership's organization chart. A Canadian military intelligence officer looked back at his tour of duty with satisfaction in the spring of 2008, believing that nearly all the middle ranks of the local insurgency had been killed or captured during his nine months in Kandahar. The elimination of those field commanders, he calculated, would leave the insurgents with little remaining capacity for the summer fighting season. Sadly, he was proved wrong: the summer of 2008 was the deadliest period Kandahar has witnessed in the latest war. It could be argued that the violence might have been worse if certain Taliban commanders had not been killed, but so far attacks on insurgent commanders have shown no signs of weakening the insurgency. In fact, some analysts argue that the quick turnover in the Taliban's leadership has swept away an older, more cautious generation of leaders and created opportunities for promotion of younger radicals.

An exception to this trend was the killing of Mullah Dadullah. At one point in 2006, an Afghan official estimated that Mullah Dadullah commanded 75 per cent of the Taliban fighters in Kandahar and held sway over insurgents across most of southern Afghanistan. While that percentage may have been an exaggeration of his power, he was clearly the most influential Taliban field commander in the south. Profiled by Western intelligence as a sadist who enjoyed fighting for its own sake, Dadullah showed enthusiasm for blood-thirsty executions, video propaganda, and suicide bombings. His death in May 2007, during an apparent commando raid, was followed by a small but noticeable shift away from all three activities in Kandahar: a spate of Taliban executions ended, and illicit Taliban videos from the southern battlefields became less plentiful in the local DVD markets. Suicide bombings also fell, relative to other kinds of attacks; the analyst Kovanen compared the first 29 weeks of 2008 against the same period in 2007 and found a slight decline in suicide bombs in Kandahar, while other types of attack increased dramatically. It is impossible to know whether Dadullah's death was directly linked to these changes in Taliban behaviour, but it is a fair assumption.

Such guesses about the internal workings of the Taliban are necessarily fraught with risk of error, however. I have spent weeks having friendly arguments with Western security officials about whether certain figures in the insurgency are alive or dead, and NATO or the US military sometimes issue statements claiming that Taliban leaders have been killed, only to suffer the embarrassment of the supposedly slain commander proving himself very much alive. The mistakes are understandable; by definition it is difficult for an outsider to gain insight into a xenophobic group. The Taliban are even harder to understand because they might physically harm a researcher. I have had several meetings with insurgents since I took a full-time assignment in Kandahar for *The Globe and Mail*, a Canadian newspaper, but those conversations rarely left me satisfied. The risks involved with face-to-face contact made it difficult to cultivate any of the Taliban as sources, because the relationship between a journalist and a source usually involves a measure of trust, and you cannot trust somebody who might kill you. Nor can you always trust the information provided by the Taliban, because of their strong incentives to inflate achievements, misdirect enemies, and protect the vital secrets of their operations.

By the summer of 2007, I had grown frustrated with usual journalistic methods of learning about the Taliban, and decided to try something more ambitious: a survey. My editors approved a small budget, and we sent a researcher into the rural districts around Kandahar city to interview Taliban using a standard list of questions. It was highly unscientific, and the process was sometimes disappointing; we discovered, for instance, that asking Taliban foot soldiers how they get paid does not yield much insider detail about insurgent financing. It is important to emphasize how little can be gleaned from a series of short statements by masked men, and surveys in general have a tarnished reputation in Afghanistan as other samples of public opinion have generated some clearly inaccurate results in recent years. But our final product, 42 video interviews with 512 pages of English-language transcript, does provide a starting point for understanding the Kandahar insurgency. We treated the Taliban as a social movement and asked for opinions from ordinary members—less a formal survey than a crude sampling of views. This made the survey different from the usual analysis of the Taliban's hierarchy of military, administrative and judicial units. Such formal organization does exist, but reveals nothing about the movement's centre of gravity. At its core, the Taliban is an uprising by rural Afghans. These simple fighters must be understood with an examination of their demographics, sources of motivation, and attitudes about the world.

The limited geography covered by such a small survey probably makes the results less relevant to other parts of Afghanistan. The Taliban's leadership is reputed to divide the country into areas of operation, with the insurgents' definition of the southern region roughly mirroring the cluster of provinces in NATO's Regional Command South. Experts differ on the exact boundaries of these Taliban zones; some describe two major insurgencies—one centered on Kandahar and directed from Quetta, and the other centered in eastern Afghanistan and directed from the Federally Administered Tribal Areas (FATA) in Pakistan—while others see three, four, or five insurgencies. These theories of parallel insurgencies may explain why the Taliban we found in Kandahar seem so different from the insurgents described in studies of eastern Afghanistan, especially in the low level of influence by non-Pashtun fighters in the south. It also fits with Kandaharis' self-aggrandizing view of the southern region as a universe apart from the rest of Afghanistan. The impression that Taliban fighters rarely travel into the south[7] from the eastern battlefields was supported by the tribal profile of the 42 fighters, which will be detailed later in this chapter. In other words, the opinions of Kandahar's insurgents might sound bizarre to the ears of their comrades in other provinces.

The researcher has worked with us since 2006 and learned the basic skills of journalism. He previously served as a police commander for the Taliban regime and we often send him on fact-finding trips to places that would be off-limits for anybody without strong insurgent connections. This project involved tasks at which he has already proven capable: find a specific person, point a video recorder at them, ask questions from a list, and, most challengingly, listen to the answers and formulate further questions. He is still learning the art of follow-up questioning, but otherwise he has appeared to be fairly disciplined about obeying the rules described below. He started work in August 2007, supervised by a staff translator, who watched the videos and roughly interpreted them into English. I met the researcher as he returned from his visits to the districts. We hired the academic Alex Strick van Linschoten to provide a second verbatim transcript in English, with coding for subtitles, and in March 2008 published all the material on the internet.[8]

Instructions for Taliban researcher

1. Find small groups of Taliban and try to speak with them individually. They do not need to show their faces or give their names, although displaying their weapons might support their claim to be fighters. (Persuading the insurgents to speak by themselves proved difficult, and clusters of three or four interviews often contain answers that echo each other, as Taliban apparently waited to hear what their comrades would say. In fact, this makes our project more like a series of small focus groups than a formal survey.)

2. Visit as many districts as possible. (He visited five: Zhari, Panjwayi, Maywand, Arghandab, and Daman. Access to each district was negotiated by him and a staffer for *The Globe and Mail*, in each case requiring permission of a local Taliban commander.)

3. Ask a standard list of 20 questions, in the same order every time. (He largely obeyed this request, with a few major exceptions: for instance, he sometimes dropped a question about the insurgents' loyalty to Mullah Omar when he felt it would be dangerous to push them on a sensitive topic.)

4. Try to get enough elaboration for the interview to last a minimum of 10 minutes. (This improved during the course of the project, with durations varying from 4 to 15 minutes.)

The Taliban in the survey guessed their own ages at 18 to 42 years, with an average in the early 20s. They usually described themselves as religious students, which may have been a euphemism for unemployment. The other largest groups were farmers and labourers. Others claimed similarly modest occupations as drivers, landowners, shopkeepers, a shepherd, a home-schooled student, a trader, and a house painter. Results from other questions, discussed later in this chapter, also suggested that many Taliban earn money from the flourishing opium industry.

Only one of the Taliban fighters, a Kuchi nomad, described himself as something other than an ethnic Pashtun. The rest of them claimed membership in 18 different Pashtun tribes: Noorzai (10), Ishaqzai (6), Alizai (3), Kakar (3), Taraki (3), Popolzai (2), Baloch (2), Barakzai (2), Andar (2), Nasir (2), Alokozai (1), Sayyed (1), Yusufzai (1), Moghulzai (1), Achakzai (1), and Navid (1). That is a confusing array of tribal names for the uninitiated, but learning about the structure of Kandahar's tribes is essential to understanding why the

Taliban fight. Although our sample was not large enough to draw firm conclusions about the tribal makeup of the insurgency, the findings support the anecdotal impression that the insurgency draws fighters most heavily from outside the triumvirate of tribes that dominates the local government.[9] It is a variation on the power struggles that happen in many countries, as those in power support their own clans and those denied power jealously fight for their share.

The divisions between Pashtun tribes can seem insignificant to an outsider, because they generally share the same culture, religion, language and ethnicity, but they are separated by ancestral lines that resemble the branches of an incredibly complicated family tree, dividing and subdividing almost infinitely. In Kandahar the Pashtuns are usually divided into three main groups: Zirak, Panjpai, and Ghilzai. Those categories are considered a bit abstract by most Afghans, however; I have never encountered anybody who described himself as a "Zirak", for instance, and nobody refers to themselves using even the names of broader tribal groupings such as the Durrani tribal confederacy.[10] Tribal politics is local. Hamid Karzai, the President, belongs to the Popolzai tribe, which falls into the Zirak branch of the Durrani confederation along with other major local Zirak tribes such as the Alokozai, Barakzai, and Achakzai. But when local shopkeepers want to curry favour with the government they do not paint the word Zirak or Durrani on their signs; instead, it is usually "Popal's Auto Mechanic" or "Popal's Bakery". Even smaller units of tribal membership can become vitally important in local politics, too; in Kandahar, for instance, the Barakzai tribe is subdivided into two branches that occasionally feud against each other. These are essentially squabbles among families, but they are the foundation of politics in Kandahar.

Such local dynamics are the most important factor in this insurgency. A US intelligence report on tribes, completed in the spring of 2008, found that the Taliban are not primarily driven by external forces; although support from Pakistan's border region is important for the insurgency, the analysts saw much of the fighting driven by local rivalries. The foundation for many such rivalries is tribal, as Karzai uses the instruments of official power to support his own Popolzai tribe and selected allies within the Zirak Durrani confederacy. The Taliban have exploited the resulting anger among the other Pashtun tribes, many of whom find themselves on the wrong side of disputes over money, land, opium, or water. Our survey results supported this theory.[11] Only two Taliban fighters identified themselves as Popolzai in our sample, and they appeared to have personal reasons for participating in the insurgency: one said his family was bombed by international forces and the other said the government repeatedly eradicated his opium fields. There was a similar lack of insurgents from other tribes sometimes aligned with the local government—Barakzai, Alokozai, and Achakzai—although most of the survey was conducted before dissatisfaction among the Alokozai became a major problem in Kandahar, and so it is possible that the government's tribal support has narrowed even further. The US assessment concluded that the Taliban do not support any tribe wholeheartedly, but the insurgency is increasingly coloured by tribal rivalries. No foreigners appeared in our survey, and the impression of their scarcity on the battlefield was supported by our researcher's observations. Most of the fighters appeared to be Pashtun tribesmen from the southern region, probably not straying far from their homes. Those results do not fit the stereotype promoted by Afghan politicians who describe the Taliban as heavily composed of Arab and Pakistani extremists.

The tribal aspect of the war also seems to be a touchy subject for the Taliban leadership, which prefers to describe religion—not tribe or ethnicity—as the insurgency's unifying force. Another reason for this sensitivity may be the tribal tensions within the Taliban movement itself, as rumours from Quetta suggest feuds between the Kakar, Ishaqzai, and Noorzai tribal leaders within the Taliban command. Our researcher was sharply criticized by Taliban leaders when they discovered he was surveying the tribal background of insurgents and found some tribes more heavily represented than others. Perhaps even the Taliban understand the terrible dangers of tribal war in southern Afghanistan. One of my Afghan friends looked at the results of our survey and concluded that the war was not yet a genuine tribal conflict; in such a situation, he said, neighbours would be killing neighbours, and the scale of fighting would be vastly greater.

We also asked a variety of questions about why the Taliban fight, sometimes approaching the issue directly— "Why do you fight against the Karzai government?"—and sometimes asking about related issues, such as whether any of their family members had been killed by bombs, or had their poppy fields eradicated. When faced with the open-ended questions about their war, Taliban from disparate parts of the province often repeated the same lines, sometimes verbatim, suggesting that these ideas are part of their indoctrination. A majority used some variation of two lines: "Afghans must expel infidels" and "infidels enslaved the government". Several others referred to religious teachings, quoting textual sources even though they are probably illiterate. Some raised objections to the behaviour of the Afghan government and foreign troops, usually the killing of civilians.

Asked specifically about bombings by foreign troops, almost a third of respondents claimed their family members had died in such incidents during the current war. Many of them denied seeking revenge after these deaths, but said other civilian deaths inspired them to fight. About half of those who claimed bombing deaths in their family said they joined the Taliban after the killings occurred. Those for whom the bombing was a trigger for joining the Taliban generally fell into two categories: young men replacing older relatives who died fighting in the Taliban ranks ("call-ups") and men who took up arms against the government after their civilian relatives were killed.

When asked whether foreigners had bombed their families, the Taliban often complained about bombings by Russian aircraft in the 1980s in addition to recent air strikes under the Karzai government, suggesting that memories of the Soviet invasion fuel some of the current opposition to US and

NATO troops. Even those who have not lost family in the bombings clearly identify themselves as defending Afghanistan against such attacks: in response to the question "Has your family been bombed by foreigners?", four fighters said something fatalistic, such as "Not yet". Two others gave variations on a declaration of solidarity: "No … but the families of my friends have been bombed, and other Muslims are like my own family." One described the air strikes hitting even closer to home: "No, but our neighbours and relatives have been bombed". A 25-year-old Alizai tribesman said he joined the Taliban after two of his uncles died in air strikes in Pashmul, a village about 15 kilometres west of Kandahar city that saw heavy combat, especially during Operation Medusa in September 2006. He initially used civilian deaths as a justification for *jihad*—"The foreign troops came to Afghanistan, killed many innocent people and elders and bombed them, so I started *jihad* and joined with the Taliban"—but he did not claim a personal vendetta. When asked whether he joined the insurgents to get revenge, he said: "I became their friends as our grandfathers fought with non-Muslims and our elders fought with non-Muslims, [and] the Prophet Mohammad fought with them." He may have been an example of the family replacement mechanism, by which younger members of a family feel obligated to stand in for older fighters if they are killed. Certainly that appeared to be the case with a 30-year-old farmer from the Taraki tribe, who said his brothers were killed recently. "They were older than us," he said. "They were fighting and I was working. But when they died I started to fight." He also denied a desire for personal revenge, but acknowledged that the event triggered his desire to fight: "When they became martyrs, I also wanted to become a martyr."

Another example of the call-up mechanism was the case of a 25-year-old farm worker who said three older members of his family were killed in air strikes—but he specified that all of them were Taliban fighters. "All of them were with the Taliban and when one of them was killed in war, after that another was killed, and then the third one was also killed," he said. "So after that I decided to join the Taliban." He was asked: "But what is your motivation? Do you want to take revenge or what?" "No, no, no," he replied. "I would never fight to take revenge for my family or something else. I am fighting only to remove the non-Muslims from my country because they are here to destroy our religion."

Others did not dwell on the rhetoric of *jihad*. A 22-year-old farmer from the Kakar tribe initially said he abandoned his farm work because foreign troops arrived in his area, but later specified that three of his relatives, two elders and one child, had been killed in an air raid in the previous year. He joined the Taliban after the bombing. "Are you fighting because of that bombing?" he was asked. "Yes," he said. "Because of the bombing, and also because the foreigners are here." Bombing was the only reason given when an Ishaqzai farmer in his 40s described his motives: "The non-Muslims are unjust and have killed our people and children by bombing them, and that is why I started *jihad* against them," he said. He claimed his family was bombed several times. "They have killed hundreds of our people, and that is why I want to fight against them." The self-defense rationale was also strong for a Noorzai tribesman in his late 20s, who claimed he gave up shopkeeping and joined the Taliban "because non-Muslims have attacked us". A dozen members of his family were killed in Panjwayi district, he said, referring to a swath of farmland southwest of Kandahar city that has seen heavy fighting in the last three years. Still, he used a religious justification for the war instead of a desire for personal revenge:

"What did you feel after the bombing?" he was asked.
"I thought that I should fight against them [foreign troops]."
"So you want to take revenge against the foreigners?"
"No, I am not fighting to take revenge for my family. I am fighting only for God's approval."

For some, civilian bombings of their immediate family do not appear to have inspired them to join. A 20-year-old Popolzai tribesman who described himself as a religious student and "painter"—likely a house painter—said recent air strikes had killed ten members of his family, including children. The killings did not change his mind about the foreigners, he said. "Before this bombing I also had this feeling that non-Muslims were here, in our country, and that we should fight against them. And after the bombing I had the same feelings." But his hatred of foreigners may have had older roots—he said his family was first bombed during the Soviet occupation. From the survey responses, and other anecdotal experience in Kandahar, it is clear that civilian casualties inspire the insurgents.

The war on drugs also seemed to give many insurgents a strong reason to fight. A majority of the Taliban admitted a personal role in the opium industry, with more than 80 per cent of respondents saying they farmed poppies themselves and a similar percentage saying it was farmed by their family or friends. Those numbers are not surprising in rural Kandahar, where poppies rank among the most common crops, but perhaps more significant is the fact that half the Taliban surveyed said they had been targeted by government eradication efforts—and sometimes their fields were destroyed more than once: "Yes, several times," said one farmer. Eradication efforts in Kandahar were not widespread in the years before the survey was conducted; it appears either that the Taliban exaggerate the government's counter-narcotics program, or that there is a connection between farmers who face eradication and those who join the insurgency.

The Taliban seemed bashful about admitting a profit motive for their war, saying it was a secondary reason for fighting after the primary concept of *jihad*, but a few described the connection bluntly: "Previously they were cutting them [poppies] down, but now those areas are controlled by *mujahidin* and now they cannot cut them down," said one fighter. A 21-year-old Ishaqzai tribesman, who said his main occupation since the age of six was memorizing the Koran, said the government often preferred to collect bribes instead of eradicating poppy.

"No, they can't [eradicate]," he said. "They do not want to cut our poppy. They collect money." The interviewer asked him, "How many times did you pay money for poppies?"

"About two or three times, and I have paid around 12,000 [Afghani]."

The conversation continued: "Why do you grow poppies even when it creates problems for you?"

"We grow it because it damages the non-Muslims. And that is why we're growing it. And we should do whatever harms non-Muslims."

"Before this drug reaches the non-Muslims, won't it destroy our own people first?"

"[Even] if it harms Muslims, most of the foreign countries are using it."

"What does Islam say about growing poppies?"

"Islam says that it is not permitted. But we do not care whether it is permitted or forbidden. But we are only saying that we will grow poppies against non-Muslims."

Another fighter, a 25-year-old Alizai tribesman who described himself as a farmer, summarized the economic and jihadist arguments in a similar dialogue.

"Why are you growing poppies? You can grow wheat or corn instead," our researcher suggested.

"This is harmful for non-Muslims and wheat gives less profit than poppies. We irrigate our fields with machines [water pumps] and spend a lot of money for the fuel. If we grow wheat we can't afford those prices."

"It doesn't offer profit enough to cover the fuel?"

"No."

"What does Islam say about poppies? Is it good or bad?"

"We have heard that it is harmful for non-Muslims. When they use it a lot it is harmful for them."

"You grow it for this reason?"

"Yes."

A 23-year-old religious student alluded to the idea that opium should only be a temporary industry for Afghanistan, perhaps reflecting the fact that the Taliban once banned the crop: "It should be grown," he said. "These days it is good, because it is harmful for the non-Muslims. But Islam says that it is wrong." A 23-year-old Nasir tribesman was among the very few who said opium was banned by Islam. "No, we do not grow poppies," he said. "It is not a good thing, and it is not permitted in the [Koran]." But others even suggested that opium could be a decisive factor in the war: "We can defeat the non-Muslims by growing poppies," said one fighter.

Another rationalization for the opium industry was that the arrival of international forces in Afghanistan has hurt the country's economy, which forced farmers into growing opium. This argument ignores the fact that Afghanistan's GDP had double-digit growth in the years after 2001, but it appeared to be a commonly accepted thesis among the Taliban: "Non-Muslims have come here and now there is no trade," said a fighter. "And there are a lot of problems in Afghanistan's fields, and we have to grow it." A 25-year-old former driver said he grew poppy, and "of course" the government had eradicated it.

"So what was your reaction to the government then?" he was asked.

"We are fighting against them."

"Ok, so you mean to say that you are fighting for poppies?"

"No, no. We are only fighting for the approval of God. But as I said, they attacked us and it is our responsibility to fight against them. When non-Muslims attack they always attack your home, or they attack your country. So that is why we are fighting."

"What is your opinion about growing poppies?"

"Muslims here do not have any other income. They had orchards which are destroyed."

"What does Islam say about growing poppies? Is it permitted or forbidden?"

"When Mullah Omar was the 'prince of the faithful' he did not allow poppies. But now the *mujahidin* are growing it for their own use or for other Muslims."

A 28-year-old Noorzai tribesman complained that a lack of development had forced him into growing opium, which put him into conflict with the government as it repeatedly eradicated his fields.

"We are forced to grow it. We do not have car or a road or anything, so what should we eat if we do not grow it? Tell me. If we had factories, we would not grow the poppies," he said.

"I am not fighting for poppies, but it is our income. We do not have factories, and when we are growing it with water in the fields we need fuel [for water pumps] and it is a big expense, and everyone knows that it is not good."

A similar explanation came from one of his fellow Noorzai tribesmen: "All of us are growing poppies," he said. "There was nothing in Afghanistan for a long time. And if we did not grow this we would not even be able to pay for the expenses of our fields."

For all their talk about the economics of opium, the Taliban revealed very little about their sources of income. From these interviews and other contacts with the insurgents it seems the primary cash inflows arrive from Pakistani territory, sometimes originally from donors in other countries. Other funding sources appear to be opium dealers and ordinary Afghans. Farmers pay *"ushr"* an Islamic tithe, which amounts to one tenth of their crop, and business is taxed through a similar system called *"zakat,"* usually considered 2.5 per cent of annual profits from business, although the real percentages seem to vary wildly in practice. These religiously mandated payments are regularly shared with the Taliban, sometimes 50 per cent to the insurgents and 50 per cent to the local mullah for other kinds of charity. One fighter said: "All the Muslims give us money, whether they are Afghans or from Saudi Arabia or somewhere else."

As with the illegal drug trade, suicide attacks have received specific endorsement from the Taliban's religious teachers, and the Islamic rationale used to justify their actions is widely disseminated among the front-line fighters. At times, suicide bombing has been a contentious issue within the Taliban; an insurgent faction even took out a newspaper advertisement in Kandahar in 2006 to disavow the tactic.[12] None of the insurgents we talked with, however, was willing to publicly voice any concerns about suicide attacks. A surprising number even said they were ready to volunteer for martyrdom, which seems to support a comment from a mid-level Taliban organizer I met in Quetta in late 2006, who said the insurgency's supply problems—ammunition, money, winter clothing—do not include any shortage of eager young men. A few of the Taliban made reference to a story they believe supports the idea of sacrificing oneself during a war. "There is a story from the time of the prophet," a fighter said. "There were two companions of the prophet, and when they were taking [attacking] a place the walls were high so they could not jump over the wall. One lifted the other over the wall and he died in the attack. He knew he would be killed, but it was his duty."

We did occasionally break through the responses that fighters had obviously memorized by rote. Some departures from the usual Taliban messages occurred when our researcher started asking questions about the fighters' willingness to negotiate peace and their loyalty to Mullah Mohammad Omar, the so-called Commander of the Faithful. We were interested in attitudes towards Mullah Omar because any negotiated settlement of the conflict would likely require some sort of compromise on the issue of leadership, as the international community (not to mention the warlords of northern Afghanistan) would balk at any deal that returned power to the former Taliban head of government. But the question about Mullah Omar's leadership was the only item on our list of questions that caused our researcher to worry that he was risking the insurgents' anger, and he was initially shy about raising the issue at all. When he did pose the question, many of the responses were so evasive that they could not be categorized. It clearly caused discomfort.

The responses that could be categorized, however, showed a fascinating lack of loyalty to the insurgents' leader. Twenty-four fighters, more than half those surveyed, were willing say that their Commander of the Faithful was not necessarily required for their war, nor necessarily the best leader for Afghanistan. This was especially curious when their other responses suggested they were strongly committed to the insurgency. A few of them set tough conditions for replacing Mullah Omar, such as a decision by the leader himself, but the largest group offered variations on the same phrase: "It makes no difference whether Mullah-sahib[13] is in the government." Some even suggested that there need not be a Taliban government in Kabul at all, only that they wanted to influence the selection of a new leader. "We are not saying that it should be our government," a fighter said. "But we want only a Muslim king, and do not want a non-Muslim." One fighter went so far as to suggest that the Karzai government would be acceptable after the expulsion of foreign troops: "Then, if it is Karzai or Mullah Omar it doesn't matter." Others said the opposite: "We accept an Islamic government but not Karzai's government."

One version of why the Taliban want Mullah Omar as leader of Afghanistan held that it depended on his behaviour, and there was nothing intrinsic about his personality: "We want an Islamic leader to implement Islamic rules and regulations, whether he is Omar or not," one said. "We have accepted Mullah Omar because he is an Islamic person and wants Islam in the country." In response to the question, "If foreigners leave Afghanistan, would you accept a government without Mullah Omar?" some were emphatic: "Yes, if he is a Muslim man and implements Islamic rules in the government, then of course we would accept [him]." Others were more equivocal. "No, we would not accept, but if it is an Islamic government then we would accept it." Many placed extra conditions on such a change in leadership; one said another leader was only acceptable "if that person is like Mullah Omar." Of the various conditions, the toughest were posed by those who said Taliban elders must choose Afghanistan's leader: "If there is someone who has been selected by our leaders, and if he implements Islamic rules in the government, then we would accept that." One even appealed to higher authority: "If God is convinced of that, it will happen."

One of my friends in the Afghan government suggested that the Taliban's lack of insistence on Mullah Omar's return to power reflected the same kind of false humility they displayed in 1994, when they seized control of Kandahar under the guise of a temporary regime. But it is also possible that ordinary Taliban are feeling a lack of competence at their highest level. Mullah Omar has never been mentioned as playing an active role in organizing any of the Taliban attacks or offensives that I have covered from 2006 to 2008; he is widely regarded by Afghans as a figurehead. Perhaps the Taliban are not insisting on his return because they know their movement can survive without him.

There were several exceptions to the trend, of course, fighters who said they would serve nobody but the current Taliban leader. A 21-year-old Ishaqzai tribesman pledged unwavering allegiance to his leader: "Mullah Omar is the commander of the faithful selected by 1,000 mullahs in the time of the Taliban," he said. "So if he is alive he remains 'Commander of the Faithful.' There is no other man." Another said: "There can be no Islam in the government if Mullah Omar is not part of it." Another who was counted among those who consider Omar indispensable was only willing to consider an alternative leader who was named by Omar himself: "Without Omar, no one is acceptable for us." Also counted in the same group was a man who said he would consider an alternative only if Omar were killed or incapacitated.

Whether any softness in support for Mullah Omar could be turned into an opening for negotiations was not clear. Several of the respondents who lacked enthusiasm for their leader also declared themselves committed to the most bloodthirsty kind of *jihad*: "We are not fighting for Mullah Omar; we are fighting for Islam." Most answers to a general question about negotiations started with a refusal to talk under current conditions, with nearly all respondents saying they did not want to negotiate, for reasons that usually included the presence of foreign troops in Afghanistan and the perception of the Karzai government as a puppet regime. None admitted any willingness to accept money, work, property, or immunity from prosecution in exchange for peace. Still, nearly all of them described themselves as working towards a new political order within the borders of Afghanistan, with a majority saying they want to bring "Islamic rules" or "Islamic government" to the country. Very few respondents seemed to go beyond those aims, with only a small number of extremists saying *jihad* would continue "until the end of the world."

A handful of the Taliban specifically mentioned they were ready to stop fighting if they got an order to halt. The proper authority to give such an order was described as that of "leaders," "big mullahs," or "the *shura*," the latter presumably referring to the Quetta council. Several said they were not qualified to discuss such political matters, making a distinction between "talkers and fighters" in the Taliban ranks (a distinction so common that it is become part of my verbal shorthand with local staff, referring to "fighter Taliban" and "political Taliban"). For such proud warriors to declare willingness for a ceasefire, no matter how theoretical, seems to indicate they are not entirely against negotiations.

Unfortunately there was also generally a lack of faith in Karzai's ability to negotiate, even if he wanted to: "It can never happen because Americans brought Karzai to power. It is not possible," said one fighter. Many insurgents gave a very narrow definition of their reasons for war. A 26-year-old Ishaqzai religious student said: "Until Karzai tells the foreigners to leave we won't accept that offer, and if they leave then we are all Afghans and we will sit together." Some responses even suggested the Taliban felt guilty about killing fellow Muslims among the government forces. "Why are you fighting against this government?" our researcher asked a 25-year-old former driver, from the Ishaqzai tribe. "Because they are with the non-Muslims," he replied. "If there were no non-Muslims we would not fight with them, because one Muslim does not fight with another Muslim. But when we are fighting an Afghan soldier, it is because they are in an American convoy."

"If they weren't in a convoy with Americans, you wouldn't fight with them?"

"No. Then we would not fight."

Still, the bold question about whether a fighter would accept money, a job, or offer of immunity in exchange for peace always elicited strong rhetoric against laying down arms: "Even if you give me so much money that I can't spend it in my entire lifetime, I will not stop. I would not accept it and would continue my fight because I do not want non-Muslims and the people of other religions in my country." The same man said he would accept a government without Mullah Omar, but never the Karzai government. "No, I will not accept a non-Islamic government. I want my king to be a Muslim but never a non-Muslim." Another said: "As long as non-Muslims stay here, I will not stop fighting and even if he were to give me a million million. [I would say] I do not need your money nor your rupees."

Several of our questions touched on the insurgents' relationship with Pakistan: Do you accept the Durand Line as the real border between Afghanistan and Pakistan? Do you think Quetta and Peshawar belong to Afghanistan? Or do you think the Pashtuns should have their own country, Pashtunistan, separate and different from Afghanistan and Pakistan? Elsewhere in the survey, the name Pervez Musharraf was included in a list of leaders as we tried to gauge their impressions about major figures.

Finally, one of our last questions was a general query: Some countries are enemies of the Taliban, some countries are friends. What countries are good? All experts agree that sanctuaries inside Pakistan are hugely important to the insurgency, but these Taliban expressed deep ambivalence about their hosts.

I had previously interviewed alleged Taliban bombers at the Kandahar governor's palace, under the supervision of local NDS officials, and those prisoners described themselves as Pakistanis who attended *madrasas*, where they were persuaded to wage *jihad* against the foreign troops in Afghanistan. Other anecdotal evidence also suggests that the Taliban draw support from elements of Pakistan's security and intelligence services. But it is interesting how the widely accepted notion of Pakistani support for the Taliban seems at odds with the Taliban fighters' own ideas about Pakistan. Many described Pakistan as an enemy and criticized Musharraf with the harshest language in their vocabulary, raising questions about whether any outside actors—even the Taliban's alleged sponsors—control any majority share of the insurgency.

Every fighter said the Pakistani cities of Quetta and Peshawar belonged inside Afghanistan, and rejected the Durand Line as the official border between the two countries. Sometimes these attitudes betrayed a loose grasp of history: "Sind and Punjab used to belong to Pakistan. Those areas of Pakistan were small. In the time of Zahir Shah or someone else, then they made this line." Another said: "The King Zahir Shah sold them, but when Mullah Omar was in Kandahar, he saw the contracts and the contracts were expired. They can never be a part of Pakistan and it is a part of Afghanistan." A third fighter said: "We sold Quetta and Peshawar to Pakistan, but it is part of Afghanistan." Some of the Taliban seemed to be appropriating the cause of Afghan nationalism, and reclaiming the territory beyond the Durand Line, as part of the insurgency's agenda. "They [Quetta and Peshawar] absolutely belong to Afghanistan, and if we become successful in our war we will take it back from Pakistan, because it is a part of our holy Afghanistan." Another said: "Now they belong to Pakistan but originally they belong to Afghanistan. But unfortunately at the moment Afghanistan is in a big pressure: non-Muslims are here. But when the non-Muslims leave Afghanistan then it can never be a part of Pakistan. We will erase the Durand Line."

When asked why Pakistan now controls the territory past the Durand Line, the fighters usually found creative ways of laying the blame on foreign invaders and local governments that serve Western interests. "Because the British handed it over to them," one fighter said, referring to that territory. "Where is the government? It belongs to the Americans now." Another elaborated on the same theme: "Because there is no Islamic government, all of them are non-Muslims, and the government of Pakistan is also a non-Islamic government, and that is why."

Despite all their talk about Pakistan's unfair seizure of the Pashtun lands, the Taliban were strongly reluctant to accept the idea of Pashtunistan as a separate country. Only four respondents said they favoured the creation of a new country for ethnic Pashtuns. "Whether it is Pashtun, Tajik or whatever, all of them are our brothers, and we will live together," said one. Another explained why he opposed the Pashtunistan concept by suggesting that his ethnic identity transcended borders: "We are all united Pashtuns and united Muslims." One of my friends laughed when he saw these results, suggesting they revealed less about the Taliban's attitude towards a Pashtun homeland and more about their unrealistic ambitions. By claiming an historical right to the Pashtun lands inside Pakistan, and the parts of northern Afghanistan never entirely conquered by the Taliban government, he said, the Taliban were merely setting lofty ambitions. "Basically, they want everything," he said, dismissively. But recent statements from Taliban leaders have also reinforced the idea that the Quetta council has explicitly nationalist aims inside Afghanistan.

The Taliban became synonymous with ignorance during their years in government. As insurgents, however, they have shown signs of sophistication: distributing video propaganda, sending press statements via text message, and apparently choosing some of their tactics with the intention of swaying public opinion in NATO countries. I wanted to gauge the Taliban foot soldiers' general level of understanding about the world, because this might reveal how easily they are manipulated by their commanders, how they would react to a politicization of the insurgency, and whether they have evolved from their primitive roots. We asked for fighters' reactions to the names of well-known leaders—George Bush, Hamid Karzai, Pervez Musharraf, Gulbuddin Hekmatyar—and even obscure names such as the Canadian politicians Stephen Harper and Stephane Dion. We asked them to define "NATO," to describe the difference between soldiers from United States, Canada, and Britain, and to tell us the geographic location of Canada in relation to the United States ("If you are looking at a map, and you can see the United States in the middle, where is Canada? On the left side? The right side? The top? or the bottom?"). Because I am working for a Canadian newspaper, and the insurgents we interviewed were all located near Kandahar city, I included questions about their knowledge of the Canadians specifically, asking whether they could muster even the smallest bit of information about Canada: "The Taliban have been fighting against Canadian soldiers in Kandahar for more than one year. What do you know about these Canadians? Can you tell me something about the country where they come from? Is it a big country? Small country? Rich or poor? Hot or cold? What kind of food do Canadians eat? How do they behave with their women? Are there any Muslims in Canada?"

Almost none of the fighters volunteered any correct information in response to any of these questions. Only one fighter correctly guessed that Canada is located to the north of the United States, with the sample performing worse than randomly in response to the question. Four said Canada is "right" of the US on the map, two said "south," one said "left," and one said "to the side." The vast majority refused to hazard a guess. "If you gave me a map, I wouldn't be able to find it," one said. "As long as we are busy with *jihad* we do not know anything," said another. A lot of the responses were monosyllabic mumblings. I have previously encountered well-groomed Taliban operatives near Quetta, intelligent men well-versed in global politics, but at the level of ordinary fighters the insurgents are still deeply ignorant of the outside world. Many of them appeared to filter news from beyond Afghanistan using their understanding of religious history, as shown in this exchange:

Q: Who is Bush? What do you think of him?
A: He is a great injustice, and he is a big terrorist, because he attacked our country and he surrounded the whole world, and he put bases every where, and if they kill one person in Afghanistan he loses many of his NATO soldiers, and he is a very unjust man.
Q: Why did he attack Afghanistan? And why is he against the Afghan people?
A: Because he is against us.
Q: But why?
A: Because non-Muslims have been against Muslims for a long time, just as they attacked the Prophet Mohammad and broke his teeth, so they are against us since that era.

Combing through the pages of transcripts from these interviews, some of the passages that seemed most revealing were the instances when the conversation slipped away from the original list of questions. Spontaneously, without prompting, two of the insurgents started complaining against the modern way of life that has arrived in Kabul. These simple fighters probably did not have much personal experience in the capital, hundreds of kilometres away, but rumours about the sins and excesses of Kabul are a favourite topic of conversation in faraway villages. "There are some things forbidden by Islam and the Koran, like alcohol, adultery and cinemas," said a 27-year-old farmer, with a belt of machine-gun bullets draped around his neck. "Why do they not stop these things which are clearly going on in Kabul and some other provinces? Instead they beat those who are poor." Another insurgent focused on the corrupting influence of foreign movies. Street vendors have started a black-market trade in video discs since the arrival of international forces, selling Indian movies and hardcore pornography—sometimes in the same market where other vendors are selling Taliban propaganda videos that denounce these foreign influences. "They are enthusiastic about the dollar and cinemas," a fighter said. "That is why we are fighting them."

Such perceptions are not exclusive to Taliban fighters, as many ordinary Afghans also say they are disgusted by the lifestyles that the foreigners have recently brought to Afghanistan. But it was revealing that Taliban raised these issues in the context of their motivations for war. I have noticed similar themes in my face-to-face conversations with insurgents. My translator recently invited his trusted friend, a Taliban organizer, for a meeting in Kabul. The black-bearded little man plopped himself down on a cushion beside me and we enjoyed a few hours of conversation. Towards the end of our chat, perhaps feeling more comfortable with me, the insurgent patted my pillow and gave me a knowing look: "You have girls in your guesthouses, yes?" he said. I told him I did not have any female companions in Afghanistan, but he clearly did not believe me. These people feel strongly that the foreign influence brings moral rot to Afghanistan, a corrosive process that undermines values they have cherished for hundreds of years.

The Taliban are a growing force in Kandahar. An intelligence report at the beginning of 2008 suggested that the insurgents controlled more of the provincial districts than the pro-government forces. Any ordinary Afghan can tell you the insurgents hold sway over most of Kandahar's roads, and they have started exercising that influence in worrying ways. I drove the highway between Kabul and Kandahar in 2005, and took a bus between the two cities in 2006. By the following year, 2007, that same road trip would have been considered suicidal. At this point in 2008, I do not even allow my Afghan staff to travel along the highway, because the insurgents are running checkpoints where they interrogate travelers about their sources of employment and kill people suspected of collusion with foreigners. Trucks carrying fuel for military bases are getting attacked with increasing frequency, threatening the supply chain for the foreign troops. Thousands more US soldiers are expected in southern Afghanistan in the coming year, but few observers are predicting the influx of international forces will quell the insurgency in the short term. Some analysts have started referring to the conflict as an uprising, or insurrection, and a frightening number of the ordinary fighters we surveyed in Kandahar fit that description. Pashtun farmers are defending their opium fields against a government that has outlawed their primary industry. They are rising up against foreign forces that bombed hundreds of civilians in recent years. They are fighting a system in Kabul that they accuse of tribal bias and corruption both financial and spiritual. Most fundamentally, they are rejecting the Western influences that flooded into Afghanistan after the collapse of the Taliban regime. Lurking behind these foot soldiers is probably a sophisticated network of insurgent organizers with more complicated motives, but the leaders are not the Taliban who make me worry for the future of Kandahar. The heart of the conflict involves these ordinary insurgents, too numerous to be killed off and too stubborn to give up. As more troops arrive, the people of Kandahar are bracing for an even bigger war.

Notes

1. Author's correspondence with Sami Kovanen, September 2008.
2. US Department of Defense, "Report on Progress toward Security and Stability in Afghanistan", Report to Congress in Accordance with the 2008 National Defense Authorization Act, June 2008, p. 11. http://www.defenselink.mil/pubs/Report_on_Progress_toward_Security_and_Stability_in_Afghanistan_1230.pdf
3. Mullah Naqibullah's death by heart failure in October 2007 happened after months of ill health as a result of a bomb attack in March 2007.
4. See, for example, a forthcoming study by the Afghanistan Independent Human Rights Commission. Other accounts are documented by Human Rights Watch, "The Human Cost: The Consequences of Insurgent Attacks in Afghanistan", April 2007, Volume 19, No. 6 (C). http://www.hrw.org/reports/2007/afghanistan0407/afghanistan0407web.pdf
5. "Administrative Structure of the Taliban Islamic Movement", Al Samood Monthly Islamic Magazine, 2nd Year, 21st Issue, Rabi al Awal 1429, March 2008, pp. 14–17.
6. Major Shahid Afsar, Major Chris Samples and Major Thomas Wood, "The Taliban: An Organizational Analysis," Military Review, May-June 2008, p. 67
7. The United Nations' analysis of genetic clusters found in polio samples also suggests that fighters from Afghanistan's east and south form separate groups, without extensive contact between the two regions.
8. http://www.globeandmail.com/talkingtothetaliban
9. The Popolzai, Alokozai, and Barakzai tribes have the majority of official government power in Kandahar. Their tribal grouping, the Zirak Durranis, have generally held dominance since the 18th century, as noted in Antonio Giustozzi and Noor Ullah, "The Inverted Cycle: Kabul and the Strongmen's Competition for Control over Kandahar, 2001–2006", Central Asian Survey, 26:2, 2007, pp. 167–84.
10. Many tribal charts show the Durrani confederacy encompassing the Zirak and Panjpai groups of tribes, but interviews in Kandahar suggest the categorization of the Panjpai may not be so clear. Panjpais sometimes describe themselves as Ghilzais—particularly, it seems, if they oppose the government and its heavy concentration of Zirak Durranis. The difficulty in classifying the Panjpai as either Durrani or Ghilzai has led some researchers to treat them as a separate group. See for example Tribal Liaison Office, Musa Qala/Helmand Rapid Assessment, July 2006, p. 17.
11. Among the first to emphasize the tribal nature of the Taliban were the authors Thomas H. Johnson and M. Chris Mason, with publications such as "Understanding the Taliban and Insurgency in Afghanistan", Orbis, 51:1 (January 2007), pp. 71–89. The survey results from Kandahar do not entirely fit the theory of a Ghilzai tribal uprising described by Johnson and Mason, but the idea is broadly similar: a rebellion by tribes excluded from government.
12. Terry Pedwell, "Taliban leaders distance themselves from suicide attacks against civilians," The Canadian Press, 25 August 2006. The authenticity of the statement could not be verified, which means that this may be an example of information warfare by the international forces, but other sources confirmed that some Taliban were privately uncomfortable with the tactic.
13. "Sahib" is a term of respect in South Asia, which can be translated as "Sir," "Master," or "Mister".

10

THE TALIBAN'S MARCHES

HERAT, FARAH, BAGHDIS AND GHOR

Antonio Giustozzi

Historical background

The time of *jihad* in western Afghanistan (1979–92) was characterised by the relative weakness of the insurgent movements, due to a number of factors: the remoteness of most of these provinces from the sources of supply on the other side of the Pakistani border, the refusal of the Iranian government to supply the insurgents, and the flat landscape in the centre of Herat and in much of Farah, which allowed government and Soviet forces to use armour relatively effectively and reduced the availability of hiding places for the insurgents. Gradually most insurgents in Farah and Herat were subdued or forced to make deals with Kabul ("reconcile"). Baghdis was too remote to attract much interest either from the Soviet/Kabul side or from the insurgents, and the war there was an occasional occurrence. The collapse of the government of Dr Najibullah in 1992 offered an unexpected chance to the surviving insurgents, among whom the leading figure was Mohammad Ismail "Khan". After occupying Herat and seizing the supplies stockpiled there by the Soviets, Ismail Khan set out to consolidate his control over the whole region. His autocratic ways rapidly alienated many of those who had initially sided with him, and before the end of the year he faced a revolt of former government militia and the forces of Hizb-i Islami. Having defeated the revolt, he faced another at the beginning of 1993, which he fended off easily. His efforts to extend his power to Baghdis, Farah and Ghor were not quite as successful. He never had solid control over either of the first two provinces, while his success in imposing his dominion on Ghor was short-lived.

Even Ismail Khan's control over Herat province was not to last long. In early 1995, having been rebuffed in their attempt to take Kabul, the Taliban started directing their attention towards western Afghanistan. Although Ismail Khan had successfully established a monopoly of force in the province, there were clear elements of disfunctionality in the system that he created ("The Emirate of Herat"). After an early failure, the Taliban managed to conquer Herat in September 1995, facing little resistance after the fall of Shindand, the southern gateway to the province. Once in power, the Taliban enlisted significant levels of local support in all of these provinces, particularly among the Pashtun tribal population. In Ghor, it was Aimaq commanders linked to Hizb-i Islami and previously defeated by Ismail Khan who helped the Taliban conquest.

Some rugged areas of Baghdis and particularly Ghor were never taken by the Taliban and became the centres of an anti-Taliban insurgency. Until 2001, such insurgency achieved very little beyond annoying the regime. With American and Iranian support, however, after 9/11 Taliban control quickly collapsed and Ismail Khan was able to re-establish his control over Herat, appointing himself as governor, even though his leadership had been significantly discredited and weakened because of his earlier defeat. As his autocratic ways had not changed, he soon faced opposition both among the Pashtun tribes of Shindand, Gulran and Ghuryan and from former allies in Ghor and Baghdis. He was never able to re-establish even a semblance of direct control over any of the provinces surrounding Herat, while at the same time he antagonised the central government because of his refusal to hand over the plentiful customs duties of Islam Qala, on the border with Iran. The emergence of Herat as an alternative power centre in the west clearly worried Kabul, while Ismail Khan's links to Iran (which, in contrast to its non-intervention in the 1980s, helped Ismail Khan against the Taliban) worried the Americans. In the summer of 2004 a concerted effort to unseat him was launched by an alliance of all his rivals, allegedly sponsored by Kabul. Ismail Khan was forced to leave the position of governor and accept a ministerial post in Kabul. However, it seems did not renounce his ambition to bring Herat back under his control one day.[1]

Factors favouring the spread of the insurgency

Until 2005, western Afghanistan had been almost completely unaffected by the insurgency. Some incidents occurred in 2003 in Baghdis between Pashtuns and Tajik militias loyal to Ismail Khan, where some of the local Pashtuns had some previous links to the Taliban. A similar conflict in Shindand and in some other spots of Herat province was similarly only very indirectly related to the insurgency and was largely motivated by local grievances. Kabul was involved as part of an effort to discredit and weaken Ismail Khan.[2] In Ghor, conflicts between local commanders were frequent, but none of this was taking the form of opposition to the central government. The presence of Taliban in the southern district of Pasaband, which has a significant Pashtun population, was reported already in 2002, but like in other parts of the country these were inactive groups who were trying to escape retribution and showed no interest in joining the insurgency at that stage. In Farah, there was a modest presence of elements linked to the Taliban in the far eastern corner of the province only.[3] Former Taliban living in the province were again mostly lying low and being quiet, while political tension was mostly between elements associated with Ismail Khan and others linked to the central government and to the strongman of Kandahar, Gul Agha Shirzai.[4]

At that point in time the Taliban were simply not in a position to exploit local rivalries and state weaknesses in the west, owing to their long lines of supply and limited overall resources. Nonetheless, opportunities in the west existed and the ground for the later penetration of the Taliban there was being laid during this period, as the state structure started decaying as a result of internicine conflict and political paralysis at the centre. In 2004 elements within the central government encouraged the mobilisation of armed groups to fight against Ismail Khan, in order to deligitimise and discredit him, to expose his weakness and ultimately to make it possible to remove him from the governorship of Herat.[5] Although the plan was successful, it also proved destabilising in a number of districts, where the government and the new local authorities had no strength to restrain or control armed groups. The most prominent example of anti-Ismail Khan declining militias into banditry and/or hijacking by anti-government forces was to be found in Shindand and more precisely in Zeerkoh, a mountainous area south of the town, inhabited mostly by Noorzai Pashtuns. As early as the first few days of the post-Ismail Khan era, the militias were already indulging in looting and thievery. The death of the militias' leader, Amanullah Khan, in 2006, was a key development in the decay of the Zeerkoh militias, which fragmented under several leaders, some of whom then established a direct connection with the Taliban.[6]

If the governance of Herat left much to be desired, the three remaining provinces of the west were all basket cases of extremely bad governance. Although the spread of Taliban influence in Farah owed much to a massive influx of Taliban from Helmand, there are clear indications that state institutions were in a deep state of crisis long before that. Banditry affected Farah already in the immediate aftermath of the American invasion, but appears to have grown worse over time. Some Noorzai notables from Farah present it as a kind of popular revolt against a provincial administration largely controlled by their traditional rivals, the Barakzais. There seems to be a fair degree of truth in this assessment. Although Noorzais represent the largest portion of Farah's population, an estimated two thirds of the administration is in the hands of the Barakzais. Eng. Ibrahim, deputy head of the NDS, member of the NSC and close confidant to Karzai, turned into a major power broker in his home province of Farah, where several of his relatives were incorporated in the administration or formed armed militias. Allegations of harassment and abuse at the hands of government agencies and militias linked to Kabul were plenty among Noorzais. Many members of the tribe supported the Taliban regime and served under it, a fact which made it easier to target them within the context of the counter-insurgency effort. The same might hold true for Alizai communities, which rank third among the Pashtuns of Farah in terms of numerical strength and have likewise been excluded from the provincial administration. Elements of both tribes maintain links with fellow tribesmen in the southern provinces. The absence or weak presence of Noorzais and Alizais within the administration is likely to have encouraged lawlessness in the remote districts, as the provincial administration became unable to maintain relations with the local population. Even before the Taliban became a major threat in Farah, the provincial administration had no reach in districts such as Gulestan and Pur Chaman, where the Taliban maintained a low level presence, intermingled with high levels of banditry.[7]

The authorities of Baghdis might have been in an even weaker position than those of Farah, owing partly at least to the particularly bad road network, which made reaching out to the eastern districts very difficult. In Bala-i Murghab and Ghormach an extremely weak government presence, bad roads and rivalries among local communities created an environment in which the Taliban managed to linger on after 2001, even if the distance from the Pakistani border made logistical support very difficult. During 2003–4, violent incidents in Baghdis were attributed by local authorities to efforts of the Taliban to remobilise; other sources indicated a component of ethnic strife in the fighting, pitting supporters of Governor Ismail Khan against some local Pashtun communities, or inter-tribal clashes among Pashtuns.[8] What is clear is that the lack of governance presented opportunities for the Taliban to exploit local rivalries and infiltrate the region as soon as logistical supply lines were in place. The militia leaders who were in control of the provincial capital, Qala-i Naw, were based among some Aimaq communities surrounding the town; other militias existed near the Turkmen border, which were also based among Aimaqs and linked to Ismail Khan in Herat. The Pashtuns of Bala-i Murghab and Ghormach were therefore largely marginalised and had no access to the administration or the police. Quite the contrary, they tried to stay as far from them as possible.[9]

There is no doubt that Ghor was as much affected by local rivalries and bad or nonexistent governance as Baghdis or Farah. During 2002–6 the main militia leaders, based among specific communities, competed for the control of Chaghcharan and the drug route crossing the province. The losers in this conflict had to look either for alternatives such as becoming MPs or for external linkages that would allow them to maintain influence and accumulate some capital, but their valley strongholds were never threatened. As Ghor was the least affected by the Taliban insurgency as of the autumn of 2008, it is necessary to ask why. The argument that the Taliban insurgency relied on tribal Pashtun networks as a key tool of expansion, as much as on religious networks, is plausible in this case: apart from some pockets in the southern districts, where the Taliban often deploy, the ethnic composition of Ghor is entirely non-Pashtun (Aimaq with an Hazara minority in the east). However, another plausible explanation is that the absence of a major player in Ghor, able to fundamentally challenge the interests of local power brokers, prevented the emergence of imbalances of power sufficiently strong to motivate opening of the doors to the Taliban.

One factor which might have facilitated the re-enlistment of former Taliban into the ranks of the insurgency throughout the region was the attitude of the Afghan security services, which seem to have been arresting former Taliban on the potentially flimsy basis of possession of weapons and allegations that they were about to hand these over to the insurgents, even before the insurgency manifested itself in any significant way.[10]

The insurgency takes off

It took until 2006 for the situation in Herat to show dramatic changes, apparently as a result of British deployment in Helmand. The official British version of events, that the Taliban entered Farah to escape the pressure of British forces in Helmand, is only a partial explanation. The Taliban had invested few resources in Farah previously, despite its almost perfect profile as a target for infiltration and subversion: very weak police and governance, plenty of former Taliban hanging around. It is likely that as in Helmand, this was due not to a lack of interest on the Taliban side, but to insufficient resources, difficult logistics and lack of response among the local population. As the Taliban suddenly gained greater resources and freedom of movement in Helmand owing to popular reaction to the British presence, and recruited new cadres for the insurgency, they were now able to deploy significant resources in Farah for the first time. The role of Taliban infiltration from Helmand needs to be relativised, as the Taliban's main strongholds during 2007 emerged in Bakwa and Bala Buluk districts, as opposed to those closer to Helmand (see map). It is these concentrations of Taliban which represented the real threat to the central districts of Farah and were able to carry out relatively effective military operations, as opposed to the loosely organised and more opportunistic armed groups of Pur Chaman, closer to Helmand. From those districts, by 2008 the Taliban were in a position to carry out attacks and infiltrate the western districts of Farah province as well.[11]

Given the very weak government presence described in the previous paragraph, the eastern and southern district of Farah, populated by Pashtuns mostly from the Noorzai tribe, rapidly fell under the influence of the Taliban, who re-mobilised a number of their old local supporters and started new recruitment. Farah's police proved completely unable to cope; often the Taliban were even able to take police stations. The presence of foreign troops was also very limited at this stage, and largely concentrated in the provincial centre. Throughout 2006–7 the Taliban had limited success in penetrating the western districts of Farah, where a significant percentage of the population is Tajik; some instances of local armed resistance to Taliban infiltration were reported. Between the end of 2007 and the early months of 2008, their efforts intensified and seemed to be achieving a greater degree of success; even the border post of Qalat-e Nazar Khan on the Iranian border was attacked twice and several policemen defending it were killed.[12]

Much has been said about the symbiosis of Taliban and bandits in Farah, particularly in the eastern and southern districts. In reality banditry was widespread in Farah even before the Taliban spread their influence to the province, and occurred in areas that as of mid-2008 had not been taken over by the Taliban yet, such as Anardara. Hence the equation Taliban = criminal organisations is simplistic.[13] By 2008 the Taliban clearly appeared to enjoy widespread support among the Noorzais of Farah, but not only among them. The Alizai community in Bala Buluk was considered among the keenest supporters of the Taliban, although one author puts this down to their links to their community of origins in Musa Qala (Helmand). The village of Shaiban allegedly functioned as a sort of HQ for the Taliban of Farah.[14] Another spot of support for the Taliban was an Ishaqzai nomadic community in Anardara, near the border with Shindand.[15]

Another factor behind the rising popularity of the Taliban in Farah is to be identified in the fear of local poppy growers that they would soon be targeted by eradication efforts. Such fears are likely to have been magnified by their lack of influence within the provincial administration. Eradication efforts were never very intense in Farah, but in August 2005 US$20 million were allocated to this purpose specifically for this province.[16] The impact on the ground seems to have been very modest, but it might well have sounded as a warning for local farmers that the age of impunity might soon be over. What is certain is that already in early 2006, that is before the fall of Helmand under Taliban influence, some security incidents not attributable to bandits were beginning to occur and the Taliban were considered to be responsible for them.[17] At this point the Taliban had already appointed a provincial leader in the person of Mullah Qudus, though they were unable to boost their efforts by sending supplies or by transferring fighters from other provinces.

Once they had destabilised most of Farah, the Taliban were in a strong position to infiltrate Herat province. The presence of Taliban agents as far as Herat city itself was already reported in 2005, but they clearly were still receiving little local support anywhere in Herat province. From December 2005, the Taliban carried out a few suicide attacks in Herat city, but failed to cause a stir. At that time the Pashtun strongmen opposed to Ismail Khan were still hoping that the central government would continue to support them and reward them with official appointments. The assassination at the end of 2006 of the leading Pashtun strongman in Shindand, Amanullah Khan, together with the failure of Kabul to deliver on its promises, created new opportunities

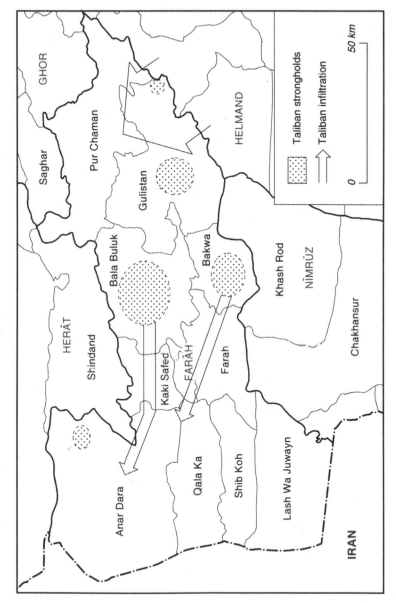

Map 6: The Taliban in Farah, 2008. The map is based on information contained in the text

for the Taliban. During 2007 their presence in Shindand became very significant and as early as in April it led to the first large scale military confrontation
in the west between foreign troops (American) and Taliban. The heavy loss of
life among civilians consolidated the Taliban's role in the local political landscape. The conflict between the small Barakzai community, supported by
Ismail Khan, and the dominant Noorzais contributed to make the Taliban a
welcome presence among the latter. The conflict cannot be described exactly
as tribal: Noorzai communities in neighbouring Adraskan district were left
largely unaffected. Even among the Noorzais of Shindand, although sympathy
for the Taliban seems to have been widespread, only a relatively small number
of tribesmen were at this stage actively involved with the Taliban, while others cooperated with the government and many sided with neither. However,
the Taliban gained freedom of movement in the Zeerkoh area, from which
they started attempts to infiltrate the rest of the province.[18]

More opportunities for the Taliban to infiltrate the rest of Herat province
started appearing during 2007. Turf wars for the control of the province
among local notables intensified during this year. Ismail Khan seems to have
calculated that governor Anwari, a pro-Kabul Shiite, was now so weak that
unseating him and replacing him with one of Ismail's cronies was a real possibility. The spread of banditry to many districts of this once safe and secure
province had already given Ismail Khan sufficient leverage to obtain the
appointment of one of his men (Juma Khan Adil) as chief of police of the
province. Ismail Khan had always claimed that in 2004 Kabul had been
behind efforts to unseat him and in 2008 he was accused of resorting to the
same tactics of destabilisation to discredit Anwari and force a change of governor. Reports and rumours abounded in 2007–8 about how he clandestinely
sponsored armed resistance and favoured the spread of insecurity throughout
the province. What was observable was the paralysis of the police, divided by
the contrast between a component of pro-Ismail Khan former militiamen
and the professional officers who opposed him. In order to clear part of
Guzara district of a gang of kidnappers in early 2008, the governor had to
bring in the border police, who intervened with backup by American special
forces.[19]

NDS sources estimated in spring 2008 that 50 armed groups operated in
Herat province; most of them did not appear to have anything but a merely
criminal agenda, but about 22 groups were believed to entertain some connection with the Taliban. They had by then appointed a provincial leader in
the person of Mullah Abdul Manan Niazi. The main concentration of Taliban
was in Shindand, where 15 Taliban groups were reported to be operating
with an overall strength estimated between 100 and 300. Amanullah Khan's
son Nanghialay was in charge of military operations, while his uncle Nasrullah Khan had become the political representative of the Taliban in the district.
There were other Taliban groups in Herat, as shown in the map.[20]

The two commanders in Ghuryan (Mullah Sangin) and in Guzara (Esma-
tullah) had previously been with the Taliban in the 1990s. Another former

Taliban official, Qari Mohammad Amin, was allegedly involved in the insurgency when he was arrested in Farsi in June 2007. Many other former Taliban were still lingering around in parts of Herat province, particularly Ghuryan and Gulran, but had not yet been mobilised by the spring of 2008. One factor in this reluctance to engage in open warfare might have been the difficulty of waging guerrilla activities in mostly flat and sparsely populated lands like these two districts. Moreover, several small armed groups are active in Adraskan district, which might have something to do with the Taliban. Apart from a single group of about 15 men, which had been seen operating near the highway and had no links to the Taliban, the others were smaller and seemed to stay away from the highway; since there is little worth grabbing in the remote villages of this extremely poor district, it might well be that these were armed propaganda teams deployed by the Taliban to expand their influence there, but there is no confirmation of that.[21]

Groups of Taliban coming from Farah and Helmand often entered Shindand and Farsi district too, but did not deploy permanently there. The assault on Farsi district centre in September 2007 seems to have largely been the work of Taliban coming from Farah or Helmand.[22] An interesting aspect of Taliban activity in Herat has been the proactive attempt to recruit other groups, including some disaffected Jami'atis who "went up the mountains" during 2007. A typical example is that of Ghulam Yahya "Shawshan", a former Jami'ati commander of Guzara district who became an active opposition member. He had been working in the provincial administration until his sacking in 2006. He is known to have received a visit by a delegation of Taliban, who appear to have asked him to join their movement. He was reported to have initially refused to join because of a number of disagreements (for example his alleged refusal to shut down girls' schools), but maintained contacts with them. The number of men under him has been reported to be as high as 170 at one point, but after border police and US special forces launched an operation in Guzara, many followers allegedly deserted, even if Ghulam Yahya himself was not the target of the operation.

By the autumn he had recovered, and was openly proclaiming his allegiance to the Taliban.[23] In the 1980s Ghulam had been a popular Jihadi commander in Guzara; he had his own judicial system and always refused to submit to Ismail Khan.[24] However, since 1992 his relations with Ismail Khan had been good and he still allegedly maintained links to the old Amir. Faiz Ahmad, another Jami'ati linked to Ismail Khan and formerly a police officer, operated in Enjil district until his killing in January 2008 in an operation by the border police, along with four of his men. The group however survived and the leadership was taken over by Bismillah Diwuneh. It counted an estimated 100–120 men.[25] Both commanders were Tajiks, with a record of fighting the Taliban. The fact that they accepted the latter's approach is significant. By the summer of 2008 the Taliban seemed to be working out a formula which would attract significant numbers of non-Pashtuns to their ranks.

The political turf wars which were tearing the Herati establishment apart continued even after the Taliban started showing up in Herat, and helped to

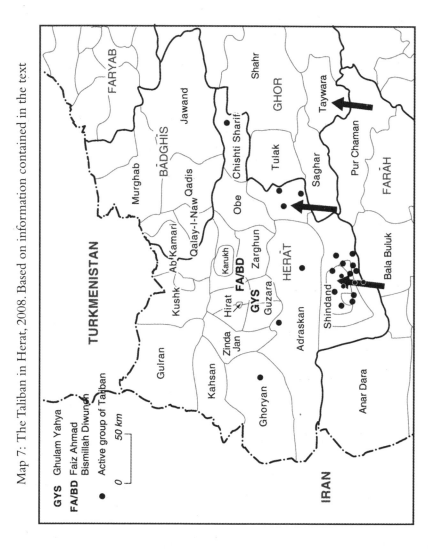

Map 7: The Taliban in Herat, 2008. Based on information contained in the text

GYS Ghulam Yahya
FA/BD Faiz Ahmad
Bismillah Diwunah
• Active group of Taliban

0   50 km

create a climate of insecurity, which favoured further penetration of Herat province by Taliban elements. Ismail Khan remained a major player in local politics, despite spending most of his time in Kabul as Minister of Energy. The death of Amanullah Khan in 2006 deprived the opposition to Ismail Khan of a unifying figure, but the gap was gradually filled at least in part by Mawlawi Khodaidad, the president of the Council of the Ulema. The two rivals had once been allied, but they broke relations relatively soon after the fall of the Taliban regime. Ismail Khan's militias survived their formal disbandment in 2005 in relatively good shape, affected more by internal organisational problems than by the disbandment itself. By comparison with 2004, when he was removed from the position of governor, Ismail Khan's military force seemed to have declined significantly. This was the result of his distance from Herat (he spent most of his time in Kabul and did not have a reliable deputy to represent his interests in Herat) and reduced financial resources (he no longer had control over the customs revenue). Nonetheless, Ismail Khan was still believed in 2008 to have the capability to quickly mobilise a force of 2,000–3,000 men. The organisational centre of his forces seemed to have moved to Guzara and Enjil districts, which include part of the city, from Zindajan, Koshk and Koshk-i Kohne which used to be his strongholds in the past. The rationale of this move would seem to have been that having the militias based at the outskirts of the city facilitates the task of controlling them and would allow faster mobilisation in the event of an open conflict. Controlling militias widely dispersed in the villages is of course a much more complex task, which requires a stronger organisational structure and would not allow a quick call-up.[26]

Although Ismail Khan's military superiority among non-state armed groups was still beyond doubt in 2008, during 2007 Khodaidad was reported to be encouraging the emergence of armed groups in the vicinity of the city, presumably to counterbalance Ismail Khan's reduced but still substantial military strength. Such groups were reported to be engaging in criminal activities as a way to raise funds, contributing to the climate of insecurity which started affecting Herat in 2007. Khodaidad seemed to be focusing most of his efforts on gathering behind him the opposition to Ismail Khan among Pashtuns. Because of his limited success in mobilising armed support and his even more limited success in managing it effectively, Khodaidad does not seem to have functioned very well as a pole of attraction for the province's Pashtuns; indeed, as pointed out earlier, many of Amanullah Khan's old followers joined the Taliban after his death.[27]

The dynamics of the other western provinces were in many regards similar in 2006–8. The growing influence of the Taliban in Helmand in 2006–7 was felt in Ghor as it did in Farah, although the impact was much more modest. As of mid-2008 little evidence of in-depth penetration by Taliban elements within Ghor had emerged, except for a few agents, who were establishing connections with a number of local commanders. The Taliban from Helmand were using the southern districts of Pasaband and Taywara as a logistical rear and resting place (see map), but of the many security incidents which occurred in Ghor from 2006, only a few taking place near the border with Helmand were attributable to the Taliban. One exception was the case of Mawin Ahmad, a *qazi* and former Jihadi commander who may have had links to the Taliban in Dawlatyar; a community mobilisation seems to have followed his arrest in February 2008, and the district centre was stormed.[28] In general, the Taliban may have been more interested in keeping their supply route open than in quickly turning Ghor into a battlefield. As mentioned earlier, the fact that the provincial authorities and the Lithuanian PRT were so weak, under-resourced and unable to challenge the strongmen was a reason for not starting an open conflict: there was no reason for the strongmen to openly challenge the authorities.

This does not mean that the attempts of the Taliban to establish contacts were completely unsuccessful. One of the erstwhile contenders for control over Chaghchran, Ahmad Morghabi, was reported to have established relations with the Taliban and facilitated movement of their supplies towards north-western Afghanistan, possibly to make up for his marginalisation from the few sources of revenue in the province. The former Hizbi commanders of northern Ghor were similarly reported to be re-connecing to the Taliban. Despite being Aimaqs, they had been associated with the Taliban regime in the late 1990s and until the collapse of Mullah Omar's regime and had been excluded from power and influence after 2001.[29]

In Baghdis the efforts of the Neo-Taliban to re-mobilise their former companions, as well as "fresh blood", seem to have been under way no later than 2007. They took the usual form of the despatch of agents and agitators ("preachers"), but their eventual success was rather the result of a renewed crisis of bad governance. In the autumn of 2007, probably stimulated by news of the arrival of such agents, the border police of Baghdis raided the Pashtun populated areas of Ghormach and Bala-i Murghab as a preventive measure. However, the Tajik-dominated and Ismail Khan-affiliated border police had a long standing grudge against some of the local Pashtun leaders, who had been associated with the Taliban. Moreover, it was a badly disciplined force. The result was a wave of looting and rape at the expense of Pashtun villagers. The ensuing tribal revolt was intercepted by the Taliban agents, who offered help and found it much easier to argue that it was necessary to fight against an impious state. Local police forces turned out to be unable to cope with the scale of the revolt; the deployment of police units from Takhar only made the situation worse as they too indulged in abusive behaviour.

The deployment of a relatively strong contigent of ANA and of some ISAF forces towards the end of 2007 put only a temporary lid on the expansion of the Taliban. The insurgents' control over Bala-i Murghab remained unchallenged as poor or non-existing roads hampered the ability of the armed forces to deploy there. With this stronghold available, despite heightened attention by the ISAF, low intensity guerrilla operations spread throughout Baghdis, including to areas populated by Aimaqs. A large-scale attack on a supply convoy, escorted by the ANA and ANP, which took place in Bala-i Murghab in

November 2008, also showed a significant improvement in the tactical capabilities of the Taliban of Baghdis.[30] The poverty of the province did not allow local strongmen opposed to the Taliban to mobilise sufficient forces to oppose them effectively; in all of the eastern districts, it was reported that only one community in Bala-i Murghab (the Dawdi)[31] was actively fighting the Taliban. Significantly, even this community refused any cooperation with a state seen as utterly corrupt and ineffective. Some sources alleged that a dirt road was being built by the Taliban over an existing track in Jawand, suggesting that the aim was to improve the supply line into Baghdis; according to other sources the improvement effort was being funded by drug smugglers. Jawand is the district of Baghdis worst served by roads and one of the worst in the country in this regard. In any case, the building of this road by non-state agents bears witness to the extreme weakness of the state in Baghdis. The Taliban also used Baghdis in 2007–8 as a platform for infiltrating the neighbouring province of Faryab.[32]

Map 8: The Taliban in Baghdis, 2008. Based on information contained in the text. Strategic rationale of Taliban expansion to the west

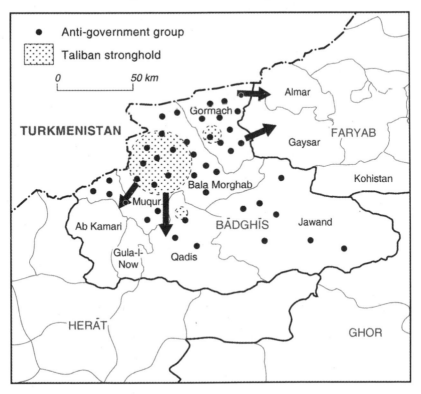

The debate on whether the Taliban have a strategy or not is far from being resolved.[33] This author's opinion is that a strategy exists, even if it is loosely and sometimes clumsily applied. In this case, there are at least two possible reasons for the Taliban's move westwards. The first is the establishment of supply lines with Iran and the second a more general desire to expand the insurgency geographically. Most observers believe that most of what crosses into Afghanistan from the Irano-Afghan border is smuggling in which the Iranian authorities might well have no role, though even Taliban sources confirm that some modest amounts of aid have been delivered to them by the Sepah-i Pasdaran. Nanghialay (from Shindand) reportedly went to Iran and brought back some weapons, while Ghulam Yahya is also reported to have links to Iran. Given the modest size of these commanders' forces, it should be assumed that little help must have come from Iran, especially as support was also reported to have come from other Taliban through Farah. In any case, what matters for the present chapter is that supplies came through the Iranian border. Although already in 2006 some individuals within the ISAF were speculating about Iran's links to the Taliban, evidence of supplies actually coming in only surfaced in the spring of 2007.[34]

In other words, Taliban infiltration into the west coincided with supplies beginning to cross the border in significant quantities. What is not clear, from available information, is whether the growing quantity of supplies reaching the Taliban from the Iranian border was cause or effect of their expansion westwards. Although most of the supplies coming into Afghanistan from the western neighbour in 2007–8 were aimed at the southern fronts, until the Taliban had established a presence in the west they had little reason to develop supply lines from Iran, which would have been very long and unsafe. Given the growing wariness apparent among the Taliban leadership of the long-term reliability of their Pakistani supply lines and logistical rear, establishing alternative supply routes with Iran might well have been a strategic objective in its own right and the expansion of an armed presence in the west might have been a side-effect of this. Some observers even believe that a fairly sophisticated supply network was gradually developed in the west and that the expanding military presence of the Taliban in the area might be primarily conceived as a kind of protection of this network.[35]

Available evidence is indecisive. A relatively large cache of weapons was captured in the summer of 2007 by Afghan security forces in Ghuryan district, an area where the Taliban had a minimal presence. Similarly a cache was found in January 2008 in Anardara district, also an area of very modest Taliban presence.[36] These incidents could be seen as confirming that the Taliban hardly needed an armed presence to build a supply network, but also as an indication that in the absence of military forces such a supply network was vulnerable to disruption by the security forces.[37] In the areas of Farah where the Taliban had a strong presence, regular and extensive patrolling of rural areas by ISAF or Afghan government forces was obviously not possible. There are also clear indications that the Taliban considered geographic expansion a major strategic priority. For example, in Baghdis a small group of as few as 50 "cadres" (or "core fighters" in the ISAF's parlance) was used to lead 2–5,000 tribal warriors, while another 200–250 "cadres" dedicated themselves to trying to infiltrate Faryab.[38] This allocation of human resources seems quite eloquent. At the end of the day establishing what was the main driver of the Taliban's expansion westwards is not so important, and the two reasons discussed here are not mutually exclusive.

Tactics and organisation of the Taliban

As in many other places throughout Afghanistan, there are indications that Taliban mobilisation occurred in the west through several stages. The dispatch of agitators and preachers was the first such stage and was reported in Shindand in 2005 and in Baghdis in 2007 (or earlier); there is no precise information available about other areas. The next stage—the infiltration of small groups of armed men in charge of armed propaganda, consolidating the propaganda work of the agitators and intimidating potential opponents—seems to have occurred in Farah and Shindand mainly in 2006–7. At the same time, the "political agents" already deployed were trying to mobilise armed groups among the local population. The arrival or formation of larger groups of armed men, coinciding with the launch of a relatively intense guerrilla campaign, was already happening in parts of Farah in the autumn 2006. It is important to point out that even when the Taliban moved forces to neighbouring provinces to escape ISAF operations, as often happened in Ghor, Uruzgan, Daikundi and Farah among others, they usually did not carry out military operations there unless a support network was already in place. For example, no major attacks were carried out in either Ghor or Daikundi in 2006–7, despite the weak government presence, even when large groups of fighters were available. The participation of Taliban fighters from Helmand in the fighting in Farah in late 2006 and in 2007, therefore, suggests that the Taliban had already made significant progress in the establishment of such a support network. Similarly, once local strongholds in Bakwa and Bala Buluk were consolidated, the Taliban started raiding the other districts, where support structures of "facilitators", informers and sympathisers had meanwhile been established.[39]

As usual the Taliban tried to build a network of armed groups as interconnected and as wide as possible, in order to guarantee a measure of territorial "control". For example, efforts by the Taliban leadership in Farah were reported to be underway in 2007 to integrate the military fronts of Bakwa and Baba Buluk with the Taliban presence in Pur Chaman.[40] On top of this structure, essentially manned by full-time fighters, whenever possible the Taliban mobilised local communities to provide part-time fighters. Helped by bad governance and a host of local rivalries, their success in this regard was considerable, although quite uneven. In Baghdis, despite the small number of cadres (estimated at around 50), they could mobilise between 2,000 and 5,000 tribal warriors, mainly in Bala-i Murghab and to a lesser extent in Ghormach. Here the organisation was particularly loose, owing to the long distance from the Taliban headquarters in Pakistan and the small number of cadres. Visits from representatives of the leadership were rare and communications difficult. In Farah and Shindand too the Taliban had a significant ability to mobilise part-time fighters among locals, mainly in parts of Bala Buluk and Bakwa, but also in Gulistan, in Pur Chaman and in a single spot in Anardara. Their success was much more patchy even among Noorzai communities, hence the cooperation with independent armed groups and bandits.[41]

The Taliban practice of appointing provincial governors and chiefs of police in every province had little meaning in the west. This was of course particularly true in the case of Ghor, where both Taliban "authorities" were in fact based in Helmand and were relatively low rank field commanders.[42] Where the presence of the Taliban in the territory consolidated itself, establishing even the simplest formal governance structures proved quite a challenge for the loosely organised and weakly structured movement. In Shindand, for example, differences were reported between "governor" Manan (a relatively high ranking "old" Taliban activist) and the district military commander Nanghialay, who seemed to be refusing to recognise the authority of the former. It appears that the differences originated over the control of the position of Taliban "governor" of Shindand; Naghialay wanted the position, but the Taliban leadership, which opposed plurality of positions in the hands of a single individual, refused his request and appointed Mullah Tazeh Gul instead. Nanghialay appears to have tried to mobilise the Noorzais behind him in order to put pressure on the Taliban, but apparently without success.[43]

The military tactics and technology of the Taliban in the west have not been shone in their sophistication, but they achieved their aim of creating chaos, particularly in Farah. Targeted assassinations of government officials, particularly police officers, were carried out even in the provincial centre. IEDs were used, although not in large numbers. Ambushes of convoys also occurred, although the impression from the reports is that they were not carried out in a particularly skilful way, at least until the November 2008 attack in Baghdis (mentioned above). In other words, Farah and the west do not seem to have been particularly prioritised by the Taliban in terms of capacity building among their ranks. By contrast, there is evidence that the Taliban have been posting a substantial number of "cadres" to the western provinces from the south and from Pakistan; a number of Helmandis were reported to be operating in Farah and Shindand from late 2006 onwards, and some might have travelled as far as Baghdis. Taking into account the limited absorption capacity of the western provinces in 2007–8 (none of them being fully engulfed in the insurgency yet), the deployment of human resources there seems quite significant.[44] This seems to suggest that "political" work has been prioritised over military activities, an attitude also justified by the less than proactive attitude of the foreign forces deployed here.

Future prospects

Although the penetration of Herat province by the Taliban was by early 2009 still quite limited, there seemed to be additional potential. In the past, this area was a theatre of clashes between Ismail Khan's militias and a number of local Pashtun leaders. In the western districts of Ghuryan and Gulran, where the Noorzai tribe is present in strength, even if it has been largely Persianised and its members speak Dari as first language, during the 1990s the Taliban found a strong base of support. One source estimates that in all 18,000 men from Herat served under the Taliban, in large majority Pashtuns. Using tribal connections, Taliban agents could easily penetrate and find hosts in this area, then exploit local rivalries between Pashtun groups and supporters of Ismail Khan, dating back to the 1980s or to the period of Taliban control. Mullah Manan, the provincial "governor" of the Taliban, has indeed been reported to have travelled to these two districts to meet tribal elders.[45] In the presence of an effective police force, these two districts would not provide many safe hideouts for the insurgents, as they are sparsely populated and offer a limited numbers of hideouts; given the current paralysis and ineffectiveness of the police, however, the chance of a successful spread of the insurgency is not so remote. It is significant that one of the first acts of the new Minister of the Interior, Hanif Atmar, was to start sacking police officers in Herat in November 2008.

There is a strong Pashtun presence in Guzara and Enjil too, both areas which are close to the city. Here too, in the past, Pashtun leaders experienced rivalry with Ismail Khan and his militias.[46] The settlement of the conflict between Ismail Khan and forces opposed to him did not seem to be within reach at the time of writing this chapter. The division was so deep that even a change in the local authorities would probably fail to satisfy at least one of the main factions. Moreover, as long as Kabul's hold is perceived as failing, the opposed factions have little incentive to reach a settlement, which leaves a window of opportunity for the Taliban open.

The potential for the Taliban to expand their activities beyond Pashtun territory is less obvious. Attempts are clearly being made, as the above mentioned example of former Jami'ati commanders from Herat show. There are other examples too: pro-Taliban propagandists were distributing leaflets in a Tajik district like Karokh in 2007, while a weapons cache was found in Pashtun Zarghoon in July 2008.[47] As of July 2008, however, the results were modest. In fact, in a number of cases the decayed but not extinguished Tajik militias responded militarily to Taliban infiltration. A case occurred in a village of Anardara in 2006 and another was reported in the district centre of Farsi in 2008.[48] There might be some potential to use networks belonging to other parties as a tool of mobilisation among the non-Pashtun population. The approaches towards the former Hizb-i Islami commanders of Ghor have already been mentioned. Karokh district, mentioned above, also used to be a stronghold of Hizb-i Islami. In most cases, however, Hizb-i Islami networks among non-Pashtuns were not very strong in the west. Moreover, by 2008 there were signs that Hizb-i Islami itelf was trying to reorganise in Herat province at least. A commander of an armed group with a background in Hizb-i Islami was present in Gulran, but his current affiliation was unclear. A military presence of the party was reported with certainty only in Shindand, where a brother of Amanullah Khan had joined the party, but there were indications of some activity by the party also in Turghundi (Koshk) and Pashtun Zarghoon.[49]

Notes

1. For more on western Afghanistan until the emergence of the Neo-Taliban, see A. Giustozzi, *Empires of Mud*, forthcoming.
2. See A. Giustozzi, *Empires of Mud*, forthcoming.
3. Giustozzi, *Koran, Kalashnikov and Laptop: the Neo-Taliban Insurgency in Afghanistan*, London: C. Hurst & Co., 2007, p. 5.
4. See A. Giustozzi, *Empires of Mud*, forthcoming.
5. Ibid.
6. See A. Giustozzi, *Koran, Kalashnikov and Laptop*.
7. Personal communications with Noorzai notable and with members of provincial council, April 2008.
8. "Seven killed in Afghanistan 'Taliban' battle", AFP, 26 March 2003; personal communication with UN official, Herat, April 2004.
9. See Giustozzi, *Empires of Mud*, forthcoming.
10. See for example *Sada-ye Jawan* Radio, 6 August 2006 (BBC Monitoring).
11. Personal communication with British officers and diplomats; Rahmani; provincial *shura* members.
12. The attacks on Qalat-e Nazar Khan were attributed by the authorities to "smugglers", but there are doubts about this version of the story. Members of provincial Shura Farah, Kabul 6 May 2008, Roshan and Abd al Ahak; MP Farahi; UN official.
13. ISAF sources; Provincial council members.
14. W. Rahmani, "Farah Province: The New Focus of the Taliban Insurgency", *Terrorism Monitor* 5:23 December 2007.
15. "ISAF secures release of kidnapped Italians", *Pajhwok Afghan News*, 24 September 2007; Dad Nurani, in *Arman-e Melli*, 3 January 2008.
16. "Afghanistan's Farah gets US$20 Mln for Poppy Eradication", *AsiaPulse News*, 22 August 2005.
17. Personal communication from Thomas Ruttig, April 2008.
18. A. Giustozzi, *Koran, Kalashnikov and Laptop*, pp. 68–9; personal communication with members of Herat Provincial council and with UN officials.
19. Provincial council members, officials of international organisations; NGO workers; Herat MPs; ISAF sources
20. NDS source; ISAF sources; personal communication with Herat MP.
21. NDS source, ISAF sources; personal communication with Herat provincial *shura* members; National Afghanistan TV, 26 June 2007.
22. *Herat Pagah*, 15 September 2007.
23. "Afghan Mayor turns Taliban leader", *Aljazeera.Net*, 17 October 2008.

24. On Ghulam Yahya in the 1980s see Giustozzi, *Empires of Mud*.
25. NDS source, ISAF sources; personal communication with officials of international organisations; personal communication with with Herat provincial *shura* members; personal communication with Herat MP.
26. Officials of international organisations; ISAF sources; Herat provincial Shura members; Herat MP; Herat police sources. On the opposition to Ismail Khan in 2002–7 see Giustozzi, *Empires of Mud*, forthcoming.
27. Officials of international organisations; ISAF sources; Herat provincial Shura members; Herat MP; Herat police sources.
28. News dispatch of the Islamic Emirate of Afghanistan, 1 February 2008; "Protestors release district chief, commander", *Pajhwok Afghan News*, 3 February 2008
29. Personal communication from British researcher, with experience of travelling to Ghor, February 2008; personal communication from officials of international organisations; ISAF sources; ANSO sources.
30. Kirk Semple, "Ambush raises unsettling questions in Afghanistan", *New York Times*, 21 December 2008.
31. A small ethnic group born out of the fusion of Pashtuns and Aimaqs.
32. Personal communication with MP from Baghdis; diplomatic sources; personal communication officials of international organisations.
33. For example, in a workshop organised by Rand Corporation in Virginia in July 2008, some participants were convinced of the existence of a Taliban strategy, while others were resolutely opposed to the idea.
34. Officials of international organisations; diplomatic sources; ISAF sources; Herat police sources; "Iranian land mines found in Taliban commander's house", *RFE/RL*, 25 January 2008; Mark Townsend, "Special forces find proof of Iran supplying Taliban with equipment to fight British", *The Observer*, 22 June, 2008; Giustozzi, *Koran, Kalashnikov…*; Con Coughlin, "War on two fronts in Afghanistan", *Daily Telegraph*, 22 December 2006; Robin Wright, "Iranian flow of weapons increasing, officials say", *Washington Post*, 3 June 2007
35. Personal communication from ANSO official, Herat, April 2008.
36. "Iranian Land Mines Found In Taliban Commander's House', *RFE/RL*, 25 January 2008; Ron Synovitz, "Afghanistan: Official says Iranian mines found In Taliban commander's house", *RFE/RL*, 25 January 2008.
37. "Large weapons cache discovered in Western Afghanistan", *RFE/RL*, 7 September 2007.
38. Diplomatic sources; NDS sources; personal communications with officials of international organisations.
39. On the presence of armed Taliban groups in Shindand see "NATO: 'High-priority' Taliban leaders killed", *CNN*, 17 July 2008. On Taliban support networks in Farah see for example "Iranian land Mines found In Taliban commander's house", *RFE/RL*, 25 January 2008; "ANA detains Taliban facilitator, recovers weapon caches in Herat", Combined Joint Task Force-82, Combined Press Information Center, Release # 112, 18 April 2007 (which erroneously refers to Gulistan district as being part of Herat province); Carlotta Gall, "Afghans catch 2 Taliban figures sought in violence and bombings", *The New York Times*, 6 June 2005.
40. W. Rahmani (note 334).
41. Diplomatic sources; ISAF sources; personal communications with officials of international organisations; Sébastien Pennes, "L'Insurrection talibane: guerre économique ou idéologique?", *Politique Étrangère*, 2: 2008.

42. They were Mullah Jalil (governor) and Mullah Abdul Saraj (police), both killed during a clash with police in Ghor in May 2008. See "Taliban 'governor, police chief' slain in Afghan operation", Agence France Presse, 8 May 2008; "6 Taliban fighters killed in a clash with police in western Afghanistan", The Associated Press, 8 May 2008.
43. Personal communication with officials of international organisations; NDS sources; ISAF sources.
44. Personal communications with officials of international organisations and police officers; ISAF sources; diplomatic sources.
45. Personal communications with officials of international organisations; ISAF sources.
46. See Giustozzi, Empires of Mud, forthcoming, for background
47. Mohamad Reza Shir Mohamadi, "Weapons cache in Herat uncovered", www. quqnoos.com, 28 July 2008 [accessed 29 July 2008].
48. Personal communication with UN official, Kabul, May 2007; Herat Pagah, 15 September 2007.
49. Personal communication with Provincial Shura members; police sources; personal communication with officials of international organisations.

11

TALIBAN AND COUNTER-INSURGENCY IN KUNAR[1]

David Kilcullen

During the summer and autumn of 2006, and again in the spring of 2008, I led field assessment teams in Afghanistan. In each case the aim was to conduct an independent expert review of the Afghan campaign, to identify best practices and challenges. During 2006 and 2008, my team conducted numerous debriefings, round-tables, structured interviews and analysis sessions with US and Coalition military, diplomatic, intelligence, aid and counternarcotics personnel. I also met many Afghans—officials of the Government of Afghanistan, provincial governors, local officials, intelligence officers, police and military officers, tribal and community leaders, and recently captured or reconciled Taliban. I spent time with senior commanders of ISAF, representatives of the United Nations and members of commercial firms, aid agencies and NGOs working in rural Afghanistan. I visited Kunar several times after 2001; the last time I was there was in the spring of 2008.

Although it is often described by the aggregative shorthand term "Taliban", the insurgent coalition in Afghanistan is actually a fragmented series of shifting tactical alliances of convenience, especially in the East. Insurgents in the South are comparatively unified under the Taliban Quetta *shura*, the core leadership group of the old Taliban regime now based, as a *de facto* "government-in-exile", in Pakistan's Baluchistan province, while in the East extremist groups—such as Lashkar-i-Tayba (LeT), Hizb-i Islami Gulbuddin (HiG), Tehrik-i-Nafaz-i-Shariat-i-Mohammadi (TNSM) as well as al Qa'ida, and the "Pakistani Taliban" under leaders like Baitullah Mehsud and the Haqqani network in Waziristan—are loosely cooperating toward roughly similar objectives. Paradoxically, their disunity makes them harder to counter—they have no central leadership that can be dealt with, co-opted or eliminated.

Setting the scene[2]

On a small-scale map Kunar Province looks like a wedge-shaped block, resembling a distorted pine tree lying on its right-hand side along the Afghan-Pakistan border north-east of Jalalabad, with the province of Nangarhar to its south and, to the east across the Durand Line, Mohmand and Bajaur Agencies of the Federally Administered Tribal Areas (FATA) and the districts of Chitral, Swat and Dir (a rumored location for Usama bin Laden), in the Malakand Division of Pakistan's North-West Frontier Province. But thinking of Kunar province as a solid block of undifferentiated territory and regularly administered population is entirely wrong. Topographically Kunar is not a block but a tree, its trunk running southwest to northeast along the Kunar River Valley on the province's eastern edge, anchored by the towns of Jalalabad (capital of Nangarhar Province) to the southwest, Asadabad (the Kunar provincial capital) in the center and the large village of Asmar (in Bar Kunar district) to the northeast. The "branches" are tributary valleys of the Kunar, running west into Afghanistan and east to Pakistan, each dividing into smaller branches in a twig-like capillary drainage system. The Kunar River is about 480 kilometers long, rising in Pakistan (where it is called the Chitral) and flowing south into the Kabul River just east of Jalalabad. It is a perennial, shallow braided stream system, non-navigable except by small boats, rarely and—until recently—poorly bridged outside major towns, with a rocky stream-bed and high gravel banks, fed by snow-melt from the mountain ranges (Hindu Kush to the west, Hindu Raj to the east). Tributary creeks and streams are intermittent, some flowing in the spring and early summer while others are dry *wadis* that only experience occasional flash flooding during storms or the spring thaw. Although there are some glaciated landforms in Kunar, in general the valleys are V-shaped, with steep bare craggy mountains sloping down to narrow basins dominated by the rivers and their flood plains (less than 500 meters wide in most places, much narrower in others). The province is rich in natural resources, especially timber, in which there has long been a lively cross-border smuggling racket, prompting a recent moratorium on timber movement by the Provincial Governor, Fazlullah Wahidi: I saw several overstocked lumber yards in March 2008.

In its human geography the province is also tree-like, its population clustering in villages on the valley floors and along the tributaries of the river system, like leaves on branches. Most villages and all towns are in valleys, while the mountainous interstices between the valleys are barren and largely unpopulated. The total population, last estimated in 2006, is approximately 390,000[3] across the province's fifteen districts. Since almost all these people live in villages along the valley floor, and securing the province means securing them where they live, operations tend to focus on securing valleys not hills. Also, because each valley feeds into the next, parts of the population are isolated from the rest, and movement from a minor capillary valley to the main Kunar valley, or further to Jalalabad or Kabul, requires passing through multiple terrain compartments and chokepoints. Areas like the Korengal or Watapur districts, for example, have traditionally been very isolated because of this: their populations have a general clannishness and suspicion of outsiders as a result and, at least in the Korengal, the population has long been vulnerable to religious indoctrination by extremists.[4] Thus securing routes is also critical. Holding the valleys and routes is not the whole security problem, though: critical points in the hills also have to be held, because they dominate routes and allow observation and fire onto populated areas; it is a tenet of mountain warfare on the frontier that whoever holds the high ground at dawn tends to have the upper hand.[5] But mountain picquets and outposts are supporting activities for the main security effort, which is to create a protective "bubble" around each population center, then link each bubble to the next through measures that hold and protect the valleys and the routes along them (traditionally unimproved dirt tracks, more recently paved roads).

In counterinsurgency the population is the prize, and protecting and controlling the population is the key activity. The war, therefore, is where the people are: you win or lose it a village at a time, and you secure villages and gain access to the people by controlling valleys, roads and the heights that overlook them, in that order of priority. Politically, also, the province is a tree not a block, with political power centering in the major towns, and state influence attenuating sharply with distance from the main valleys and their population centers. Shifting the metaphor, we might consider towns and their associated valley-based infrastructure as magnets that draw in population, information, resources and also predators, with a field of attraction and influence that weakens with distance. This has always been so, and indeed the state has never been particularly influential in this part of the country. As my colleague Chris Mason has argued, most Afghans have historically had little interaction with the central state, and they like it that way.[6] Recent World Bank governance assessments support this view,[7] as do detailed analyses spanning many years by the highly-respected Afghanistan analysts Thomas Johnson[8] and Barnett Rubin.[9]

Ethnography of Kunar

The population of Kunar can be divided into three groups: the Nuristani people, who populate Naray district in the far northeast of the province; the Pashais of Bar Kunar and Dangam districts, in the east, who speak their own language although in some areas have been increasingly Pashtunised; and Pashtuns who represent the large majority of the population. The latter are in turn divided into a number of major tribes: the Safi who dominate the center and west of the province in Asadabad, Marawara, Narang, Darya-e Pech, Chawkay and Chapa Dara districts; the Mohmand, a major cross-border tribe dominant east of the Kunar river, the Ghilzai of Nurgal and Sirkanay districts, and the Khugiyani of Khas Kunar district (see map). As in other societies in the Pashtun culture area, Kunar's social structure is based on what anthropologists call a "segmentary kinship system", with tribes divided into sub-tribes, clans, sections (usually inhabiting one, or sometimes several villages) and sub-sections (extended families) based on lineage segments that are defined by descent from a common apical male ancestor.

In Akbar Ahmed's terms, the remoter mountain tribes are *nang* Pashtuns, while lowland people in the main Kunar valleys might be considered *qalangi*. *Nang* Pashtuns (those driven by *nang*, honor), who typically live in low-production zones, mountains and areas distant from the reach of the state and tend to be warlike and predatory; *qalang* Pashtuns (those who pay *qalang* or *kandar*, taxes or rent) typically live in richer, fertile irrigated lowland areas under greater control of the state. Like mountain tribes everywhere in the world, *nang* Pashtuns look down on lowlanders and have traditionally regarded

Map 9: Tribes and ethnic groups of Kunar

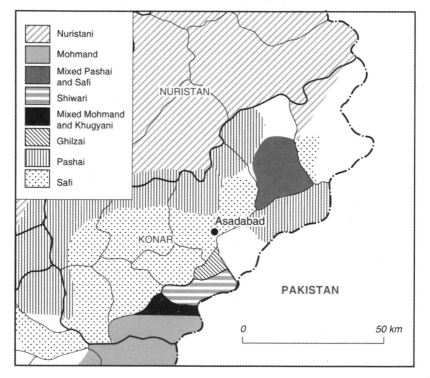

234

them as fair game for raiding and pillaging. Except for the *kuchi*[10] (nomadic Pashtuns, of whom there are virtually none in Kunar) all Pashtun tribes—even the most honor-driven, remote *khel* outside government control—tend to make their livelihood as sedentary agriculturalists (crop-growing house-dwellers tied to their villages and fields) rather than nomadic pastoralists (mobile tent-dwellers who live by their flocks). This means that the traditional recourse of nomadic tribes when threatened by the encroachment of enemies or state authorities into their independence—namely, to escape into inhospitable terrain where adversaries cannot follow—is not open to Pashtun hill-tribes, tied as they are to households, fixed landholdings and immobile crops. Thus when threatened they tend to stay and fight, banding together to resist intrusion and re-establish their independence from external control (a hallmark characteristic of tribes as distinct from peasants) through violent resistance rather than withdrawal. This cultural ecology perspective, though perhaps subject to charges of environmental determinism, may at least partly account for the extremely warlike nature of Pashtun tribes, as well as for their tendency to fragmentation (or "fission") into feuding sub-groups when the unifying "fusion effect" of an external threat is withdrawn.

The martial character of Pashtun tribes is something of a clichéd stereotype, though it is rarely remarked on in contemporary conflict literature (where most analysts tend to focus on the war-weariness of Afghans after decades of conflict). Still, over the years the warlike nature of Afghans has become very evident to me, repeatedly when coming to Afghanistan between tours in Iraq and visits to other theaters in the "war on terrorism". At the risk of reinforcing cultural stereotypes that provide a partial picture, and a caricature at worst, I would be remiss if I failed to record my observation that while Iraqi insurgents like to win, and they certainly enjoy killing people who cannot hit back, they do not particularly like to fight. They do not exactly *dislike* fighting, and will do so willingly in protection of relatives or hope of plunder or profit, but it is a rare Iraqi who loves the fight itself. Afghans do: they like to win, and are certainly not averse to killing, but what they really love is the fight, *jang* (battle), for its own sake. An illustration was an incident in 2006 where local farmers in Uruzgan took part in a Taliban ambush, not because they supported the Taliban politically or hated the coalition, but for reasons of honor, adventure, and love of the fight.

Patterns of political authority in Pashtun tribes traditionally reflected a shifting internal balance of power, conditioned by these phenomena of balanced opposition, generalized reciprocity, honor (*nang*), extremely warlike behavior, the fusion-fission cycle of response to external threat, primary group cohesion, and a desire for partial or total independence from government control. The authority system was well adapted for maintaining social order and collective security in an inhospitable frontier environment which typically saw little government presence, if any. Like other forms of tribal organization it was, in essence, a self-regulating social system for governance without government.

The tribal governance triad

There were three main poles of this informal power system, which I call the "tribal governance triad". These were the *khan* or, collectively, the *jirga* as a group of tribal elders, the *mullah* as a member of the Islamic religious establishment (the *'ulema shura*), and the government intermediary or representative (the government-approved *malik* or Political Agent in parts of Pakistan, or the district governor in Afghanistan). It might be tempting to liken these functions to those of a modern democratic state, with the *jirga* representing the legislative branch, the *malik* the executive and the *mullah* the judiciary. Some Pashtuns do this: one tribal leader I met in mid-2006 asked why Americans want to bring democracy to Afghanistan through the medium of national elections: "We already have democracy", he said, "but at the level of the tribe, not the central state. How will elections improve things?"[11] The analogy is a limited one, since women and children are excluded from it and it does not cover the full range of state functions, but for male Pashtuns tribal governance is in principle very egalitarian—in ideal terms; except when appointed as a temporary war leader in time of conflict, no adult male Pashtun can tell another what to do. All have a theoretically equal voice in the *jirga* and a right to be heard.

Actions of leaders are sharply circumscribed by group consensus and judgments about what tribal public opinion will bear. In this sense, public opinion is the ultimate sanction, a potent force indeed in one of the most inhospitable regions on earth, where withdrawal of tribal protection can literally be a death sentence. But in theory all hold themselves equal and independent members of a free association based on lineage, rather than slaves of the state or followers of a *khan*. Members of the tribe traditionally positioned themselves for advantage by shifting allegiances and re-balancing among the three competing poles of authority, like middle children in a large family. More broadly, tribespeople participated in business, governmental, party-political and religious hierarchies, simultaneously occupying rungs on multiple ladders. This allowed individuals to deploy supporters and resources from one hierarchical system (say, tribal kin) to neutralize a challenge emerging from another hierarchy (perhaps, an over-eager district governor), but then to shift opportunistically as power relations changed (later making an ally of the governor to outmaneuver a pushy business rival). As Gluckman showed elsewhere,[12] such patterns are very common in "eroded" or "de-tribalizing" systems where traditional authority patterns are disrupted, like Afghanistan. This traditional authority structure can be represented graphically, as in Figure 1.

In Kunar, corrosion of this traditional authority structure through war and its attendant social chaos has been especially heavy, with the introduction of new actors (religious extremists, foreign fighters including the Coalition, and the Afghan government) and the growth of an unemployed, traumatized, deracinated youth vulnerable to recruitment by groups like Gulbuddin Hekmatyar's Hizb-i Islami, the Taliban Peshawar *shura*, associated networks like

Figure 1: Tribal Governance Triad

Pashtun tribes of Eastern Afghanistan an the Frontier
[Ideal-type informal authority structure prior to disruption]

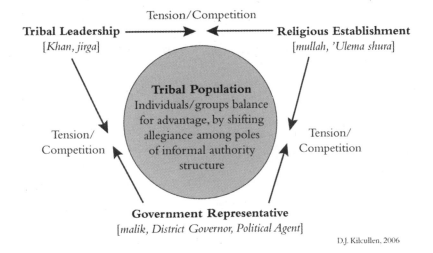

D.J. Kilcullen, 2006

those led by Jalaludin and Siraj Haqqani, or al Qa'ida itself. This in turn has marginalized tribal elders, government representatives, and sometimes also mullahs (though in many cases extremists cooperated with the traditional religious establishment through alliances that super-empowered the mullahs).

Traditionally, the mullah's authority derived from his status as a sanctioner of social practices, an arbiter of faith and morals and a provider of religious and educational services, dispute resolution and mediation to the tribe. As Akbar Ahmed shows, the *mullah* (unlike the *sayyed*, a person with traditionally ascribed authority deriving from his lineage as a descendant of the prophet, similar to a *sharif* among Arabs—governor Wahidi of Kunar is a *sayyed*) had little traditional prestige, but mullahs frequently sought to achieve authority by building a personal following through a network of dyadic patron-client relationships with followers, often provoking rivalry with tribal elders whose authority derived from different sources and who sought to resist the economic or political self-aggrandizement of religious leaders.[13]

This process of change in the internal authority dynamics of tribes can also be represented graphically as in Figure 2.

This process of disruption is critical for the security situation, since many tribal elders and some relatively moderate religious leaders in Kunar have felt dispossessed, which has given them a motivation for revenge and a strong desire to get "back into the game" by driving out extremists and recovering their traditional authority. A series of coalition commanders going back to Colonel Mick Nicholson, who commanded the Brigade in this area in

237

Figure 2: Disrupted Governance Triad
Pashtun tribes of Eastern Afghanistan and the Frontier

Disrupted Governance Triad
Pashtun tribes of Eastern Afghanistan and the Frontier

Terror/Intimidation

Tribal Leadership ←————————————→ **Taliban**
[*coopted, terrorised, or*   [*traditional religious establishment*
allied with Taliban]   *supplanted or coopted*]

Tribal Population
Individuals/groups respond to
Taliban "normative sytem" or
regulations and sanctions, seeking
security and order by conforming
to tribal or Taliban direction

Taliban
[*government representative*
supplanted or eliminated]

D.J. Kilcullen, 2006

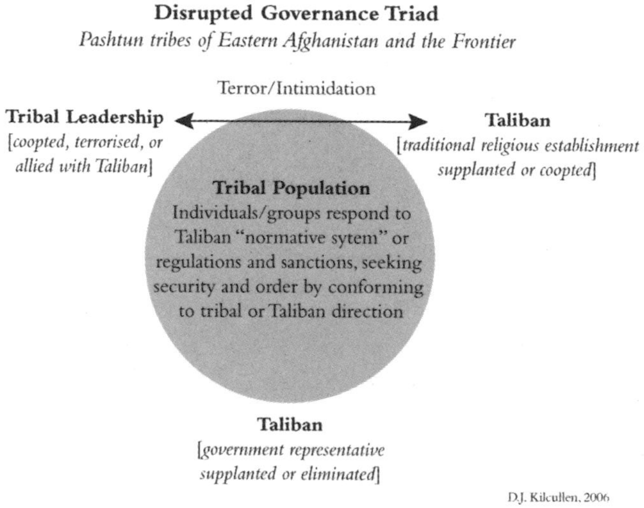

2005–6, Lieutenant Colonel Chris Cavoli, his battalion commander for the Kunar valley, and Provincial Reconstruction Team leaders like Navy Commanders "Doc" Scholl and Larry Legree at Asadabad, worked closely with tribal leaders on this basis, while projects like a new road provided a source of patronage, employment and income to the tribes which traditional leaders, in conjunction with representatives of the Afghan state, were able to disburse to the people—thus cementing their positions of influence, re-establishing tribal cohesion and social norms, and undermining radicals in the tribal power structure and their external extremist sponsors. The road—not the road itself, but the process of constructing it (like the bridge that saved the regiment in David Lean's 1961 film *Bridge on the River Kwai*)—became for some the means of restoring and reintegrating the tribe's honor and cohesion, regaining their status and redressing the erosion of social structure caused by war and extremism.

The Taliban operating system

As described in generic terms earlier, the Taliban are far from unified: they include competing or cooperating factions and, especially in Kunar, are not the only threat since religious extremists like Hizb-i Islami and AQ are also important. Moreover, the term *talib* ("student" or "seeker") applies broadly in Pakistan and Afghanistan to people with varying motivations and characteristics. So any attempt to describe a "Taliban operating system" is to some extent a caricature, a distorted snapshot of one stage in the constant and rapid evolutionary process of a highly adaptive social movement. This description, therefore, is illustrative only.[14]

There are seven basic elements in the system, three located inside Afghanistan ("in-theater") and four in Pakistan (the "active sanctuary"). In-theater elements include full-time fighters (operating as a "mobile column"), local guerrillas (who typically operate on a part-time basis in their local area only), and village cells (providing a clandestine infrastructure for the movement and linking local guerrillas to full-time fighters). The active sanctuary elements, located in Pakistan, include training and logistics support systems, political and religious leadership, the recruiting base for full-time fighters, and external sponsors and financial backers. Terrorist cells operate semi-independently on both sides of the frontier.

The in-theater system works like this: full-time fighters, recruited in either Afghanistan or Pakistan but usually trained in Pakistan, move around the area in groups of varying size (sometimes a dozen or fewer but sometimes up to several hundred, with the ability for small groups to concentrate into larger columns within hours to days). They operate as a mobile column, working in one valley for a period of days or weeks and living in villages or compounds alongside the people or (only when absolutely necessary) out on the hills. They do this until the security forces' response to their presence becomes too intense, at which point they disperse into smaller groups and melt away across the hills into the next valley, where they reassemble at prearranged points and start the process again. Their main activities are political and religious indoctrination, armed propaganda, intimidation and killing of those who support the government or breach their extreme interpretation of *shari'a* law (such as schoolteachers educating girls, active local officials, or tribal leaders working with the government); publicly killing criminals and corrupt or oppressive local figures, in the manner of vigilante justice; attacks on symbols or infrastructure of the coalition or the Government of Afghanistan; collection of taxes; levying of help in kind; and laying of ambushes and Improvised Explosive Devices (IEDs) against government projects or infrastructure.

These fighters operate almost entirely on foot, though pack animals are also sometimes used, and they almost always avoid roads, preferring to move across country, usually by night, and relying on the local knowledge of their part-time guerrilla guides to find neglected passes or mountain trails. Long distance transport of supplies sometimes occurs by road, but in general their use of the road system is incidental, occasional and light. They communicate using radios and cellphones or satellite phones, and carry small arms (rifles and machine guns), rocket launchers, sniper rifles, mortars, mines and explosives for IEDs, and sometimes anti-aircraft weapons. In some cases (as in Nuristan in 2006), a better class of fighter has emerged, appearing to have benefited from professional military training and equipment and operating in a more "regular" fashion; in other cases they operate in a looser, less technology-enabled manner. They function like "flying columns", the technique pioneered by the early IRA in the 1920s,[15] working at a high level of intensity for several months (a typical "tour" for Pakistan-based full-time fighters is four to six months[16]) before returning to Pakistan for rest and refit, to be replaced by another mobile column as it comes on line.

Full-time fighters (sometimes called "Tier 1 Taliban") are usually therefore "foreigners" in any valley where they operate, unless it happens to be their actual home valley, and the mobile column is usually made up of people from several tribes, reinforced by foreign fighters (often Uzbeks, Tajiks, Chechens, Arabs or Pakistanis) acting as embedded trainers or advisers. These embedded foreigners often hang back in the fighting, directing the column's operations, coordinating heavy weapons or logistic support, and generally avoiding direct contact with coalition or government forces, though their presence is well known. Some Afghan tribal leaders I spoke to said that, since many full-time fighters come from refugee communities or originate outside Afghanistan, they do not really fit into the tribal structure: "their tribe is the Taliban".[17] This might create difficulties for the full-time column in terms of local knowledge and support were it not for the next element in the system, the local guerrillas.

Local guerrillas (also known as "Tier 2 Taliban") fight almost entirely in their home valley, usually within a day's march of their village, close to the roads, on a relatively casual "pick-up team" basis and almost always in support of the full-time column; rarely on their own. The arrival of the mobile column in a valley tends to serve as the signal for a general activation of local guerrillas, who fight in support of the column while it is in their valley, then go back to farming as the column melts away and the full-time Taliban depart in the face of reaction from the security forces. Local guerrillas seem mainly to act as guides, conduct reconnaissance, carry ammunition and supplies, support full-time fighters during combat, provide guards and sentries for full-time fighters, and gather intelligence. They are normally motivated by economic self-interest (the Taliban leaders pay local guerrillas for specific activities such as attacking the road or placing an IED), desire for excitement, honor and prestige, fear of retaliation if they fail to support the Taliban, and tribal and local identity (supporting nearer relatives against outsiders). Some exhibit individual motivation along these lines, others fight through tribal loyalty, as in the case of the Mahsuds (a legendarily well-organized, dangerous and cohesive tribe whom the British colonial administrator Sir Olaf Caroe described as a "wolf-pack"[18]) in Waziristan, where tribal elders told me that the tribe had decided to allocate a certain number of their young men, two per family, to fight with the Taliban; in this case the motivation is tribal solidarity, while the tribal leaders themselves are driven by more instrumental motivation.[19] Religious extremism and support for the old Taliban regime are uncommon motivations, according to Afghan intelligence officers and local officials with whom I discussed this,[20] but desire for revenge (badal) and anger arising from the loss of relatives in the fighting or from killing of bystanders and destruction of property through "collateral damage" are more common.[21]

The connective tissue between local guerrillas and full-time fighters, and a key coordinating mechanism in the overall operating system, is the third in-theater element: the village underground. This varies in sophistication between villages but usually comprises a cell of a few individuals, perhaps led by an elder with a traditional or personal connection to the old Taliban regime, along with a few relatives. The cell operates clandestinely, gathering intelligence, reporting on Afghan government or coalition activities, intimidating those who support the government (often, as discussed earlier, via threatening notes—"night letters"—as well as intimidatory visits and assassinations or beatings), managing caches of explosives and ammunition in the local area, and sometimes acting as a shadow governance structure or "guerrilla mayor" of the village (indeed, in some cases I observed, the leader of the local cell was the actual former Taliban "mayor" of a village). The cell rallies local fighters to meet the "flying column" when it is in the valley, coordinates local support work for the full-time fighters, conducts armed propaganda, and provides leadership for local guerrillas. In these ways, the village infrastructure is the key link in the in-theater system.

The external, active sanctuary components of the Taliban operating system, located on Pakistani territory, require only a brief mention here since they do not directly affect the situation inside Kunar. Out-of-theater elements include training and logistic systems (training camps, supply and infiltration routes and depots, contracting and purchasing arrangements for weapons, ammunition and other supplies, medical support for wounded fighters and recreational/leave services); political and religious leadership (including the Quetta *shura*, the Peshawar *shura*, the Hizb-i Islami, the Haqqani network, TNSM, LeT and other Taliban or associated leadership groups); the recruitment base for full-time fighters (largely drawn from cross-border tribes, large-scale Afghan refugee communities in Pakistan and *madrasas*); and sponsors and financial backers. This last category includes both private and unofficial sponsors, and sponsors associated with governments outside Afghanistan. The degree of official endorsement of such sponsorship has been the subject of debate; the fact that members of the Pakistani armed services, civil armed forces[22] and other government agencies have directly and indirectly supported the insurgency (whether on their own initiative or under official direction) is not disputed. It is something of an open question whether the insurgency inside Afghanistan is now self-sustaining, or whether it would wither without its active sanctuary on the Pakistani side of the Durand Line. In my view, since there is very little practical prospect of the active sanctuary diminishing any time soon, the point is rather moot: the sanctuary's role in enabling the insurgency is a fact of life.

The counter-insurgency effort facing the Taliban in Kunar was stronger and more effective than in most Afghan provinces. A series of local outposts, partnering coalition and Afghan forces and police, was established to protect the population centres. The road construction project enabled them to link each bubble to the next. The building of a road gave the sense to the local population that the American presence was not short-term. This persistent presence is essentially a "counter-punching" strategy that relies on a cycle of defense and counter-attack, in which the presence of the road and coalition forces protecting and interacting with the population draws the enemy into attacking defended areas, causing him to come to the population and the government—the opposite of the "search and destroy" approach in which security forces "sweep" the countryside looking for the enemy within the population as if for a needle in a haystack, and in so doing often destroy the haystack in order to find the needle. More particularly, search and destroy operations tend to create a popular backlash and contribute to the "antibody response" that generates large numbers of accidental guerrillas and pushes the population and the enemy together.

The road created an opportunity for the creation of an auxiliary police force, which district chiefs had been trying to get the government in Asadabad and Kabul to authorize; once these chiefs were able to justify the need for local police as a guard force for the road, the Afghan government gave its approval to raise five men from each population center to the road. US forces created a program to equip, train and jointly operate with these local police.[23] Like the raising of local security forces in Iraq (which was partly modeled on the Kunar program), this program was hugely successful in terms of improved security and the beginning of government. Just as in Iraq, however, providing consistent, long-term funding to support local auxiliary forces is a critical requirement and, in the Kunar case, lack of this almost led to disaster: after approving the force, the authorities in Kabul refused to release funds to pay the men in it, who would go for months at a time without pay, creating very significant problems. In the fall of 2006, with the formation of the Afghan National Auxiliary Police, this local force was merged into that organization to give it centralized training, uniforms and equipment, place it on a permanent payroll, and make it a recruiting base for the ANP (which after a year each man had the option to join).

The construction of the roads resulted, over the long term, in a very substantial drop in the number of IEDs being placed along roads,[24] primarily because IEDs were easier to spot and harder to emplace on paved roads, as distinct from the already-existing dirt tracks which were easier to mine.[25] Coalition commanders initially spent considerable time considering how paving would affect IED emplacement—they initially expected that paving would simply lead to side-mounted IEDs in the cliff faces (an escalating response-counter-response situation). In some places the road contractor understood this and cut a wide shoulder, but on balance commanders decided that side-mounted IEDs would still be easier to spot than IEDs buried in the roadway, and that they would still therefore be better off on balance with paving.[26]

However, while the roads eventually brought a drop in IED placement, on the Asadabad-Jalalabad road the construction process (including the digging of more than 200 culverts under the roadway, the presence of piles of loose dirt and gravel along the roadside and the need to park road-building machinery on site overnight) facilitated a temporary spike in IED emplacements. The reduced IED threat also means that security forces can adopt a lower threat posture, allowing them to interact more closely and in a more friendly and collaborative manner with the local population.

Separating the people from the Taliban and connecting them to the government was also a key aspect of the Kunar approach. As noted above, unlike in a conventional development scenario, in a counterinsurgency environment it is much less effective to apply governance and development assistance on a purely needs-based or universal basis. This soaks up resources with minimal political effect, and does little to counter the "accidental guerrilla" phenomenon. By 2006, the Americans had learned to combine kinetic operations (i.e. the use of lethal or potentially lethal force) with engineering activity, civil development assistance, route and population control, and targeted humanitarian and economic assistance, in cooperation with Afghan government officials who applied political negotiations and civil population control measures, all in support of a political strategy to extend government control into an enemy-dominated area. This disrupted the Taliban operating system we have described above, separated the enemy from the people, and gave the population an incentive to support the government. In response to this full-spectrum political maneuver, the enemy mounted their own political maneuver: a campaign to remove the effective local district administrator.

The role of local Afghan officials has already been discussed, and the quality of these officials, especially provincial governors and district administrators, is central. The Kunar governor in 2008, Fazlullah Wahidi, has played an extremely important leadership role in the province. Previous governors in this district, Governor Wafa and Governor Didar, had less of a positive reputation among local people, being seen by some as lacking in energy and prone to influence by third parties.

But the effects described in this case study accrue not just from the road itself, but rather from a conscious and well-developed strategy that uses the road as a tool, and seizes the opportunity created by its construction to generate security, economic, governance and political benefits. This is exactly what is happening in Kunar: the road is one component, albeit a key one, in a broader strategy that uses the road as an organizing framework around which to synchronize and coordinate a series of political-military effects. This is a conscious, developed strategy that was first put in place in 2005–6 and has been consistently executed since. Thus the mere building of a road is not enough: it generates some but not all of these effects, and may even be used to oppress or harm the population rather than benefit it. Road construction in many parts of the world has had negative security and political effects, especially when executed unthinkingly or in an uncoordinated fashion. What we are seeing here, in contrast, is a coordinated civil-military activity based on a political strategy of separating the insurgents from the people and connecting the people to the government. In short, this is a political maneuver with the road as a means to a political end.

Conclusion

The case of Kunar shows that the Taliban are not invincible and that their weaknesses can be successfully exploited. Since my last visit, in 2006, this area has seen a significant improvement in security, largely the result of a consistent US strategy of partnering with local communities to separate the insurgents from the people, bring tangible benefits of governance and development to the population, and help the people choose their own local leaders through elections. Road-building has been a key part of this effort. The Kunar case study emphasized the importance of consistency and a full-spectrum approach in the east of the country, where a road-building program integrating civilian and military effort into a single political maneuver has proved surprisingly effective since 2006. As the case study demonstrated, the reason for this program's success appears to have had relatively little to do with the road itself, and much more to do with insightful American and Afghan leaders who used the process of the road's construction as a vehicle for political maneuver designed to drive a wedge between the local people, the local guerrillas and the hard-core Taliban leadership in this area, and thus undo the "accidental guerrilla" phenomenon which had hampered previous efforts. To generate the effects listed above, a road-building project probably needs to be consciously approached as an integrated form of political maneuver, and the approach taken probably needs also to take into account the human, topographic, political, cultural and economic environment in which that maneuver will occur. All this is happening in Kunar today, with substantial positive effects on the counterinsurgency campaign in the province. But replicating this success in other places is likely to demand detailed study of the environment and an understanding of political maneuver as a counterinsurgency technique.

Notes

1. This chapter is an abridged version of a chapter of my book, *The Occasional Guerrilla*, forthcoming.
2. This section is largely drawn from my fieldnotes, compiled over the period from mid-2005 to mid-2008, drawing on a variety of published and unpublished primary and secondary sources, as well as three periods of fieldwork in Afghanistan in May-June 2006, October-November 2006 and March 2008.
3. Source: Afghanistan Information Management Services, http://www.aims.org.af/
4. Wahhabi presence in eastern Afghanistan and Northwest Pakistan is not a new phenomenon: it was remarked on by Olaf Caroe (1958), Fredrik Barth (1959) and Akbar Ahmed (1982).
5. For a detailed description of mountain warfare techniques on the Afghan frontier, see Timothy Robert Moreman, *The Army in India and the Development of Frontier Warfare, 1849–1947*, Basingstoke: Palgrave MacMillan, 1998.
6. Personal communication, May 2006
7. World Bank, *Service Delivery and Governance at the Sub-National Level in Afghanistan*, July 2007, online at http://siteresources.worldbank.org/SOUTHASIAEXT/

Resources/Publications/448813–1185293547967/4024814–1185293572457/report.pdf

8. Thomas H. Johnson, "Afghanistan's Post-Taliban Transition: the State of State-building after War", *Central Asian Survey*, Vol. 25, No. 1–2, March-June 2006, pp. 1–26.

9. See Barnett R. Rubin, *The Fragmentation of Afghanistan: State Formation and Collapse in the International System*, 2nd Edition, New Haven and London: Yale University Press, 2002.

10. The term *kuchi* is generically applied by non-nomadic Pashtuns to pastoral nomads, of whom there are several million in Afghanistan, traditionally inhabiting the Registan desert in south-eastern Afghanistan, and other low-production zones astride the border regions of Afghanistan and Pakistani Baluchistan.

11. Discussion with tribal leaders, Peshawar, Pakistan, May 2006.

12. See Max Gluckman, *Order and Rebellion in Tribal Africa*, London: Cohen and West, 1963 and "Some Processes of Social Change, Illustrated with Zululand Data", *African Studies* Vol. 1, 1942, pp. 243–60.

13. Akbar S. Ahmed, *Resistance and Control in Pakistan*, Revised Edition: London and New York: Routledge, 2004.

14. For an alternative analysis of Taliban organizational structure which is somewhat at variance with mine, see Shahid Afsar, Chris Samples and Thomas Wood, "The Taliban: an Organizational Analysis", *Military Review*, May-June 2008, pp. 58–72.

15. For a detailed description of the flying column technique and its invention by the IRA in the early 1920s, see Tom Barry, *Guerilla Days in Ireland*, Dublin: Anvil Books, 1981.

16. For an excellent and extremely detailed description of Taliban operational methods, recruitment and organizational development, see the comprehensive study in Antonio Giustozzi, *Koran, Kalashnikov and Laptop: The Neo-Taliban Insurgency in Afghanistan*, London: C. Hurst & Co., 2007.

17. Discussion with tribal affairs officers, Kabul, November 2006

18. Sir Olaf Caroe, *The Pathans 550 B.C.–1957 A.D.*, London: St Martin's Press, 1958, p. 393: "The nearest I can get to it is to liken the Mahsud to a wolf, the Wazir [the other main tribe of Waziristan] to a panther. Both are splendid creatures; the panther is slier, sleeker and has more grace, the wolf-pack is more purposeful, more united and more dangerous."

19. Discussion with tribal leaders, Peshawar, Pakistan, June 2006.

20. Discussion with Afghan intelligence officials in Kabul, Kandahar and Asadabad, May 2006 and March 2008.

21. Discussion with surrendered Taliban leader and local tribal elders of Musa Qaleh district, Helmand Province, March 2008. Discussion with Provincial Governor of Kandahar, police officials, Afghan Army officers and local community leaders, Kandahar, March 2008.

22. In Pakistan, the Civil Armed Forces (the Pakistan Rangers, Frontier Corps and Pakistan Coast Guards) are the field organizations of the Ministry of Interior, while the Armed Services belong to the Ministry of Defence.

23. LTC Chris Cavoli, personal communication via email, May 2008.

24. Interviews with CDR Larry Legree, Asadabad, Kunar Province, 13 March 2008 and Washington DC, 1 May 2008.

25. Dr Carter Malkasian, Center for Naval Analyses and Asadabad PRT, personal communication via email, April 2008.

26. Cavoli, loc. cit.

12

NORTHERN EXPOSURE FOR THE TALIBAN

Sippi Azarbaijani-Moghaddam

Many years ago, when the Taliban was still a fresh phenomenon and had not yet taken Jalalabad or Kabul, some aid workers were trying to locate and accompany a lost convoy of medicine in the remoter valleys of the Hindu Kush. When their vehicle was swept away in a fast flowing river, they were stranded in a remote district of Badakhshan in the northeast of Afghanistan. They had heard of the Taliban but they had never seen a Talib, so that encountering any of the militant students so far from Kandahar, in a non-Pashtun area, was absent from their minds. After negotiating horses with local villagers they were picked up by *mujahidin* guarding the wild borderlands with Pakistan and taken to their base at Tupkhaneh. From there, they negotiated a vehicle to Chitral but were asked to transport friends of the local commander. Thinking nothing of it they took three men, bearded, armed and unable to speak a word of Dari. The men stopped the car frequently to pray, they were completely ignored by the Chitrali scouts on the other side of the border, and once inside Pakistan, they asked to be dropped off in a small village where they disappeared into the dusk. It was only later that the aid workers were surprised to find that these men were Taliban and the border commander was thinking of accepting money offered to him for access to Badakhshan through the Dorah pass[1] and the surrounding hinterland that he and his men knew so well. This chance encounter in 1996, along with a number of others in other provinces, has puzzled the author for many years, and raised questions about the possibility of Taliban advances in the north. The same questions arise today.

A year after the encounter described above, much had changed and the Taliban had advanced rapidly almost to the borders of Badakhshan. The

Taliban captured Kunduz in 1997 and Taloqan, the centre of Takhar, for the second time in September 2000. They had captured, lost and recaptured territory in the north, tensions had built up and human rights abuses on a significant scale had been perpetrated both by them and their Northern Alliance opponents. By this time the Taliban offensive was apparently bolstered by the presence of foreign forces which had been put in place to ensure victory, although the number might have been overestimated. The Taliban consolidated their gains in Takhar by taking district centres along the Tajikistan border. Attempts to enter Badakhshan through Keshm and Tupkhaneh on the border of southern Badakhshan and Pakistan were repulsed at the time. The Taliban never took Badakhshan as events after September 11, 2001 overtook them. Since then much has been glossed over and for many the northeast has become a bastion of anti-Taliban sentiment. The identity of the Taliban has been distilled down to basics and ignores the complex politics of the region, the country and northeast. The distillation process has also led to the neglect of events and processes which have created convenient footholds for the Taliban should they have occasion to use them.

Rising Taliban attacks in the north, in non-Pashtun areas, are seen as opportunistic expansion into areas with pockets of aggrieved Pashtuns. Much of the analysis of the Taliban is post-2001, frequently opportunistic and repetitive. It is based on a process of stereotyping Afghan ethnicities, resulting in the construction of myths that are repeated as fact and thereby perpetuated. This mythology presents the Taliban as a fundamentally rural, Pashtun movement. It posits that certain Pashtun tribes are particularly poor, marginalised and neglected and that the Taliban movement arose from the grievances of these groups in the underdeveloped south and east, especially among the impressionable, uneducated and unemployed young. Additionally, in creating the Taliban pantheon, the Pakistani Inter-Services Intelligence (ISI) staunchly supports their Pashtun creations and has hostile relations with the leaders of other ethnic groups. On the basis of such stereotyping it is assumed that the north-eastern region of Afghanistan is a mountainous backwater with a non-Pashtun majority of moderate Tajiks, Uzbeks and others, inimical and impervious to the advances of the Pashtun Taliban and related insurgent groups.

This chapter questions stereotypes and assumptions by demonstrating that the northeast is much the same as the Taliban's so-called heartlands. It suggests that using such a paradigm to analyse the Taliban's popular appeal may be flawed. It may be wiser to seek answers in the Taliban's understanding of the nature of leadership, which is for the most part divorced from notions of protecting the communities under one's rule. It becomes clear that leaders only manipulate identity markers such as ethnicity or Wahhabism if it is advantageous to their pursuit of power. The neglect of the northeast, in terms of security, governance and development, both by the Afghan government and by the international community may be precisely what the Taliban need to strengthen their foothold there.

There are two main parts to this chapter. The first part examines ethnic stereotyping of Afghans and questions the validity of models of the Pashtun

Taliban which have led not only to the creation of a monolithic identity taken as a basis for their strategizing, and reflected in "hearts and minds" programming, but also to notions of a moderate, non-Pashtun north that is safe from the advances of the conservative, Pashtun Taliban. It demonstrates that, ethnicity aside, the north and south share many similarities which should lead us to question why the Taliban or similar movements did not gain popularity sooner, and cast doubt on notions of the Taliban's popular appeal based on Pashtunism, conservatism and poverty. It also touches on recruitment opportunities among the youth.

Part two briefly looks at the Taliban's search for allies in the northeast, whether through opportunistic recruitment, mobilising of old Hizb-i Islami networks or manipulating of power struggles among warlords and leaders in the area. What becomes clear is that winning over ordinary people may not figure in their calculations and that there is no need to look for Pashtun grievances in the northeast to explain the Taliban's ability to expand their operations there.

It must be clear from the outset that the Taliban is not one united movement, that the various parts have hierarchies and that the leadership and full-time members have a different worldview from the part-time fighters and occasional sympathisers who are recruited in various localities. The term "Taliban" when used broadly covers all of the various categories but mainly the leadership. It goes without saying that, for the sake of brevity, there is a certain amount of generalization.

The Taliban: made in Pashtunistan

A Pashtun movement? Every nation has stereotypes about its own members and its neighbours. In jokes recounted in Afghanistan, Wardakis do everything back to front, Laghmanis are sly enough to trick the devil, Badakhshis are sheepish, and the list goes on. Since 2001, with the constant need for speed in analysing and acting, perceptions of many Afghan politico-military, social and ethnic groups have been stereotyped and crystallised, the result being short lists of characteristics, presented as immutable facts. Stereotyping in analysis as well as in the media has tended to lead to perceptions that some ethnicities may be more mild-mannered or less prone to fundamentalism than others. Ethnic and even provincial stereotypes abound in writing on the Taliban. The make-up of the typical Talib, if there is such a thing, includes a Pashtun and tribal provenance, preferably from the south, and some form of grievance born of poverty, underdevelopment or an underdog status. Religious conservatism is also included in the list.

It is not an easy task to define or profile the Taliban and related insurgent groups. Since 2001 there has been a swarm of books and articles offering different explanations, attempting to provide definitions to an audience that was largely ignorant of the Taliban presence until late 2001. What is clear is that the Taliban's family tree has roots which are entangled with those of various *mujahidin* factions and Islamist movements that have operated in the region in the past decades and maybe even centuries. Much of the literature on the Taliban, following on from connoisseurs like Rashid, stresses the Pashtun provenance and character of the movement[2] and largely ignores the role played by Afghanistan's minorities. More important, frequent alliances between the Taliban and various political, military and religious leaders of Afghanistan's diverse ethnic groups are neglected. The Taliban are consistently viewed through a monochromatic Pashtun lens and described as one hundred per cent Pashtun, part of the "complex historical and tribal phenomenon of the Pashtuns".[3]

We are blinded to other alternatives by this stereotype of the Taliban. Articles frequently refer to the Southern provinces of Afghanistan as the Taliban heartlands and the stalwart bases of support for them, the map being cut up into distinct provinces which either wholeheartedly support the Taliban or despise them. In response to the International Council on Security and Development's[4] claim that the Taliban had a permanent presence in 72 percent of the country, NATO spokesman James Appathurai recently said: "We don't see the figures in this report as being credible at all... The Taliban are only present in the south and east which is already less than 50 percent of the country."[5] As soon as the Taliban have a foot in the door, in any region with a non-Pashtun majority, commentators try to link related events to the local grievances of the nearest Pashtun pockets and experts in tribal affairs are tasked with isolating the small conflicts which apparently lead to alienation from government and support for the Taliban. With reports that Kunduz once again may be turning into one of the Taliban's operational centres in the north, for example, explanations are based on ethnicity: "[O]ne-third of residents are Pashtuns from the Ghilzai tribe, originally from the southern provinces of Kandahar and Helmand, where the Taliban enjoys strong support."[6] In other words, the appeal of the Taliban is popular and must therefore have a Pashtun flavour.

There are few sources, especially in English, which deal with non-Pashtuns within the ranks of the Taliban and with dealings between the Taliban and former leaders of the *mujahidin* and Northern Alliance, especially in the period since the fall of the Taliban in 2001. In 1998, Marsden[7] was cautious about calling the Taliban a Pashtun movement. Maley,[8] also writing in 1998, provides a detailed explanation of the Pashtun groups, such as the Kandahari *Pai Luch* brotherhood, which were absorbed into the ranks of the Taliban, but he still refrained from calling them a Pashtun movement. The Taliban themselves have never categorically stated that they are a Pashtun movement and often stressed their readiness "to accept anybody who shared their views and accepted their rules, regardless of ethnicity and tribe".[9] However, the reported presence of non-Pashtuns in their ranks has consistently been interpreted as tokenism.[10]

From the start there were a number of Tajiks and Uzbeks involved with the Taliban, although their presence is explained away as a result of their living in Pashtun areas for a long time. One was Mawlawi Sayed Ghiasuddin, a Badakhshi, who was a member of the original ten-member Supreme Shura of the Taliban.[11] The Taliban placed in charge of Paktia province were young, *madrasa*-educated Badakhshis, from areas around Baharak and Jurm.[12] In 2003, a number of Uzbek ex-Taliban from Badakhshan were apparently picked up by the Disarmament, Demobilization and Rehabilitation process in Paktia.[13] They explained their presence by saying that they had escaped conflicts and punishment for crimes in their native provinces and ended up with the Taliban in Paktia. Afghan analysts in close contact with the Taliban explain that even if they started out as a Pashtun movement their strategy, under the influence of ISI and others, soon altered to include other ethnic groups in order to expand their influence in non-Pashtun parts of Afghanistan.[14] They still have influence and supporters among the Tajik and Uzbek commanders of the north, especially former Jami'at and Hizb-i-Islami commanders who were assimilated into their ranks many years ago. These sources report that almost half of the current leadership of the Taliban is non-Pashtun.

Ethnicity is an excellent focus for manipulation, but it may not be the most important factor in determining conflicts and alliances in the region. Tajik and Uzbek leaders have accommodated all sorts of violent incursions against the defenceless communities they rule as long as they have been allowed to hold on to power. Evidently there is the array of old festering multi-level conflicts in every part of Afghanistan, including the inevitable land and water conflicts which can take on an ethnic dimension in their latest incarnations, but not every development in favour of the Taliban can be laid at the door of ethnic conflict. A longer-term perspective reveals wave upon wave of displacement. Delving into the history of such displacements makes it clear that it is not just Pashtun grievances that can be isolated and manipulated. For example, a large number of Uzbeks—from Afghanistan as well as Uzbekistan—have been settled in Azam Warsak area of South Waziristan, in Pakistan, for many years and have married locals. The Afghan Uzbeks are largely former supporters of Dostum. Some believe they used to serve in the Afghan Army of Najibullah in southern and eastern Afghanistan. Apparently, when Dostum deserted Najibullah in 1992 and linked up with CIA-trained *mujahidin*, these Uzbek soldiers deserted and settled in South Waziristan.[15] Others think they may be remnants of Dostum's units trapped in Khost when it fell in 1991.[16] This area also has many fighters from Uzbekistan belonging to the Islamic Movement of Uzbekistan. This demonstrates clearly the existence of multiple, multi-ethnic layers of desertion, migration, recruitment and manipulation with histories linked to the *mujahidin*, ISI, and Islamist groups. In addition, South Waziristan has been the scene of violent clashes between local tribals and Uzbeks living in the area following the alleged murder of an important tribal personality by an Uzbek. It is reported that to dissipate tensions a number of Uzbeks will be relocated to northeastern Afghanistan and other areas where they can blend more easily while furthering the aims of insurgency.

An analysis focused exclusively on Pashtuns leads many to consistently link the Taliban to Pakistan as the only other country in the region with a substantial Pashtun population. It then usually leads to the conclusion that the Pakistani government and ISI are trying to keep the Pashtuns occupied, ensuring that they will not revive the Pashtunistan issue. Clearly, there are other actors involved with the Taliban, although their relations with Afghanistan's other neighbours, in particular Iran, are not covered here. In comparison to the attention given to Pakistan's role, interference from other nations which participated in the Afghan civil war by proxy is largely neglected, but it would shed light on some of the Taliban's latest strategies. Taken on its own, Pakistan's attempts to encourage the inclusion of non-Pashtun elements in their policies and programmes has a history which stretches back to Pakistan government and ISI support for a range of *mujahidin* movements and their leaderships in the refugee context. Cordial relations have been maintained between key actors in Pakistan and non-Pashtun leaders in the north. Afghan sources report, for instance, that the retired general Mirza Aslambeg is in close contact with Uzbeks and Turkmens, mobilising an identity which may include Uzbek ancestry. He is reported to have close ties with Khairudin Tatar, a deputy of Dostum, Aka Yassin from Saripul province, a number of other influentials and commanders from the north, and is currently making overtures to leaders in Samangan province.

The conservative South, the moderate North?

Is northern Afghanistan so very different from the so-called Taliban heartlands of the south? Is it only popular appeal based on a Pashtun identity, conservatism and poverty that explain the Taliban's expansion? Is it mass popular appeal that allows them to gain ground?

The task of explaining culture and history to new arrivals in the military and diplomatic corps in Afghanistan's current context is often left to young, urbanised interlocutors because they are English-speaking and computer literate and foreigners can relate to them more easily. Many, having grown up in middle-income refugee families and distanced from the reality of the outlying refugee camps[17] or Afghanistan under the Taliban, perpetuate the stereotypes and explain the Taliban as a sudden upsurge of religious influence based on the southern, rural, underprivileged, Pashtun provenance of the movement. Some may even claim that the Taliban are not Afghans but Punjabis and Arabs, emphasising the strong sense of the Taliban as "other"[18] in comparison to urbanised Afghans of a particular background. There is almost a creation myth of the Taliban emerging as a spontaneous uprising of mullah-fighters in response to the depravity of *mujahidin* commanders in Kandahar[19] and in relation to the waning influence of tribal leaders in the south and east. This is, however, misleading and leads us to think that the south was the only area ready for such a flowering of religious ideals. This myth ignores long term trends in Afghan society as discussed by authors such as Edwards[20] and Dorronsoro[21] who noted the growing influence of mullahs as a result of the *jihad*, tensions with tribal leaders and the creeping influence of Saudi-funded and ISI-backed fundamentalist groups across Afghanistan, a process which has spanned three decades or more. As with so many developments in Afghanistan, the seeds were planted long before. The resulting changes, as various phases of conflict and resistance in Afghanistan played out their course, have simply taken time to come to fruition.

Whether the Pashtun-dominated south is more prone to religious influence of an Islamist or militant nature than the non-Pashtun north is another argument in the "fixing" of characteristics of ethnic groups. In this regard, Badakhshan with its Ismaili population may be seen as a "benign" province and districts such as Warduj with its pockets of Taliban support may be seen as exceptional. In this model, it is assumed to be the conservative Pashtuns whose children fill the *madrasas* who have lent themselves so well to processes of indoctrination and recruitment by militant Islamists. It is well documented that *madrasas* operating in Pakistan produced the Taliban[22] as they had produced generations of fighters and activists for previous insurgent groups.[23] *Madrasas* did not start out as factories turning out Islamic militants, however, and an interest in *madrasa* education cannot be equated with support for the Taliban. *Madrasas* originally provided, to varying degrees, an all-rounded, albeit dated, education[24] and produced polymaths. Radicalisation of the North West Frontier Province's (NWFP) *madrasas* took place in the 1980s in response to the Soviet intervention in Afghanistan and involved external influences:

Thanks to the CIA's 51 million US dollar grant to the University of Nebraska to produce pictorial textbooks glorifying jihad, killing, maiming and bombing other human beings was made sufficiently entertaining. Sadism could now be cultivated as a virtue. That was when madrasa doors were opened to the mass of the poor. The new "education" they received was to hate the Russians, later generalised to include any non-Muslim. Jews, Hindus and Christians figured prominently…[25]

The largest number of foreign students in Pakistani *madrasas* is Afghan, from within Afghanistan as well as from the refugee camps in the NWFP and Baluchistan.[26] There are no breakdowns of the ethnicity of Afghans receiving *madrasa* education, nor are there accurate indications of the percentage of these children swelling the ranks of groups such as the Taliban. There are well-established but largely undocumented links between communities in the northeast and the Deobandi and Wahhabi *madrasas* of Pakistan. A strong interest in sending boys (and even girls) to *madrasas* is a trait shared by all Afghans regardless of ethnicity. There is the important issue of *sawab*[27] and possibilities for upward social mobility that having a mullah in the family can bring for all Afghans. For a God-fearing Muslim, enrolling children in religious schools removes any doubt about the devoutness of a family and reduces the risk of the wrong sort of indoctrination by secular or "godless" regimes. It is also reported that many poor parents choose to send their children to *madrasas*, sparing them the responsibility of finding money for their upbringing.[28]

Poverty, like conservatism or support for insurgent groups, cannot be neatly categorised according to ethnicity or province in Afghanistan. Other factors are also indicative. Many women in the northeast still wear *burqas* and feel nervous about participation in public life.[29] With the exception of certain pockets, secondary education for girls is still frowned upon and not long ago there was an international outcry when a community in Badakhshan stoned a woman accused of adultery.[30] There is no gradation of conservatism according to ethnicity or province, but it can probably be safely hazarded that non-Pashtun communities in the northeast are as conservative as Pashtun communities in other parts of Afghanistan. It does not automatically follow, however, that people in either region support the Taliban.

Some might also argue that the level of education in the northeast offsets religious influence; patterns of clericalisation in the northeast coincide with areas where there is an absence of state schools.[31] Table 2 below shows that Badakhshan has one of the highest rural literacy rates in the country, followed by Kunduz, while the literacy rate for Takhar is quite low.

Table 2: Rural literacy rate by province, circa 2006[32]

Badakhshan	25.3	Kunar	26
Baghdis	9.9	Kunduz	26.8
Baghlan	17.2	Laghman	12.2
Balkh	31.9	Logar	24.4
Bamyan	23.6	Nangarhar	20.8
Daikundi	22.9	Nimruz	20.6
Farah	20.6	Nuristan	22.2
Faryab	22.2	Paktika	2
Ghazni	30.9	Paktia	32.5
Ghor	17.1	Panjshir	32.2
Helmand	4.1	Parwan	34.7
Herat	30.2	Samangan	15.7
Jowzjan	20.3	Sar-i Pul	10.2
Kabul	31	Takhar	12.6
Kandahar	11.4	Uruzgan	4.7
Kapisa	34.2	Wardak	24
Khost	25	Zabul	0.3

Within Badakhshan itself, however, there are variations in literacy by district, with the highest density of secondary schools in areas around Faizabad and Baharak and in some Ismaili areas. Ragh, Argu and Keshm have the lowest education rates, the most conservative clergy and a history of strong Taliban support. It is difficult to ascertain whether lack of attention to education in these areas has allowed mullahs to dominate the population or whether well-established clerics have consistently resisted the establishment of schools in their areas. Giustozzi[33] suggests that a high density of mullahs signals radicalisation because penetration of state education threatens their influence and livelihoods. It is these radicalised mullahs who are likely to put religious commitment ahead of ethnicity and coerce communities under their influence into an alliance with the Taliban.

It must be noted here that a high percentage of *educated* and unemployed youth with expectations of a better life can prove problematic, putting the northeast at disadvantage compared to the south. Urdal[34] tested claims that youth bulges[35] may be causally linked to internal armed conflict. Youth bulges are believed to strain social institutions such as the labour market and the education system, thereby causing grievances that may result in violent conflict. The study found robust support for the hypothesis that youth bulges increase the risk of conflict, particularly under conditions of economic stagnation. Urdal also found that although unemployment is believed to cause grievances, especially if expectations are raised through expansion in education, poverty in itself was not a strong enough cause for grievance and resulting social unrest. Using his analysis, if educated youth are radicalised the northeast may be more at risk of social unrest than the south.

The poor South, the prosperous North? It is also common to see the Taliban explained as a popular movement emerging from the rural poverty and underdevelopment of a neglected south. This type of analysis leads to aid being seen as a prop in achieving military or political objectives, by, for example, assuaging the rural Pashtuns at risk of being manipulated by the Taliban and similar groups. This has resulted in massive investment in assistance in southern provinces:

If it were a state, Helmand alone would be the world's fifth largest recipient of funds from USAID, the US Agency for International Development. These disparities are also reflected in the pattern of combined government and donor spending: for 2007–2008 the most insecure provinces of Nimruz, Helmand, Zabul, Kandahar and Uruzgan have been allocated more than $200 per person, whereas as many other provinces are due to receive less than half this amount, and some, such as Sari Pul or Takhar, are allocated less than one third.[36]

Table 3: Proportion of population below National Poverty Line[37]

Badakhshan	60.1	Kunar	11.8
Baghdis	52.3	Kunduz	17.6
Baghlan	20.0	Laghman	47.0
Balkh	22.9	Logar	7.2
Bamyan	53.7	Nangarhar	25.8
Daikundi	77.0	Nimruz	68.4
Farah	24.2	Nuristan	47.0
Faryab	30.9	Paktika	61.2
Ghazni	40.0	Paktia	18.9
Ghor	51.9	Panjshir	19.1
Helmand	53.5	Parwan	8.0
Herat	25.6	Samangan	29.9
Jowzjan	14.1	Sar-i Pul	47.9
Kabul	15.7	Takhar	45.3
Kandahar	20.0	Uruzgan	33.5
Kapisa	18.6	Wardak	36.6
Khost	23.2	Zabul	60.8

"Satisfying the rural Pashtun"[38] may be a simplified approach to a phenomenon which is not only complex but constantly evolving. Table 3 above indicates that the north is equally underdeveloped and underserved in comparison to the south, making it vulnerable to Taliban advances if poverty is a key factor in community mobilisation. Access to basic needs such as drinking water and sanitation is as bad in northeast Afghanistan as it is in southern provinces.[39] More households perceive themselves to be food insecure in the northeast by comparison with those in the provinces of the south. And yet the northeast, and especially Badakhshan, is largely neglected in terms of assistance because only the Pashtun populations of the south and east are believed to be at risk of falling for overtures from Taliban and related insurgent groups. Families and communities in the northeast were as adversely affected by drought from 1999 to 2001 as those in other parts of the country, and burdened with the additional impact of the war from 1997 until 2001.

Already in 2001 this situation created fertile ground for recruitment, and the Northern Alliance was able to enlist 14–18 year olds on a large scale in northeastern Afghanistan. Stated reasons for becoming soldiers among this age group at the time were "poverty, family and peer influences, pride, and ideology":[40] The Taliban also recruited from this age group, both sides having to use force because war-fatigued families and communities demonstrated reluctance. The longer-term generational impact of the sequence of natural and man–made disasters that have afflicted the northeast, especially on socioeconomic networks and processes, together with an endemic neglect of children and young people, has not been studied. If a recruitment drive was to start among the youth of the northeast at this stage in Afghanistan's history, it would be difficult to predict where loyalties would lie if not to the highest bidder.

Young people form the largest group across Afghanistan, with over half of the population estimated to be below the age of 19.[41] Despite this there are no comprehensive, nationwide government policies targeting children or adolescents and their particular needs. Evidently young people have different expectations based on socioeconomic background, gender and a range of other variables, but Afghanistan will have an estimated 5.7 million children of school age within five years, and if the education system cannot absorb them other, informal systems will. All over Afghanistan young people are faced with unemployment and lack of viable livelihood opportunities leading to out-migration with attendant problems, which can include exploitation and exposure to criminals, insurgents, drugs and other negative influences. In the northeast there are other ills for the young, such as gambling which leads to debt and possibly recruitment into the military:

[V]illages in Kunduz province identified gambling debts as a pathway for young people into the military. Around the age of ten years, boys in those villages played high-stake card games on the streets and in some cases incurred such debt that payment could have been made only by having parents sell off their major assets. Parents' inability to support such children or children's recognition that they were putting their families at risk led some boys to join the military to prevent the accrual of such a burden.[42]

Afghanistan remains a gerontocracy where old leaders cling to power[43] and the young find little opportunity to participate in matters which impact their lives, especially at provincial and district level, except by ingratiating themselves into existing networks and rising through the usual channels of crime and violence. There are very few initiatives to give young people a say in governance and security in their communities, without recourse to corruption and violence. It would seem that young people in the lowest strata of society learn that if they do not resort to exercising power with recourse to violence, they will be neglected or exploited.

To conclude the first part of this chapter, it is clear that conditions in the northeast are not too different from those in the south, and can create at best fertile recruiting grounds for the Taliban at village level and, at worst, passive support. If there is not an automatic gravitation towards the Taliban and other insurgent groups, the reasons are probably more complex than the much emphasised ethnic dimension of conflict in Afghanistan and need to be sought elsewhere. The plight of young people across Afghanistan requires attention. Reports warn that recently recruited foreign fighters support younger Taliban commanders,[44] leading to a waning in the influence of the older, more traditional leadership based in Quetta. It is becoming clear that, regardless of the scale of problems for young people, in the face of the insurgents' policy to tap into the energies and resourcefulness of disgruntled youth needing a channel for their ambitions, the Afghan government needs to counter with a comprehensive, nationwide approach.

Meltdown in the northeast

A steady rise in attacks[45] clearly demonstrates that it may be ill-advised to see the northeast as a low priority area in terms of insurgent infiltration and insecurity. Senior Taliban commanders are appearing in the area; for example Mullah Usman, killed recently in Kalafgan district in Takhar, was described as "the most senior commander in the northeast region".[46] The Taliban's self-styled military commander in Kunduz, Qari Bashir Haqqani, has issued threats to the Germans, warning that Kunduz "will soon become the Kandahar of the north".[47] The main focus of the Taliban is reportedly on Kunduz as the base of operations, followed by Takhar, while Badakhshan will be used as a transit zone.[48] Some see the Taliban's northward shift since 2006 as a result of reaching spatial limitation in the south and southeast. Others see it as a repeat of their 1996–98 campaign in the area, making a pincer movement towards the north.[49] Afghan sources[50] allege that the Taliban and Al Qaida advisers decided about a year ago to focus operations in the North of Afghanistan. There are three main explanations for the shift to the north. The first is that insurgent groups have scattered their resources across Afghanistan to protect them from international forces. The second is that they have sought to improve their ability to influence insurgent activities throughout Afghanistan. The third is that their aim is to position Central Asian and other insurgents on the Afghan border with the "Stans" for expansion of cross-border terrorist activities. Evidently the volatility of foreign guests in NWFP and recent tensions between Uzbeks and Pashtuns in Waziristan may also have contributed to this decision. The question is how the Taliban and their friends expect to advance and find support outside their southern and eastern "heartlands".

Cashing in on failures in security, governance and development? The answer to the Taliban's ability to reappear in the north is not based on manipulation of Pashtun grievances. Similarly, if poverty and conservatism fuelled Taliban support they would have appeared long before. They may resort to their tactic of cashing in on opportunities provided by the Afghan government and the international community, swelling their ranks through random and opportunistic recruitment of a motley hotchpotch of disgruntled groups. Jalali portrays the "new Taliban" as "an assortment of ideologically motivated Afghan and foreign militants, disillusioned tribal communities, foreign intelligence operatives, drug traffickers, opportunist militia commanders, disenchanted and unemployed youth, and self-interested spoilers. It is more of a political alliance of convenience than an ideological front."[51] Theories on the Taliban's growth and popular appeal are variations on the same theme which include mistakes by the international military coalition, slow economic and social progress, lack of governance and the rule of law, rampant corruption, and frequently repeated quotes about the Taliban's staying power in relation to Western actors who famously and short-sightedly abandoned the Afghans once Soviet forces withdrew in 1989.[52] Also listed is Afghanistan's "history of foreign interference, ordinary people's distrust of foreigners and the grassroots strength of Islam",[53] all playing into the hands of insurgents. These explanations are all based on the assumption that ordinary Afghans can have a say about insurgent operations in their areas and decide to provide or withhold support, but the truth is they rarely can. Apart from rumours judiciously spread by the Taliban, there is little evidence to prove active community-level support for them without intimidation.

In fact the "sources of the insurgency are…to be found in the intrinsic weaknesses of the Afghan state".[54] The Afghan wars ushered in a period when support was provided to warlords and leaders by actors who largely ignored the impact their actions had on ordinary people of all ethnicities, whether it was murder, torture, rape, displacement or impoverishment. Hizb-i Islami was the only group that focused on social organisation and social outreach programmes, but it was still difficult to stop unsupervised commanders falling back into their old ways. The period after the fall of the Taliban saw those leaders reinstated. At no stage were people truly given the chance to exert any influence on their lives, and most understand that to effect change in their lives they must embrace warlordism which then perpetuates the status quo.

NORTHERN EXPOSURE FOR THE TALIBAN

Leaders have rarely if ever been accountable to their followers[55] in a democratic sense, and occasional acts of generosity do not equate with felt obligations to provide for or protect one's followers. The Afghan government has not provided alternative modes of governance in the northeast or any other region of Afghanistan.

The case of the northeast combines this previous planning with current neglect. The focus on Pashtuns of the south and east has seen much discussion and analysis and attempts to support initiatives empowering tribal leaders and tribal militias by funding and strengthening them. Analysis of leadership models has been rare in recent years[56] and once again conducted rapidly. There is a fascination with tribal structures and the notion of integrated communities contained within Pashtun tribes with tidy boundaries, sub-tribes and clans, easily distinguishable to the tribal expert, sharing one political or religious view, cohesive, gathered behind a traditional leader with the prerequisite biblical image of long white beard and old-fashioned garb, who has the interests of his constituency at heart but may be misled by insurgent elements because of a nasty falling out with the Karzai regime or its lackeys. Much is based on assumptions that Afghanistan is a "tribal" society and that we need to understand tribal structures, which are in turn assumed to be a well-liked, egalitarian model of rule based on a democratic *jirga*. But leadership models vary across the country and even within single ethnic groups, based on local history; hence little is understood and much assumed about the strongmen and leaders of the predominantly Tajik and Uzbek northeast. Non-Pashtun leaders are assumed to care about their non-Pashtun followers. This ignores the history of neglect, brutality and barbarity from many commanders, at times directed at their own communities and ethnic groups—the typical exercise of power which has alienated ordinary people and left them cynical and indifferent. The question is whether it is the ruling classes or ordinary people who would throw in their lot with the Taliban.

Taliban allies in the northeast. The Taliban are the product of an Old Boys' Network of Islamists and *mujahidin* which is still serviceable:

All the leaders and cadres of the Sunni extremist Sipah-e-Saheba Pakistan (SSP) and the Lashkar-i-Jhangvi (LEJ) and the Shia extremist Siph Mohammad, almost all the leaders of the Taliban and over 90 per cent of its cadres and over 70 per cent of the leaders and cadres of the Harakat-ul-Mujahidin (HUM), the Harakat-ul-Jihad-al-Islami (HUJI), the Jaish-i-Mohammad (JEM), and the Lashkar-i-Tayba (LET) are products of the *madrasas*.[57]

Established Islamist networks disregarding ethnicity will provide multi-level support to the Taliban. Some Hizb-i Islami forces joined the Taliban when Kunduz and Takhar fell. When the Taliban fell in 2001, Hekmatyar tried to regroup his forces in the northeast, a strategy which apparently failed as they remained more strongly affiliated to the Taliban and Al Qaida.[58] It would appear that those forces still loyal to Hekmatyar have little contact with the Taliban, use different routes, but do not obstruct the Taliban and Al Qaida,

259

since Hekmatyar has relatively cordial relations with the leaderships of both groups.[59] Ability to utilise parts of the Hizb-i Islami network is of tremendous advantage to the Taliban in their activities in the northeast. A history of Hizbi activity, and fundamentally anti-Western and anti-American sentiment which appears to be there, make Kunduz an important place for the Taliban movement,[60] a veritable Kandahar of the north. Qari Bashir Haqqani, a Taliban commander in Kunduz, claims that he has 13 *mujahidin* groups under his command, three created for the sole purpose of attacks on German and other foreign "invaders". It was claimed that in the provinces of Kunduz, Takhar and Badakhshan there were close to 1,000 armed Taliban in mid-2008.[61] Haqqani is not isolated:

If there is one man who fuels this animosity more than anyone else, it is Mullah Salam from the Imam Sahib district. As the radical Islamic extremists' military chief for north-eastern Afghanistan, Salam's influence within the region under German ISAF command extends well beyond Kunduz Province to Baghlan and Takhar and the region bordering Tajikistan... Salam's fighters are already the de facto rulers of entire districts in Kunduz Province...Three senior Taliban leaders are on the target list assigned to the Germans in northern Afghanistan. One of them is Mullah Salam.[62]

It is unlikely that these commanders appeared in the past year or two, brought forward by grievances of Ghilzai sub-tribes in the north. Long before the Taliban arrived in the northeast, Hizb-i Islami had extensive and well-organised networks radiating outward from Kunduz. According to some, ISI operations in northern Afghanistan can be traced back to Islamabad's efforts to ensure that Gulbuddin Hekmatyar, their protégé at the time, would take over Kabul following the collapse of Najibullah's Communist regime.[63] According to some reports, in the spring of 1990, ISI also helped establish the "Afghan" Takhar Regiment:

It was the most tightly controlled "Afghan" unit, and the best equipped. Ostensibly, this unit belonged to Hizb-i-Islami Gulbaddin Hekmatyar and had been prepared by the ISI for resistance operations near the Soviet border. The troops were provided with the most comprehensive military training given to Afghans. Resistance sources described this unit as being turned into "a conventional army" by the ISI. In early April 1990, the force was virtually combat ready and ISI expected to commit this Afghan Army to battle within a month, once the mountain passes leading into Badakhshan were completely open.[64]

It is claimed that the remnants of this force, controlled by ISI, constituted the core of the Afghan force that supported the Islamist insurgency in Central Asia. A history of radicalisation and previous experience with local warlords provide other entry points for the Taliban in the northeast. "Safe" areas such as Badakhshan provided fertile ground for the seeds of Deobandi and Wahhabi influence long before the Taliban threat appeared. The northeast has long been a focus for external actors building up a cadre of religious leaders and a sphere of influence. The northeast was never neglected in the long history of *mullah-bazi*[65] in Afghanistan and it was certainly not impervious to religious influence. After the Partition of India in 1947 most Afghan religious students at the *madrasas* of Deoband and Patna in northern India dispersed to the border areas. Apparently these were mostly Pashtuns, Nuristanis and Badakhshis[66] who formed the *ulema* in their respective areas upon their return. In relation to this Begzad,[67] an Afghan journalist, describes the history of Ahl-i Hadith, listed as one of the dependent groups of the Deobandi *madrasa* network in Pakistan,[68] together with Jami'at-i Ulema-i Islam and Sipah-i Saheba. The second group has been influential in the politics of Afghanistan while the other two have been engaged in cultural and military activities. Ahl-i Hadith expanded its religious programmes within Pakistan and into the eastern provinces of Afghanistan, particularly Kunar, Badakhshan and Northern Nuristan, through the support of Saudi charitable organisations. Mawlawi Badakhshi was one of the activists of this group and completed his studies at the Haqqaniya *madrasa* close to Akora Khatak refugee camp. He supported one of his students, Mawlawi Shariqi Badakhshi, in the establishment of "an Emirate" in Badakhshan. Rivalry with *mujahidin* commanders in the areas led to the eventual murder of both these leaders in the 1990s.[69]

In an accommodation of militaristic and religious interest, local commanders tend to support mullahs in the northeast, an attitude that has allowed them to retain authority and influence in their communities. Not all mullahs, however, support the government: "[M]ore traditionalist religious leaders—believed the ulema should be independent of the government and viewed government support to the clergy as co-optation to gain legitimacy. In this perspective, mullahs and ulema that associate with the government are illegitimate and political opportunists."[70] Giustozzi[71] reports that in 2000, Massud barely managed to repress an attempt by military leaders and clerics of the areas of Ragh, Argu and Keshm to side with the Taliban. The Ikhwani network is strong in the northeast and is in direct contact with members of the Taliban and Al Qaida network including Mawlawi Abdul Qadir Takhari and Mawlawi Mohammad Sharif Deobandi, a Badakhshi.[72] For such groups the presence and influence of foreign military forces is an irritant. Giustozzi also mentions reports of mullahs in Jurm, Yumgan, Keran-o Munjan and Warduj— well-known conservative enclaves—urging their communities to join the *jihad* against the government and foreigners.[73]

The Taliban know that both they and leaders in the northeast can afford to ignore the populace should they find it convenient to do so. In line with ethnic stereotyping, it is often assumed by those new to Afghanistan that former Jami'ati commanders unanimously abhor the Taliban for committing atrocities against ordinary people from their respective ethnic groups. Despite being cornered by the Taliban in Badakhshan in 2001, former President Burhanuddin Rabbani of Badakhshan recently set up an initiative for dialogue between the Taliban and President Karzai, claiming that the "Taliban has moved away from their militant ideology and is partial to open dialogue with the government".[74]

Rabbani was largely sidelined after the establishment of the Afghan interim government in 2001. He created the Jabhe-ye-Motahed-e-Milli or the

United National Front (UNF) in March 2007, "a conglomeration of former politicians, disgruntled ex-ministers, warlords and Mujahedeen-government leftovers like Rabbani".[75] At the time of its creation, some saw attempts by UNF leaders to push a mediation role with the Taliban as an opportunistic move to put pressure on the Karzai government and to increase their power and access within the current administration. It was alleged that they did this on the basis of good relations with the ISI leadership rather than specific relations with or overtures towards the Taliban or Al Qaida.[76] Others saw the UNF as a negotiating committee in case of power collapse in Kabul and a possible need to bargain with the Taliban. Another possibility was that a "pre-negotiation ceasefire with the Taliban could take place before the collapse and essentially concede the southern provinces to the Taliban. In such a deal, analysts predict the UNF would likely carve out their respected fiefdoms, reinstalling the former warlords as governors."[77] Some interpreted Rabbani's move as "protecting northern Tajiks from marauding Taliban forces",[78] once again interpreting events through the ethnic lens which assumes ethnic solidarity and responsible or principled leadership.

The Taliban understand full well how to do business with Afghanistan's latest ruling classes. Myriads of examples exist of brazen and opportunistic alliance shifting driven by money, power and, infrequently, ideology throughout the *jihad*, during the internecine warfare of the 1990s and from late 2001 when many Taliban and Al Qaida commanders were allowed to escape by non-Pashtuns. Regardless of where they operate, north or south, the Taliban seem to be very skilled at finding fault lines and weak spots:

[W]hen the Taliban, supported by Islamabad entered the Afghan arena, there was a clear strategy of targetting local commanders of regional warlords in a piecemeal fashion. This would explain in large measure their blitz through southern and central Afghanistan, capturing 14 provinces without encountering resistance. Even in 1997, this policy has been pursued with even greater success in ensuring that their non-Pashtun opponents like Ahmed Shah Masood, Abdul Rashid Dostam, Karim Khalili and Sayyed Naderi have been weakened not through battles but by desertion of men, local commanders and equipment.[79]

Had they not been interrupted by the events following September 11, 2001, the Taliban would probably have entered Badakhshan relying on their preferred "indirect strategy of subversion in a conservative and now isolated province that has never been solidly behind Massud".[80] As they are skilled at exploiting grievances, it was even claimed that in the districts bordering Badakhshan they negotiated with Ismaili Shiites who were still smarting after a string of abuses inflicted by and conflicts with Rabbani's commanders.[81]

At the end of 2008, the time appeared right for the Taliban to start agitating. Leaders of the north, especially the northeast, may have been pushed out of central government, but in some cases they have effectively been left to their own devices. Warlords marginalised by the current administration are harbouring a great deal of resentment[82] and, together with their militias, are apparently turning increasingly hostile to the government in Kabul.[83] The

Karzai administration may have attempted to sideline some of these figures, but it never managed to neutralise them by dismantling their networks. Instead the government has responded with concessions and mollifications to local strongmen, allowing them to strengthen and, in some cases, even to create their networks as businessmen, land grabbers and military brokers. Attempts to dismantle these local fiefdoms are met with threats to security. Governance and security reforms are focused more on power plays from Kabul and in the provinces of the northeast than on containing the potential threat of insurgency.[84]

Non-Pashtun parliamentarians and leaders with small spheres of influence, who come from districts in the northeast which bore the brunt of Taliban atrocities prior to 2001 and who embraced the ideals of disarmament and democracy, feel they have lost out. They appear to be in denial and are reluctant to admit Taliban activities and acceptance in their localities, for a variety of reasons—ranging from reluctance to admit "betrayal" by their own leaders to their own fears of being assassinated, and their apprehension of being seen as having failed to deliver to their constituencies and protect them. One parliamentarian interviewed denied any Taliban presence in Badakhshan and finally, after extensive questioning, blurted out locations in different mountain valleys where Taliban leaders are being entertained by former Jami'at and Hizb-i commanders.[85] This further underlines the uncomfortable truth that ordinary people do not have direct or significant influence on how insurgency pans out in their areas.

Finally, it is only in recent years that the Taliban have had to build substantially on their strategy of bribing their way to victory and recruit fighters of a high calibre with specialist skills to engage in combat with the foreign forces of Operation Enduring Freedom and the International Security Assistance Forces. It would seem that the Taliban are recruiting according to job descriptions. There is currently an influx of many more violent, extreme and uncontrollable foreign fighters, who seem to be making regular appearances in the north. The foreign advisers to the Taliban and insurgent groups are counterparts to those brought in for the *mujahidin* in the 1980s and for the Afghan National Army in recent years:

In Afghanistan, the foreigners serve as mid-level commanders, and train and finance local fighters, according to Western analysts. In Pakistan's tribal areas, they train suicide bombers, create roadside-bomb factories and have vastly increased the number of high-quality Taliban fund-raising and recruiting videos posted online.[86]

Now that the Taliban are fighting a different type of war, they may no longer require the manpower available in the villages of the northeast and can afford to sideline communities in favour of their armed and dangerous leaders.

Conclusion

As the insurgents' areas and modes of operation expand with new recruits, our zones of operation and interactions with Afghans, limited as they have always been, decrease. We have less opportunity for chance interactions which trigger new lines of inquiry and analysis, while the situation on the ground is changing at a rapid pace. We work with tired old assumptions and many of our perceptions are slow to change. Overall, for most the minimal level of interaction with the Taliban and other insurgents, or even with ordinary Afghans, makes it increasingly difficult to draw up a reliable typology able to provide a more three-dimensional image of the Taliban and their allies. Much of the rapid post-2001 analysis of the Taliban and their allies fails to take into account layers of socio-political sediment in communities, districts and regions, a history of complex, multilayered interactions, and a piecing together of movements and leaders long since disappeared but whose ghosts haunt the living. It is clear that the inclusion of non-Pashtuns in the Taliban movement requires a framework for analysis going beyond tribes and ethnicities and beyond events shortly before and after September 11, 2001.

Ethnic and tribal dimensions of insecurity are sought at every twist and turn of the insurgency, but there is plenty of evidence suggesting that the Taliban movement was not and is not a Pashtun movement fighting for ethnic hegemony. An erroneous notion of stereotyped Taliban, leading to an international focus on Afghanistan's Pashtun provinces and on Pashtun areas of Pakistan, plays into the hands of the Taliban and insurgent groups, potentially giving them greater room to manoeuvre in the non-Pashtun north and into the countries beyond.

This chapter has highlighted the need to look for answers in processes of social change, in shifting alliances of Pashtun and non-Pashtun leaders based on multi-faceted identities and circumstances which are manipulated to great advantage by a variety of actors. The main recommendation of this chapter is to move away from the dogged adherence to the same set of stereotypes that seem to determine the majority of perceptions and approaches to the Taliban and other insurgent groups, particularly at this time when their focus appears once again to be shifting to the north.

Similarly, analysts who insist on pushing poverty and underdevelopment as underlying causes of the success of the Taliban should look to the north as well as the south. One has to ask whether the massive investment in stabilising the south is justified when the north could soon be in jeopardy. The northeast suffers from the same symptoms of poverty as other parts of Afghanistan. If there is one issue requiring special attention, it is the plight of young people who suffer as older leaders cling on to old positions, networks and practices that do nothing to improve the daily lives of their increasingly cynical and indifferent constituencies. With regard to problems faced by young people, especially in poorer strata of society, that are facilitating recruitment by groups like the Taliban, then once again the northeast is more vulnerable to recruitment drives compared with other parts of the country, because the young are educated, underserved and disgruntled.

The failure to explain the advance of the Taliban using the community-level, Pashtun grievance model should underline the uncomfortable truth that ordinary people do not have direct or significant influence on how insurgency pans out in their areas. The northeast is slowly coming apart at the seams as old warlords and a new struggle for power go unheeded by central government. The Taliban can find allies and support from their old networks of leaders in the northeast. Like their allies in the north, it is painfully clear that atrocities committed in their past against ordinary Afghans will not necessarily impede or halt their progress.

Notes

1. It is also referred to as the Shah Salim pass.
2. Ahmed Rashid, *Taliban: Islam, Oil and the New Great Game in Central Asia*, London: I. B. Tauris, 2001.
3. Thomas H. Mason and M. Chris Mason (2007) *Understanding the Taliban and Insurgency in Afghanistan* http://www.nps.edu/programs/ccs/docs/pubs/understanding%20the%20taliban%20and%20insurgency%20in%20afghanistan.pdf
4. Formerly known as the Senlis Council.
5. Jon Hemming, "Taliban in 72 percent of Afghanistan, think-tank says," *Reuters* 8 December 2008.
6. Konstantin von Hammerstein, Susanne Koelbl, Alexander Szandar and Sami Yousafzai, "Expanding violence: Germany discovers a war in Afghanistan", Spiegel Online International, 8 September 2008.
7. Peter Marsden, *The Taliban—War, Religion and the New Order in Afghanistan*, London: Zed Books, 1998.
8. William Maley (ed.) *Fundamentalism Reborn—Afghanistan and the Taliban*, New York University Press, 1998.
9. Antonio Giustozzi, *Koran, Kalashnikov and Laptop: The Neo-Taliban Insurgency in Afghanistan 2002–2007*, London: C. Hurst & Co., 2007.
10. Robert Crews, Amin Tarzi and Robert D. Crews (eds), *The Taliban and the Crisis of Afghanistan* Cambridge, MA: Harvard University Press, 2008.
11. Ahmed Rashid, *Taliban: Islam, Oil and the New Great Game in Central Asia*, London: I.B. Tauris, 2001.
12. These were regularly encountered by the author during her work in the area in 1997–98.
13. Vikram Parekh, in his capacity as Senior Analyst with the International Crisis Group, interviewed in November 2008.
14. Interview with Afghan analysts who choose to remain anonymous, December 2008.
15. B. Raman, *"Attacks On Uzbeks In South Waziristan"*, *International Terrorism Monitor* No. 208, 23 March 2007.
16. Personal communication with Antonio Giustozzi, December 2008.
17. A number of Afghan refugees lived in suburbs of cities such as Peshawar or Islamabad rather than the refugee camps proper.
18. The concept of alterity or "otherness" is borrowed from anthropology. "It is... more than likely that ethnocentric constructions of the stranger always follow a process through which alterity is reduced to a familiar form that is easily accessible to the self. All systems of otherness are structures of identity and difference that have more to do with the establishment of *self*-identity than with the empirical

reality of the other..." Nigel Rapport and Joanna Overing, *Social and Cultural Anthropology: The Key Concepts*, New York: Routledge Taylor & Francis Groups, 2005.

19. Ahmed Rashid (2001), op. cit.

20. David B. Edwards, *Heroes of the Age: Moral Fault Lines on the Afghan Frontier* (Comparative Studies on Muslim Societies; 21), University of California Press, 1996.

21. Gilles Dorronsoro, *Revolution Unending: Afghanistan, 1979 to the Present (The CERI Series in Comparative Politics and International Studies)*, London: C. Hurst & Co., 2005.

22. Ralph H. Magnus *et al.*, *Afghanistan: Mullah, Marx and Mujahid*, Boulder, CO: Westview Pres, 2002.

23. One example is the Jami'at-ul-Uloom-il-Islamiyyah, run by Maulana Mohammad Yusuf Binnori in Karachi. The seminary has 8,000 students from different nationalities.

24. For an interesting and readable account of education in a Shiite *madrasa* and life in a clerical family see Roy P. Mottahedeh, *The Mantle of the Prophet: Religion and Politics in Iran*, New York: Simon & Schuster, 1985.

25. Ishtiaq Ahmed, Associate Professor of Political Science, Stockholm University quoted in B. Raman, "Pakistani Madrasas: Questions & Answers", Paper No. 1487, 5 August 2005 http://www.southasiaanalysis.org/%5Cpapers15%5Cpaper1487.html

26. Mariam Abou Zahab and Olivier Roy, *Islamist Networks—The Afghan-Pakistan Connection*, London: C. Hurst & Co., 2004.

27. This can best be explained as religious brownie points in return for good, appropriate or charitable acts.

28. B. Raman, *Pakistani Madrasas: Questions & Answers*, op. cit.

29. Personal observations of author and interviews with women engaged in different activities, 1995–2006.

30. "Afghanistan: Focus on warlordism in northeast", *Integrated Regional Information Networks*, 1 Jun 2005

31. Personal communication with A. Giustozzi, December 2008.

32. Source: Ministry of Rural Reconstruction and Development.

33. Personal communication with A. Giustozzi, December 2008.

34. H. Urdal, *The Devil in the Demographics: The Effect of Youth Bulges on Domestic Armed Conflict, 1950–2000*, The World Bank Social Development Papers Conflict Prevention and Reconstruction Paper No. 14, July 2004.

35. Extraordinarily large youth cohorts relative to the adult population.

36. Matt Waldman, *Falling Short: Aid Effectiveness in Afghanistan*, ACBAR Advocacy Series, 2008.

37. Source: The Recovery and Development Consortium, DFID, *Understanding Afghanistan: Poverty, Gender And Social Exclusion Analysis 4.4.4 Poverty Technical Annex Final Report*, November 2008

38. Thomas H. Mason and M. Chris Mason, "Understanding the Taliban and Insurgency in Afghanistan," 2007 http://www.nps.edu/programs/ccs/docs/pubs/understanding%20the%20taliban%20and%20insurgency%20in%20afghanistan.pdf

39. Ministry of Rural Rehabilitation and Development and The Central Statistics Office, Kabul, *The National Risk and Vulnerability Assessment 2005: Afghanistan*.

40. *After the Taliban: A Child-Focused Assessment in the Northern Afghan Provinces of Kunduz, Takhar and Badakhshan*, CCF International/Child Fund Afghanistan, April 2002.

41. The figure given was 59.33 per cent in UNFPA, *Afghanistan—A Socioeconomic and Demographic Profile and Household Listing 2003–2005*.

42. *After the Taliban: A Child-Focused Assessment in the Northern Afghan Provinces of Kunduz, Takhar and Badakhshan*, op. cit.

43. For example, Rabbani's reluctance to let go of his position and status is demonstrated by Sayyed Haider Akbar who quotes a verse in his book *Come Back to Afghanistan*, which centres on his *chowk* (which can be translated as both chair and position or status): *"My beloved chair. I've worked so hard for you. I've fought jihad for you. My beloved chair, I'll take you to the mountains of Badakhshan. I'll take you everywhere."* Matt Dupee, *The United National Front: Warlord Redux*, 2007, 03/04/2007 Afgha.com

44. David Rohde quoting Western officials in "Rising Violence: Foreign Fighters of Harsher Bent Bolster Taliban", *Spiegel Online International*, 30 October 2007

45. Ibid. on the capture of Kuzeubaev, a bomb maker, arrested in Badakhshan; Jaffar Tayar, "Taliban attack radio transmitter in Badakhshan", *Afgha.com*, 11 August 2008; Kirk Semple, "Afghan ex-militia leaders hoard arms", *The New York Times*, 28 October 2007; Konstantin von Hammerstein, Susanne Koelbl, Alexander Szandar and Sami Yousafzai, "Expanding violence: Germany discovers a war in Afghanistan", *Spiegel Online International*, 8 September 2008.

46. "Taliban commander killed in north Afghan Takhar province", *Deustche Presse Agentur*, 26 July 2008; "Takhar police kill Taliban commander", *Quqnoos.com*, 27 July 2008, http://quqnoos.com/index.php?option=com_content&task=view&id=1237

47. Susanne Koelbl and Sami Yousafzai, "Interview with a Taliban commander: 'What's Important Is to Kill the Germans'", *Spiegel Online International*, 21 May 2008.

48. Afghan sources with close links to former Taliban leaders who choose to remain anonymous, interviewed in December 2008.

49. M.K. Bhadrakumar, "Bhutto's death a blow to 'war on terror'", *Asia Times Online*, 3 January 2008.

50. Afghan sources with close links to former Taliban leaders who choose to remain anonymous, interviewed in December 2008.

51. Ali A. Jalali, "Afghanistan: Regaining Momentum", *Parameters*, winter 2007 (http://www.carlisle.army.mil/usawc/parameters/07winter/jalali.pdf)

52. See for example Robert Fisk, "Nobody supports the Taliban, but people hate the government", *The Independent*, 27 November, 2008.

53. Daniel Korski, "French deaths highlight NATO's other challenge", *The European Council on Foreign Relations*, 19 August 2008

54. Antonio Giustozzi, *Koran, Kalashnikov and Laptop: The Neo-Taliban Insurgency in Afghanistan 2002–2007*, London: C. Hurst & Co., 2007.

55. The case of leaders handling an extended family is much more complex.

56. The last substantive work that dealt with leadership in the region is Fredrik Barth, *Political Leadership among Swat Pathans*, London: Athlone Press, 1954. There have been no major detailed studies since then.

57. B. Raman, *Pakistani Madrasas...*, op. cit.

58. Afghan sources with close links to former Taliban leaders who choose to remain anonymous, interviewed in December 2008.

59. Ibid.

60. Susanne Koelbl and Sami Yousafzai, 21 May 2008 *Interview with a Taliban commander...*, op. cit.

61. Ibid.

62. Ibid.
63. Basir Begzad, "The Godfathers of the Taliban," 8 May 2008: translated by Amin Wahidi http://aminwahidi.blogspot.com/2008/05/godfathers-of-taliban.html
64. Yossef Bodansky, *Islamabad's Road Warriors*, Freeman Centre for Strategic Studies, 1995..
65. This is a colloquial Dari term which means "playing with mullahs" and refers broadly to manipulation of religious leaders and groups to gain influence.
66. Gilles Dorronsoro,*Revolution Unending*, op. cit.
67. Basir Begzad *The Godfathers of the Taliban*, op. cit.
68. See also Mariam Abou Zahab and Olivier Roy, *Islamist Networks*, op. cit.
69. See Dorronsoro (2005) for a detailed explanation of the rivalry between Ahl-i Hadith and Hizb-i Islami in eastern Afghanistan
70. Kaja Borchgrevink, *Religious Actors and Civil Society in Post-2001 Afghanistan*, International Peace Research Institute, Oslo (PRIO), November 2007.
71. Antonio Giustozzi, "Centre-periphery Relations in Afghanistan between Patrimonialism and Institution-building:The Case of Badakhshan", *Central Asian Survey*, no. 1, 2009, forthcoming.
72. Afghan sources which choose to remain anonymous.
73. Antonio Giustozzi, *Koran, Kalashnikov and Laptop...*, op. cit.
74. "Rabbani:Taliban quits militant policy, may sit for talks with Karzai", *Fact International*, 7 February 2008 [http://www.factjo.com/Factjo_en/fullnews.aspx?id=401]
75. Matt Dupee, "Dangerous liaisons: Rabbani endorses direct talks with the Taliban, Hekmatyar", *Afgha.com*, 3 September 2007
76. Afghan sources with close links to former Taliban leaders who choose to remain anonymous, interviewed in December 2008.
77. Matt Dupee, "Dangerous liaisons...,", op. cit.
78. Matt Dupee, "The United National Front: Warlord Redux", *Afgha.com*, 3 April 2007.
79. Aabha Dixit, *Soldiers of Islam: Origins, Ideology and Strategy of the Taliban*, New Delhi: Institute for Defense Studies and Analysis, 13 November, 2001]http://www.idsa-india.org/an-aug-2.html]
80. Anthony Davis in *Jane's Defence Weekly*, 4 October 2000; Ahmed Rashid, "Massud Ready To Fight On" *Eurasia Insight*, 10 June 2000.
81. Personal interviews with Ismaili religious leaders in Badakhshan, 1996.
82. Matt Dupee, "The United National Front..." op. cit.
83. Antonio Giustozzi, *Koran, Kalashnikov and Laptop...*, op. cit.
84. Antonio Giustozzi, "Centre-periphery relations in Afghanistan ...," op. cit.
85. Interview with parliamentarians who prefer to remain anonymous.
86. David Rohde, "Rising violence: foreign fighters of harsher bent bolster Taliban", *Spiegel Online International*, 30 October 2007.

13

THE TEHRIK-E TALIBAN PAKISTAN

Claudio Franco

Introduction

Where the Pakistani Taliban phenomenon is concerned, in particular with regard to the Pakistani militants' contribution to the wider conflict in Afghanistan, it seems clear that Western policies are marred by an inadequate approach, as inadequate as the one devised by Pakistan to assist the US-led campaign against the Afghan Taliban insurgency.

Since the onset of the Pakistani insurgency there has been a tendency, among Western and Pakistani observers,[1] to treat the Pakistani Taliban as an autonomous entity, a group aligned with but separate from the mainstream Afghan Taliban. This assumption rests mainly on the Western idea of a Durand Line functioning as a proper border, although the peoples inhabiting the Pashtun areas along the border do not seem to see it as such.

The idea of a Pakistani Pashtunistan, or land of the Pashtun, existing alongside the main Afghan Pashtun body, arises mainly from the Western predisposition to trust maps and diplomatic treaties between nation states. Fundamentally, the misunderstanding was induced and, to some extent, perpetuated by Western geography itself, which shaped the land while interpreting it. In that process the work of geographers and politicians also affected, at least to some extent, the attitude of the eastern Pashtun tribes towards the foreigner. This radical misconception proceeded to perpetuate a certain idea of Western-Pashtun interaction, from the point of view of both sides, and this tradition of enmity has played a significant role during the conflict. The British deployed en masse in Helmand, for example, fighting their own war, was one the worst strategic mistakes NATO, or Britain, could conceive, reviving

269

the century-old hate towards the *Anglesi*, the British, a term that had extended its semantic reach to mean the *farang* or foreigners in general.

However, in order to interpret and confront tribal dynamics effectively, a radical shift of perspective may prove to be indispensable. More precisely, if the aim is a lasting resolution of the conflict in the border area, the first necessary condition is probably a radical methodological shift in cultural approach, which will inevitably affect policy-making when the Pashtun issue is concerned. Reading the eastern Pashtun tribes as they are, or as they think about themselves, and not as we have learned to interpret them may be a first step towards a renewed international effort to stabilize the Pak–Afghan theatre.

The Karlanri tribes of the Pakistani frontier are an integral part of the Afghan-Pashtun family,[2] a section of it that was absorbed within Pakistan after Partition. Because of their relative isolation from Persian-speaking peoples, they are often regarded as the guardians of true Pukhtun identity. There is no difference of nature between the eastern tribes, loosely ruled by Pakistan since 1947, and the other branches of the Pashtun tree, the eastern and western Serbanri, the Bitan and the Gurghusht.[3] Although the classification relayed by Olaf Caroe is essentially based on genealogical myths which may or may not be entirely reliable, it is undeniable that in practice the Pashtun think of themselves as an homogeneous and coherent entity, notwithstanding the specific traits characteristic of each tribe or grouping of tribes. Furthermore, in today's context, what is required is not to engage in a historically accurate analysis of the genealogy of the Pashtun tribes but to confront their "national"/tribal identity as they perceive it.

The fact that the Federally Administered Tribal Areas (FATA) have belonged to a modern nation state since the Partition of British-ruled India threatens to alter our objectivity, as we tend to consider whatever happens east of the Durand Line as something that concerns Pakistan. According to the tribes' point of view, however, those Pashtuns, or Pukhtuns, based in Pakistan remain an integral part of the tribal structure of the Afghans' homeland. There is a noteworthy difference, in fact, between a greater Pashtunistan (the proper homeland of the Pashtun people as a village elder would intend it, without always having a name for it) and Afghanistan as a nation state. The former is an ideal territorial entity that exists notwithstanding the Durand Line and includes the eastern Pakistani tribes. The latter is the territory where the Pashtun are the ethnic majority and the country where Pashtun dynasties have ruled for centuries a multi-ethnic kingdom,[4] a state for which the Pashtun have always played a role very similar to the one they are playing today in the FATA: allied or hired, but never controlled, by the Amir in Kabul.

An understanding of Pashtun national identity coherent with the self-perception of the Pashtun people itself would enable the international community to deal with the tribal insurgency more effectively, as the behaviour of the tribal peoples certainly does not depend on what we expect from them but, most probably, on how they think about themselves. Such a shift of perspective may result in a radically improved understanding of the reasons for the Pak-Afghan Taliban conflict, a war prolonged by a series of strategic mistakes linked to what we expected from the interaction between the two sides of the Durand Line. There are visible fallacies disseminated over the last seven years, mispredictions and flawed assessments that led to where we stand today. A humble reconsideration of the problem's root causes is the least the international community can do, if the target is indeed a stabilization of the area for the long term.

Mullah Omar's Pakistani Wilayat

The Taliban phenomenon in Pakistan is the most visible symptom of the long-standing links and ideological proximity between the tribes of Pakistan's Federally Administered Tribal Areas (FATA) and the Afghan Taliban proper. It was born from a reciprocal sympathy between cousins cultivated during the years of the anti-Soviet *jihad*, and flourished with the rise of the right circumstances, in the form of Taliban fleeing to safety across the border.

The Pashtun regard the arrival of a guest as an opportunity to demonstrate their honour, in line with their tribal code, and will often offer asylum unconditionally. When, in the autumn of 2001, the trickle of Taliban fugitives became a stream, their regime routed by a foreign superpower that was merely flexing its muscles, the tribes of the Frontier responded warmly: they opened forgotten mountain trails and cleared the bush, took dollars and delivered supplies and transport. They provided donkeys and guides, pick-ups, Corollas and trucks, and led Taliban and al-Qaeda fighters to safety, whether they were lower ranks or leaders, paying guests or penniless fugitives.

Besides their religious, ethnic and tribal links, the Pakistani comrades were often motivated by a personal and ideological sympathy which had developed on the front lines of Afghanistan and in the refugee camps of Miramshah, Parachinar, Peshawar and Pabbi. Many tribesmen had grown to adulthood fighting with the Afghan *mujahidin* or providing them with support, ambushing Soviet tanks with them or carrying ammunition and bread to the combatants. Many of these fighters turned to the Taliban cause as a consequence of their disillusionment, disgust or desperation with the fratricidal breakdown of the civil war between the *mujahidin* factions, but the old support networks in the NWFP (North-West Frontier Province) and the FATA remained intact. When America began knocking at the door with 1,000 lb laser-guided ordnance, Afghan Taliban fighters began to head east, and in their time of need their tribal brethren became guides and hosts, providing support when needed and a hiding place when possible.

Most probably, it was this logistical effort that sowed the seeds of an organized Taliban movement within Pakistan—or, at the very least, this is suggested by the tribesmen of the FATA working with the Afghan Taliban in an organized fashion after 9/11. Providing sanctuary to the Taliban, tribesmen and former *mujahidin* were inspired by those energetic Afghan cadres and firebrand clerics who had established Shariat law and Pashtun rule in Afghanistan, militants who had manned an authentic Islamic revolution just miles away across the border. Those tribal *mujahidin* who had joined the Islamic Emirate became their natural hosts and protectors in the Tribal Areas, and mediated between the local population and the unexpected "guests". In addition, the tribesmen were naturally fascinated by the regime of the mullahs: the Afghan Taliban revolution, grown out of sheer desperation with an intolerable situation, had transformed a band of puritan vigilantes into an all-conquering Islamic army led by an *Amir-ul-momenin* in perfect accordance with Quranic precepts.

In late 2001, in the immediate aftermath of September 11, that very same Commander of the Faithful had renounced his kingdom out of loyalty to a guest on the run, a Saudi Islamist organizer named Osama bin Laden. Islamic piety and the Pushtunwali tribal code's tradition of asylum were both upheld by Mullah Omar, as had seldom been done before by a head of state. We might say that the near-suicidal determination of the Taliban Amir, followed by the complete annihilation of his regime, represented a spiritual and perhaps quasi-divine act of renunciation to his followers, an ultimate proof that the Taliban state was indeed a blessed entity led by a saint-like Commander of the Faithful.

A fragment of a speech of 6 October 2001, contained in an unreleased book written in 2004 by Amir Khan Muttaqi, a former Taliban minister and currently a close adviser to Mullah Omar, provides an insight into Mullah Omar's interpretation of unfolding events at the time. The book was banned by the Taliban leadership upon completion[5] in order to safeguard confidential information. A day before the start of the US bombing campaign, Omar harangues his men in a speech which emphasizes that the Taliban are confronting the most powerful of enemies and sets the stage for the long run: eventually the forces of Islam will be victorious, he says, but do expect death and defeat to begin with. In an inspired piece of rhetoric, he considers his own likely demise in the imminent conflict. Mullah Omar admits he is scared, for himself and his family, and he makes a clean breast of his own weak human nature. Accordingly, he questions the sincerity of his thoughts. "It is very strange that I am not greedy," he says, and he clearly knows already that he will likely lose everything in this battle, "for I know my power; my position; my wealth; and my family are in danger". But, Omar continues, there is something worse than losing power, family and wealth, and that is becoming a friend of non-Muslims. "However, I am ready to sacrifice myself and I do not want to became a friend of non-Muslims, for non-Muslims are against all my beliefs and my religion." "My family, my power, and my privileges," he concludes, "are all in danger, but still I am insisting on sacrificing myself, and you should do likewise."

The *Amir-ul-Momenin* is "ready to leave everything, and to believe only in Islam and in my Afghan bravery", and it is worth noting that Afghan/Pashtun identity and Muslim faith are given the same rhetorical status in this case. But

Afghans tired and disheartened by three decades of war, "those who will not lose anything" in Omar's words, were probably the least responsive to this exhortation to renounce everything for the Taliban cause and for a leader who was certainly, by his own admission, on his way out. The tribal populations across the Durand Line might, however, have had a better disposition towards Mullah Omar's words, in particular considering the cyclical nature of Islamic insurgencies in what are today the FATA uprisings led, more often than not, by charismatic clerics who were not dissimilar from Mullah Omar.[6] The financial opportunities linked to providing for the needs of a low-intensity war across the border must have represented a further encouragement. Undeniably, the tribals were very much at ease with Omar's rhetoric, and unlike the Afghans, they actually had something to sacrifice for the cause.

Inspired by the Taliban reaction to the post-9/11 events and motivated by foreign hard currency, the tribesmen set their support mechanism in motion and thereby, starting in 2002, joined the Taliban by proxy, relying on the mediation of the tribal Taliban cadres who had returned home and were becoming increasingly influential within the movement. Hence, selected tribes, primarily those to which the Taliban contacts belonged, opened their hearts and compounds to the Taliban doctrine, turning the tribal belt into the rear staging area and launching pad of choice for the resurgent militia.[7]

The human raw material needed to kick-start a Pakistani Islamist insurgency was certainly already there in late 2001, as it had been when the fundamentalist militia first emerged in the Kandahar area seven years before. Besides Pakistani fighters "attached" to the Taliban "proper" and *madrasa* students, the first Pakistani Taliban, the insurgency's core, were often former *mujahidin* who had fought the Soviets in Afghanistan, mainly under Nabi Mohammadi and Younis Khalis. Once the Soviets had crossed the Amu Darya on their way back to a dying USSR, most of them had returned home while a suicidal civil war escalated across the border, a conflict that inflicted more damage on the country than the Soviets ever had.

This was not a pleasant sight for those who had contributed to liberating the country from a godless foe, and when the Taliban first emerged they were perceived as paladins of faith and homeland, in Afghanistan as well as in the FATA. But there was a crucial difference: while the Afghans as a people experienced first-hand the Taliban revolution since 1994, their tribal cousins could only observe it from afar, or through the eyes of those who joined the Emirate's troops. The events of 9/11 and Mullah Omar's momentous decision freed the Taliban ideal from its Afghan national dimension. If in 1996 the Taliban had taken Kabul as a formidable Islamic army, the FATA were instead "conquered" by defeated fighters who crossed the border fleeing from "crusaders" and Tajiks. The *mujahid* ideals had filtered through to Pakistan with the refugees throughout the 1980s, while it was the fleeing Taliban who were now exporting the praxis of the Taliban ideology to Pakistan. Geographically, Taliban infiltration was not a limited phenomenon by any means: it was reported that the Gomal and Tochi border passes, leading directly to Miramshah and Mirali, were left open by Pakistani forces even when theoretically, according to Islamabad, the border was sealed;[8] and militants found their way across the Durand Line wherever they could, always relying on personal networks. Anecdotal evidence, for example, is available regarding a substantial flow of fighters crossing into Bajaur and Mohmand Agencies from Afghanistan's Kunar Province: the TTP spokesman and central *shura* member Mawlawi Omar quietly stated that his tribal militants had set up camps for foreign fighters led into Pakistan by Lashkar-i-Taiba and Jaish-e-Mohammad members.[9]

We have seen that the Pakistani Taliban phenomenon was born in the aftermath of 9/11 as a support network for the defeated Taliban army, but it was not until mid-2003 that the embryonic movement evolved from being a fifth column of the Afghan organization into an organized entity aimed at the establishment of Sharia Law in Pakistan's FATA. The early days of the Pakistani Taliban—the months during which the tribesmen were nothing more than a support network for the Afghan insurgents, between the collapse of the Islamic Emirate in December 2001 and the first large-scale clashes between tribal militants and the Pakistani Army around Kalosha (South Waziristan) in January 2004[10]—can be regarded as a gestation period. The birth of an authentic Pakistani Taliban insurgency, however, was prompted by General Musharraf's compliance with the requests made by the Bush administration. It was the deployment of Pakistani military personnel deep inside the Tribal Areas in pursuit of fleeing Taliban and al-Qaeda operatives that ignited the tribal insurgency.

Even earlier than that, once the Taliban had reorganized their ranks to meet the needs of a low-intensity guerrilla war, local like-minded tribals began contributing to the incursions against Karzai's government with manpower, funds, weapons and expertise. Hence the Pakistani Taliban were born as a vital component of the Afghan insurgent network and their cadres were integrated within Afghan units for most of the first year following the 9/11 attacks. The original core of the Pakistani insurgency was formed of Afghan fugitives, Pakistani militants and foreign operatives, a concoction of fighters based in areas where the local population was supportive of the Jihadist cause. These villages and rural areas are the ones that constitute the territorial backbone of the tribal Taliban insurgency to this day. Bajaur, for instance, played a critical role in terms of hosting foreign operatives who would engage in terrorist activities in the West;[11] Abu Faraj Al Libi, it was reported, led the foreign network in the northern FATAs until his arrest[12] in May 2005 in Mardan, in the NWFP.

The "labour phase" of the Pakistani insurgency was, as mentioned, the result of Islamabad's compliance with America's requests. Since 9/11, Washington's clear priority on the international stage was to smoke out the remnants of al-Qaeda and annihilate its Taliban hosts. When the Pakistani Army deployed to the FATA to plug the escape routes, their target was to arrest and root out foreign al-Qaeda affiliated fighters, be they Chechen, Uzbek, Arab or Uighur: exactly what the army had refrained from attempting in the past few decades. Many of these foreign Islamists had established themselves in northwestern Pakistan as settled guests and, in accordance with local customs, the local population had every intention to protect them. In this context, we should keep in mind to what extent a politically-motivated escape is integrated within the conservative Islamic system of thought favoured by the tribes. The fleeing militants could be seen as *muhajirun*, and neglecting a *muhajir* implies that the Prophet's band of followers might have been neglected if he had asked for Khair in the hands of that Pashtun clan or family. The *muhajir* logic is a well known leitmotiv of Islamist rhetoric, in particular in its Anti-Crusader-Western incarnation[13].

Musharraf's circle certainly neglected the extent of tribesmen's sympathy for the Taliban-Al Qaida cause and, to this day, it is extremely difficult to believe that such a strategic oversight was even possible among the well-trained Afghan specialists within the Pakistani Army. It was when the army went in to hunt down the foreigners that they found out to what extent the locals were ready to protect them. During the first Azam Warsak operation, for example, launched on 22 June 2002, the tribesmen cooperated with the Uzbeks so well that all of them, approximately three dozen, managed to escape. In Azam Warsak, however, the tribesmen abstained from fighting the Army, even though they voiced their anger aloud, criticizing a regime which they perceived of as having become the enemy's ally.

The Pakistani Army deployed for the first time in the Tirah Valley in Khyber Agency and along the Pak-Afghan border in Kurram Agency in the autumn of 2001, trying to plug escape routes from the Tora Bora area, where the Taliban and al-Qaeda were making their last stand, to safety in Pakistan. The Tirah Valley is among the remotest locations in Khyber Agency and the Army HQ knew that extreme caution was required in dealing with the local Afridis: and yet Washington's "with us or against us" ultimatum was enough for Musharraf to kick-start deployment in the FATA.

It should be noted that for anyone fleeing Tora Bora through the Spinghar range, Tirah represents the most immediate path to safety. The Taliban holed up in Tora Bora, however, opted mainly for Kurram, where the fugitives could rely on swathes of territory controlled by sympathetic Sunni villagers, who had long shared a fundamentalist stance and an anti-Shia sentiment with the Taliban and al-Qaeda. From Kurram, Taliban and al-Qaeda operatives filtered through to Waziristan, where the rebels could rely on assets and support networks, while others proceeded to the settled areas of the NWFP and the rest of Pakistan. The bypassing of Tirah suggests that there was no sign yet of an immediate local reaction to the presence of the Pakistani Army.

Just over a year later things had already radically changed course, and when the army launched the Kalosha offensive on 8 January 2004, Nek Mohammad, the first Pakistani Taliban leader, had given orders to treat the Pakistani soldiers as legitimate targets. The army sustained scores of casualties, losses inflicted by fellow countrymen; a nuclear-capable army had been humiliated by a formidable Islamist *lashkar*, a tribal rendition of the Taliban motive.

The Kalosha operation was meant to "root out" the foreign militias led by Tahir Yuldashev, the Uzbek commander closely associated with al-Qaeda and the Afghan Taliban. As it turned out, the most notable result of the battle of Kalosha was the emergence of Nek Mohammad Wazir as the first significant leader of the Pakistani insurgency. At the height of the fighting, Nek Mohammad famously drove his vehicle through army lines in order to recover the wounded Yuldashev. Within a few months of the call to arms, Pakistani tribal insurgents had gone from providing support to playing a key strategic role in the FATA theatre, their determination demonstrated by their readiness to compromise their peaceful coexistence with Pakistan's Federal Government for the sake of the Jihadist ideal.

The first phase of the Pakistani offensive in the FATA had therefore achieved a threefold result: the population was now supporting the foreigners openly as a sign of widespread regional opposition to Western interference in the area, the Army had been humiliated, and most important, the Pakistani militants were now fighting alongside the Afghan and foreign militants both in Afghanistan and within Pakistani territory.

While Pakistan's FATA were witnessing the emergence of their own Jihadist insurgency, the US-led Coalition was still utterly oblivious of this decisive by-product of Operation Enduring Freedom: America had sanctified Mullah Omar and idealized his regime, even while its military was annihilating the malfunctioning, inherently failed Taliban state. The Western "Coalition of the Willing" turned a fundamentally botched governance system into the perfect expression of moral rectitude. The US-led invasion had freed the mullahs from the obligation to govern, an activity for which they did not appear to be particularly well qualified, to consign them instead to the ambit of ideological strife and guerrilla warfare, incomparably better suited to the movement's characteristics. Born seven years before as a Ghilzai-dominated, Deobandi-inspired revivalist faction rooted in the southern Pashtun belt of Afghanistan, by 2006 the Taliban had become a transnational, pan-Pashtun insurgency and a leading protagonist of political life in the Pak-Afghan region. The quasi-suicidal defeat of 2001 did not wipe out the Taliban but simply reduced them to their ideological hard core while granting them a moral high ground that, in the years to come, would prove to be their most significant asset in the eyes of the Muslim world.

The weight of the tribal element

We have seen how the relative isolation of today's FATA preserved an eminently tribal structure which is still the defining trait of the eastern Pashtun tribes. Whereas the Afghan Pashtun tribes were somehow influenced by the Afghan national state, although with a varying degree of success, Pakistan's FATA remained the exclusive domain of Pushtunwali.

From its inception the Pakistani Taliban movement was influenced by the tribal element, which soon emerged as an invaluable underlying network, a basis for the insurgents to develop their organization rapidly and effectively. Nonetheless, although it undoubtedly provided Taliban organizers with the best of connective tissues, on the other hand tribal allegiance emerged immediately as the most likely cause of a sudden fragmentation of the Pakistani Taliban along tribal faultlines. Tribal rivalries were also the main tool used by the organization's enemies to thwart any serious attempt to bypass traditional tribal enmity using religion and ideology. The tribal allegiances that are observable here are critical to our understanding of the Taliban phenomenon on the Pakistan side.

We have seen how the first nucleus of insurgents in Pakistan—composed of a mixture of tribal militants, Afghan Taliban and foreign fighters—filtered through the Durand Line from late 2001 to early 2002, establishing a sizeable presence in the Wana area of South Waziristan. Here they were hosted by the Yargulkhels, a sub-clan of the Wazir tribe. Among the newly arrived fighters, the Uzbek contingent was one of the main components in this heterogeneous fighting force, and the first significant clashes involving the Pakistani Army would almost invariably involve al-Qaeda-affiliated Central Asian militants.

The fact that Wana was strategically situated for fighters on the run from the Shahikot range, where the Americans had cornered a substantial group of al-Qaeda and Taliban fighters led by Saifurrahman Mansur,[14] does not in itself suffice to explain why the area emerged as a high-density hideout for foreigners fleeing Afghanistan. We must look at the role played by those tribals who had fought alongside the Taliban in the second half of the 1990s, Nek Mohammad Wazir being the best known among them, to make sense of why Wana became the first destination of choice for the militants.

The first recognizable leader of the Pakistani uprising, Nek Mohammad,[15] grew up during the years of Zia ul Haq's Islamization drive, and dutifully studied in a *madrasa* associated with the Jemaat-e-Ulema Islami-Fazlur (JUI-F) network, a Deobandi political party well known for the extreme flexibility of its leader, Maulana Fazlur Rehman, where politics was concerned. After graduation, the young Nek Mohammad opted for *jihad* in Afghanistan and was recruited to the Taliban in the mid-1990s by Mohammad Gul—an Afghan commander close to Saifurrahman Mansur, a leading light of the Taliban resurgence immediately after 2001 and, together with Jalaluddin Haqqani and Mullah Dadullah, an initiator of the anti-US campaign.

After a spell in Kargha, a well known training camp for foreign fighters near Kabul, the young Waziri fighter ascended rapidly through the hierarchy and in 1998 was promoted to lead a Waziri contingent based in Bagram, a unit that happened to be regularly posted to the most problematic frontline hotspots. His time in Kargha under Saifurrahman Mansur, rubbing shoulders with the foreigners training there, and in the neighbouring Rishkor camp was crucial in positioning Nek Mohammad near the very top of Mansur's likely contacts when he needed an exit path across the border for the substantial Taliban and foreign contingent escaping from Rohani Baba. Nek

Mohammad provided safe passage and support and was generously rewarded by those who made it through to the FATA. Suddenly solvent and extremely well-connected, within months this obscure Waziri commander became a go-between among the various factions involved in the insurgency. The 2004 Army operation in Kalosha,[16] Nek Mohammad's own area, marks the apex of his brief career at the helm of the Pakistani component of the Taliban movement.

The early prominence of the Yargulkhel Wazirs within the movement depended directly on being the foreigners' main local contacts, but they were not the only clan involved in the support network. Besides occasional tussles with other Yargulkhel commanders, Nek Mohammad vied for funds primarily with Mawlawi Nazir, a Kakakhel Ahmedzai Wazir. The tribal dimension of the insurgency is well represented by the rivalry between these two branches of the Ahmedzai Wazirs, the Yargulkhel and the Kakakhel. According to the tribals' pragmatic rule of thumb, proximity will encourage commanders to coalesce around the best positioned member of the group, as in the case of Nek Mohammad among the Yargulkhels for example. As a reaction, rival groups will produce a contender whenever they feel that their interests are not being upheld by the ruling clan or subtribe; the Kakakhels' apparently unanimous support for Nazir offers an example of this mindset.

The opposition between Mawlawi Nazir and Nek Mohammad is also instructive about the role of state actors aspiring to control or annihilate the Taliban movement. Nek Mohammad's death had the effect of coalescing most Ahmedzai Wazirs around his family and friends, and confirmed their pro-foreign-militant and anti-government stance, thus helping to construct/perpetuate a faction around the foreign Jihadis. Mawlawi Nazir, on the other hand, had given himself up following Nek Mohammad's triumph in Kalosha and, cleared by the government of any previous sins, disappeared from the radar for the best part of the following 18 months.

It is at this stage, during this apparent lull in Kakakhel-dominated areas, that anti-Taliban state actors began to shore up support for Mawlawi Nazir's party. The future make up of Nazir's faction, coupled with the role played by his group through the following four years, clearly indicate the intervention of some invisible hand in the process. Mawlawi Nazir kept a low profile until 2006, when his organization appeared refreshed by a new injection of operatives hailing from Pakistan's sectarian groups, known as "Punjabi Taliban". These operatives' connections to Pakistan's security apparatus, which used them as a proxy against India in Kashmir, are a further sign that someone with an agenda within Pakistan's intelligence establishment was directing the effort, entire departments more often than loose individuals.

The breach between Yargulkhel and Kakakhel however was not the result of external intervention. It certainly was a "natural" occurrence in terms of tribal rivalry. What the invisible hand did was to select Mawlawi Nazir to be the recipient of state aid and army resources. So one cannot escape the impression of a concerted attempt to exploit traditional tribal rifts to split the pro-foreigner front while also gaining a proxy within the wider Taliban movement. The fact that Nazir's Kakakhels and the Pakistani state had a shared interest in getting rid of the unruly al-Qaeda-oriented Uzbeks is not in itself enough to explain the extent of the support provided to Nazir's men by army medics and other support units during his April 2007 clash with the Uzbeks[17].

Unquestionably, tribal allegiance has remained a crucial aspect to consider when dealing with the Pakistani insurgency. The most ambitious attempt on the part of the wider Taliban movement to defuse the destructive potential of the tribal element has been the creation, in December 2007, of an all-inclusive Taliban umbrella group, the Tehrik-i Taliban-i-Pakistan (TTP).[18]

Bypassing the tribal factor: the TTP era

This section will examine how the centre of gravity of the Pakistani Taliban movement shifted north towards the traditional heartland of tribal unrest: central Waziristan. The TTP's creation marked the apex of a new era for Pakistani Taliban militants.

We have seen how the rivalry between Mawlawi Nazir and Nek Mohammad in Wana between 2002 and 2005 evolved into a split between a pro-foreigners faction and a pro-government bloc, largely thanks to the interference of Pakistan's security apparatus. After Nek Mohammad's death, given the Kakakhels' cooperation with the army against the Uzbeks, Wana ceased to be the safest of places for operatives on the run. As a result, between 2004 and 2007 the centre of gravity of the Taliban phenomenon moved progressively northwards with the foreign militants. Aware of the risks posed by coalescing the insurgency around a specific tribal grouping, the Pakistani Taliban attempted to neutralize the weight of the tribal factor while at the same time anti-Taliban forces were trying to maximize its destructive effect. Neglecting the tribal element in this context means losing sight of the axis around which the conflict has been "played" by Islamabad.

We have mentioned how the epicentre of Taliban militancy had shifted north towards the Mehsud-inhabited areas of South Waziristan, along the border with North Waziristan, where in 2005 a young Shabikhel commander emerged from obscurity. Baitullah Mehsud entered the fray of the tribal insurgency and, within three years, would lead a formidable fighting force that managed to impose the Taliban as one of the key players in tribal politics. In 2008, Baitullah was named one of the world's 100 most influential figures of the year by *Time* magazine. It is worth noting that the Shabikhel Mehsuds had already produced an eminent Jihadi Amir: Mullah Powinda, who had been a nightmare for the British over a century ago, during one of the many tribal revolts that afflicted the British between the 1850s and 1947.

Baitullah had first emerged as a noteworthy figure in 2004, reported to be acting as a second[19] of Abdullah Mehsud during negotiations that followed the kidnapping of two Chinese engineers by the militants. In 2005 Baitullah was already leading his own Mehsud faction, and by February that year he had already been deemed significant enough by the army to be the signatory of a peace accord covering the Mehsud areas of South Waziristan. According to unconfirmed media reports Mullah Dadullah Akhund, on behalf of the Taliban leadership, officially named Baitullah as the Amir of the Mehsud tribe between 2005 and 2006;[20] but what is significant is that after the Sargodha accord of February 2005, Baitullah's supremacy was essentially unopposed.

It appears that even if the tribes select their local leaders though their traditional consultation procedure, it is the Pakistan military that eventually sanctions the prominence of a given leader definitively, often with the idea of encouraging internal strife among the tribals. Baitullah, for example, was probably regarded as a lesser evil than Abdullah Mehsud when the army selected its negotiating partner for the Sargodha Accord.

The Accord was short lived and with the US increasing their pressure on Pakistan, Islamabad confronted Baitullah and was repeatedly humiliated in the field: between 2006 and 2007, Baitullah's Taliban forces overran several army forts and, in August 2007, took 240 soldiers hostage in one single incident, confirming Baitullah's status as Pakistan's public enemy number one, on a par with Osama and Mullah Omar.

Baitullah's masterstroke, however, was his involvement in the creation of the TTP in December 2007. Not many details are available on the month-long talks that led to the organisation's inception, although according to well-informed sources,[21] who witnessed the first stages of the insurgency first hand, it was Faqir Mohammad who first conceived the idea of the TTP and encouraged Baitullah to accept the leadership. Certainly the creation of the TTP was a collective effort, and we know that representatives from all the agencies composing the FATA and most of the Frontier regions and adjacent districts were present during the negotiations.

Definitely, the TTP was established on the basis of an anti-tribal, or perhaps pan-tribal, agenda, an attempt to circumvent the difficulties due to tribal rivalries by reiterating the importance of the Taliban ideology for the Pakistani insurgents. The Taliban, in fact, in accordance with the early-Islamic stance favoured by the Deobandi clergy, tend to be an all-inclusive movement, and during the years of the Islamic Emirate they strove, at least officially, to widen their power base beyond their Pashtun core. In other words, in the eyes of the future TTP leaders, the remedy to the tribals' internal problems was theoretically built into the Taliban movement, which itself was originally conceived as a reaction to the ethnic and factional conflict among the *mujahidin*.

Treating the FATA like a section of the Muslim Ummah, and the tribals as a single community of believers, the brains behind the TTP were able to introduce a mutual assistance mechanism designed to break the government's strategy, which was based on the tribes' structural propensity for internal conflict. Islamabad, in fact, had learned to engage the various local Taliban factions one by one, hoping either to defeat them outright or to buy them off once the army had softened their position militarily. It had worked with Mawlawi Nazir in Wana and even the Yargulkhel "Wana Five" had eventually been split into two factions.

The TTP aimed to unify the Taliban fighters under one flag, building a single entity from along the border of South Waziristan up to the Bajaur Agency. According to this scheme, fighters would have been able to move freely within the TTP-controlled areas to provide reinforcements or support as needed, without having to transit through government-controlled settled areas. At the same time, the government would lose the possibility of negotiating in one agency while fighting in another, as the TTP would only negotiate or fight as a whole.

The TTP was launched with confidence and fervour, following an extraordinary year for Baitullah and his allies, and its first statement[22] consists of nothing less than an ultimatum to the army: in order to avoid a coordinated attack on Pakistani targets, the government was told to cease its operations in Swat and close its checkpoints there and in Waziristan, and release the former *khateeb* of Islamabad's Lal Masjid, Maulana Abdul Aziz Ghazi. The importance of the Lal Masjid episode in the creation of the TTP must not be neglected; the TTP can be considered the military-political expression of the Red Mosque generation, a new breed of young and determined Islamist militants who were not necessarily willing to talk to Islamabad, as their precursors had been. If Mawlawi Nazir had accepted dealing with the government, it was in accordance with a model which developed during the years of the anti-Soviet *jihad*; Baitullah's TTP appears rather to be the result of the tribals' interaction with aggressive al-Qaeda ideologues, the same preachers who had influenced the Red Mosque. Baitullah was the natural Amir of the new organization, and two deputies were selected to support him: Hafez Gul Bahadur, from North Waziristan, and Maulana Faquir Mohammad, the movement's head in Bajaur.

The TTP was promptly recognized by Pakistan as an entity out of control, prey to al-Qaeda-leaning and Takfiri ideologies, and was immediately engaged by the army on multiple fronts, in Waziristan, Swat, Bajaur, Mohmand and Darra Adam Khel. Islamabad's aggressive approach in 2008 is probably one of the reasons why the original TTP project could not be pursued as planned. There may still be no territorial continuity between TTP-dominated areas, and the movement has indeed lost fighters and assets as of early 2009; writing the TTP off, however, would certainly seem premature. Furthermore, the TTP remains the most organised attempt to change the splintered Islamist militias of the tribal areas into a structured organization led by a central Amir.

The link between Baitullah's TTP and the Afghan Taliban has been repeatedly questioned by several observers[23], but speculating to what extent the TTP is or is not integrated with the Afghan movement presupposes that we are in fact dealing with two distinct entities. It may sound provocative, but our knowledge of the phenomenon points towards the Pakistani Taliban being nothing more than a limb of the mainstream Afghan Taliban. Certainly it was not Mullah Omar, nor others on his behalf, who decided to create the Tehrik-i Taliban-i-Pakistan (TTP), but then he was not necessarily involved in the setting up of other prominent regional commands either. Further, if we examine the leadership of the Pakistani Islamist insurgency, wherever we look we find close personal links to the Islamic Emirate, in the form of direct involvement by the leading Pakistani commanders with the Taliban regime, fighting under them as members of tribal or all-Pakistani units attached to the chaotic Taliban war machine. Nek Mohammad, Baitullah, Mawlawi Nazir, Faquir Mohammad, Mawlawi Omar and Omar Khalid were all Taliban fighters long before 9/11, and Mullah Omar had been their leader for years when his regime crumbled.

The proximity of the TTP to the Afghan Taliban was confirmed repeatedly by the movement's top leadership in 2008. Both Faquir Mohammad and Mawlawi Omar, respectively Naib Amir[24] and official spokesman of the TTP, made clear that there is no difference in nature between the Pakistani outfit and its counterpart across the border. Asked if the TTP entertained relations with the Taliban, Faquir Mohammad answered: "No questions about it. They are the true Muslims and everybody has acknowledged them as such. We still support the Afghan Taliban, as they were the ones who implemented Shariah in Afghanistan. We are their staunch supporters and there is no difference in our beliefs." Further, al-Qaeda is regarded as nothing less than the international face of the Taliban ideology. According to Mawlawi Omar's own words:

There is no difference between Al-Qaeda and the Taliban. The formation of Taliban and Al-Qaeda was based on an ideology. Today, Taliban and Al-Qaeda have become an ideology. Whoever works for these organizations, they fight against Kafirs. (...) However, those fighting in foreign countries are called Al-Qaeda while those fighting in Afghanistan and Pakistan are called Taliban. In fact, both are the name of one ideology. The aim and objectives of both organizations are the same.

In addition, the extent to which the Pakistani Taliban are part of the Taliban movement as a whole is confirmed by the weight of their contacts with Afghan leaders: it was always a visit from one of the Afghan heavyweights, notably Dadullah or Haqqani, which heralded a commander emerging as a key leader, as can be seen with Nek Mohammad, Baitullah and Mawlawi Nazir. Anecdotal evidence may be of use in this case, in order to provide a snapshot of the TTP mindset: in Bajaur, where the Taliban in 2007–8 controlled over 60 per cent of the Agency, Faquir Mohammad won the leadership over Waliur Rahman, an extremely powerful commander controlling the area across the border. According to witnesses interviewed by the author,[25] Ziaur Rahman launched a bid for the leadership of the Taliban in Bajaur on the strength of his proximity to Arab Al-Qaeda-oriented commanders and their associates; he had married his daughter to an Arab commander; Al-Qaeda had become "family" and this clearly constituted a badge of honour of critical importance. Faquir Mohammad, a charismatic commander and more importantly a qualified cleric, was eventually perceived to be a more balanced leader, one who could represent the TNSM soul of Bajaur, a Tribal Agency that has historically been influenced by events in the neighbouring former Malakand Division.

In the case of Baitullah, his close links with the leadership of the Afghan Taliban are also substantiated by his involvement in the spread of suicide operations in Pakistan, with 56 suicide attacks in 2007[26] and 28 in the first eight months of 2008, causing a staggering 461 victims; in 2008 Pakistan suffered worse than both Afghanistan and Iraq in the number of *shahid* operations. Suicide bombing as a tactic was imported to Afghanistan by Mullah Dadullah, who in early 2004 had sent a team to Iraq to train with an old acquaintance, Abu Musab al Zarqawi.[27] According to well-placed sources in South Waziristan, Dadullah, who was killed in a special forces attack in 2007, had begun training suicide recruits in Waziristan in areas controlled by Baitullah. As a result, the vast majority of the suicide bombers in 2007 were young Mehsud boys aged from 16 to 20, allegedly handled by Baitullah's men.[28] They rapidly became the most proficient trainers and organizers of martyrdom operations and the perfect conduit to export the new technique across the border. This is to say that suicide bombing spread to Pakistan because of the Afghans' need for a safe training ground and adequate logistics, but the attacks were originally primarily devised for Afghanistan. Although today suicide attacks are as much a Pakistani phenomenon as an Afghan one, this kind of operation first spilled over into Pakistan as a by-product of the know-how being acquired by Afghan Taliban operatives in 2004. We have seen how Baitullah's links to the Taliban leadership and the critical importance of an extra-territorial training infrastructure and logistical rear base did the rest, in order to export the phenomenon across the Durand Line.

As far as suicide bombings are concerned, after Dadullah's death in May 2007, Baitullah became the nearest thing to his designated heir. Once again, the leader in Pakistan appears to act as a divisional commander, or a minister perhaps, but certainly as a subordinate to higher command and not as someone leading an autonomous entity. On the basis of recent communications between the Taliban leadership and Baitullah, analysed by the author in 2008, it is impossible to ignore the influence of the Afghan leadership where the Pakistani Taliban, both the TTP and the Wazir bloc, are concerned. And the same applies to the leadership's will to unify the two factions or, at the very least, to avoid confrontation between them. Nevertheless, the primacy of Baitullah as the representative of Mullah Omar in Pakistan is unquestionable, and the TTP leader appears to be a higher-ranking commander than Sirajuddin Haqqani himself, where the Pakistani areas are concerned. Likewise, the primacy of the TTP as the most formidable fighting force within the FATA is also beyond question.

The Uzbeks contribute substantially to Baitullah's fighting force, constituting both a liability and a unique asset. In fact, while Arabs act as sources of inspiration for the Pak-Afghan Taliban, able motivators and often qualified religious *ulema* or highly specialized operatives, the Uzbeks appear to function as a commando unit, the Taliban's very own crack force. Mullah Omar communicates with Baitullah often, and has frequently made clear that the Mehsud leader stands as Pakistan's own Taliban Amir, notwithstanding Omar's recognition of Nazir's and Hafez Gul Bahadur's influence (see below) among the Waziris.

The two souls of the Taliban, epitomized by the Pakistani case

It is worth noting here that where the Pakistani Taliban are concerned, whenever we set out to analyse specific events and their wider significance, we always confront two tendencies and two sets of players who visibly influence the game, Pakistani state actors and al-Qaeda-oriented foreigners—never three, as would be the case if Afghan and Pakistani Taliban were two separate entities. The Afghan Taliban never appear as an external actor: they direct the Pakistanis as if they were another of their regional Wilayat, or governorates.[29] Policy may be dictated by Mullah Omar's circle, but the central leadership does not interfere in local matters unless there is an acute conflict between the interests of the Emirate and those of the regional Amir.

Possibly, the Pakistani Wilayat epitomizes better than any Afghan Province the two different souls of the movement, each one linked to an important ally of the Islamic Emirate, neither of whom can be disregarded or offended. It was natural, for example, that the Afghan Taliban would deny any association with Baitullah at a time when Mehsud's Taliban were inflicting substantial casualties on one of the Taliban's allies, Pakistan. Mullah Omar can only be expected to distance himself from an anti-Pakistan campaign, as he did in December 2007, but this does not mean that the TTP has ceased to be a Taliban entity. It means that it will be spun, in Pakistan, as being out of control. Baitullah's problem in that case was of the kind encountered by charismatic leaders within a loose but highly centralized movement; Mullah Dadullah had the same problem during the Emirate, and the same applies to his brother Mansur Dadullah,[30] expelled in December 2007. All the conflicting tendencies within the Taliban leadership, however, would doubtless agree that it is advisable to keep some degree of influence over an outfit, the TTP, that could attack Peshawar if pushed towards a suicidal, *shahid*-like strategy. Baitullah is to some extent Mullah Omar's knife held at Islamabad's throat, too precious an asset to be alienated.

In other words, Mullah Omar's determination to safeguard his relationship with Pakistan does not signify that a pro-government attitude will halt any trend within the movement that might prove dangerous or hostile for its powerful ally. The Taliban have also displayed an exceptional attitude to play on more than one table, when the circumstances require it.

At the time of the Islamic Emirate, for example, both the Pakistani advisers seconded to the Taliban regime and the leaders of the foreign contingents attached to the Islamic Army—Osama bin Laden and Qari Tahir Yuldashev—played critical roles where policy-making was concerned: two souls for one Taliban entity, one could say. In the case of the Pakistani insurgency, the same elements are active in the background, but they champion different factions while vying for the attention and approval of the one common denominator they share: Mullah Mohammad Omar Mujahid, Servant of Islam and *Amir-ul-mominin*. Somehow in the tribal context these two souls evolved into two distinct groups, the Waziris and the TTP.

The reason why Mullah Omar's circle continues to deal with both factions, and they do not try to discredit each other, is that although they do represent different tendencies, neither of them has ever questioned the other's Taliban credentials or its loyalty to Mullah Omar. Being a Talib is an indisputable and integral part of the personal history of these commanders, not a feature that can be assumed or discarded according to the circumstances. Further, allegiance to Mullah Omar's leadership can be described as a necessary and sufficient condition for someone to call himself a Talib. There is, however, also a second common denominator among the rival Taliban commanders in the FATA, and possibly a second condition to be satisfied in order to be numbered among the Pakistani Taliban ranks, and that is some degree of proximity to the ideological stance of Maulana Fazlur Rehman.

These two trends, which had coexisted during the Islamic Emirate, clashed when Pakistan complied with American demands and hit al-Qaeda repeatedly on Pakistani territory with a series of notable arrests, between 2002 and 2003. As a direct consequence of Islamabad siding with the US in the War on Terror, al-Qaeda and Jaish-e-Mohammad targeted Musharraf twice in 2003,[31] and encouraged their tribal allies to focus on Pakistan as the main enemy of the Jihadist cause. Al-Zawahiri's message calling for an anti-Musharraf revolt[32] in the country epitomizes the confrontation between these two tendencies, and can be read as a motivator and a go-ahead for the Pakistani militants to attack the General's regime. The tribesmen, like most fundamentalist Muslims, are particularly hesitant where killing believers is concerned. The most common device to convince them that Muslims can be killed is to appeal to the principles of *Takfir*,[33] a doctrine that regards apostates as on a par with infidels, and this is essentially what al-Zawahiri was appealing to with his video address. The pro-foreigner Pakistani Taliban faction, which had meanwhile metamorphosed into the TTP, accepted this interpretation within the framework of a "defensive *jihad*" and declared war on Islamabad.

The reaction of the pro-government faction was as far-reaching as Baitullah's initiative: the engineering of a second umbrella organization, the Local Taliban Movement (LTM), an alternative entity to the TTP and one capable of steering the tribal Taliban movement towards becoming the proxy army Islamabad wants. Such an organization would focus exclusively on the Afghan *jihad*, and there would be no more attacks in Pakistan conceived in the FATA by Pakistani nationals. In short, if the al-Qaeda-inspired faction of the Pakistani Taliban had found representation in the TTP, the pro-government faction found its own vehicle in the Local Taliban Movement.

Given the broad appeal of the TTP and the substantial success of its platform, the one option available to anti-TTP strategists was invoking tribal identity as a weapon to fragment the TTP. Given the Mehsud primacy within the TTP, and the fact that Pakistan's best friend in the FATA was an Ahmedzai Wazir, appealing to the centuries-old rivalry between the two cousin tribes inhabiting Waziristan, Mehsuds and Wazirs, must have appeared the natural option if the target was stirring troubles among the local Taliban.

The opportunity to build this pro-Islamabad Wazir bloc came soon after the TTP's creation, in January 2008. The army had launched its latest offensive against Mehsud-held territory and Baitullah, relying on the TTP charter, requested the help of his allies. The commander best positioned to alleviate Baitullah's troubles was one of his two deputies, Hafez Gul Bahadur, the scion of an important Jihadist family[34] who, unusually by Taliban standards, led his own tribe as well as the Taliban in North Waziristan. Following the TTP Amir's call for help, however, Bahadur rebuked him on the grounds that his people had already endured enough deaths and material losses and he could not bring himself to involve them in a conflict once again. Attempts were made to convince Bahadur to revise his position, but eventually the North Waziristani commander left the TTP, probably the movement's most significant loss to this day.

Interestingly, at the very same time, Bahadur was negotiating with the government on behalf of his Agency, not as part of the TTP leadership but as a tribal leader. It would therefore seem that Bahadur was already talking to the government before the rift with Baitullah emerged, and it would be naive not to factor this in, given the events that followed. Indeed, the definitive proof that Bahadur's defection had somehow been orchestrated came when, on 30 June 2008,[35] Hafez Gul Bahadur and Mawlawi Nazir, representing respectively North Waziristan's Uthmanzai Wazirs and South Waziristan's Ahmedzais, announced the formation of a Waziri bloc aimed at "defending the Wazir tribe's interests in North and South Waziristan", according to the words of Nazir himself.[36] During a sustained media campaign Nazir made clear that the movement, named the Local Taliban Movement, was openly in disagreement with Baitullah over attacks on Pakistani territory. The leader made clear, nevertheless, that the new outfit would continue to support the Afghan *jihad* from the FATA. Indeed, *jihad* in Afghanistan was their own main motivator and raison d'etre, or they would not be Taliban at all.

Playing the anti-Mehsud card must have appeared the most effective and least problematic option if the target was to stem the growth of the TTP insurgency. At the same time, the inherently tribal character of the Wazir bloc would function as a self-limiting mechanism preventing the group from spreading among other tribes. In other words, the Local Taliban Movement represented the polar opposite of Baitullah's ambition of tribal unification. If the TTP was inherently out of control, the Local Taliban Movement had been devised with a deeply ingrained safety mechanism, as the safest of proxy armies.

Given the chain of events that led to the creation of both organizations, it is inevitable to discern in this opposition between the TTP and the Local

Taliban Movement the motives of each faction's allies. On the one hand, Pakistani state actors supported a Taliban movement focused militarily on fighting the Coalition in Afghanistan, its tribal connotation ensuring that followers would be few and all Wazirs. On the other hand, al-Qaeda and al-Qaeda-affiliated advisers and financial backers aimed for nothing else than a Takfiri Taliban movement let loose to kill as many Pakistani apostates as possible, a movement which should ideally spread far and fast. Here we come to the extraordinary spillover potential intrinsic to the TTP.

The TTP spread at an exceptionally fast rate in the FATA, and that was made possible by the movement's adherence to the always successful Taliban doctrine of law, order and (whatever they meant by) revivalist piety. The groups' tactics to make their case heard were simple and effective: identify and confront the strongest criminal network in the area in question, and annihilate it while possibly making as much noise as possible over the whole affair. As a consequence, criminal leaders in the area would experience a sudden religious awakening and present their weapons to the local Taliban Amir. Taliban ranks would then be inflated with the usual brand of tribal dacoits who were suddenly presented with a cause to pursue by kidnapping for ransom. Turbans were donned and white pick-ups became the vehicle of choice, but more often than not little else changed in relation to aims and attitude of the former bandits. Although never a majority, criminal networks have certainly played a role in the fast territorial expansion of the TTP and may constitute a liability for the movement, if they are left free to discredit the organization.

The TTP strategists should have known that such an effective vehicle, one capable of unifying the tribes under one Jihadist pan-Pashtun banner, and one which was at the same time linked to a powerful military entity across the border and to the international Jihadist Ummah, would have not been allowed to exist by Pakistan. This would amount to allowing a Punjabi, Sindhi or Mohajir tendency to make its case militarily and hope to achieve results. The TTP is far too dangerous because it pre-empts the very possibility of inter-tribal enmity, and therefore nurtures the potential of an authentic Islamist pan-Pashtun movement. The Wazir bloc devised to counter the TTP had still the capability to be an effective proxy army, and that is everything Islamabad needs and expects from a Pakistani Taliban outfit.

Conclusion

Pakistan is certainly a "governorate" more important to the Taliban than many others, and one that requires particular attention and a specific degree of autonomy, but the model remains the one favoured by the Taliban since the years of the Islamic Emirate: the Taliban rule all their provinces with directives, more often than with specific orders. The chain of command relies on a presumption of loyalty towards the central Amir, which confers ultimate authority on the leader via a given chain of command. During the guerrilla years, the Taliban have further refined a tendency that had already appeared in the years of the Emirate, deriving from a total lack of efficiency: the almost proverbial loose chain of command favoured by the Taliban was perfect for a low intensity guerrilla war. Difficult to intercept because of their rare occurrence, orders are few and always delivered by hand, but the central leadership, known as *Rhabari Shura*, does promulgate orders for the provincial Amirs; the Pakistani case does not differ from other "provinces", although it may be regarded as strategically more important. It certainly is an extra-territorial Wilayat, but the ideological nature of the Taliban phenomenon does not necessarily exclude direct control by the *Amir-ul-Momenin*. In addition, the de-territorialization of the Taliban Emirate favoured the strict integration of militants on both sides of the Durand Line. In the words of Mawlawi Omar, in becoming an ideology, the Taliban have widened their scope and further enhanced the flexibility of the movement and its potential appeal.[37]

We have seen how the tribal dynamics of the eastern Pashtun tribes, preserved intact in the FATA by their relative isolation from both the Persian-influenced Afghans and their Pakistani brethren—invariably accused by the Pathans of representing the Punjabi soul of Pakistan first and foremost—emerged as the defining feature of the Pakistani Taliban movement. Accordingly, Pashtunwali certainly remains the dominating factor and affects the very nature of the brand of political Islamism practised in the region.

The tribes of the Pakistani Frontier have adjusted the Taliban praxis because of the unique circumstances affecting their territories during the last decade, but they play, from the eastern side of the Durand Line, the very same game played by their Afghan colleagues across the border. They are somehow more royalist than the king, as they vie for a prize which lies in Kabul and for a victory that would affect them only marginally. But this is a customary consequence of the very nature of the interaction between Kabul's Amir, or King, and the Karlanri tribes. It has certainly happened cyclically since the 18th century.[38]

Where Taliban history is concerned, the structure of the FATA power game reflects exceptionally well the political dynamics of the Taliban Emirate, concerning the role of al-Qaeda-oriented foreigners or that of Pakistani actors for example. There is an exceptionally high degree of consistency between Mullah Omar's interaction with Osama bin Laden and Juma Namangani in Kandahar, in the late 1990s, and Baitullah's dealings with Qari Tahir for the central Asians and Abu Yahya al Libi on behalf of the Arabs. That is, the quasi-ambassadorial role played by the foreigners' leaders during the Emirate apparently functions as a blueprint for the relationship between Baitullah and his *muhajir* guests, the Islamic Movement of Uzbekistan (IMU) and al-Qaeda central.

On the other hand, the union with al-Qaeda translates the Taliban ideal into the language of international Jihadism, traditionally dominated by Egyptians and Saudis. We have seen how the TTP represents the merger between the al-Qaeda-oriented model and the Deobandi-inspired radical Islam favoured by the tribals. According to the TTP leadership, "Taliban" is the name of al-Qaeda's ideology at home, and home means both Pakistan and Afghanistan, the land inhabited by the Pashtun militants.

Ultimately, the Pakistani Taliban phenomenon finds the primary reason of its existence in the Afghan *jihad* against the US-led coalition. A defensive *jihad* against Pakistan has been necessary in order to guarantee the movement's survival east of the Durand Line, once Islamabad aligned itself with the American ally. This all-out war was certainly favoured by the Takfirist stances of those al-Qaeda-oriented leaders and preachers who have roamed the Pashtun territories along the border since the early 1980s. This union of intents between international Jihadists inspired by or associated with al-Qaeda and the Pashtun Taliban movement was unquestionably exacerbated by the Western and Pakistani attitude towards the problem. A flawed assessment of the nature of the problem contributed to coalesce militants around a common cause.

Only a profound revision of the Western post-9/11 assessment, an assessment that was never really questioned or even critically probed, may facilitate a lasting resolution of what has become a regional, transnational conflict with Pashtun roots. A dangerous convergence of interests with international Jihadism is certainly perceived as a threat by Western policy-makers, but that must be regarded as a consequence and not a cause of the problem. What can and should be addressed is the Western understanding of what the eastern tribes, still governed by the Raj-implemented Frontier Crime Regulations (FCR), want for the future of their people. Misunderstandings can be lethal in this context, and between 2001 and 2009 Washington must have learned the lesson: acknowledging that a fundamentally flawed evaluation has informed Western strategy to this day may be a first constructive step towards a thorough reappraisal of the Taliban conflict. Certainly there is no room left for manoeuvre, nor for further strategic mistakes.

A radically new peace platform, and not an inherently flawed adjustment of the existing Afghan Reconciliation Programme, should seek the involvement of the Pakistani Taliban, as a condition necessary in order to move towards a comprehensive resolution of the Pak-Afghan quandary. Islamabad should not be left out of the process, and neither should Pakistan refrain from entering the fray of a complex multilateral negotiation because of its instinctive fear of Kabul's revanchist sentiments.

Notes

1. H. Abbas, "A Profile of Tehrik-i-Taliban Pakistan", *CTC Sentinel*, Vol. 1, issue 2, 2008, pp. 1–4.
2. O. Caroe, *The Pathans*, Oxford University Press, 1983.
3. Ibid.
4. M. Ewans, *Afghanistan, A New History*, Richmond: Curzon, 2001,.
5. Amir Khan Muttaqi, *Mam*, unpublished volume, 2004. [Nefa Foundation].

6. D.B. Edwards, *Heroes of Age, Moral Faultlines of the Afghan Frontier*, Berkeley, Los Angeles, London: University of California Press, 1996.

7. Interviews by the author, Kabul, 2007.

8. F. Grare, "Pakistan-Afghanistan Relations in the Post 9/11 Era", Carnegie Papers South Asia Project No. 72, 2006, available at http://www.carnegieendowment.org/files/cp72_grare_final.pdf.

9. Mawlawi Omar interviewed by the NEFA Foundation. http://www1.nefafoundation.org/multimedia-intvu.html.

10. "Pak tribal elders back military's anti-Taliban, al-Qaeda drive", INRA 11/1/2004http://www.globalsecurity.org/military/library/news/2004/01/mil-040111-irna01.htm.

11. Interviews by the author. Shabqadar, District Charsadda, Pakistan.

12. "Pakistan and the key al Qaida man". 4/03/2005, BBC Online. http://news.bbc.co.uk/1/hi/world/south_asia/4513281.stm.

13. Al Muhajiroun, a UK-based Islamist group let by Mohammad Bakri, famously joined Osama Bin Laden's anti-Crusader charter in 1998. (N.b.A.).

14. Rahimullah Yusufzai, 3/3/2002, *Time Magazine*, "Battle creates new Taliban legend" http://www.time.com/time/world/article/0,8599,216053,00.html.

15. Nek Mohammad Wazir, *Monthly Herald*, Pakistan. 2004. http://www.dawn.com/2004/06/19/latest.htm.

16. FATA Timeline 2004. SATP http://www.satp.org/satporgtp/countries/pakistan/Waziristan/timeline/2004.htm.

17. H. Abbas, "South Waziristan's Mawlawi Nazir: The New Face of the Taliban", The Jamestown Foundation *Terrorism Monitor*, Volume 5, Issue 9, 10 May 2007 [http://www.jamestown.org/programs/gta/single/?tx_ttnews%5Btt_news%5D=4147&tx_ttnews%5BbackPid%5D=182&no_cache=1.

18. Faquir Mohammad interviewed by the NEFA Foundation. http://www1.nefafoundation.org/multimedia-intvu.html.

19. I. Khan, "Baitullah, Pakistan's biggest dilemma", *Dawn*, 31/12/2007 http://www.dawn.com/2007/text/nat10.htm.

20. "Omid Marzban Mullah Dadullah: The Military Mastermind of the Taliban Insurgency," The Jamestown Foundation *Terrorism Focus* Vol. 3, Issue 11 (21 March 2006). http://www.jamestown.org/programs/gta/single/?tx_ttnews%5Btt_news%5D=707<0x0026>tx_ttnews%5BbackPid%5D=239<0x0026>no_cache=1.

21. Interviews by the author, Peshawar, November 2008.

22. H. Abbas, *A Profile of Tehrik-i-Taliban Pakistan*, op. cit.

23. Ibid.

24. Deputy leader (N.b.A).

25. Middle-level Taliban operative interviewed by the author, Bajaur Agency, April 2008.

26. "Pakistan tops Iraq, Afghanistan in suicide bombing deaths", PakTribune, 15/09/2008 http://www.paktribune.com/news/index.shtml?205698.

27. Amir Khan Muttaqi, Mam…, 2004.

28. http://www.guardian.co.uk/world/2009/jan/10/pakistan-taliban-intelligence-report.

29. Confidential documents seen by the author confirm the organization of the Taliban movement in 18 Provincial Governors.

30. *The New York Times*, 31/12/2007, "Taliban leader expels Commander" http://www.nytimes.com/2007/12/31/world/asia/31afghan.html?fta=y.

31. "Arrests follow Musharraf attack" http://news.bbc.co.uk/1/hi/world/south_asia/3351207.stm.
32. "Al Zawhairi calls for overthrow of Pakistan government" 25/03/2004. Translated by BBC. http://www.why-war.com/news/2004/03/25/alzawahi.html.
33. G. Kepel, *Jihad*, London: I.B. Tauris, 2002.
34. Gul Bahadur belongs to the same Wazir family that gave birth to another legendary Islamic leader, the Faquir Ipi. J. Stewart, *The Savage Border, The History of the North Western Frontier*, Stroud, Gloucestershire: Sutton Publishing, 2007.
35. Sadia Sulaiman, "Empowering "Soft" Taliban Over "Hard" Taliban: Pakistan's Counter-Terrorism Strategy", The Jamestown Foundation *Terrorism Monitor*, Volume 6, Issue 15, 25 July 2008 http://www.nytimes.com/2007/12/31/world/asia/31afghan.html?fta=y.
36. *Daily Times*, 2 July 2008, http://www.dailytimes.com.pk/default.asp?page=20080702story_2-7-2008_pg1_4.
37. Mawlawi Omar (TTP official spokesman) interviewed by The NEFA Foundation. http://www1.nefafoundation.org/multimedia-intvu.html.
38. Haroon, S., *Frontier of Faith, Islam in the Indo-Afghan borderland*, London: C. Hurst & Co., 2007.

CONCLUSION

"Command and control", as explained in the introduction, is the main focus of this book. At first sight, the picture emerging from the different chapters of the book seems contradictory: the Neo-Taliban appear as better organised and disciplined in some provinces and less in others; Uruzgan in particular, despite being a province of "old" Neo-Taliban settlement, appears quite chaotic and ineffectively managed from Quetta. The influx of many loose fighters into the Taliban ranks can also mislead. It seems appropriate to distinguish between a core insurgency and an "auxiliary" component, which the Taliban leadership does not directly control. Many self-proclaimed Taliban, also, increasingly complicate the picture, but they should not deceive the analyst. Moreover, the quality of the Taliban's command and control should be examined in perspective: the effort of the leadership to impose a certain discipline and even a certain structure is evident, even if the outcome is uneven. Uruzgan, often described by the Taliban themselves as a "resting place" and a logistical rear and not as the frontline, is probably not their first priority in terms of enforcing stricter discipline, though even this might have been changing in 2007–8 as ISAF pressure has been growing in parts of Uruzgan.

Greater efforts in the same direction seem to have been made in other provinces, again with varying results. In Helmand, for example, the Taliban seem to have struggled to establish a system which would keep communities and individual commanders on board, not least because of the competition of the British and the financial autonomy of most local commanders. In places such as Ghazni, Wardak and Logar, the Taliban seem more independent of local communities and it might have been easier for the leadership to maintain a degree of effective command and control. At the tactical and operational level, this has also increasingly become the case in the Southeast, as the Haqqani network has gradually been absorbing "rival" Taliban networks in the region. The Taliban have only managed to break through in a few cases, most notably in Zurmat, whose density of Taliban presence was in 2007–8 high even by the standards of southern Afghanistan. However, they displayed considerable flexibility in adapting to local situations, treading carefully in tribal territory. For all the eagerness of the UN and others to describe the Haqqani network as "tribal", clearly even that network only enjoyed limited access among the Zadrans; it is remarkable how the Haqqanis refrained from establishing a permanent presence in Zadran villages, as if they had some kind of agreement with the tribal leadership, enforced across several districts and three provinces.

The limitations of the Taliban may seem nonetheless obvious, at least when compared with abstract models of insurgents, but they have to be considered against previous experiences of insurgents in Afghanistan, most obviously the *mujahidin* organisations active in the 1980s and 1990s, a period in which the contemporary Taliban have their roots. There is no question that today's Taliban have made great strides compared to the old *Harakat-i Enqelab-i Islami* of Nabi Mohammadi, in whose ranks many of their leaders fought once. *Harakat* was one of the most disorganised *mujahidin* parties, even if a few individual commanders, such as Qari Baba in Ghazni, set up a quite efficient system in limited areas. *Harakat* made no attempt to control or direct its field commanders from the top, contenting itself with distributing weapons to commanders who claimed allegiance to the party and sent delegations to Peshawar to collect. The Taliban are instead making a serious, if somewhat flawed, effort to organise their struggle down to the district level. The only *mujahidin* party whose leadership stood out for its effort to establish a real system of command and control from the top was Hizb-i Islami of Gulbuddin Hekmatyar. The sophistication of Hizb's centralised system has not been equalled by the Taliban yet; in fact they still lag well behind even if they seem to have taken inspiration from Hekmatyar's model.

The Taliban do not appear to have established anything resembling a system of political commissars regularly travelling to the provinces to assess the performance and loyalty of individual commanders, as Hizb-i Islami did, although there are signs that they have been putting a counter-intelligence system in place. Their ability to supervise field commanders is therefore significantly more limited. In particular, they seem slower in assessing the decay of their organisation on the ground, as in the case of Ghazni, or in dealing with rivalries among commanders. The enforcement of the leadership's decisions also seems more problematic, as it depends mostly on the good will of field commanders. The system has been described as a kind of franchise, which might be correct at least in part, but again there are franchises and franchises. The *mujahidin* parties of the 1980s were also mostly operating like franchises, but the conditions imposed on franchising partners varied and were sometimes much more restrictive than at other times.

Although Hizb-i Islami was the most sophisticated of the parties involved in the *jihad* of the 1980s, it is of course important to point out that it failed to achieve its aim of conquering power. In a sense it could be argued that Hizb-i Islami's organisational structure was too sophisticated for Afghanistan. To function it relied on educated cadres, whose recruitment grew increasingly difficult during the war. Centralised command and control did not allow field commanders to exploit local opportunities and build strong power bases, so that the whole party became dependent on correct decision making at the top. The leadership, on the other hand, faced a tremendous task in gathering reliable information about local realities and in assessing tactical situations or strategic opportunities. Although its information gathering system was the most advanced among the *mujahidin* parties, it was not quite powerful enough. Hizb-i Islami was a product of urban society, transplanted in a rural environment; although it was initially very successful in penetrating that environment, Hizb-i Islami did not really have a firm rural constituency. It was anti-clerical and opposed to the power of the village elders. As a result, it rapidly started experiencing difficulties in recovering from losses and defections; from the early 1980s onwards it gradually lost strength. Its area of influence was particularly fluid in the Pashtun belt, dependent on the constant influx of reinforcements from the refugee camps that it controlled in Pakistan. Once it lost Saudi support, sometime after the Soviet withdrawal in 1989 Hizb-i Islami's long-term prospects as a viable military organisation were doomed.

This short discussion of Hizb-i Islami's model of insurgency serves my purpose of demonstrating how it does not necessarily follow that greater sophistication brings more success for an insurgent movement (a similar argument is developed by A. Sinno in his volume *Organizations at War* [Cornell University Press, 2008]). On the basis of these considerations, the Taliban's effort at organising an insurgency deserves to be considered in a different light. Although it might have been possible for them to do more in terms of managing the insurgency in a centralised way, that would have increased the movement's vulnerability. In fact it could be argued that the Taliban decentralised their insurgency as much as they could, while at the same time retaining an ability to exercise a degree of control over their fronts operating throughout Afghanistan. The mostly indirect character of this control (threats of withholding supplies, assassination/punishment, ideological discredit, demotion) means that it is not always effective, but also that it is quite resilient to counter-insurgency. Faced with an adversary immensely more powerful, the priority for the Taliban was to be in a position to absorb as much damage as possible without compromising their operational capability too much.

Considering that Hizb-i Islami counted among its ranks many more educated and semi-educated people than the Taliban, the greater "bureaucratic" sophistication of its structures does not surprise. Quite the contrary, it is surprising how far the Taliban managed to go if we take into account that their rank and file (and many of their commanders too) are in fact illiterate or nearly so. After all, primitive as their organisation and technology might be compared to what industrialised nations can field, they have still been able to to force the American armed forces and their ISAF allies to a virtual standstill. The earlier Taliban fronts (1980s) were a far cry from what the Taliban managed to do after 2001. The tactical adaptation of the Taliban, which occurred in a number of distant provinces although not uniformly, is a major indication of how inputs come from above and are received at the base of the movement.

In this regard the effort to build an effective propaganda machine deserves particular attention. Not only is the effort to address a worldwide audience remarkable, but even inside Afghanistan the production of propaganda material and "night letters" clearly receives considerable investment of human resources; it would seem that the few Taliban educated to university or high school standards focus their efforts on propaganda. Nothing even remotely comparable existed in *Harakat-i Enqelab* in the 1980s and only *Hizb-i Islami* managed to produce something comparable, considering that the World Wide Web and VCD/DVD technology were not available at that time. The improvement can be explained by at least two different factors. The first is the gradual absorption into the Taliban of segments of the educated or semi-educated youth, particularly when coming out of Pakistani establishments. The second has probably to do with the ability of the Taliban to learn from the experiences of the past and with the fact that the Pakistani, Arab and other pro-insurgency advisers, who once may have nurtured Hizb-i Islami cadres, after 2001 dedicated their efforts to the Taliban.

As already stated in the introduction, the most controversial issue is the role of narco-trafficking in the funding of the Neo-Taliban. It is difficult to distinguish between genuine Taliban, whose presence in the movement is acknowledged by the leadership, and mere bandits or opportunists who use the label for their own convenience. Some of the "auxiliary" insurgents mentioned at the beginning of this Conclusion, moreover, might just capture narcotics revenue and keep it for themselves, without contributing it to the coffers of the movement. As a result it is easy to overestimate the amount of drugs revenue accruing to the Taliban as a movement. Still, the evidence that the core Taliban too cooperate with traffickers and tax farmers is overwhelming; at the same time it seems clear to me that the Taliban are not spending more than US$70–80 million a year in funding the insurgency, a figure that an extrapolation of Gretchen Peters' evidence seems to support. Only recently have they started acquiring sophisticated (and expensive) weaponry and in small quantities. It is also clear that narcotics are not the only source of funding to the Neo-Taliban; all sorts of economic activities are taxed whenever possible, while international Jihadist networks send money to their Afghan allies and friends too. UNODC's and Gretchen Peters' high end estimates, therefore, are exaggerated or else imply that the Neo-Taliban are accumulating large financial reserves. Of course, some cash might be moving towards personal bank accounts in the Gulf or elsewhere, but it does not seem that corruption and personal greed are a major issue as far as the Taliban leadership is concerned. Probably the truth lies somewhere in between: the actual revenue is likely not as much as the high end estimate claims (UNODC and ISAF/Coalition might have their own, different reasons for overstating the involvement of the Taliban in the narcotics trade), but the Taliban are also likely to be accumulating substantial financial reserves for a "rainy day".

Several implications of this are obvious. First, the Taliban may become increasingly autonomous of their sources of funding, having cash reserves sufficient to keep going for years. Secondly, they could be acquiring the ability to manoeuvre strategically to an extent unknown until 2006, when they acquired influence and control over large swathes of poppy-growing areas. In particular, the cash reserves could also be used for an intensification of the conflict. Available evidence shows that the Taliban are already intensifying the conflict, in particular by expanding geographically, but it is clear that they are still spending significantly less than what they seem to be collecting.

This book's survey of most provinces where the Taliban were active in 2008 shows that by and large their priority had up to that point remained the expansion of control over the population. The investment in new tactics and even more so in new technologies has been limited. At the time of writing there were few indications of any effort to change the typical mix of weapons used by the Taliban in the battlefield. The Taliban started purchasing, or trying to purchase, anti-aircraft or anti-tank missiles, but have not yet been able to use them effectively. A few firings of anti-aircraft missiles were reported as early as 2006-7, but they never inflicted significant casualties. The influx of large numbers of sniper rifles reported by Christoph Reuter and Borhan Younus for Ghazni is interesting, although it is not clear whether it is being matched by any specific training and whether the same trend is taking place elsewhere. As illustrated earlier, if the Taliban do not buy more technology it is probably not because they cannot afford to. There appears to be a conscious decision to keep the technological level of the war low, either for lack of skilled personnel to operate guided missiles or other advanced weaponry, or because technological escalation is seen as counter-productive. The Taliban might well have experimented at purchasing higher technology (hence reports and statements about the acquisition of missiles) and realised that they could not handle it successfully enough to justify the expenditure.

The chapters of this book highlight well, I believe, how possibly the greatest weakness of the Taliban mirrors the weaknesses of the Afghan state: once they gain the upper hand, they have big difficulties in enforcing their kind of governance. Their reliance on the good will and commitment of their members for command and control to function is undoubtedly a weakness; the decay experienced in Ghazni might well have inflicted permanent damage, and it occurred after just a couple of years of Taliban establishing their *de facto* hold over the Pashtun districts of the province. The impact of the effort to reform Ghazni's Taliban is difficult to assess at this stage, but it appears unlikely that the same kind of cooperation which existed among the population will be regained. The chapters on Zabul, Uruzgan and Helmand also raise this issue explicitly. In Logar and Wardak the successes of the Taliban are still too fresh to have led to this type of problem, whereas in the Southeast the Taliban have not been sufficiently successful yet to face these kinds of issues. Some of the Taliban's problems derive from the fact that even if they are somewhat more effective than the current government in Kabul, they do not have access to the same scale of resources, particularly in the field of reconstruction. Even after extensive pilfering because of corruption, still more is delivered in terms of services and benefits to the population from the government side than from the Taliban. Their attitude towards education, now in part being reversed, also proved self-defeating. As long as the Taliban's governance is impeccable and Kabul's is disastrous, this may suffice to offset the lack of redistribution; however once the Taliban's own governance system enters a crisis (or once Kabul's should improve, which is still in the realm of hopes), they become more vulnerable.

A crisis in Taliban governance is by no means a guarantee of the movement's defeat, for a number of reasons. The Afghan state, with its international patrons, might simply be tempted to exploit the situation by pushing the Taliban out and then re-establishing the *"ancien régime"*, the system as it was. In this case, the gains might be very short-lived. The importance of the quality of state-delivered governance is highlighted particularly clearly in David Kilcullen's chapter on Kunar. What his chapter also shows is the importance of state building as a *project*. In the case of Kunar from 2006 onwards, that was mostly fortuitous: road building provided the project needed at the local level to motivate state agents and provide a focus to their efforts. In Afghanistan as a whole, the project dimension of state building has clearly been completely lacking, a key weakness which contributed to making the response to the insurgency fragmented, ad hoc and ineffective. It also explains why dynamic new elites, forged as a united group in years of hardship and struggle, motivated ideologically around a project of state and nation-building (no matter how flawed that might be), tend to be much more successful in counter-insurgency than heterogeneous, opportunistically assembled and externally sponsored regimes usually are: they have a project around which to gather and synchronise their efforts.[1]

It would also be misleading to assume that a decline in the popularity of the Taliban and the failure to maintain any large social base would doom the movement to a rapid decline and ultimate defeat. The mythology of hearts and minds as the decisive aspect of insurgency and counter-insurgency survives and continues to be repeated in the literature, but its importance is greatly exaggerated. As Sippi Azerbaijani Moghammad points out in her chapter and Thomas Coghlan shows particularly well in his, the lack of extensive popular support does not prevent the Taliban from operating, as long as they have a core of committed militants, who will use coercion whenever necessary to impose their will, and the opposing side does not enjoy extensive support in its own right. What is true is that the lack of widespread popular support does increase the cost of waging war and limits the efficiency of asymmetric warfare as it is carried out by the Taliban. This, however, is a common trend in insurgencies, particularly in prolonged conflicts. However careful or well-intentioned an insurgent group might be in the beginning, war weariness will sooner or later emerge among the population and support will become problematic. As a result, it is very common for insurgencies to increasingly rely on coercion towards the civilian population. This did not prevent a number of insurgencies from being successful in achieving their aims.

The issue of "command and control" in its widest implications throws light on the much debated problem of the unity of the Neo-Taliban. Claudio Franco, writing on the Pakistani Taliban, shows that the leadership gathered around Mullah Omar extends its authority over the various 'Taliban' movements operating in the FATA and increasingly also in the NWFP. Indeed, the Pakistani Taliban were initially mobilised in direct support of their Afghan companions. Although different currents or wings clearly exist within the movement and they have even been at odds sometimes, they have been kept together by Mullah Omar, who remains in a position to issue directives as well as to negotiate among different networks and components within the movement. Thomas Ruttig discusses the role and position of the Haqqani network at length in his chapter. In my view it is quite clearly inappropriate and misleading to describe the Haqqanis as a separate insurgent movement, although it is true that of all the many Taliban networks it is probably the one with the greatest potential to turn into a separate insurgency one day, mainly because of its autonomous sources of funding. To achieve that, however, the counter-insurgents would probably have to remove the threat that unites the different strands of the Taliban; that is, their own presence on the ground. Haqqani aside, the issue remains of determining the vulnerability of the Taliban to "reconciliation" approaches, meant to lure individual commanders away from the movement in order to weaken it, or possibly even obtain a breakaway of a moderate wing of the Taliban, amenable to a separate peace deal. To the extent that the Taliban will face a crisis of governance (or any sort of crisis for that matter), it would be relatively easy to win back several of the less ideological commanders aligned with them, and indeed this has been already done in a number of cases, mainly in Helmand and Uruzgan. However, the more successful these "reconciliation" efforts are, the more the weaknesses of a state governance system saturated with contradictions will come under stress, reproducing the cycle which allowed the Taliban to expand in the first place. Several examples of "reconciled" Taliban are known and even mentioned in this book (see for example Martine van Bijlert's chapter), showing a remarkably high tendency of the "reconciled" to be assassinated or at the very least harassed by their new allies on the government side.

When listening to the strategic debate in Western capitals, it is difficult to escape the feeling that what drives it is not an understanding of the situation on the ground, or even an effort to achieve it, but bureaucratic politics. The policy makers seek some quantifiable indicators of success to show to their superiors; the old-fashioned body count is no longer seen as politically correct, or at least it is not seen as sufficient, so that the count of "reconciled Taliban" assumes a new attractiveness.

It is important to keep clearly in mind that the role of the core activists is crucial: it is they who are able to inflict casualties, able to move around as required by the leadership, disciplined enough to take orders and motivated enough to risk their lives. Among them we find the preachers who spearhead any attempt of the Taliban to penetrate a new region. Although local recruits, local commanders without an ideological profile, and mobilised communities make up the majority of the Neo-Taliban insurgency, their strategic importance is very modest. They are "auxiliary insurgents" or even "decoy insurgents" in some cases, and wars (or peaces) are not won by focusing on auxiliaries. Indeed, one of the main reasons why the Taliban recruit these "auxiliaries" and "decoys" is probably to confuse their adversaries, to offer a multiplicity of targets and create chaos. Any major political or economic effort targeted at luring away these "auxiliaries" and "decoys" could well end up resembling an attempt to empty the sea with a bucket. Such a reconciliation effort might produce satisfying statistics to be shown at the highest policy-making levels, but not necessarily contribute as much to the defeat of the Taliban.

The potential for local leaders with their retinues of followers to join either side is immense: they number several hundreds of thousands in Afghanistan, and more could see an incentive in adding to that number if the perception emerges that violence is rewarded.[2] The government side might "reconcile" many thousands at great financial and political cost and yet achieve very little, just driving the Taliban to recruit other disgruntled groups in the villages. Indeed, because the uneven and unfair distribution of government favours is one of the factors driving Taliban recruitment, more recruitment and a wider dispensation of favours might just translate into wider Taliban recruitment, particularly if we assume as we realistically should that taking everybody on board and rewarding them equally is an impossible task. As Sippi argues in her chapter and I also show in mine on western Afghanistan, there are large reservoirs of disgruntled "commanders" with their retinues of armed men north of the Hindu Kush, whom the Taliban have just begun to court.

Are negotiations then a non-starter then? Reconciling sections of the Taliban in my view only makes sense as a short-term strategy, aimed at strengthening the government/international hand in the event of wider negotiations towards a full political settlement. It should also be considered that such a short-term strategy entails the risk of making a final political settlement more difficult, as the Taliban leadership might react by raising the ideological stakes. Otherwise, reconciling only the "moderates" has rarely if ever been conducive to victory in counter-insurgency. In order to be meaningful, negotiations have to be carried out with those who control the real fighting power and financial resources of the movement.

This raises the issue of whether the Taliban leadership is really amenable to any kind of peace settlement. Indications are that it was in 2003–4, when the insurgency was still little more than a nuisance from Kabul's perspective. Today, when the Taliban have grown rapidly and seemingly become confident in final victory, the prospects of having genuine peace negotiations with the movement's hierarchy seems debatable. This is of course one of the reasons why negotiations are not popular in Washington, at least until a position of strength has been reached. It might well have to get worse before it can get better.

Notes

1. Although it might not be politically correct to point this out, the Sandinista government of Nicaragua (1979–1990) was striking successful against all odds in its counter-insurgency effort against the Washington-sponsored "Contras", who were militarily defeated before the Sandinistas were voted out of office.
2. For a discussion of non-state armed groups see A. Giustozzi, "Bureaucratic Façade and Political Realities of Disarmament and Demobilisation in Afghanistan", *Conflict, Security & Development*, no. 2, 2008.

NOTES ON CONTRIBUTORS

Sippi Azerbaijani Moghaddam is a consultant currently working on community-level organisation and leadership models and links with sub-national governance in Afghanistan. She has worked in Afghanistan for fourteen years and is a fluent Dari speaker. Although her most recent work has been on local perceptions of civil-military relations in the Pushtun-speaking provinces of the south and east, she is primarily a rural development specialist with long-term experience with civil society and social exclusion issues in the Afghan context. She has worked for a range of donors as well as the United Nations, the International Committee of the Red Cross and NATO-ISAF. Under the Mujahidin and Taliban she worked in the NGO sector, focusing on gender and social protection both in Afghanistan and in the refugee camps of the North West Frontier Province of Pakistan. She holds a BA in Persian and Old Iranian from Oxford, and a Masters in Rural Development Sociology from the University of Birmingham. She has published numerous articles and papers on Afghanistan.

Thomas Coghlan is the Afghanistan correspondent for *The Times* of London and *The Economist*. He has been based in South Asia since 2003 and has lived in Afghanistan continuously since September 2004. He has worked previously for the *Daily Telegraph* and *The Independent*. Much of his work since 2006 has been focused on Helmand and he has made approximately 15 different trips to the province, many of them conducted outside the auspices of the British military. He has been a journalist since 1999.

Claudio Franco is a writer and journalist specializing in Islamist terrorism and the Pakistani-Afghan region. Since 1999, he has conducted extensive research in the field, working with the Taliban insurgents as often as with NATO and the Karzai government (or as often as possible). He has been working at the NEFA Foundation since 2007. He also collaborates with JSAS (Jane's Information Group) and The Hudson Institute. As a journalist, Franco has contributed to several print media and broadcasters in Europe, including NBC, BBC, *La Repubblica*, the *San Francisco Chronicle*, *The Times*, ISN, *The Independent*).

Antonio Giustozzi is research fellow at the Crisis States Research Centre of the London School of Economics). He is the author of several articles and papers on Afghanistan, as well as two books, *War, Politics and Society in Afghanistan, 1978–1992* and *Koran, Kalashnikov and Laptop: the Neo-Taliban Insurgency, 2002–7*. His next book, *Empires of Mud: War and Warlords in Afghanistan*, will appear in 2009. He is currently researching issues of governance in Afghanistan, from a wide-ranging perspective which includes understanding the role of army, police, sub-national governance and intelligence system.

David Kilcullen has served as the Senior Counterinsurgency Adviser to General David Petraeus in Iraq and is one of the world's most influential experts on counterinsurgency and modern warfare.

Joanna Nathan has lived and worked in South Asia since 2001. Since May 2005 she has been a Senior Analyst for the International Crisis Group, focusing on issues of conflict prevention and security sector reform in Afghanistan. Her chapter is largely drawn from research for Crisis Group's 2008 report *Taliban Propaganda: Winning the War of Words?* This work has built on her experience in communications, as she has worked in media development in Kabul and Mazar-i Sharif in 2003/4 on a project which later became the country's first independent news agency. Trained as a journalist, she previously worked for the UK Press Association and CNN. Ghulam Sakhi Darwish also provided media monitoring, translation and valuable input for the chapter.

Gretchen Peters has covered Pakistan and Afghanistan, with one brief break, for more than a decade, first for The Associated Press and later as a reporter for ABC News. A Harvard graduate, Peters was nominated for an Emmy for her coverage of the 2007 assassination of Benazir Bhutto and won the SAJA Journalism Award for a Nightline segment on the former Pakistani president Pervez Musharraf. Her work also has appeared in leading media outlets including *The Christian Science Monitor*, *The New Republic* and The National Geographic Channel, and she has been a commentator on NPR and CNN. She now lives in the US with her husband, photojournalist John Moore, and their children.

Christoph Reuter and Borhan Younus have been covering the Taliban in Andar since 2006. They visited the core group (with Mullah Farouq) in July 2006 (together with photographer Karim Ben Khalifa) and have since then done several pieces about the re-emergence of the Taliban in the South. Christoph has been covering Afghanistan since 2002, while Borhan is a trainee of the Institute for War and Peace Reporting. Originally he is a Mullah from Ghazni, and he therefore knows many people in the area, including

Taliban who went to *madrasa* with him. They continue to research the topic, although the task is becoming more difficult since even Borhan cannot go to Andar district any longer for security reasons.

Thomas Ruttig is an independent researcher and political consultant on Afghanistan. He has been working on and in Afghanistan from 1980 onwards, spent nine years living and working there and speaks both Pashto and Dari. His last postings were as a Political Affairs Officer at the UN Special and Assistance Missions in Afghanistan (2000–3), Deputy of the Special Representative of the European Union (2003/4) and political adviser to the German Embassy in Kabul (2004–6). In 2006–8, he was a Visiting Fellow at the German Stiftung Wissenschaft und Politik. He lives outside Berlin. He is the author of *Islamists, Leftists—and a Void in the Center. Afghanistan's Political Parties and Where they Come from (1902–2006)*, as well as several briefings and papers in German.

Graeme Smith has devoted more time to southern Afghanistan than any other Western journalist, since the arrival of NATO forces in that region. After previously working for the *Toronto Star*, he was hired in 2001 by *The Globe and Mail*, a nationally distributed Canadian newspaper, and named Moscow Bureau Chief in 2005. The war in Afghanistan became his full-time project in 2006. His awards include the Canadian Association of Journalists' prize for investigative reporting; the Edward Goff Penny Memorial Prize; the Amnesty International award for Canadian print journalism; a National Newspaper Award for international reporting; the Michener Award; and an Online Journalism Award.

Mohammad Osman Tariq Elias is currently working as governance adviser with the Asia Foundation Afghanistan. He holds an MA degree in Governance and Development (IDS). Tariq fought as a *mujahid* against Soviet forces in Afghanistan in the 1980s and then worked as a development worker. Later, he worked in the Taliban government's foreign affairs ministry. He then assisted the UN special mission for Afghanistan after the fall of the Taliban regime to organise and reactivate tribal Jirgas in the Southeast region. He was also coordinator of the National Solidarity Program in the Southeast region of Afghanistan.

Sébastien Trives has a Master in International Relations (Boston University) and a diploma in European Studies (Université Catholique de Louvain). He served as Head of the Southeast regional office of United Nations Assistance Mission in Afghanistan (UNAMA) until the end of 2005. He had previously worked as Afghanistan country Coordinator for the French aid agency ACTED (Agency for Technical Cooperation and Development) and for the OSCE (Organisation for Security and Co-operation in Europe) Mission to Tajikistan. He is currently deputy director of UNRWA (United Nations Relief and Works Agency).

Martine van Bijlert has served as Political Adviser to the European Union's Special Representative for Afghanistan since May 2004, and has concurrently worked as an independent consultant on Afghanistan since August 2007, among others for the Netherlands Embassy in Kabul, providing political analysis in the fields of governance and institution building, insurgency and tribal politics, and democratisation in (post-) conflict societies. Previous experience includes work for a humanitarian NGO in Kabul, during the Taliban regime.

Abdul Awwal Zabulwal is the pseudonym of an Afghan author, who does not want to use his real name for security reasons. He has been working in Zabul for many years and has extensive knowledge of the province.

INDEX